THE
SHRIEKING SIXTIES

BRITISH HORROR FILMS 1960 TO 1969

THE
SHRIEKING
SIXTIES

BRITISH HORROR FILMS
1960 TO 1969

Edited by Darrell Buxton

Midnight Marquee Press, Inc.
Baltimore, Maryland, USA

Thanks to:

Roy Spence
Henry Green
Colin B at www.bosharts.com
Chris Wood and britishhorrorfilms.co.uk
Sally Griffith
Vic Pratt
Paul Cotgrove and The White Bus
The Gothique Film Society
The Society of Fantastic Films
James Murray and Kathy Tipping
Tony Earnshaw
Michael Wesley
Des Glass
of Arrowe Hill
Dave Gold
Andrew and Teresa Clark
John Grieve and the Manchester and Salford Film Society
Mark at 'Hard To Find Films'
James Stanger
M J Simpson
Jonathan Rigby
Russell Kearney
Quad, Derby
Nicky Henson
Hilary Dwyer
Paula Fay and Mitch Morgan
Kate Bailey
Carol Otter
Chris Barfield–whose enthusiasm
will never be forgotten and continues to inspire

Copyright © 2010 Darrell Buxton
Cover Design/Layout Design: Susan Svehla

ISBN 978-1-936168-06-4
Library of Congress Catalog Card Number 2010933213
Manufactured in the United States of America

First Printing by Midnight Marquee Press, Inc., July 2010

**Dedicated to
Harry Alan Towers
(1920-2009)**

Table of Contents

"It begins…"
—Christopher Lee, *The Devil Rides Out*

Foreword

by Michael Armstrong

During the 1960s, there was the crumbling Hollywood, star-driven studio system crippled by budgetary overheads, and a growing subculture of independent producers making low-budget exploitation for the lucrative teenage market that had evolved during the previous decade.

British film, slowly being starved of Hollywood support, struggled to compete with its homegrown product in the world marketplace while, at home, two major cinema chains, ABC and Rank, dictated a film's fate. Without their screens, there was virtually nowhere to have your film shown, let alone see a chance of breaking even.

Unlike America, where exploitation thrived in the drive-ins, British horror was forced into a trickle of small independent cinemas and occasionally granted limited circuit release by ABC for British quota purposes (a government incentive to insure British cinemas screened a certain number of British films per year). It was within this system that the horror double-bill, popularized by Hammer and its competitors, flourished.

If getting films before a large enough public for recoupment was next to impossible, trying to make them was even more difficult. Film investment was, as always, hard to find. Trying to recoup from sales outside the U.K. was even harder. As with all low-budget filmmaking, schedules were tight and salaries minimal.

A need for cheap labor, therefore, was ideal to open the door for aspiring new filmmakers—or it should have been. During the 1960s, the British unions held the industry in a Catch-22 stranglehold whereby you couldn't apply for a job—any job—unless you were a union member, and you couldn't apply to be a union member unless you already had a job.

Get out of that one!

For people to get even a runner's job was virtually impossible, and as for thinking about becoming a film director without decades of industry experience…? The existence of Santa Claus was a more likely reality.

But during the mid-1960s, this impassable brick wall was finally breached. A young aspirant, Michael Reeves, raised the financing for a low-budget horror feature that he shot abroad; then, armed with this director's credit, he was allowed by the unions to direct *The Sorcerers* for producer Tony Tenser.

Having won one battle, Tony Tenser challenged the system again, barely a year later, but this time championing an even younger feature-film neophyte whose screenplay he'd purchased. And that's how I became a British feature film writer and director at the age of 23. In those days it was unprecedented—and it finally helped open the floodgates.

The 1960s may have started by shrieking with horror at a cruelly restrictive industry, but it ended by shrieking with joy at the opportunities low-budget horror films provided for new talent—more than any other genre has ever done—and for that I shall always be, personally, eternally grateful.

May this new millennium continue to shriek as joyfully!

Julian Barnes and Jill Haworth with wrtier/director Michael Armstrong during filming of *Haunted House of Horror*.

Introduction

"Beware the beat of the cloth-wrapped feet!"
—publicity for *The Mummy's Shroud* (1967)

The beat. It's what 1960s Britain was all about, really. This decade spawned a kaleidoscopic explosion of English music, fashion, satire, art and style, most of which has been documented, celebrated, imitated and regurgitated in subsequent years. Even U.K. cinema of the time grabbed global attention: From kitchen sink to musical extravaganza, the likes of *Saturday Night and Sunday Morning*, *Lawrence of Arabia*, *Tom Jones*, *The Knack* and *Oliver!* were festooned with awards and acclaim everywhere, and the cream of the world's most exciting young directors visited our shores to lend a flavor of whatever we had to their own filmmaking endeavors.

So much British culture of the era has been written about, pored over, discussed and analyzed that it seems few areas of the scene have been neglected. This book is intended to fill one of the remaining gaps.

Despite the fact that domestic cinema seemed to boom during the 1960s—add the international success of the James Bond franchise or the twice-yearly treat of the *Carry On* series to the glittering array noted earlier—and the continued box-office demand for themes of a shocking or supernatural type, British horror films of this vibrant period have rarely been studied or considered. The glory years of the preceding decade, with the impressive and influential impact of tiny Hammer Films reviving and reinvigorating the horror genre, have received due and proper attention.

The previously accepted wisdom that 1970s "Britsploitation" was a worthless embarrassment has been successfully challenged in recent times. (See Simon Sheridan's reappraisals of the "Dirty Mac Brigade" sex films, Matthew Sweet's applecart-upsetting perspective, and Harvey Fenton and David Flint's reclamation of the seemingly haphazard 1970s U.K. terror output as a coherent, daring, and connected body of work.) Yet the intervening years filled with what might be referred to as "Carnaby Carnage" have been strangely untouched.

My own latent fascination with the British horror movie, an indefinable form that had long held a peculiar interest for me, was piqued and prodded by the publication of Andy Boot's *Fragments of Fear* (Creation Books, 1996). At last, here was someone who had tapped into the vein my own mind had flitted and skirted around for years, someone who understood exactly why the sight of unconvincing bikers haring around tarmacked curves in *Psychomania* or the collision of cod-psychedelia with a cast of fright-flick veterans in *Curse of the Crimson Altar* (*The Crimson Cult* in the US) worked on levels way beyond the conventional. I was so thrilled to discover another admirer of this type of palaver—a person who reveled in the buried delights from the scene to the point where he'd even penned an entire chapter on Anglo-Amalgamated—that I was inspired to commence in-depth research into British horror eventually leading to the compilation of a would-be exhaustive filmography. And then I contacted Andy Boot, with whom I briefly discussed the possibility of an updated "Fragments 2."

Sadly this never came to fruition, but others have since taken on the mantle: Jonathan Rigby's tremendous *English Gothic: A Century of Horror Cinema* filled many of the gaps in Andy's pioneering but patchy history of the scene; David Pirie, who arrived at the party before all of us, has lately revised his legendary overview *A Heritage of Horror*; and, as previously mentioned, Harvey Fenton's FAB Press published *Ten Years of Terror* in 2001, another pivotal and cathartic moment for me, as I gleefully threw myself into this tome's revelatory pages, and I still haven't come up for air.

Michael Reeves, Tony Tenser and Boris Karloff (Photo courtesy John Hamilton)

Naturally, the Internet was hot on the literary world's heels, and Chris Wood's "does what it says on the tin" website "British Horror Films" (www.britishhorrorfilms.co.uk) has been a spiritual haven for me and for dozens of fellow aficionados during the recent past. The website's message board is something of a "net" rarity, an online community rife with considered debate rather than argument, friendship as opposed to malice, and a willingness to share information, swap rare material, and generally talk about all things horrific and far beyond. The sense of camaraderie among the board's regulars is palpable, and ultimately manifested itself in physical form when Wood, impressed with the quality of the fiction and artwork posted at the forum's "Your Creations" section, compiled several Pan-style anthologies of macabre tales written by the contributors. Published via lulu.com and with magnificent cover designs by Paul Mudie, these collections are highly recommended.

The success of this risky venture served to plant another seed in my mind. The BHF board's "films" platform contained plenty of informed musings on our favorite movies, often to an extremely high critical standard. I'd pondered, while perusing *Ten Years of Terror*, how a prequel to Harvey and David's book on the 1970s might take shape and, when the light bulb went on, one night in the autumn of 2006, I realized that one way to find out would be to undertake such a project myself. Requesting assistance from the trusty BHF crew, plus other interested parties picked up along the way, I mooted the concept of a publication examining British horror of the 1960s. More than three years on, you hold the results of our collective's toil in your hands.

A few brief words concerning the contents. How did films qualify for inclusion? You'll spot the likes of *Jason and the Argonauts* and the two *Dalek* pictures alongside the more expected Draculas and Frankensteins. These are surprises perhaps, but bear in mind that the Harryhausen classic is chock-a-block with monsters and scares, and that the Daleks, supposedly responsible — as TV legend has it — for forcing successive generations of viewers to take cover "behind the sofa," are as malevolent a foe as any hero has faced in speculative fiction. Indeed, the plot of their second movie displays considerable parallels with the mechanoid invaders in *The Earth Dies Screaming*, so I figured we could hardly feature one of those titles while omitting the other.

Jess Franco's prodigious output is also represented. Students of the so-called "jazz filmmaker" will be all too aware of the minefield of his oeuvre, and we've included Señor Franco's 1960s works that feature both significant "horror" content and confirmed British production involvement and

finance. For those of you who enjoy debate along the lines of "Is it horror?" "Is it British?" or even "Is it a film?" we've also included a "Problem/Borderline" appendix where you'll find examples of contentious titles which didn't quite make the final cut but deserve a mention in our survey: films with minor terror elements; fright fare often referred to as "British" but funded and produced overseas; and feature-length output made for television.

Credits information has been compiled by Dave Simpson, and we've kept it fairly minimal and streamlined. As far as I'm concerned, this is a book in which opinion and viewpoint take center stage; and, in this day and age, if you want to find out

more about the third assistant director or the name of the character who gets his head chopped off in reel three, there are copious ways and means. Additional appendices list the many British horror shorts of the period in question (you'll spot the recurring names of Harrison Marks, Michael Armstrong and Delta Film Group) and Tim Rogerson's meticulously researched look at the British Board of Film Censors' wary approach to the feature titles reviewed in the main body of the work.

Please bear in mind that many of our reviews contain spoilers and plot revelations and giveaways. Ideally, you're advised to read these pages after viewing the movies concerned, although we also hope that we can introduce you to a smattering of hitherto obscure and perhaps unknown items. We make no apologies for certain aspects of the prose in which

you are about to immerse yourselves. We've tried to retain the unique zest, essence and vernacular (rhymes with Dracula) of the British Horror Films website without being too "in about it all." I'd like to think that more than a few readers will pick up on the house style and shorthand — for example, our playful reduction of the names of favorite actors, whom we at the BHF fondly refer to as "The Cush," "The Plezz," etc. — and that, if you like what you experience here, maybe you'll mosey on over to Chris Wood's site before long.

Above all, I hope you enjoy *The Shrieking Sixties*, and that our humble efforts bring some deserved attention to an under appreciated decade of U.K. genre cinema. Now, do you mind if I smoke?

—Darrell Buxton
Editor

1960

The Brides of Dracula

The most obvious point to make about this film is that the titular Dracula never actually appears. Made two years after Christopher Lee created his iconic role, in this second stab at the vampire myth Hammer decided to dispense with his services, saving him up for a sequel still another six years in the future. Clearly though, they hoped to get some box-office oomph out of the big D, but frankly he is never missed, such is the quality of this picture. In many respects, *The Brides of Dracula* remains *the* perfect Gothic Hammer horror. Its production design, cinematography, music, costumes, direction and performances are all quite brilliant. Even the crazy, jagged opening credits are memorable.

Brides opens with a shot of that same flippin' lake at Black Park that appears with dreary predictability in so many Hammer films, standing in for everywhere from Switzerland to Canada. Here, we're back in Transylvania again, with the delicious Yvonne Monlaur ending up in the usual tavern full of "colorful" locals muttering veiled threats and exuding all the friendly hospitality of a Soviet-era bakery.

She's invited by the local grandee, Baroness Meinster, to spend the evening at her château (cue much uneasy rustling among the slack-jawed yokels). Martita Hunt is perfect as the batty old Baroness, sadly never exclaiming, "A handbag!" though she plays the part with tremendous Bracknellesque spirit. From her bedroom window Monlaur spies a gloomy young man apparently about to throw himself to his death. When she locates his room in an attempt to rescue the chap, it turns out he is going nowhere, as his ankle is chained to the wall.

Falling for his Romantic poet mien and his enormous Hammer trademark blond quiff, she resolves to find the key to his links and free him. Thus, the silly girl unleashes an ancient evil on the world: the young vampire, Baron Meinster, whose first job is revenge upon his mother, who chained him up in the first place. It is a quite obscene act of incest. Fortunately for all, Dr. Van Helsing, in the shape of Peter Cushing, is still in the area, making sure Christopher Lee stays out of sequels for a few more years to come.

A series of superlative set pieces follows, including the resurrection of vamp victim Marie Devereux, coaxed from her grave by the cackling Freda Jackson as the Baron's nurse, in a perverted inversion of midwifery,

urging her to "Push, push!" Add to this the destruction of the Baroness at Cushing's hand—her utter shame when she is confronted by Van Helsing is unique in Hammer horror—she covers her fanged mouth as though it's some kind of tumor too ghastly to reveal to anybody else humiliated by the pathology of her sickness.

Cushing again is superb, leaping around and putting the young-uns to shame with his energy in the action scenes, and exhibiting unnerving stillness in his more serious dialogue exchanges. His moment of self-cauterisation remains genuinely nasty, and his dispatching of the Baroness, even though at her own request, almost comes across as cold-blooded murder.

The Technicolor cinematography by Jack Asher is sumptuous, if unnaturalistic (where's all that lilac light supposed to be coming from?), perfectly suiting the grand mood of the vampire's castle. The control of the lush color throughout the film is always fascinating: Note the way that Cushing's tie matches his eyes perfectly when we first see him. That Asher's career ended just five years later was a bloody disgrace, Hammer becoming impatient with the time he would spend bathing the sets in wonderful colors, sacrificing quality for budgetary concerns. Hammer films would never look this good ever again. Speaking of which, Andrée Melly (sister of George), playing the small role of Gina, must be one of the all time great vampire beauties, with those big, brown, doe eyes and incredible figure.

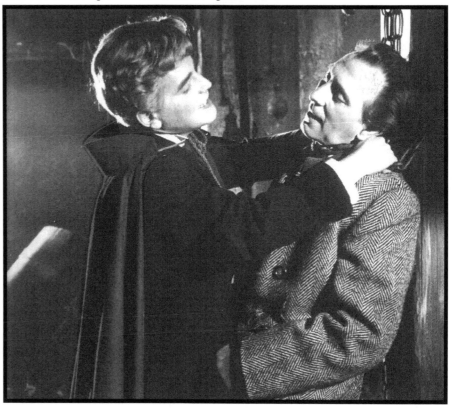

David Peel and Peter Cushing in *The Brides of Dracula*

A few script niggles remain. If Meinster can turn himself into a bat (which he does frequently), how could a chain round his ankle have kept him locked up for years and years? Why does Van Helsing always say he'll be back before sunset, only inevitably to show up in the dead of night, when he *knows* he'll be too late?

Finally, as to our Lee substitute, David Peel: He's rather bland when being a charming, human pretty boy, but once he gets those fangs on, he makes a terrifying, bestial baddy. He's a greedy little Count, though. Three brides?

Sadly, the rubber bat flapping about on a string, uttering, "Weeeek! Squeeeeak!" is rubbish.
—John Rankin

Credits: Director: Terence Fisher; Writers: Peter Bryan, Edward Percy, Jimmy Sangster.
Leading Cast: Peter Cushing, Martita Hunt, Yvonne Monlaur, David Peel, Freda Jackson, Andrée Melly, Miles Malleson.

Circus of Horrors

When compared to director Sidney Hayers' later masterpiece *Night of the Eagle* [*Burn, Witch, Burn!*], *Circus of Horrors* comes off as lurid, garish melodrama, unfeasibly plotted and stuffed full of sadism and busty babes to keep less discerning minds occupied. But, let's face it, you're probably one of those less discerning minds, or you wouldn't be reading this. And in that case, you'll love *Circus of Horrors*.

It's 1947, and shady plastic surgeon Dr. Rossiter (Anton Diffring) and his assistants are on the run after a botched operation. Rossiter, sporting the worst fake beard ever, hits on an idea: He'll transform his own face and therefore evade the authorities! Brilliant! Except, when the bandages come off, he looks *no different*. What a testament to your skill, doc!

Having escaped to France, Rossiter, now calling himself "Dr. Schuler," stumbles across a young girl with, wouldn't you know it, a scarred face. It turns out she's with a circus (not because of her scarred face, don't be mean) run by her father, a somewhat sozzled Donald Pleasence. Seeing an opportunity, Schuler fixes the girl's features in return for the running of the circus, because it's "the ideal front" (you tell me).

Overjoyed that his daughter will no longer have to go through life with an arse for a face, a drunken Pleasence promptly molests Bosco the bear and is crushed to death for his trouble, conveniently leaving the circus in the hands of the wicked Dr. Schuler. After a run-in with a shiv-wielding streetwalker who just happens to have (you guessed it) a scarred face, Schuler hits upon the idea of staffing his circus with facially reconstructed criminals (mostly top-heavy female ones) whose fealty will be guaranteed by means of blackmail. Well, it's a plan…

Fast forward ten years, and Schuler's circus is now pulling in crowds all over Europe, but with one caveat: His performers keep getting offed in fatal accidents (maybe for not being top-heavy enough). Diffring goose-steps around, being the most German man *ever* in a polo neck, jackboots and whip combo. The little girl, meanwhile, has since blossomed into Yvonne

Monlaur (possibly *zee* most French *wooman evair*), while another Yvonne of early '60s Brit horror, Yvonne Romain, wobbles into view as a prospective new attraction and muse for Schuler. There's no danger of her being bumped off for not being top-heavy enough.

Of course, the "jinx circus" doesn't go unnoticed, and a reporter starts snooping around. On the verge of leaving, the top-billed Magda gets it in the neck (literally) when a knife-throwing stunt goes awry. Having stumbled across a few clues and being ever so close to revealing Schuler's secrets to the reporter, second-billed Elissa also meets a sticky end. Oy vey, Schuler, you'll have no circus left in a minute! He takes everything in his stride, though, saying, "Send ze clowns in" (oh no, not ze clowns!), maybe because he still has Yvonne Romain's lion taming act up his sleeve—for a few moments, anyway, until she gets mauled to death by one of the beasts (or somebody throws a rug over her, you decide). By this point, Schuler has been recognized by his victim of 10 years earlier and, realizing the net is closing in on him, makes his escape, only to be killed by a gorilla. Well, they do say never work with children or animals…

It has to be said, *Circus of Horrors* looks great (that Eastman color stock works a treat here) and, for all its ludicrousness, it's a hoot. For any Brit horror fan with a sense of humor, it's required viewing.
—Jed Raven

Anton Diffring plays a completely focused (yes, he's crazy) plastic surgeon whose hands can seemingly perform miracles—sometimes. Fleeing a badly botched operation in England that drove his patient insane, he and his sidekicks, Kenneth Griffith and Jane Hylton (playing a weak willed brother and sister), end up in France, having changed their identities. Indeed Diffring claims to have a whole new face constructed by his protégé, Griffith, which seems to have involved shaving off his beard and most of his eyebrows. Remarkable surgery!

Accidentally meeting a child disfigured in the war (the film begins in 1947), whose father (Donald Pleasence) owns a run-down circus, Diffring instantly concocts a cunning plan. He'll make the little girl beautiful, buy the circus, staff it with disfigured murderers, prostitutes and other ne'er-do-wells, cure them through his experiments, blackmail them into staying with his carnival after they have learned complex acrobatic and animal training skills, travel Europe with his successful show and then—via all this—triumphantly re-enter the legitimate world of medicine.

No, it made no sense to me, either, and poor Donald Pleasence isn't around long enough to see it happen: He is almost instantly killed by a bear after drunkenly trying to dance with it, celebrating his daughter's beautification. Diffring shows his true villain colors by standing back and cruelly watching as Pleasence rolls around on the ground with a motionless, stuffed, moth eaten bruin plonked on top of him. Cut to "10 years later" in Berlin, and the "Circus Schuler" is seemingly Europe's biggest attraction, though it also has a reputation as

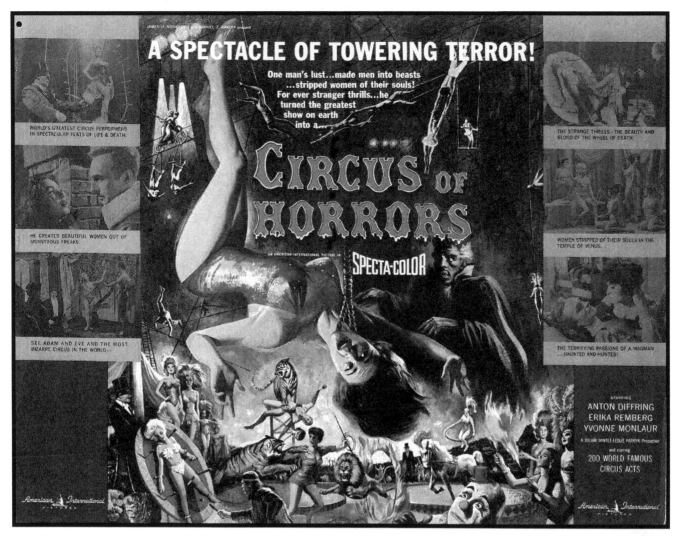

the "jinx circus," as so many of its lovely young performers are killed in bizarre accidents. And what a collection of beauties Diffring has created. One of the film's chief pleasures is the amount of buxom flesh on display. Yvonne Monlaur (who also graced *The Brides of Dracula*), Vanda Hudson and the incomparable Yvonne Romain (of *The Curse of the Werewolf* fame) all look magnificent, and the whole thing has a risqué feel, which is surprising, given that this was a British film made in the very late 1950s.

Another novelty is the extreme gore as various members of the cast meet grisly ends in blood gushing color, at a time when color film itself was still a box-office draw. As such, the film's real star is Douglas Slocombe, whose sumptuous cinematography still looks vibrant, intense and almost lurid, with its saturated palate of rich primary reds, greens and blues, combined with powerful framing. (Slocombe also shot *Dance of the Vampires*, *The Servant*, *The Music Lovers* and *The Sailor Who Fell from Grace with the Sea*, ending his career with the Indiana Jones films). It's a fabulous picture to look at from start to finish.

Where it does drag a bit are during the seemingly endless circus acts. We see horses, elephants, chimps and lions in various Busby Berkeley-type formations, which were entertaining

back in the '50s and '60s, but are very dated and yawnsome to watch today (never mind the contemporary animal welfare issues). And there are *a lot* of these scenes, as well as having to sit through Erika Remberg's entire aerial act three times, with its truly horrible accompanying Tony Hatch song, "Look for a Star."

Some may ask, "Is it a horror film?" It certainly has gore, and the plastic surgery and madness theme has enjoyed a long shelf life in international horror. If you look at the movie more closely, Diffring is compared to Frankenstein and even God, performing not just surgery, but creating new beings of unnatural loveliness. The first exhibit the undercover policeman investigates when the circus arrives in Britain is a tableau of "Adam and Eve," and he later comments on the remarkable beauty of the carnival performers crafted by Diffring's knife — all solid genre worrywarts. Another of the film's themes is essential essence. Despite her beautiful, new external appearance, the Elissa Caro character remains a dangerous, warped whore, while the kindly child, Nicole, retains her compassion as she grows up to be a woman.

Circus of Horrors is still an enjoyable picture, particularly on its dazzling surface. It would be rare that a cinematographer at Hammer could wring out quite such a range of tones from

300 years old! Human blood keeps them alive forever!

HORROR HOTEL

Just ring for doom service!

DENNIS LOTIS · CHRISTOPHER LEE · BETTA ST. JOHN · PATRICIA JESSEL · VENETIA STEVENSON

viewer would be forgiven for thinking it's an *American* film with all its American accents, American settings and generally American-ness (even Christopher Lee is sporting a New England drawl), but it's as British as fish and chips, bangers and mash, or Crufts. Venturing into the same kind of chiller territory as *Night of the Eagle* or *Night of the Demon*, *The City of the Dead* is every bit as intelligent, scary and well made.

The film begins with a flashback to witch burnings in Whitewood, Massachusetts. As Elizabeth Selwyn (Patricia Jessel) is dragged to the pyre (complete with Pythonesque chants of "Witch!" and "Burn her!"), she calls out to a man called Jethrow (Valentine Dyall) for help, but he denies being in league with her. Then, quick as a flash, he offers up a prayer to Lucifer (the little fibber) and a huge shadow falls across the village.

The story is being told by college lecturer Driscoll (Christopher Lee), who bookends it by leering into the camera and chanting, "Burn witch, burn witch, burn!" in a comedic American accent ("Dig that crazy beat," cracks one of his male students). Token attractive blonde Nan Barlow wants to study witchcraft "in situ" (?) and stays behind after class to ask Driscoll's advice. He immediately points her towards Whitewood, where Elizabeth "Charcoal Briquette" Selwyn was rumoured to have risen from the grave and sucked the blood of her victims.

Being the feisty young gal that she is, Nan immediately sets off on her own, arriving at a fog-bound petrol station, where the attendant tells her, "Not many God-fearing folks visit Whitewood these days…" She carries on regardless (nothing is putting this girl off, not even the thickest fog ever committed to celluloid), and when a figure looms out of the mist, she stops and gives him a lift to the village. Despite his modern dress, the man is immediately recognizable to the audience as Jethrow from the witch-burning shenanigans at the beginning, so that can't be good. And things get worse when Nan arrives at Whitewood. First, her miserable passenger does a disappearing act, and then it turns out that the hatchet-faced owner of the only hotel in town (the Raven Inn) is none other than—you guessed it, Elizabeth "Kindling" Selwyn.

Whitewood is an astonishingly well-realized spooky place. Silent figures drift in and out of the fog, seemingly uninterested in Nan as she wanders about. Reverend Russell, the local vicar, doesn't lighten the mood much, either: "For 300 years the devil has hovered over this city… made it his own," he tells Nan without a great deal of prompting. "I have no parish, no one worships here! Leave before it is too late!"

But our feisty heroine is having none of this, and it's roughly about this time that you begin to think she might be a bit thick. After reading up on Candlemass Eve and the rites that occurred on that day, she doesn't seem at all worried by the singing coming from beneath her room ("There is nothing underneath but earth," the hotelier tells her), the fact that it actually *is* Candlemass Eve, and the disappearance of an "item

the same Eastmancolor film stock as Slocombe does here, and its performers all dive into it with a relish again lacking in contemporaneous productions, thanks in part to Scottish-born Sidney Hayers' efficient direction. However, the plot's utterly absurd premise and the overexposure of Billy Smart's Circus acts remain caveats. The film is a real curiosity. Look out for an uncredited Kenny (R2D2) Baker and Kenneth Griffith's fellow *The Prisoner* star, Peter Swanwick.

—John Rankin

Credits: Director: Sidney Hayers; Writer: George Baxt.
Leading Cast: Anton Diffring, Yvonne Monlaur, Donald Pleasence, Yvonne Romain, Erika Remberg.

The City of the Dead (aka *Horror Hotel*)

Few films in the Brit horror canon are as surprisingly good as *The City of the Dead*. (I thought I'd get the gushing praise for this gem out of the way right from the start.) The casual of value" (an integral part of the rites she's so interested in). There's a rather wonderful scene when Nan walks out of her bedroom to find a group of people dancing (we don't see their faces), rushes back to get ready to join them, and then bursts back into a suddenly empty room. But that's nothing compared to what happens next, as (in a moment of *Psycho*-like plot mechanics) we see our supposed heroine brutally stabbed to death.

After a while, Nan's brother (who happens to work with Lee's character) gets worried about his missing sibling and calls the police, who fail to find a trace of her at the Raven Inn. Concerned, he visits Lee (stopping a sacrifice to the "Lord of Light"), who gives veiled warnings about trying to track her down.

Lee is then visited by the Reverend Russell's granddaughter (whom Nan struck up a friendship with during her brief stay), looking for Nan's family. After getting the brush-off from Lee, she heads back to Whitewood, picking up Jethrow on the way. For some reason, her brief sojourn away from the place has gotten her marked as the next sacrifice, as the devil worshippers have decided they now need "a living descendant of those who were cursed." Luckily, she's being followed not only by the suspicious brother but also by Nan's boyfriend, Maitland. And it turns out that *everyone* in Whitewood is undead: The locals were granted eternal life in a pact with the Devil.

The City of the Dead is an astonishing monochrome feast. The fog-bound sets are incredible, the shocks are extremely shocking (a brilliantly executed body-in-the-cupboard moment, and *every* time someone looms out of the fog), and the performances are uniformly great. Halfway through the film, you get *that* death, which adds to the unsettling nature of the proceedings, but it's the graveyard ending which will blow you away. It has to be the most spectacular set piece that '50s and '60s British horror produced, and the film is worth sitting through for the last 10 minutes alone. Noble teenage sacrifice and dozens of exploding monks—does it get any better than that? —Chris Wood

Credits: Director: John Moxey; Writers: Milton Subotsky, George Baxt.
Leading Cast: Patricia Jessel, Christopher Lee, Betta St. John, Dennis Lotis, Valentine Dyall.

Doctor Blood's Coffin

"Top notch British horror. In color, too. People are mysteriously disappearing near a lonely Welsh village where a mad doctor conducts weird experiments with life and death in an underground cave. A stylish film reminiscent of the Hammer horror films of the same time period. The dead return to life in a very gruesome climax."

This mini-synopsis from Sinister Cinema's catalogue, besides its patronizing tone ("in color too"—bloody cheek!), also contains a number of inaccuracies. For a start, it bears no resemblance whatsoever to a Hammer film (well, all right, Hazel Court's in it), the "Welsh" village happens to be on the coast of Cornwall, and the "underground cave" is, in fact,

that favorite old horror movie haunt, an abandoned tin mine (shades of *Crucible of Terror* and *The Plague of the Zombies*, and Warner Bros.' *The Mysterious Doctor* [1943]) where a mad doctor transplants living hearts into corpses in an attempt to give the dead a new lease on life. However, the fact that the partially anesthetized donors are still alive and conscious as their hearts are surgically extracted does indeed lend a truly gruesome note to the proceedings.

Although the pace is rather slow, the leading man totally inexpressive and the script overly talky, there are still a few standouts to enjoy in this movie, apart from the purely visual delights of the location photography, which manages to make Cornwall look like a highly enticing, sun drenched holiday destination. An early feature from director Sidney J. Furie, who went on to make *The Ipcress File* and *The Entity*, the disturbing "true story" of a woman repeatedly raped by an invisible monster, *Doctor Blood's Coffin* does have its moments for the undiscerning fan.

GRIPPING SUSPENSE! SEE!—a semi-paralyzed victim of the mad medico agonizingly drags himself down the hillside toward the party of villagers who are searching for him while a frantic Dr. Blood races in pursuit—who will get him first? *GHASTLY HORROR! SEE!*—the hideous decomposing zombie creature raised from the dead by Dr. Blood's sadistic surgery! *QUAINT CUSTOMS! SEE!*—the cute cottages of a typical 1960s Cornish village, and witness the age-old English ritual of "having a jar in the local." *CHEAP MORALIZING! HEAR!*—the same old "there are some things with which Man was not meant to tamper" claptrap. *SEXY DAMES! SEE!*—the ever lovely Hazel Court in a figure-hugging nurse's uniform!

This time-waster is certainly easier on the eye than many of its studio-bound contemporary competitors, as so much of the action is played out against the backdrop of some really picturesque Cornish countryside and beautifully photographed seascapes. You can almost feel the sun beating down on you, and smell the ozone on the sea breeze, as Kieron Moore races along the Cornish cliff-top roads in his snazzy two-tone Hillman Minx with the wind rushing through his hair and a luscious

lady in the passenger seat. The no-nonsense direction, the total nonsense dialogue, the luminous, airy, panoramic vistas and the sharp, bright color photography make this quite a tonic for horror fans wanting a break from an excess of bleak, gritty, unrelentingly downbeat fare—in fact, it's just what the doctor ordered!

—Mike Hodges

Credits: Director: Sidney J. Furie; Writers: Jerry Juran, James Kelly, Peter Miller.
Leading Cast: Kieron Moore, Ian Hunter, Hazel Court, Gerald C. Lawson, Kenneth J. Warren.

The Flesh and the Fiends (aka Mania)

The Flesh and the Fiends sets out its stall immediately, with two "resurrectionists" at work, stealing a nastily stiff body from a grave. We're immediately transported to the Academy of Doctor Knox (Edinburgh in 1828 for those of us who need to know these things). After being visited by his niece, Martha, Knox begins his lecture: "You men of medicine are the modern miracle makers," he tells his rapt audience of side-burned youngsters, going on to describe theirs as "the most honorable

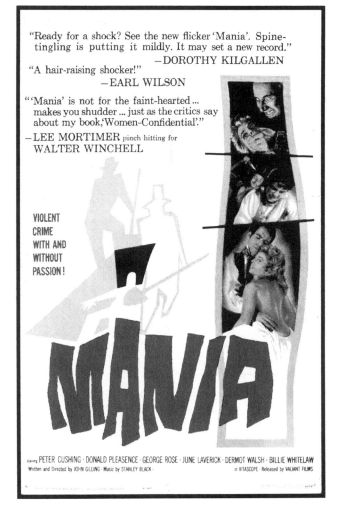

profession in the world." However, Knox's idea of "honourable" might not be the same as yours or mine: "Death is an incident producing clay," (oh-oh) "use it, mold it, learn from it…" Yes, Peter Cushing (complete with "evil" wonky eye) is once again playing a Baron Frankenstein figure—only this time the character is based on fact.

It's not long before he's taken on a failing student to help in his "laboratory," where he accepts delivery of the freshly disinterred corpse from scene one. The student (who goes by the name of Chris Jackson) is sent to a dodgy pub to pay the graverobbers for their work, but, being a complete arse, he immediately manages to get into a fight and is saved by tart with a heart, Mary (Billie Whitelaw), and her trusty bottle (ouch!). Unfortunately, the amount Jackson paid the graverobbers was spotted by none other than Burke and Hare, who decide to mug him outside the pub, necessitating a further rescue by the spunky Mary. For some bizarre reason best known to herself, Mary decides that this obvious liability is an attractive proposition (women, eh?), and Jackson finds himself with a common-as-muck girlfriend.

Back at Burke's lodging house, his tenant drops dead from natural causes, and the pair decide that they might as well earn a few bob from this and pay Dr. Knox a call. Meanwhile, the good doctor is busy insulting his friends and enemies at a party. "That man is doing the devil's work," says one scandalized fat bloke. "Aye, he does it brilliant," another adds. Burke and Hare are busy spending their not-very-hard-earned cash in the pub and, deciding they need more, entice "Old Aggie" back to Burke's house and suffocate her. "Sure, the old girl's better off," says Hare. "She bit my hand," complains Burke, who did the dirty deed. "Well, you can't blame her for that," is the reply. Jackson's studies are now suffering quite badly, thanks to Mary. In fact, the woman is a bloody nightmare, getting rat-arsed and setting fire to his work. As Burke and Hare continue to murder Burke's tenants and cart the remains up to Knox, who explains his reasoning to his partner, Mitchell: "I will continue to teach anatomy using the best specimens available, to turn out doctors to replace quacks!"

Finally, Jackson realizes that Mary is doing his college work no good at all, so he chucks her. Sadly this only serves to drive her into the waiting clutches of Burke and Hare, and she lasts approximately 30 seconds. Mrs. Burke arrives home shortly after the deed but, instead of inquiring why there's a body on her floor, she is more concerned with her husband's fidelity. "Nobody touched her!" says Hare. "Willy just killed her, that's all!" a scandalized Burke adds. So that's okay, then.

Of course it's not long before Jackson, at work in the laboratory, accepts delivery of Mary's still-warm corpse (in a moment that really needs a comedy "wah-wah" noise). He rushes around to Burke's house to confront the man, but gets a knife in the back. Burke and Hare realize they are now in serious trouble, and have to murder another innocent, the marvelously named Daft Jamie, in one of the most brutal scenes I've seen in a Brit horror flick—although I'm sure I'm not the only person who considers the sight of Melvyn

Hayes being beaten to death in a pile of pig shit a positive bonus to any film. But the mob is closing in, anyway, and the writing's on the wall for Knox, too—who, against his better judgment, has accepted delivery of Daft Jamie's body.

The Flesh and the Fiends is brilliant. Don't let its age and the fact it's black and white put you off. Cushing's portrayal of Knox displays genius, touching on the familiar Frankenstein persona at times, but eventually showing the doctor to be a misguided fool. He only wants to help the human race, and simply sees bodies as his "clay" to work with—after all, they're already dead, aren't they? Rather than being a cold and calculating killer (as Frankenstein is in many of the Hammers), he's simply turning a blind eye (ho, ho) to what he knows Burke and Hare are up to. But Cushing's performance is not the only highlight. Whitelaw is in top form as busty Mary, and Pleasence is fantastic (dodgy Oirish accent aside) as Hare. Any point where he and George Rose (as Burke) are on screen together is played for all the dark comedy they can muster. Even when they are brutally murdering people, they're still funny.

Just when you think it can't get any better, you have angry mob justice (wait till you see what happens to Pleasence) and a road-to-Damascus realization of what's going on by the misguided Knox: "As a child I believed in God and the Devil. It took a child to show me what I am now. I have failed. Yes, I have failed."
—Chris Wood

Credits: Director: John Gilling; Writers: John Gilling, Leon Griffiths.
Leading Cast: Peter Cushing, Donald Pleasence, George Rose, June Laverick, Billie Whitelaw.

The House in Marsh Road

Take some nouns: wife, husband, blonde, house, ghost. Add some adjectives: long suffering, boozy, sexy, creaky, benevolent. Now mix in a few verbs: inherit, conspire, murder, blaze, die. Include assorted words: extramarital affair, money, retribution, supernatural. Throw in a synonym: Irish char lady = Exposition/comic relief.

Now you have all the words (but not necessarily in the right order) to reconstruct the plot of *The House in Marsh Road*. You've got five minutes (believe me, that's more than enough). It shouldn't be too difficult. I'll wait for you here...

Back already? In that case, I'll lend you a hand. Long-suffering wife Jean Linton (Patricia Dainton) is sick of having to bolt from one tawdry bedsit to the next when the landlady's demand for back rent become too pressing. Her boozy, idle husband David (he's a writer, strangely enough, played by Tony

Wright) invariably blows what little money he earns from book reviews on Scotch and cigarettes. Then, in what seems a stroke of luck, Jean inherits a large, creaky old house in the country. But the pile comes complete with a resident ghost, as Mrs. O'Brien, the "woman who does" (Anita Sharp-Bolster), tells her (and us) at the first opportunity. No need to fear, though, the spirit seems quite benign provided it's not inconvenienced by the other inhabitants.

David, who's supposed to need peace and quiet to be able to write a novel and make some real money (those were the days!), actually has no intention of settling down in what he contemptuously regards as a rustic backwater. Before you can say "busty blonde in a tight sweater," he starts an extramarital affair with typist Valerie (another woman who *does*), played by Sandra Dorne, a cut-price Diana Dors. They conspire to murder the wife, sell the house for six grand to a local businessman who has his eye on the property, and steal away to the bright lights of London. But the protective poltergeist foils each murder attempt and, finally, when Jean is away for the night, sets the house on fire: The adulterers are trapped inside and die in the act (actually, after the act—evidently the old "whoever screws, dies" axiom was around long before the advent of the slasher genre) via supernatural retribution.

Directed by Montgomery Tully, who perpetrated the abominable *The Terrornauts* for Amicus seven years later, *The House in Marsh Road* could be the prototype of those cozy, monochrome Merton Park, B-movie second features spoofed hilariously by Stanley Baxter in his Christmas Special back in 1995. The cut-crystal diction of the main protagonists contrasts with the truly awful "stage Oirish" accent of the cleaning woman (which actually sounds more like a cross between Welsh and Hindustani), people smoke compulsively as if it were going out of fashion, suits and ties are worn at all times, the village pub is the center of the universe, and the local, worldly wise property developer ("If you want to keep a friend, never borrow, never lend") is portrayed with shifty relish by Sam Kydd, denizen of countless such pictures.

Though it's easy to poke fun at this typically threadbare production, there's no doubt that *Marsh Road* holds the interest for its 65-minute running time. The competent cast all play their roles with professional conviction (except the aforementioned Sharp-Bolster; Arthur Lucan would've done a more convincing job) and, after the initial nostalgic glow/piss-taking moment has worn off, the viewer is drawn into the film on its own merits. The plot moves at a brisk pace, and though the "special effects" are decidedly low-tech (a slamming door, a trundling armchair and a mirror that cracks of its own accord), Tully achieves a minimum but sufficient amount of spooky ambience and a reasonably tense final act.

In short, if you enjoy low-key, "less-is-more" British supernatural fare like *The Man in the Back Seat*, *The Halfway House*, *The Night My Number Came Up*, *House of Mystery* or *Ghost Ship*, then this *House* should be right up your—Road.
—Mike Hodges

Credits: Director: Montgomery Tully; Writer: Maurice J. Wilson.
Leading Cast: Tony Wright, Patricia Dainton, Sandra Dorne, Derek Aylward, Sam Kydd.

Never Take Sweets from a Stranger

Some of Hammer's darkest movies, both thematically and visually, emerged when the studio ventured outside of its established Technicolor Gothic horror framework and made bold black and white, genre-bending titles like the grim, fucked-up family drama *The Nanny* and the extraordinary, sci-fi-tinged, anti-nuke parable *The Damned*. The rare *Never Take Sweets from a Stranger* wears a pair of weighty influences on its sleeve. It recalls *The Night of the Hunter* (menacing older man pursues pair of vulnerable but resilient kids through the countryside) and has a courtroom-drama set piece and pre-teen protagonist that both echo Harper Lee's *To Kill a Mockingbird* (while prefiguring the Robert Mulligan film adaptation). These parallels aside, it remains a unique and brave picture for its time.

Opening with a disclaimer assuring that, while the story, adapted from Roger Garis' play *The Pony Cart,* is fiction, it could happen anywhere at anytime; but the movie has a rather awkwardly conveyed Canadian setting and suffers from some ho-hum adult performances. Flaws notwithstanding, documentary director Cyril Frankel (who returned to Hammer to make *The Witches* for the big screen and *Tennis Court* for TV) made a movie that still packs a powerful punch today.

Janina Faye, appealing in smaller parts in *Horror of Dracula* and *The Two Faces of Dr. Jekyll*, turns in an unusually good child's performance. She's naturalistic and likable as an imaginative nine year old who moves to a well-to-do Canadian town from England with her high-school-principal father (Patrick Allen) and mother (Gwen Watford). Faye's

The most challenging film of the decade . . .

NEVER TAKE SWEETS FROM A STRANGER

A HAMMER FILM PRODUCTION
Distributed by COLUMBIA

new, same-age friend (Frances Green) leads them both to get "candy" from elderly retired businessman/full-time pervert Felix Aylmer. Subsequently, the unharmed Faye calmly informs her parents that the old man gave her candy after she and her friend, at his request, stripped naked and danced as he watched (and, it is suggested, did other things aside from watching).

Faye's parents and grandma are horrified, even more so when it appears that Aylmer has earlier been incarcerated for similar misdemeanors, and the case goes to court. Different factors, however, prevent the unrepentant pedophile from being locked away; the accused is a very prominent and respected businessman in the town, the English family are "outsiders" and the little girl is unreasonably grilled in court and made to look like a liar. Aylmer walks free and the worst happens.

Although not a horror film in any conventional sense, Frankel's stark movie prefigures the genre-bound anger of Pete Walker's 1970s classic *Frightmare*, in which the justice system similarly and repeatedly fails to do its job and, as a result, a dangerous killer is let loose to kill again. The movie pulls off the rare trick of conveying anger and outrage in a muted, understated fashion; its approach to the contentious subject matter is mature and non-exploitative, and you'll find just a handful of melodramatic music cues.

The one aspect that may elicit unwarranted laughs in the wake of, for instance, Chris Morris' outstanding *Brass Eye* pedophile satire, is Aylmer's portrayal of a stereotypical child molester. Even this tabloid-worthy presentation of the character, a staggering, twitchy old man silently clutching a bag of sweets and lunging at little girls, manages to be creepily effective within the intelligent context.

The film has three distinct acts, with the central courtroom drama section paving the way for a suspenseful climactic foray into pure thriller territory, as the girls are persecuted by Aylmer. Movies focusing on children in peril, both before and since *Never Take Sweets from a Stranger,* tend to avoid anything too shocking for fear of alienating the audience. Frankel's film has no such fears, and its strongest suit, especially for its time, is its remarkably grim resolution.

Faye is found and rescued in time but, as Aylmer's shell-shocked son connotes repeatedly to a gathering crowd, her friend was not so lucky. Thus, an already bleak, quietly despairing movie closes with the revelation of a murdered child. In the wake of this understandably controversial, rarely discussed film's minimal theatrical release, Hammer sometimes chose to forsake the optimism of its earlier Gothics in favour of nihilistic outcomes more appropriate to the changing times, like the finale of *Frankenstein Created Woman*. This film's closing scene ranks high among the more emotionally devastating moments in their canon.
—Steven West

Credits: Director: Cyril Frankel; Writers: Roger Garis, John Hunter.
Leading Cast: Gwen Watford, Patrick Allen, Felix Aylmer, Niall MacGinnis, Janina Faye.

Peeping Tom

1959 produced two low-budget movies by England's greatest film directors, both about voyeuristic psychopaths. However, when they were released the following year to an unsuspecting public, one brought its creator even greater fame and acclaim, adding new iconic images to horror cinema, while the other brought disapprobation, disgust and ultimately even the exile of its director. Why were Alfred Hitchcock's *Psycho* and Michael Powell's *Peeping Tom* received so differently?

Even today it's difficult to quantify. Powell, in partnership with writer Emeric Pressburger, had a string of huge critical and box-office smash hits throughout the 1940s and '50s, usually with epic, yet experimental Technicolor productions on themes of war and, nearly unique in British cinema, eroticism. After splitting from Pressburger,

Powell seemed to have found a new creative partner in scriptwriter Leo Marks, opening their first (and, as it turned out, only) picture with the confident bull's-eye of the familiar Archers logo. There was little sense of any collective ideal, however.

Peeping Tom follows the fate of Mark, played by Karlheinz Böhm (credited as Carl Boehm), a stammering, socially awkward creature, forever lurking behind a movie or stills camera. In the film's celebrated opening sequence, we see, through the viewfinder of his cine-camera, Mark pick up and murder a prostitute in Fitzrovia. The next day he returns to the scene of the crime and films the police taking away the body, telling somebody that he is working for the *Observer* newspaper, one of the many puns and gags based around seeing and photographing, with which Leo Marks' clever script abounds. The best of these centers on Miles Malleson, playing a dirty old man at a newsstand, who inquires, "I understand you have views for sale?"

Mark works in a room above this same paper shop, creating such "views," and the rest of his professional life is spent as a focus puller at Pinewood studios, shooting awful British comedies. He rents apartments in his mansion house to lodgers, one of whom is the mousy Helen (Anna Massey). She almost instantly takes a shine to the peculiar Mark, mistaking his dangerously damaged persona for shyness, and tries to get to know him better. He seems to reciprocate these emotions and even begins to copy the actions of a "normal" human being when he is around her, promising a sort of redemption and possibly even an end to his relentless killing spree. It is probably this from whence the film's critical reaction stems. Whereas *Psycho* is all about Marion Crane, the victim, *Peeping Tom* is all about Mark, the murderer, a pornographer who terrifies his victims at the point of death so he can record their reactions on film in a series of highly sexualized rituals. It's here in these

snuff movies that his erotic imagination dwells and obtains orgasmic release. And yet he is in the main depicted by the director as a lonely, misunderstood youth just looking for love and understanding — when he's not going around stabbing women in the throat, that is.

"Ugh!," "this beastly picture," "this essentially vicious film," "the sickest and filthiest film I remember seeing" and "shovel it up and flush it down the nearest sewer" were just some of the negative responses in contemporary reviews of *Peeping Tom*. Such was the furor over the film that Powell, unable to get work again, left the U.K. to try and continue his career in Australia. The film remained buried and forgotten for 20 years. Now it's rightly considered a modern classic. So how does it compare today?

Although we are all familiar with the likes of peepers Mark and Norman after 40 years of screen nutters rampaging in their wake, both films created very modern monsters who needed their legends clarified. Both scripts drag in psychoanalyst characters to "explain" the villain's mental aberrations to mainstream audiences: in Norman's case, his psychopathy and multiple personality disorder; in Mark's case, his psychopathy and "scoptophilia," even though the correct clinical term is scopophilia (a peculiar slip on Leo Marks' part). These expository dialogue scenes feel clunky to a modern audience, especially in the Hitchcock film, as it takes up most of the ending. Its companion scene in *Peeping Tom* is played with more of a light comedy touch. What dates Powell's picture more is the factor that bedevils so many British films of a certain vintage: the accents of the performers. Massey's cut-glass voice makes the Queen sound like an oik in comparison, and most of the rest of the cast also fail to achieve a naturalistic expression (an interesting exception being "nudie" model Pamela Green, the muse of notorious smut peddler Harrison Marks — there's yet another of this film's curious "Mark" connections).

Speaking of accents, one of the big mysteries is where Mark's originated. As a little boy, he has a terribly posh, angelic little voice, and yet as a grown man he sports a Mittel Europe twang of no apparent origin. As Powell himself noted of Böhm, he was "both a triumph and a tragedy" in the role. Had *Peeping Tom* emerged in a more receptive era, and with a more suitable "realist" cast, who knows what Powell/the new Archers might have been able to achieve next?
—John Rankin

Credits: Director: Michael Powell; Writer: Leo Marks.
Leading Cast: Carl Boehm, Anna Massey, Maxine Audley, Moira Shearer, Jack Watson, Miles Malleson.

The Tell-Tale Heart

Adapted from the Poe classic, *The Tell-Tale Heart* is the story of the shy, awkward Edgar Marsh, who's had little experience with women and falls for the new girl in town, Betty Clare, played by a young Adrienne Corri. Betty is basically a decent sort who takes pity on the naïve Edgar and agrees to date

him. But unfortunately for Edgar, she then falls for his more experienced, "man about town" friend, Carl. To his credit, Carl initially tries to keep a distance but eventually can't contain his attraction to Betty, and they meet later to make love, this being witnessed by the mentally frail Edgar, who then bludgeons his friend to death in a fit of jealousy.

This is really where the story starts, but the build-up is important because there's a strong undercurrent flowing which gives a depth of insight into the characters, especially Edgar. Betty has moved in across the street from him, and he accidentally sees her stripping down to a basque and stockings. The sexual repression in Edgar is rife. He glances up to his (presumably dead) mother's portrait, as if he feels guilty about the sexual thrill in voyeuristically espying Betty in a state of undress. He has to seek Carl's advice on how to approach her, and agonizes over the simple task of asking her out to dinner. He soon becomes completely besotted with her, and Carl does his best to warn him not to get too attached, as he is clearly aware that his friend's feelings aren't reciprocated.

The portrayals of all three characters are handled really well, but it's Laurence Payne's oh-so-earnest Edgar who really stands out, capturing the inner feelings of a fragile man who is trying so hard — too hard. You really feel for him. Much of the sexual undercurrent is not really made explicit, but is all there in the subtext.

The story gets into gear with the murder of Carl. Edgar simply can't handle what he's done. And the quandary is whether the ghost of Carl is haunting him, or has his guilt finally sent his fragile mind over the edge? And although it's never stated for a fact, I think it's clear that rather than this being a case of a genuine haunting by the dead Carl, it's actually Edgar who's gone literally insane with remorse.

It begins with the sound of Carl's heart constantly beating and echoing around the room from under the floor where Edgar has hidden him. Things start to build further when some poltergeist-type activity commences, but the best scene is where Edgar retrieves Carl's corpse, and actually cuts out the heart of the dead man in order to try and stop the constant beating. In a decent visual effect for the era, the ripped-out heart is still seen beating in Edgar's hands.

Inevitably it all leads to a tragic ending, when Betty manages to arouse the suspicions of the police regarding Carl's disappearance. It's a very character-based film, and not a fast-paced movie by any means, but the well-written and performed characterizations, combined with the suitably eerie atmosphere that the film gradually begins to exude, make *The Tell-Tale Heart* worth seeing.
—Wayne Jefferies

In *English Gothic*, Jonathan Rigby calls this film a minor lost classic of British horror. The cast is headed by Laurence Payne, Adrienne Corri and Dermot Walsh, while the script was co-written by Brian Clemens, a year away from *The Avengers*.

Payne is Edgar (yes, really), a tortured young man who, in the beginning, wakes up screaming from a nightmare. He's got some hang ups, staring longingly at a prostitute before rejecting her advances. Instead, he goes home, stroking a picture of (probably) his mother on the stairs and looks at dirty postcards in his bedroom.

He's also a peeping tom who ogles the lovely new florist Betty (Corri), whose apartment is opposite his on the Rue Morgue (naturally). She obliviously cavorts around her bedroom in her undies with the curtains wide open. Early attempts at romancing her are painful; he even calls in his handsome best friend Carl (uh-huh!). When *they* meet, a light sparks in Betty's face, and it's not too long before an agonized Edgar is watching them make love in her bedroom.

Then Carl comes across to cheer his friend up. The sequence where he realizes Edgar must have seen them, a fact confirmed by a blunt instrument, is masterful. Carl's death is heavy stuff for 1960. It takes some bloody blows to kill him off. Edgar then buries him in the parlor (by the grand piano). But his heart goes boom-tiddy-boom-tiddy-boom day and night, driving Edgar crazy.

Betty, of course, suspects Edgar is the cause of her lover's disappearance. The police won't do anything, so she engages in some amateur sleuthing and gets into his house. In a wonderful moment she looks out of his bedroom window to her own and realizes he could see what was going on all the time. Well, love, if you don't close your curtains…

She finally gets the police, with no evidence, to harass Edgar. In an approximation of the climax of Poe's story, they end up in the parlor and finally there's a line from Poe! The film ends with a dubious rip-off of *Dead of Night*. This is a nicely constructed, three-hander quota quickie. The lead trio are all very good. There are hints of *Repulsion* and *Rear Window* at times, and the film foreshadows Clemens' 1970s series *Thriller*, but with a soupçon of sex and gore.
—Gerald Lea

Credits: Director: Ernest Morris; Writers: Brian Clemens, Elden Howard.
Leading Cast: Laurence Payne, Adrienne Corri, Dermot Walsh, Selma Vaz Diaz.

The Two Faces of Dr. Jekyll
(aka *House of Fright*)

One of the most obscure and unloved of Fisher's Hammer horror movies, this revisionist take on the Stevenson classic has had less exposure than most of his genre work and only recently enjoyed an opportunity for rediscovery via its official release on DVD. A rare chance to see the movie on the big screen came via the October 2007 Don Fearney-organized book launch for *The Hammer Story* in South Kensington, with juvenile costar Janina Faye (among others) in attendance.

Screenwriter Wolf Mankowitz conceived this bold, adult adaptation of the well-known book not as a genre film (it shows) but rather a dark satire of the two-faced nature of supposedly "respectable" Victorian society. Some of Hammer's best and most underrated movies (including Peter Sasdy's marvellous *Taste the Blood of Dracula*) were as effective in their commentary on contemporary hypocrisies as they were as conventional monster movies.

As a Hammer outing following the likes of *Horror of Dracula* and *The Mummy*, it's perhaps easy to see why this has failed to endure following its original disappointing box-office run (despite or maybe because of some gaudy alternative titles in different territories). There's a lack of actual horror or the kind of melodrama audiences had come to expect. The X rating allows for dashes of sex in the form of various scenes in the seedy Sphinx nightclub, where Norma Marla dances suggestively in her skimpies with snakes, though the most Hammer-like elements are sporadic musical flourishes and a climactic fire.

Mankowitz's script holds up as a companion piece to the same year's better known, more overtly violent studies of handsome, charming young men with dangerous split personalities. View this film in the context of the period of adult filmmaking that also brought *Psycho* and *Peeping Tom*, and its relevance increases. This film is no classic but it does have a unique resolution. Unlike the acknowledged masterworks of Hitchcock and Powell, it climaxes with a brave, well-executed internal fight to the death rather than the conventional battle between monster and monster-hunting, Peter Cushing-shaped, authority figure.

Paul Massie's commendable lead performance reverses audience expectations largely created by Hollywood's earlier versions of the Stevenson tome. Massie, only in his 20s at the time, somewhat awkwardly plays Dr. Jekyll as a repressed, unhappy fuddy duddy with *outrageous* Dennis Healey-style, stick-on eyebrows and a beard straight from Hammer's Big Box of Menacing Facial Hair. Mr. Hyde is clean cut, has neatly plucked eyebrows and represents the deceptively charming release of Jekyll's pent-up emotions and desires; consequently, he's as much of a nutter as he is a lady-killer. It's in the Hyde incarnation that Jekyll learns of the affair his wife (Dawn Addams) has been conducting with boozing, womanizing cad Christopher Lee. Lee, controversially *not* selected to play the dual lead role, is fun to watch as a total bastard—even those bored by

the film's meandering pace will appreciate his drunk act and a scowl that could stun a horse at ten paces.

Fisher's fondness for doomed anti-heroes and narratives built upon tragic inevitability is once again strongly apparent. This time, however, the unsympathetic characters are hard to become involved with and, in horror terms, there's no real pay-off. Still, Jack Asher's MegaScope cinematography looked gorgeous during the non-damaged moments of the 35mm showing in London, and this movie at the very least deserves recognition for diverting from the Hammer formula to deliver something thoughtful and intelligent.
—Steven West

Credits: Director: Terence Fisher; Writer: Wolf Mankowitz. Leading Cast: Paul Massie, Dawn Addams, Christopher Lee, David Kossoff, Norma Marla.

Urge to Kill

"Pretty bits!" No, not the description of the unfortunate lasses shortly to be mutilated by a dockland serial killer, but a reference to shards of glass collected by the special needs Hughie in Vernon Sewell's 1960 film *Urge to Kill*. It is a deplorable representation of a learning disability, portrayed with hunched shoulders and an infantile voice. Mental health and disability were to undergo reappraisal in the latter part of the decade as a series of training films fought to explain and understand the basic principles of dignity and care, improving the lives of those less fortunate. Filmed entertainment turned the mentally underprivileged into monsters and laughing stocks, and to this end, education and realism are distant concepts

in James Eastwood's adaptation of a Charles K. Freeman and Gerald Savory play (which in turn was an adaptation of Savory's 1942 novel *Hughie Roddis*). This theatrical version was an opportunistic second stab, the story having been filmed the previous year under its original title *Hand In Glove*, broadcast live as a play on ITV's *Armchair Theatre*.

Urge to Kill is an embarrassing but entertaining Merton Park pot noodle of a shoot, chucked into production for a quota support slot. Style was something that Sewell generally begrudged the viewers, excepting occasional welcome whims, but he opens on a promising note here as a beautiful girl, Jenny (Laura Thurlow), is seen to recognize the figure from whose perspective the camera gazes. His gloved hands fall upon her and she screams before the scene cuts to a kettle whistling in a stinging, shrieking pitch. Mind you, that's your lot for cleverness.

Jenny is the latest victim of a serial killer, and Auntie B's lodging house becomes the focus next morning as news of the grisly slaying comes to the breakfast table. Auntie B (Ruth Dunning) is responsible for Hughie (Terence Knapp, repeating the role he had taken in the television version), a grown man with the mind of a child. She has two male lodgers, a salesman, Charles Ramskill (Howard Pays), and the wiry teacher Mr. Forsythe (Wilfred Brambell), a budding Festival of Light supporter, who is quick to blame the victims. If a girl is easy to court, then she so courts her own demise, the Jezebel, or such is his opinion. It would have been amusing had Mr. Forsythe proven to be the maniac, as this film was a contemporary of *Cover Girl Killer*, in which Harry H. Corbett is the fiend, and thus we could have seen both Steptoe and Son slaying beautiful women in tandem. But the police inquiries move in another direction, and initially the wrong one.

Hughie is prone to late night wanderings, which come up in conversation, but he is not telling the reason for his after hours behavior. A broken plate is irresistible, and Hughie wants to collect the pieces but is not permitted. His obsession is such that he will return to them when the room is otherwise empty. The details of the attacks are coming through. Jenny Latham's body has been mutilated, as if gradually cut up with indeterminate, sharp objects. What! Like shards of broken glass! "Got herself strangulated…murdered and gashed." The newspaper emphasizes these details and, for the purposes of plot expediency, the press has a supernatural knowledge of events while the body is still warm.

The ugly details are read out: "The girl's body was found that night among the debris of the Old Queen's Dock…the body was severely lacerated. No weapon has yet been found.

The police believe the killer could have caused the injuries with broken glass." This story was partly recycled in a 1973 episode of Brian Clemens' *Thriller* series, *File It Under Fear*, with more action and pizzazz, and a new identity for the killer; that, too, featured a lodger prone to late meanderings while girls died and others in the house rifled the newspapers for details. Coming in 1960, the real inspiration for this household would likely have been *Peeping Tom*, which features a similar complement for a domicile, with breakfast table discussion on what the press is saying about the local murders. However, in a game

Ruth Dunning

of who came first, *Peeping Tom* would lose, as it only went into production after the original television production of *Hand in Glove* had been screened.

The police, led by Patrick Barr as Superintendent Allen (the original role had been taken by the similarly dependable Rupert Davies), make a trip to the pub to speak to Jenny's father, Curly, the landlord. Curly wants action, but the locals are not helpful, chattering on about the defaulted Hughie as the potential killer. "Seems like a gentle sort of boy—wouldn't harm a fly" (sounds familiar—1960, you say!), "but you never know with these mental cases." The real killer is the initially smooth Mr. Ramskill (Howard Pays), who is another of these murderers who retains a semblance of quintessential normalcy while capable of extreme deeds. He escorts a young beauty, Gwen (Yvonne Buckingham), who perhaps shouldn't have agreed to a first date in a shed on the allotment. Hughie is spotted by police collecting broken glass from wasteland, contributing heavily to the case against him.

Ramskill has a mind to set Hughie up for the killings. He has Lily Morris (Anna Turner) lined up as his next victim and encourages Hughie to go out again, failing this time. Ramskill strangles Lily, and the subsequent mood is grim with the assumption that she too is dead, but Superintendent Allen had found a pulse, the girl is safe, and Ramskill gets caught up in his own deceitfulness. As the Superintendent reveals that the girl is alive, Ramskill lunges not for the front door but toward the room in which he left Lily, perhaps to prove the Superintendent wrong, perhaps to finish the job, then—prevented—can only holler out protests to his victim as if his lies could ever resolve his new circumstances. The Superintendent is Patrick Barr, so he is not going to have the wool pulled over his eyes, and one suspects that, like Columbo, he senses the identity of the killer from the moment he meets him. Ramskill's traits include repeat references to himself: "That's who I am!" Rather too tellingly perhaps, when alone with the Superintendent, he responds rhetorically to a question about his own whereabouts: "Where did *yours truly* go?" the "*yours truly*" proof of kinship to a certain Victorian serial killer who also ripped up his victims.

The sets are often basic and the film is talkative, with the camera confined to a small number of unimaginative shots as if recording an early television play. The exteriors are more moodily captured, though the film's chills are dependent on the details of the murders: the time spent cutting the victims, carried as a threat to all potential victims. Running a brief 56 minutes, *Urge to Kill* is shorter than *File It Under Fear*, though at that running time it at least avoids becoming dull. Its half-time switch from murder mystery into psycho study also helps. The greatest of its offenses, though, lies in the depiction of the mentally disabled, which is unforgivable. Oh, don't forget that surprise for Auntie B. There's a giveaway clue earlier in the film from Hughie: "I know Israel—I've been there." Maybe the movie *was* ahead of its time, addressing audience fears of the mentally disabled and preaching the idea of improvement of lifestyle for unfortunates through creativity. Hughie has some faith, apparently, and he has created a cruciform gift made from the collected shards. Bless!
—Paul Higson

Credits: Director: Vernon Sewell; Writer: James Eastwood. Leading Cast: Patrick Barr, Ruth Dunning, Howard Pays, Terence Knapp.

Village of the Damned

The inhabitants of an almost unspeakably peaceful and bucolic English village fall asleep en masse for the space of about five hours, leading to official alarm and later a rash of unexplained pregnancies. Scientist Gordon Zellaby (George Sanders) is baffled, as are his wife Anthea (Barbara Shelley), brother-in-law, Alan (Michael Gwynn), and the local doctor (Laurence Naismith). The villagers are horrified, particularly the men who are pretty certain *they* haven't gotten their wives pregnant.

The plot thickens some months later as the affected women give birth to sinister, "perfect" blond moppets with the ability to read people's minds and control their wills. Zellaby, unlike everyone else, wants to study and understand the children as they grow and strengthen, taking charge of their education and separating them from the village for their own safety. His relatively principled stance becomes increasingly untenable due to the villagers' fear and prejudice, not to mention the children's opaque, ominous plans for their human guardians. As the spread of other "colonies" is reported throughout the world with disastrous consequences, and casualties begin to mount in the village, Zellaby finds he has to choose between the quest for scientific knowledge and the safety of the world that this quest is supposed to serve.

Village of the Damned is one of the classics, the children's spooky eyes alone insuring its cult status. The rural setting works brilliantly as a backdrop for alien subversion, and life in the village is presented realistically, particularly in the scenes showing the human cost of the initial pregnancies, with despairing women and angry, suspicious men. The cast is very good, with stalwarts Naismith and Gwynn despairing of Sanders' devotion to cold science, and Shelley, in one of her first major roles, wonderfully human and empathic in her attempts to connect both with her husband and her alien child. The children are memorably creepy, especially with the eye effects on the toddlers. The lion's share of the movie, though, belongs to Sanders, whose performance is up there with his Addison DeWitt in *All About Eve* (1950). In *Village*, Sanders gets to play a relatively heroic role (more so in many ways than it appears at first) and creates one of the more nuanced protagonists of horror films.

What's perhaps most remarkable about *Village* is its unusual sensitivity and thoughtfulness. On the surface, the children are a good example of the cold, alien "takeover"-type monster epitomized by the Don Siegel classic *Invasion of the Body Snatchers* (1956). But just as that film can be read either as a warning of Communist subversion or American suburban brainwashing (or both), *Village* has a number of unexpected cards up its sleeve as well. Based on John Wyndham's novel *The Midwich Cuckoos*, the film (one of whose writers was *Route 66* creator Stirling Silliphant) sets up a variety of problematic moral conflicts. The children are clearly up to no good, at least by the end, but the villagers aren't angels themselves, easily forming into mobs and suspicious of outsiders. Where *Village* is especially good is that it seems to leave the question open on moral culpability: Were the children evil all along, or did human prejudice push them into it?

The movie's ambiguous moral stance is most clearly embodied in the figure of Zellaby, whose devotion to science not only makes him the only person willing to try and connect with the children, but also complicates his relationship with Anthea, itself a little troubled due to the age difference between the characters (mentioned in passing). That *Village* can provide the chills it does and still pose these questions and issues makes it an indisputable classic.

—Wendell McKay

Credits: Director: Wolf Rilla; Writers: Wolf Rilla, Stirling Silliphant, George Barclay.
Leading Cast: George Sanders, Barbara Shelley, Martin Stephens, Michael Gwynn, Laurence Naismith, Richard Vernon, Jenny Laird

The Curse of the Werewolf

Having already revived most of the monsters in the Universal graveyard to great financial success (if not critical acclaim), it was inevitable that Hammer would take a crack at the werewolf concept. Acquiring the rights to Guy Endore's 1933 novel *The Werewolf of Paris* meant that, by the time producer Anthony Hinds came to commission a script, a fair portion of the budget already had disappeared, so he wrote his own under his soon-to-be usual *nom de plume* of John Elder. You wonder why Hammer bothered getting the rights in the first place, as the film bears hardly any resemblance to the book; it shifts the action to 18th century Spain, for a start.

And that's where we meet a beggar (Richard Wordsworth) who, in search of a handout, is directed to the castle home of the Marques Siniestro (Richard Dawson). Inside, the Marques is celebrating his wedding to his young bride (it *must* be the money). Having debased the beggar even further by having him dance for his supper, the Marques tosses him in jail where he rots for 15 years (hey, he's off the damn street). During that time, the beggar's only human contact is with his jailer and, latterly, the jailer's daughter, who blossoms into the frankly eye-popping Yvonne Romain. When she spurns the advances of the Marques, now widowed, decrepit and in dire need of a facial, he tosses her in chokey alongside the beggar. No doubt spurred on by the sight of perhaps the greatest cleavage in any Hammer film (and that's saying something), the beggar rapes her. But she escapes, stabbing the Marques and fleeing into the forest where she's found half dead.

Blimey, you think, surely things can't get any worse for the poor, unfortunate, gorgeous girl; and then she dies, but not before giving birth to little Leon. Brought up by the girl's rescuer, Don Alfredo Carido (Clifford Evans), the omens for the boy are bleak. He's born on Christmas Day, which according to Carido's maid is an "insult to heaven," and sure enough God, in his usual loving way, sees that the poor bastard is doomed from the start. Leon grows into a singularly irritating boy with a taste for rare lamb and hairy palms (nothing unusual there).

This is where Hinds puts a novel spin on the werewolf legend: Leon, as long as he is shown love, has every chance of beating his curse and for a while it seems he has, as he grows up into Oliver Reed. Ah, you wondered when we'd get to Ollie, and you will again while watching this, as he finally shows up at the halfway mark. Leon lands a job and a girlfriend (Catherine Feller), and it seems as though things are on the up. But this is a horror film, and when he's separated from his love on the night of a full moon, all hairy hell breaks loose.

While not in the top rank of Hammer horrors, this is still an excellent movie. It looks beautiful, and the cast (rounded out by the familiar faces of Warren Mitchell and Michael Ripper) provide sterling work, especially Reed, who succeeds in conveying an animal rage bubbling just under the surface. The makeup, while not especially wolf-like, is very good for the period. Yes, there's the odd gaffe (in the narration and none-too-kosher Spanish accents, mainly), and Romain's and Feller's roles should have been reversed. But as a whole, this is a werewolf movie to stand alongside Chaney's *The Wolf Man*.
—Jed Raven

The tone of Hammer's only werewolf movie—an undeserving box-office failure, now considered among their best work—is set by the close-up image behind the opening title sequence. Despite the typically bombastic Hammer titles music (forming part of Benjamin Frankel's rich original score), the image is one of pathos: a protracted shot of a werewolf's weeping eyes. While Lon Chaney, Jr., overplayed the pitiful plight of his Wolf Man to the point of earning a hearty slap, Fisher's film, which devotes more time to the central character's tragic origins than it does to his lycanthropy, triumphantly conveys the inherent melancholia of its werewolf within a story rife with blood and depravity.

Flawed only by ill-advised, intrusive voice-over narration, the movie has an absorbing first half despite the noted absence of any full moon hairy-paw action. In Spain two centuries ago, beggar Richard Wordsworth (in a role as memorable as his haunting turn as Victor Carroon in *The Quatermass Xperiment* years earlier) is humiliated and imprisoned in the castle dungeon of heartless bastard Marques Anthony Dawson. Relishing the chance to play the film's real villain, Dawson is fabulous, especially in the later scenes depicting him as a vile, cackling old man, merrily picking at facial scabs before being repeatedly stabbed by chesty, mute servant girl Yvonne Romain in one of the more visceral scenes of early Hammer horror.

Wordsworth becomes wild, hairy and horny in the dungeons, and his rape of Romain results in the fulfilment of the ancient superstition of an unwanted child born on Christmas Day leading to Bad Things. Neat casting means

25

that Justin Walters, portraying Young Leon, looks like he *could* grow up to be Oliver Reed. Born a half-hour into the movie, the budding lycanthrope munches on goats at night, while Priest John Gabriel has the Maria Ouspenskaya role: explaining werewolf lore, including the romantic notion that true love can save the wolf man. Halfway into the movie, Reed makes his first appearance as the adult Leon embarks on a doomed affair with a woman (Catherine Feller) trapped into an imminent arranged marriage.

The cast has the usual array of Brit TV actors and Hammer veterans. A pre-Alf Garnett Warren Mitchell plays a night watchman; as the mayor, Peter Sallis wins the 1961 Silly Moustache award; and that's Michael Ripper (who else?) as an old soak in a tavern where the joshing regulars sarcastically order "wolf steaks." The leads are excellent, though it's Reed who makes a big impact from limited screen time. A physically intimidating yet charismatic presence, Reed is one of the genre's most compelling werewolves, combining convincing anguish with genuine menace to startling effect. The werewolf, who doesn't attack until the final reels, is glimpsed only as a hand or shadow until a bravura, rousing bell-tower finale unveils an excellent makeup job, the usual angry Hammer mob ("Burn it!") and more blood-spurting violence as Evans reluctantly shoots the ill-fated young man he raised.

Preserved in an utterly gorgeous print by Universal's recent Region One DVD release, this superb movie has particularly beautiful cinematography by Arthur Grant.
—Steven West

Credits: Director: Terence Fisher; Writer: John Elder [Anthony Hinds].
Leading Cast: Oliver Reed, Yvonne Romain, Clifford Evans, Anthony Dawson, Richard Wordsworth, Michael Ripper.

Gorgo

Eugene Lourie's movie *The Beast from 20,0000 Fathoms* features a routine heroine playing both scientist and romantic interest. His low-budget British film *The Giant Behemoth* (co-directed with Douglas Hickox) also includes a hardy female scientist, though she vanishes without explanation halfway through the film, leaving the action to the men and the monster. Her disappearing act is unlikely to have been malicious, but instead dismissive; it may even have been the point at which one director replaced the other. Lourie was nudging the women out of his monster romps and, by the time he came to direct *Gorgo*, women were conspicuously absent. Irrespective of any actual agenda, *Gorgo* seems considerably deeper than a typical creature feature. Whether intentional or not, *Gorgo*, in which two men adopt a boy and confirm their relationship over his rescue, became the first "gay family unit" monster movie.

The story is not dissimilar to the earlier two Lourie epics. The ocean floor throws up a monster that wrecks a city until its spree is stayed, be it by military power or a satisfaction in the beast. *Gorgo*, however, is unusual, with a welter of subtext

bubbling away beneath its thin mantle. Captain Joe Ryan (Bill Travers) and Sam Slade (William Sylvester) are salvage divers arriving at the waters around Nara Island, off the coast of Ireland, when volcanic activity on the ocean floor damages their ship. Though they inform the harbormaster McCartin (Christopher Rhodes) that they will not be seaworthy for days, he refuses them more than 24 hours in port. The orphaned boy, Sean (Vincent Winter), who lives under the same roof as Mc-Cartin, catches up with the salvagers and tells them that the harbormaster is "a heathen liar," which is nothing short of the conclusion they had reached.

The undersea quake has also freed a monster that brings about the death of a couple of local divers before coming out of the sea and attacking the island village. Ryan and Slade capture the monster but ignore the Irish authorities' request for the specimen to be examined at the University of Dublin. The salvagers know full well the commercial viability in their find and set course for London, where Dorkins Circus awaits with an agreement that will net them an initial £15,000. During the voyage, the monster stirs and kills a crew member, and on arrival at Battersea Park where Gorgo is to be exhibited, a flash bulb awakens it, causing the death of another prominent team member, Mike. The exhibition is successful, but scientists assess that the monster is still in infancy and that its parent could tower to up to 200 feet. The adult indeed stands just so tall, following its young out of the sea and destroying the Nara Island village. It then follows the phosphorescent trail left by the monster, as it was kept from dehydration during transportation. The adult monster obliterates several London landmarks, killing thousands, and only desists when it reaches its offspring, returning with baby Gorgo to the sea.

The accent is on masculinity. The norm for a monster movie of the period was to have two male protagonists sparring over the female costar, but here Ryan and Slade show no interest at all in women. The two are never apart, and essentially represent the formula "couple." The idea of this union is affirmed when Ryan and Slade inadvertently adopt the boy. Sean stows away on their motor vessel, *Triton*, out of concern for the creature, and from that point on the adoption process begins. On reaching London, he is not collected by social services but joins Ryan and Slade in their temporary caravan home. The death of the sailors changes Slade, who hits the bottle out of guilt. Ryan, however, is celebratory. "I've got a suite of rooms at the best hotel in town," he insists, hinting at a night removed from their young sleeping charge, but he can do nothing to coax Slade out of his morass.

Slade later makes a drunken attempt at releasing Gorgo, allowing it back into the Thames. The final reel of the film depicts the boy being misplaced and the "foster parents" risking the raining masonry of London as the monster wreaks havoc. Recovering the boy, they reunite, seemingly cured of all ills and worries, and the family unit is restored. There is disproportionate consideration paid to others by this "family," however, suggesting a self-recognition of its freak status. Slade suffers guilt at the death of two shipmates, but the thousands of fatalities that follow are lost on him. Sean too seems almost insanely oblivious to the slaughter in his admiration for the prehistoric wild-life: He is spotted at one point, alone, crouched on steps, smiling up at the murderous beast, as others die in its path. Has the boy been the victim of abuse on Nara Island to formalize this antisocial attitude? This is not only a family unit, but also a dysfunctional one. The film is not completely averse to other aspects of family life. Most obviously it arises in Slade's own words as he marks his culpability over the death of Mike who leaves "a wife and two children." No surprise then that Ryan cracks on with the work and Slade stays home looking after the boy, assuming the maternal role in their relationship.

Images of conventional domesticity are violently rejected in *Gorgo*. Women are seen only fleetingly in small doom-mongering tableaux. A couple in their nightclothes cast themselves desperately from their bedroom window to their certain deaths in the street below. A mother and daughter, fleeing the ram-page, are depicted for several seconds, a rare acknowledgment of the other sex in this film. The screaming child drops her doll and men trample it, a declara-tion of death to the next generation. The fears of the Welfare State abound, a future in which women fall into three categories: childless, aborting, or single mothers surviving on the benefit funded by others. The capital is leveled by the largest single parent of them all, and it is too easy to assume that they are maternal instincts that send the creature in pursuit of its abducted offspring, but there is no finalizing evidence in the film that it is not the father. Much of the writing as-sumes that the parent is female, but it is never stated. The adult monster might instead be a forerunner of the "Fathers for Justice," complete with fancy dress suit, targeting landmarks in his quest for access to his child. But if the beast is female, you certainly hear her roar.

The script came from a pair of blacklisted Hollywood screenwriters, Robert L. Richards and Daniel James. Rec-ognized by the Writers Guild of America for official correc-tion in their own names in July 2000, the film will continue to credit them respectively as John Loring and Daniel Hyatt until the Guild can confirm ownership of the movie, and that owner can honor them in new release prints with an appropriate amendment. James had co-scripted *The Giant Behemoth* with

Eugene Lourie, itself the subject of a WGA correction that should already exist in the DVD releases. Where exactly the rage and anger in *Gorgo* and, to a certain extent, *The Giant Behemoth* comes from may have less to do with gender and more to do with the blacklist-ed authors' suppressed freedoms and a termination of recognition. In his personal life, Daniel James was familiar with adoption, hav-ing married into a ready-set family just prior to the war (in 1938 he wed ballerina Lillith Stanward who had one young daughter). *Gorgo* was therefore another op-portunity for a subversive writer to upset conventions, just as he had as an agitprop playwright and later in the unplanned hoax auto-biography of a young Chicano in the short story "The Somebody." This time he was flipsiding a real experience of his own, to help him write a story that would be oddly intriguing.

Lourie's third dinosaur stands on two legs, a man in a rubber suit, a model that is common to Japa-nese monster movies but rare in British creature features. *Konga* would be the next, shot almost simultaneously, and it would be another 15 years before men in big monster suits would return to Britain in the Kevin Connor adventure films and then *Queen Kong* (1976). *Gorgo* shuffles around the schedules, pretending to be a little episode in monster fun, but it is riddled with great details and secrets.

—Paul Higson

Credits: Director: Eugene Lourié; Writers: John Loring, Daniel Hyatt.
Leading Cast: Bill Travers, William Sylvester, Vincent Winter, Christopher Rhodes.

Editor's note: Gorgo lives! Inspired by the movie, British sf/horror journalist M.J. Simpson scripted a 2008 short film entitled *Waiting for Gorgo*. Jan Manthey's 2001 short *Inspector Zucker vs. Gorgo* is unrelated, however, featuring a monstrous half-ape, half-woman as its central creature.

27

The Hands of Orlac

Largely unseen, even by devotees of '60s Brit horror, *The Hands of Orlac* is far from a hidden treasure; it's simply unremarkable. While undoubtedly attractive in a *visual* sense, and of interest to lovers of "classic" terror as a remake of an earlier picture (*Mad Love*), it contains, for a horror film, very little actual horror at all. As a psychological thriller, it's neither thrilling nor particularly psychological, and whereas the melo-drama of the 1930s film is part of its appeal, this version hovers uneasily between Grand Guignol theatrics and the grittier, pre-Social Realist tendencies of its director's previous outing, *Beat Girl*, failing to align itself with either approach. Considering that, in the same year, Michael Powell had made *Peeping Tom* in the U.K., Franju had released *Eyes Without a Face* to much acclaim in Europe, and Alfred Hitchcock had helmed *Psycho* in the U.S., the film almost seems retrogressive, even with the plot shifted into a "present day" setting.

With a cast that practically reads like a *Who's Who* of sea-soned Brit horror stalwarts (Christopher Lee, Donald Pleasence, Donald Wolfit, Felix Aylmer, David Peel, Arnold Diamond, Janina Faye, Anita Sharp-Bolster, Gertan Klauber), two hot female leads (Dany Carrel and Lucile Saint-Simon) and a decent enough American ex-pat (Mel Ferrer) in the title role, expecta-tions were high, but such a cast can only work with the material they've been given. Somehow, the screenwriter seems to have taken the constituent parts of Maurice Renard's original story (to which the film actually claims to be faithful) and removed all the most interesting bits, leaving us with the standard tale (old hat even at the time of *Mad Love*) of the pianist, injured in an accident, whose hands are replaced with those of an insane killer, but with no dreamlike sequences or supernatural content (imagined or otherwise) to move things along.

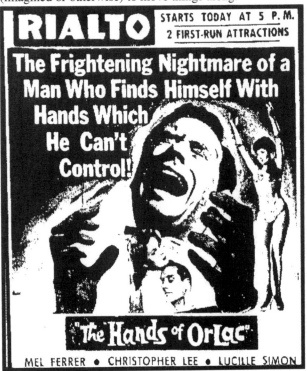

In the 1935 version, Dr. Gogol (Peter Lorre) is jealous of the pianist's relationship with the beautiful heroine, and hypno-tizes his patient into thinking he is a murderer. In the remake, there *is* no Gogol (and thus no romantic intrigue), so we're left to believe that Orlac *thinks* he *might* hurt his wife merely because he reads about the killer in a newspaper, while the surgeon who performed the operation (Wolfit) appears to have little or no ulterior motive and is almost superfluous to the plot.

What we *do* get is a turn from Christopher Lee, at the height of his fame but obviously already eager to branch out from "Gothic" roles, as the down-at-heel, unsuccessful magi-cian Nero, who just happens to live (alongside his tarty assist-ant) in the tawdry hotel Orlac checks into under an assumed name after going a bit loopy and leaving his wife "for her own safety." Clearly Lee is supposed to provide the Lorre angle, but whereas the Hungarian actor played Gogol like someone clearly in the grip of madness, Lee plays Nero as the out-and-out slimy charlatan he is, too financially motivated for us to believe he might possess any real mesmeric powers: After all, no true propagator of evil would shack up in a hotel room with an annoying ye-ye singer.

Yet, in thespian terms, he steals the show, out-acting the strangely uncharismatic Ferrer by a country mile and taking possession of the film as a result. Hamming with style, and delivering uncharacteristic dialogue such as "I couldn't stop you, you were born a slut and you'll always be one," he's at his seedy best, a natural progression from his *Beat Girl* role. After a while, you stop giving a damn about Ferrer and just want to see more of Lee, which is obviously not what the producers had in mind when they hired the American for a presumably large fee.

Ferrer here comes off as an unbelievably bland lead, con-vincing neither as a square-jawed "hunka man" nor a tortured artist. They should have stuck their necks out and brought in an Englishman (John Gregson would have been ideal), but things don't work that way, do they? You also get the feeling that Ferrer wasn't really interested in the film; and he's not the only one, with the plot meandering suspenselessly between one studio-bound conversation and another, and Orlac's arrival at the hotel more or less just "happening" with very little prior dramatic build-up.

In the role of Mrs. Orlac, Saint-Simon also seems a bit of a damp squib: One minute her husband has his hands round her throat, telling her she's "not safe with him"; the next, he's buggered off to the south of France, accompanied by some incongruously jaunty music. She doesn't seem that perturbed, with at least another 40 minutes of plot (including a show-stealing yet *pointless* cameo from Donald Pleasence, who must have just "been there" at the time, à la Lee in *Death Line* 12 years later) elapsing before she even attempts to look for him. I mean, I've heard of "noncommittal," but this is stretching things a bit, unless, alternatively, this was Gréville's attempt at a realist depiction of marriage as opposed to the fairy tale depicted in much Gothic fare, which I doubt.

If truth be known, it takes a long time for a *lot* of things to get going. Over an hour in, there still haven't been any murders (except the unnecessary and rather gruesome offing of a poor innocent dog), and the "establishment"—Felix Aylmer playing a sympathetic doctor and Campbell Singer as an avuncular copper—has only just realized (as has Saint-Simon) that the hands of hanged murderer Vasseur have been grafted onto the pianist. Leaving this revelation (which the *audience* was well aware of from the start) so near the end is an admirable attempt at subtlety, but it effectively robs the film of even more horror potential. As a result, the first remotely eerie moment (actually a *Scooby Doo* involving Lee and a mask) doesn't happen until some 70 minutes in, and the first tangible "tension" is displayed as the film heads towards its climax. The only "murder" (of a character who was quite obviously going to get it all along), at around the 90-minute mark, has nothing to do with Orlac at all! I ask you, was there any point in actually including him in the film? They could have invented another plot entirely, with Lee's cackling magician in the lead, and it would have been a whole lot better.

Is it possible to make a horror film where you *forget* to put in any scary bits and just concentrate on the outward aesthetics? I think Gréville's pulled it off here, accidentally or otherwise. It *looks* beautiful, but so does the seafront at Largs in August, and I wouldn't want to watch that for 95 minutes, either. There's a clever twist (no, I'm not telling you) that almost redeems everything, but it still doesn't stop you feeling a tad short-changed.
—D.R. Shimon

Credits: Director: Edmond T. Gréville; Writers: Edmond T. Gréville, John Baines.
Leading Cast: Mel Ferrer, Christopher Lee, Dany Carrel, Lucile Saint-Simon, Felix Aylmer, Donald Pleasence, David Peel.

House of Mystery

A cautionary little tale that shows a grim side to prospective property purchasing, *House of Mystery* is a brief but gripping marvel from the era of the British quota quickie. Its director, Vernon Sewell, did much of his most notable work under the restrictive conditions dictated by that particular form, and if such a supposed journeyman can be said to have enjoyed a golden career period, then the 1961-62 season, which spawned his startling hat-trick of *The Man in the Back Seat*, *Strongroom*, and this modern slant on cursed/haunted abode shtick, is surely it.

Dare we compare the screenplay of this throwaway to the revered output of Nigel Kneale? Certainly elements of it anticipate *The Stone Tape* by over a decade, in melding spectral loomings with state-of-the-art technology. Also beaten to the punch was 1980's celebrated small-screen *Hammer House of Horror*, whose fan-favored episode, "The Silent Scream," carries suspiciously strong echoes of *House of Mystery*. Splendid though it was to witness Peter Cushing's ruthless Nazi character and an effective shock finale in the Hammer show, "Silent Scream" is battery-powered compared to Sewell's live wire jolt to the senses.

Daring to utilize a remarkable flashback-within-flashback technique, the director pulls off the gamble so deftly that you barely notice the film's innovatively audacious structure. A young house-hunting couple with the keys to Orchard Cottage find the place rather prettier and more welcoming than its £2500 price tag suggests. Inside, they are surprised to meet an unexpected female occupant who obligingly relates the cottage's tortured recent history. It transpires that the previous owners (Nanette Newman and Maurice Kaufmann) were plagued by lighting and wiring troubles, lamps flashing on and off, and visitations by a male figure reaching out to them. At first believed to be a corporeal intruder, but soon recognized as something more vague, this spook even interrupts the evening's television broadcasts. Kaufmann rings the station to complain, only to be advised, "You must have switched to the BBC or something!"

Calling in a dapper, bow-tied expert on psychic phenomena, who theorizes that electrical energy from an unknown source is causing impulses to bombard their brains and conjure these unnerving visions, the couple next permits a Scottish medium into the house. While the boffin waves a huge tuning fork in her face, the seer takes us back to examine the preceding events which explain all.

Jane Hylton's early appearance in the flashback may tip us off to part of *House of Mystery*'s devastating final moments, but viewers who reckon on having deduced all may find themselves in for additional nagging anxiety once the true horrors of the climax sink in. Hylton and her louche lover Clive (John Merivale) plot to do away with the hubby Mark (Peter Dyneley), an obsessive bore who constantly tinkers with his experiments in electricity, while the missus and her boy toy create sparks of their own behind his back. Mark uncovers and deactivates their deadly handiwork (post-*Psycho*, they intended to see him fry while reading a book in the bathtub, having connected the heater cord dangerously to the mains) and sets about turning the tables, using his own expertise to wire up all manner of household implements, appliances and furnishings to a high voltage generator, making many of the mod cons lethal to the touch, and then trapping the faithless pair in the living room.

It's here that Hylton's earlier, apparently glib remarks to the new, would-be mortgagees take on an increased significance, especially her reply to an inquiry about the piped-in amenities: "There was no gas—*everything* was done by electricity." Elsewhere, Sewell also indicates considerable disrespect for the veneer of normality: the local bobby seen swigging hastily from a beer glass before departing to answer a call-out, relieved to be escaping his awful wife and noisy, kids; Mark using his pet dog in horrific-looking lab tests; and Newman and Kaufmann's cosy domesticity shattered almost from the moment they enter their dream home. As for the ending, I'll leave you to experience it for yourselves, but it repays careful thought and attention, revealing itself as one of the most despairing, uncompromising, and downright unfair closing shots you'll ever see. Sewell's searing sizzler is one of British horror's great hidden treasures. Track down this high-energy shocker, if you can.
—Darrell Buxton

Credits: Director and Writer: Vernon Sewell.
Leading Cast: Jane Hylton, Peter Dyneley, Nanette Newman, Maurice Kaufmann

The Innocents

Without doubt one of the very best ghost stories ever committed to film, *The Innocents* also belongs to that short list of horror pictures that have taken the genre in a direction completely at odds with what had gone before. Beforehand, haunted houses had mostly been filmed for comedy; afterwards, no one laughed when characters glimpsed movements in the shadows.

The Turn of the Screw, a novella by celebrated writer Henry James, was first published in 1898, initially in *Collier's Weekly*, then with another story, "Covering End," in the volume *The Two Magics*. James described his story as "a trap for the unwary," and it certainly is! Unlike most ghost tales, the question of whether the governess actually sees the ghosts of the former valet and governess, or whether the repressed spinster is driven mad by sexual frustration and desire is left tantalizingly unanswered. *The Innocents* (the name was very sensibly carried over from the play, written by co-scripter William Archibald, upon which the screenplay was partially based) retains this ambiguity, making the film an even more powerful experience on subsequent viewings.

The haunting, unsettling feeling that pervades the film is established from the outset, where, in an astonishing conceit, the 20th Century-Fox fanfare over the famous logo is silenced and replaced by a child's haunting, mournful singing. Thus an unnerving feeling is with us even before the film begins. An opening scene featuring Miles' funeral was wisely dropped, so the first we see of the governess, Miss Giddens, is as a nervous but hopeful applicant being interviewed by the children's cold, distant uncle. He stresses that he must never be contacted about the children, emphasizing from the outset the sense of isolation the governess will soon be experiencing. As soon as she arrives at the house, she touches some "lovely roses" and several petals promptly fall off. Thus a pervasive sense of death and decay is there right from the beginning.

And who are "the innocents?" The obvious answer is the children, but could the title not also include the governess, who certainly appears to be "innocent" in the ways of the world, and even the housekeeper, Mrs. Grose, who completely fails to comprehend the effect that the deceased Quint, the valet, and Miss Jessel, the governess, might have had on the youngsters? Alternatively, the children might indeed be experienced beyond their years; Miss Giddens might have come to this position following an extremely unpleasant relationship that scarred her, sending her to the brink of madness; and Mrs. Grose might be more complicit in past events than she cares to reveal. This multilayered approach is ably carried through from the novel and wonderfully maintained by a uniformly superb cast.

For ghost story purists, there are, arguably, two miscalculations. One comes when Miss Giddens, having seen Miss Jessel sitting at the teacher's desk in the schoolroom, finds a tear shed by her on the desk. This physical manifestation of the ghost (the tear could not have been left by anyone else) could break the spell of ambiguity that has been so carefully built up; as does the second instance, when, at the finale, the camera looks over Quint's shoulder at Miss Giddens and Miles looking up at him. How can Miss Giddens imagine this view? And why, if he still can't see the ghost of Quint, does Miles collapse and die? If we choose to conclude that he was overcome by Miss Giddens' madness, this means—as she cries out that he is now "safe" and "free"—that he is free, not of Quint, but of her. The kindly, well-intentioned governess, therefore, has driven Flora to the brink of hysteria and caused the death of Miles. Do we want to believe this, or that the children really were possessed? Just where does this leave the audience?

Following his huge success, critically and financially, with *Room at the Top*, Jack Clayton had the film world at his feet. It is to the horror genre's eternal benefit that the feisty independent director thumbed his nose at prefabricated deals to direct such properties as *Saturday Night and Sunday Morning* and *Sons and Lovers* to instead jump at the challenge to "film the un-filmable." For, in doing so, he crafted a true masterpiece, that rarity in the genre: a thinking person's horror film.
—Dave Simpson

Based on *The Turn of the Screw* by Henry James, *The Innocents* is perhaps more memorable than its source, largely because of the powerful performances and a subtly surreal quality. The eerie moments are effective because there's a more dreamlike, or nightmarish, quality to them, and the film cleverly avoids stating explicitly that what Miss Giddens is actually seeing are ghosts. In fact there are several suggestive scenes, particularly with regard to her restless nights and exhaustion because of her bad dreams, implying that this might be helping a deep-seated psychosis to manifest itself. It is quite a slow-burner, spending a full half hour setting the scene, and for a long time there's only the merest hint that something is amiss. But within 40 minutes it turns into a film that you'll want to see through to the end.

The concept of these "ghosts," who are previous occupants of the house, trying to perpetuate their relationship in some way, by possessing the two children is also an unusual and interesting slant on the "ghost story" theme. Even more intriguing is whether the controlling and manipulative personality of Quint is actually possessing Miles in some way. It would certainly explain the completely unexpected and slightly disturbing "kiss" on the lips between Miss Giddens and the young boy, which lasts a few seconds. But once again, nothing is made explicit. Miss Giddens makes no attempt to break off this "kiss," to reduce it to a half second-long peck, as you would normally expect between an adult and child—thus raising questions in the viewer's mind, since this is a seemingly lonely woman from a strong religious background who has no children of her own. Or perhaps, in her possibly unbalanced psychological state, she actually imagines she's being kissed by Quint?

Whatever the answer, it's another example, albeit the most disquieting in the film, of things being left ambiguous. That, along with some surreal imagery effectively underscoring the most eerie moments of Miss Giddens' experiences, all makes for subtle stuff. The remaining element contributing to the

film's classic status is the strength of the acting. Deborah Kerr gives a compelling performance, perhaps upstaged only by Megs Jenkins, whose portrayal of Mrs. Grose is so convincing in a solid, down to earth way. The child actors are both very good, and Martin Stephens, who appeared in many films of the period, including the landmark *Village of the Damned*, where he almost steals the film from his adult co-stars, turns in a particularly remarkable performance for a child actor, especially towards the climax.

All in all, what makes this film memorable is that it builds into a very thought-provoking story with a slightly surreal eeriness to it that appeals to one's imagination, especially throughout the latter half. *The Innocents* is rather more than just a ghost story, and definitely a film that benefits from repeat viewings. —Wayne Jefferies

Credits: Director: Jack Clayton; Writers: William Archibald, Truman Capote, John Mortimer.
Leading Cast: Deborah Kerr, Martin Stephens, Pamela Franklin, Megs Jenkins, Michael Redgrave, Peter Wyngarde, Clytie Jessop.

Konga

Britain's belated answer to *King Kong* was this cut-rate monster movie, a perfect companion piece to the later, even more bizarre Robin Askwith vehicle *Queen Kong*. An embarrassingly inept but utterly hilarious B flick from Anglo-Amalgamated, it offers Michael Gough in one of his most purely entertaining roles, on the heels of the company's memorable casting of him in the estimable early gore pic *Horrors of the Black Museum*.

Gough is your common, or garden variety, mad scientist, returning from his holidays in Uganda with an innovative growth serum, which he tests out on his chimp, Konga. The hairy pet rapidly grows into a towering ape, and Gough takes advantage of the situation by using Konga to dispense with anyone who annoys him or threatens his work, including the dean at the university where he works. Gough's loyal lover (Margo Johns) doesn't bat an eyelid for a while (referring to Konga, she notes calmly, "As big as he's become, I still have the same affection for him") but becomes restless when Gough's murder-by-proxy spree gets out of hand.

Konga gets loopier as it goes along, charting the decline of Gough's marriage via a hysterical breakfast sequence that may or may not have been intended as a parody of a famous scene in *Citizen Kane* ("What do you want with your poached egg: *Murder?*"). When she senses that her husband is planning to ditch her for a pert girl student, Johns injects Konga again and unwittingly instigates the gorilla's mini-rampage around London.

The laughable monster adds to the fun of this typically gaudy Herman Cohen production, with a lip-smacking Gough relishing an array of second-hand mad doctor lines like, "In science, a human being is only a cipher!" Some uproarious scenes involving the film's concept of hip and happening modern students place a close second in the hilarity stakes to the precious moments in which Britain's finest bobbies fail to find any witnesses who saw a massive ape stomping around in public. Eventually the police chief realizes the scale of the threat and heavy-handedly sums up the whole movie: "There's a huge monster gorilla that's constantly growing to outlandish proportions, loose on the streets." Just in case we hadn't figured it out for ourselves...

—Steven West

Credits: Director: John Lemont; Writers: Herman Cohen, Aben Kandel.

Leading Cast: Michael Gough, Margo Johns, Jess Conrad, Claire Gordon, Jack Watson.

The Man in the Back Seat

On one of those rare occasions when commercial necessity produces something approaching high art, Vernon Sewell's exceptional trilogy of fatalistic early 1960s melodramas—*House of Mystery*, *Strongroom* and *The Man in the Back Seat*—were filmed under the British "quota system"—whereby a certain percentage of a cinema bill was legally required to be home-grown and funded—and, like many of their counterparts, proved to be brisk little thrillers, offering a vigorous diversion in stark monochrome prior to the main attraction. In hindsight, however, this tense trio can be seen to intersect and entwine, forming a fuller, deeply pessimistic and resigned view of a universe controlled by cosmic higher forces, with the everyday human players reduced to mere puppets, playthings who are

Derren Nesbitt in *The Man in the Back Seat*

dangling from taut threads without any real control over their own destinies.

There are sufficiently rich pickings in the three films for some budding scholar to pen a thesis or study on the conceptual aspects of Sewell's work during the 1961-62 period, but the nature of this book dictates that we must examine the pictures in isolation. No bother, for *The Man in the Back Seat* alone manages to encapsulate the anxieties, fears and despair of this inadvertent (or intended?) series, to devastating effect.

The events are as basic as they come. A pair of small-time hoodlums, attempting to grab a briefcase filled with loot, whack a bookie over the head as he leaves his office. What Sewell, his writers and the sterling cast spin out from such gossamer proves to be nothing short of miraculous. The almost Ealing-like title could mean anything, the crime setup is simple and seems to offer little potential or possibility for development, and the film's very raison d'être, born of circuit exhibition patterns, promises orthodoxy, but what Sewell delivers is blistering, riveting and significant.

Derren Nesbitt and Keith Faulkner begin the proceedings as villains and remain so throughout; yet, as time and fate progress, we come to realize their helplessness and sheer inability to battle the unseen, corrective forces massed against them. Certain devotees of U.K. "horror" cinema have expressed doubts that this movie should be granted a place alongside the vampire, mad scientist, werewolf and mummy fare prevalent at the time, but *The Man in the Back Seat* ought to demand the attention of any discerning genre buff.

In a more understated way, the plot and execution anticipate the "coincidence—or something more?" shudders of the *Final Destination* franchise from four decades later, but I prefer to think of it as resembling *Z Cars* as if penned by H.P. Lovecraft. Everything conspires against our lead characters as their hopes and plans slowly unravel, their bid for a fast payday transforming into a nightmare, both physical and paranormal, as they anxiously attempt to rid themselves of the bookie's body, an albatross every inch as encumbering—and metaphorical—as Coleridge's. To the credit of the actors, none of the night's tribulations, from burst tires and empty petrol tanks to injuries and the dawning futility of their task, seem at all forced or over-

coincidental. This is a gripping and involving ride throughout, crammed with obstacles and spiraling into metaphysical terror.

By the desperate finale, any viewers still maintaining doubts about the supernatural influences pervading and driving this fevered episode will find their disbelief sorely tested, as Sewell climaxes the ordeal with an eerie surprise, albeit lifted wholesale from Val Lewton and Robert Wise's *The Body Snatcher* (1945), but transplanting itself perfectly into the world of the grubby British crime flick. Sewell's endings often left his players, both pivotal and peripheral, either doomed, damned or dead, and *The Man in the Back Seat* is no exception, with all passengers along this jeopardy-plagued road being ultimately judged.
—Darrell Buxton

Credits: Director: Vernon Sewell; Writers: Malcolm Hulke, Eric Paice.
Leading Cast: Derren Nesbitt, Keith Faulkner, Carol White, Harry Locke.

Mysterious Island

In the closing days of the American Civil War, a group of Union soldiers held prisoner in besieged Richmond—led by the stalwart Captain Cyrus Harding (Michael Craig)—decide to make a break for it in a nearby Confederate balloon. The noble black Neb (Dan Jackson) and callow youth Herbert (Michael Callan) end up with Spilitt (Gary Merrill), a cynical war correspondent, and booze-battered Confederate balloon expert Pencroft (Percy Herbert!) during their escape. The "greatest storm in American history" sends the balloon clear west across the continent and into the Pacific. As the balloon begins to run down, they come across an island that does indeed seem pretty darned mysterious from the get-go: Harding is pulled from the water and given a signal fire by hands unknown, and giant shellfish and chickens at first plague the castaways and then delight their palates.

Eventually, other castaways wash up on the island: the terribly English, terribly saucy duo of Lady Mary Fairchild (Joan Greenwood) and her niece, Elena (Beth Rogan), en route from Valparaiso, the latter happily ending up in revealing skins in no time at all and ensnared by Herbert's incomprehensible charms. In the course of their explorations, they find an active volcano, suffer a pirate attack, and locate a series of underground caverns. When the volcano gets frisky, the notorious Captain Nemo (Herbert Lom) shows up with his astonishing submarine *Nautilus*, anxious to leave with the blueprints for his scientific experiments to increase the world's food supply and end the root causes of war (hence the giant wildlife on the island). Can they all work together to save themselves, Nemo's research, and reach home again?

The film in general is a sneaky joy, something of a cross between the previous year's *Swiss Family Robinson* and *The Guns of Navarone* (with giant monsters as a bonus). Jules Verne wrote *The Mysterious Island* as an entertaining but

inferior sequel to *20,000 Leagues Under the Sea*, the sequel being accurately summed up by Ray Harryhausen as "How To Survive on a Desert Island" (cheekily referenced in the film as the castaways find a copy of *Robinson Crusoe*). Harryhausen and producer Charles Schneer decided to jazz it up by adding the ladies and emphasizing the "monster" angle.

The comically stereotypical nature of the original escapees is both negated and enlivened by some clever writing and the cast's obvious chemistry (anchored by Craig's mildly stiff charisma). At one point, they just start dancing in a moment that feels strangely unforced, and everyone makes fun of the deliciously game Spilitt. The women never throw off the effect, fitting right in: Rogan hardly seems out of place wearing what amounts to a *très chic* bathing suit of a century later; and Greenwood looks like she's having a blast, despite (because of?) her having to take a bead on a giant chicken. They're well-served by the screenplay, too: "Mother got married when she was my age" inspires the reply, "Darling, that was on the *Continent!*" Some weighty conversations about the sources of conflict (with two poles: Nemo torpedoing warships without warning to end war; and Harding as a soldier fighting a war which by 1865 had reached an inarguably admirable purpose) add a little starchy depth.

Everything's shipshape, and it's always a pleasure to watch Harryhausen's magic at work. *Mysterious Island* manages to be that rarity, a genuine family film that doesn't condescend to its audience while providing both thrills and food for thought (hardly surprising for a film inspired by Jules Verne).
—Wendell McKay

Credits: Director: Cy Endfield; Writers: John Prebble, Daniel Ullman, Crane Wilbur.
Leading Cast: Michael Craig, Joan Greenwood, Michael Callan, Gary Merrill, Herbert Lom, Nigel Green.

Night of the Eagle (aka *Burn, Witch, Burn*)

"...'cause it's witchcraft, wicked witchcraft and although I know it's strictly taboo…"

Overshadowed by the similarly titled and themed *Night of the Demon* (1957), *Night of the Eagle* is, in many ways, a more interesting film. Sociology professor Norman Taylor (Peter Wyngarde) discovers that his wife (Janet Blair) is a practising witch. Ever the rationalist ("If we were to investigate all of the strange rituals performed by women based on their so-called

intuition, half the female population would be in asylums"), he forces her to destroy all her charms, ignoring her pleas that they are his only defense against a gaggle of jealous academics (and their far-worse wives). That this proves to be a mistake is something of an understatement, as Taylor's charmed life soon begins to crumble.

The film was based on fantasy legend Fritz Leiber's novel *Conjure Wife*, which formed the basis of an earlier movie, Universal's *Weird Woman* (1944), starring Lon Chaney, Jr. This was brought up to date (Taylor being a teacher of that most modern of sciences, sociology) by respected genre writers Charles Beaumont, Richard Matheson and George Baxt, and relocated to '60s Britain. While the director, Sidney Hayers, was no Jacques Tourneur, here he conjures up a set of atmospheric set-pieces, ranging from a "Monkey's Paw"-inspired sequence with something nasty at the door, Blair's attempted suicide and reappearance in the house of the dead, to the climactic eagle attack (so good, you can ignore the very visible wires).

He's helped by a (largely) great cast. Forget about *Jason King* if you can, Peter Wyngarde is a superb actor and makes Taylor, a character who could easily be smug and unlikable, sympathetic. Certainly you feel his terror at the climax, and it's possibly some of the best genre acting I've seen. He is well matched by Margaret Johnston's hugely malevolent performance; in fact, she comes close to stealing the movie in her few scenes.

It's flawed, of course. The director can't seem to go five minutes without a close-up of the stone eagle, as if, you know, it could be significant and important, so the climax is less of a surprise. Bill Mitchell's character is a pain in the arse: While you could argue that he's meant to be annoying, the fact that

his accent lies somewhere in the middle of the Atlantic (is he British or American, I can never quite tell) is out of place in a cast filled with top-notch British character actors.

I'll end with a fragment of autobiography. *Night of the Eagle* was one of the first British horror movies I watched, coming across it one afternoon (of all times) when I was home from school ill, and it provided a ghostly treat on a dull Friday. Years later, it's still one of the best.
—David/"Lot 249"

Credits: Director: Sidney Hayers; Writers: Charles Beaumont, Richard Matheson, George Baxt.
Leading Cast: Peter Wyngarde, Janet Blair, Margaret Johnston, Anthony Nicholls, Colin Gordon, Reginald Beckwith.

The Shadow of the Cat

Ah, now *here's* a curious one. When is a Hammer film not a Hammer film? When it's directed by one of their great in-house directors, written by George Baxt, stars Barbara Shelley, André Morell and Andrew Crawford, and is made by practically the same crew, but for some obscure technical, contractual, political, "oh, bugger me, what's Jimmy Carreras done with the dosh?" reason, has to be released under the auspices of BHP (Baxt-Hatton-Pennington).

All quibbles over its origin aside, though, *The Shadow of the Cat* is actually a pretty neat little film with some genuine suspense, beautiful cinematography, witty "Old Dark House" dialogue and a few decent scares thrown in. Most people, with the exception of real Brit horror buffs, haven't heard of it or tend to confuse it with any of the numerous versions of *The Cat and the Canary*, but that doesn't stop it from being an enjoyable romp through the eerie corridors of traditional horror. The story is easy enough to pick up: In the pre-credits sequence, we see an old dear (Morell's wife) get bumped off by an unknown assailant, a crime to which the only witness is—surprise, surprise—her beloved mog. A while later, her scheming relatives (who all conspired to bump her off) turn up to fight over the will, followed by her favorite niece (Shelley) and her police doctor boyfriend, the only good apples in the barrel.

Sure enough, they all get picked off one by one, with a divine angel of retribution always seemingly close at hand in the form of the wily feline assassin. Eventually there's no one left except luscious, tweedy Babs, who, halfway through the proceedings, is named in the old lady's *real* will (as opposed to the false one forged by her corrupt cousins) as the sole heir of the house, the cash and her eminently suitable chap (or should that be chappish suitor?).

It's definitely an unusual film for the time, especially as there are very few characters one can identify with, and we spend most of our time watching various ne'er-do-wells get their comeuppance; yet, simultaneously, we feel we should sympathize with them. Every time a death is shown (Crawford's being particularly effective and unpleasant), it appears through the cat's eyes in a kind of widescreen-magnified wibble, something else that makes for memorable and ever-so-slightly unique cinema. Need I say that the surroundings (yes, Black bloody Park again) are as lush, atmospheric and effective as any such locations in any film, and the acting is faultless. There are some particularly effective lines of the "I'll wring its blasted neck if I get hold of it" variety, and Shelley, who had suffered pussy-related trouble of her own (oh, do pack it in, you lot, who do you think I am, Mollie Sugden or something?) in *Cat Girl*, is nowhere near the sex bomb that she would become in *Dracula—Prince of Darkness*, *The Gorgon* and *Rasputin—The Mad Monk*, yet still manages to smoulder her way through practically every frame.

Unfortunately, despite commendable performances all around, the film is let down by one major factor—let's face it, even in a widescreen, squashy, anamorphic close-up, the domestic cat just isn't that scary. As Jacques Tourneur demonstrated, what we *don't* see can often be much scarier than what we do (see what Hal Chester did to his otherwise a masterpiece *Night of the Demon* for proof), particularly in relation to feline-related horror, which is why both *Cat People* and *The Leopard Man* work so well.

Not that *Shadow* doesn't work—it's just that the cat appears so often right from the get-go (apart from the 10 minutes in the middle when it's believed drowned, until the sound of ghostly meowing is heard echoing across the grounds—now *that's* effective) that, by the end, you can't wait for it to hurry up and kill all its mistress' fiendish murderers just so it can bugger off. Maybe if it actually appeared only in shadow, it would be a lot scarier.

—D.R. Shimon

Shadow of the Cat

Credits: Director: John Gilling; Writer: George Baxt.
Leading Cast: William Lucas, Barbara Shelley, André Morell, Conrad Phillips, Alan Wheatley, Vanda Godsell.

The Snake Woman

This is a competent enough B programmer, entertaining in its own way and enjoyable enough to fit into the "cozy horror" subgenre, which seems to have formulated into today's nostalgia-obsessed culture. Despite its shoestring budget and shoddy quality, *The Snake Woman* strikes the mood of the more unorthodox Hammer output, although in no way could it be mistaken for a Hammer flick by anyone except the extremely foolish.

For a start, it features a torch-bearing lynch mob (in what should have been a pre-credits sequence) descending on the house of local "misfit" Dr. Adderson (workmanlike but personable character actor John Cazabon) and his wife as she's about to give birth. The doc, you see, must be a bad 'un, especially according to local crone/gossip/psychic/shit-stirrer Aggie, as he spends his time "consorting with wicked reptiles," which is not natural and is perceived in this part of Northumberland as tantamount to a pact with the Devil himself.

"THE SNAKE WOMAN"

starring JOHN McCARTHY · SUSAN TRAVERS
Directed by SIDNEY J. FURIE · Produced by GEORGE FOWLER
A Caralan Production · Released thru UNITED ARTISTS

Needless to say, they smash his laboratory to pieces, club him to death and set the place on fire, but not before Mrs. Adderson has delivered a cold child with the staring eyes of a demon—well, a child with slightly foreign-looking eyes, but who's splitting hairs? The good doctor had the foresight to hand her over to the other doc performing the delivery (Arnold Marlé, another link with Hammer and probably the best thing about the entire film), who leaves her in the care of the local shepherd and then buggers off to Africa to study fossils.

Some 20 years later, he returns (looking exactly the same age as he did when he left—ancient) and discovers that the girl, whom the shepherd had to raise, on account of her dad being clubbed by the locals, has now grown into a lovely 20-year-old woman—who just happens to have a penchant for disappearing onto the moors and allegedly "bewitching" people. And, as if her parentage and upbringing weren't enough to stigmatize her within the local community, she's been christened Atheris, a name that has "evil snake goddess" written all over it, even to stupid people (i.e., everyone in the village). Oh, it turns out that her kindly dad injected her mother with snake venom while she was expecting (like you do); and so the girl (the truly beautiful Susan Traver) is a cold-blooded half-human who sheds her own skin and transforms into a snake. And, once a year, there's been a murder involving death by poisonous neck bites. Mmm, methinks, could there be a connection here?

At this point, certain questions are answered and other, larger mysteries are left unsolved. Why, if her father was a trained doctor, couldn't he deliver his own daughter? Maybe he couldn't handle it himself, as his wife wasn't a reptile. I admit we don't exactly know what he's a doctor of, but it all seems a little suspicious. If he specialized in reptiles, why has it taken the villagers this long to get annoyed about it? Why does being born with reptilian traits guarantee that one will become a homicidal maniac? If deaths have been occurring for several years, and everyone knows who's responsible, why haven't they descended on her the way they did on her comparatively innocent dad? And why does Marlé, so keen to save the child's life in the early stages, and who was obviously her father's best mate, suddenly do a complete about face and decide his purpose is now to bump her off, thus resulting in his own demise?

Of course, no British film in 1961, horror or otherwise, would be complete without a clean-cut, besuited, Brylcreemed hero, and that's exactly what we get in the form of Charles

37

(John McCarthy), who is sent by Scotland Yard, or at least a superimposed pictorial idea of it, to solve the mystery. Don't they have their own police out in Pretend Northumberland? It would seem not. And before you can say, "I could have told you that was going to happen," he finds himself romantically bewitched by our forked-tongued femme fatale, largely because, as a snake, she's the only woman who's been charmed by his inept flute playing.

Seriously, where do they come up with these things? How long has he been trying this on various women, and hasn't anyone told him that a compliment and a nice glass of port and lemon might do the trick better? Anyway, the whole shebang comes to an end, as one may have guessed, on the moors, with the copper and the Colonel who sent for him suddenly realizing that old Aggie was right all along. An earlier scene, in which McCarthy finds a giant, woman-size, recently-shed skin lying atop the misty peaks, should have been enough of a clue.

Suddenly it's all over, and the deceased body of the beautiful Travers (later to go on to mild infamy as the nurse in *The Abominable Dr. Phibes* and as Barry Foster's missus in *Van der Valk*) is lying amidst the dusky stems. The handsome young policeman can go back to London, probably much to the chagrin of the local barmaid who obviously fancied him (but hated his flute playing, something he saw as a vital clue!), and the villagers who haven't been bitten to death already can return to their life of carefree rural bigotry. And in a moment that surely preempted every episode of *Kolchak: the Night Stalker* by some 13 years, the eminently sensible man from the military decides to throw McCarthy's report on the fire, "just in case anyone believes it." Poof! (That's the sound of the documents going up in flames, not my opinion of the Colonel.)

The dialogue is largely uninspired (although sometimes amusing and once even charming), the acting, with the exception of Arnold Marlé and Geoffrey Denton's performances, borders on the leaden, and the actual snakes themselves appear so fleetingly (not to mention somewhat out of focus and hidden 'neath foliage) that they might as well not be there at all.

Watch by all means, but only out of curiosity or completism. Those seeking the fulfilment one derives even from the cheesiest of films would really do well to search elsewhere, and there are plenty of better places to look. Susan Travers, though, is another matter—I could ogle her for hours. What a shame, then, that she appears so infrequently in the film in which she plays the title role.
—D.R. Shimon

Credits: Director: Sidney J. Furie; Writer: Orville Hampton. **Leading Cast:** John McCarthy, Susan Travers, Geoffrey Denton, Arnold Marlé.

Taste of Fear (aka Scream of Fear)

Taste of Fear (aka *Scream of Fear*) was a refreshing change of pace from Hammer Films. Brought on, no doubt, by the phenomenal success of *Psycho*, this is one of Hammer's most densely plotted psychological thrillers.

Penny (Susan Strasberg) arrives home following an extended stay abroad only to find her father "away on a business trip." Her stepmother Jane (Ann Todd) extends her a warm welcome, as does the live-in chauffeur Bob (Ronald Lewis). As expected with this type of "woman in peril" movie, all is not as it seems. Is her father on a trip or could he be dead? Will there be a romance with the chauffeur? And just what are the motives of the local Dr. Gerrard (Christopher Lee), who always seems to be dropping by? To top it all off, Jane is confined to a wheelchair, racking up her vulnerability level.

As scripted by Jimmy Sangster, *Taste of Fear* has enough to keep most viewers entertained and guessing right up to the end. I can only imagine that audiences of the early '60s lapped it up. When viewed today, it holds up pretty well despite a sluggish section in the middle. It's obvious from the get-go that we are either seeing the main character going out of her mind or she is being manipulated by someone close to her—but we all know it's the latter. There's only so many times one can watch someone go through the same motions and protestations before the words "get a grip" begin to go around in your head. Despite this quibble, there's still plenty to enjoy. The black-and-white film looks beautiful, especially in the well-staged night scenes filmed in and around the main house.

Christopher Lee said that he thinks this is his finest work for Hammer, and that Seth Holt was the studio's best director. I think he's overstating it by a long shot, but that's his opinion. His performance is certainly well tempered, and his French accent is spot on, but he just doesn't have enough screen time to develop the character or satisfy the average Lee fan. Hammer had a tendency to undervalue Lee, saving him for the monster roles, but he really shines in parts such as these, and I wish he had done more of them as a leading man instead of being reduced to a supporting role.

Ronald Lewis was always a serviceable actor and he certainly had the required looks to make it further in movies, but it just didn't happen for him. He's pretty good here, and is able to convey charm and suggested menace in equal measures. All the performances are nearly above reproach, with the ultimate praise being reserved for Susan Strasberg. She's perfect in the role of a would-be victim. As the daughter of famous acting teacher Lee Strasberg, it was inevitable that she would rise to the challenge. Plus, she has one of the best screams I've ever heard on film. It proved so effective that it was used extensively in advertising the movie. Her frozen scream even adorns most of the posters.

Seth Holt was undoubtedly a talented director and it shows in his staging of the many scenes involving his leading lady in jeopardy, whether real or imagined. However, I don't see anything out of the ordinary that would hold him up as Hammer's greatest director. His work on *The Nanny* shows a more confident hand and sense of style.

The bottom line is that *Taste of Fear* still performs as an above average thriller. Jimmy Sangster filled the script with so many twists and turns that most viewers should encounter at least one surprise throughout its short running time. Though not one of Hammer's best, you certainly could do a lot worse on

a winter's night than to slip this movie into your DVD player. It certainly has its moments.

—Matt Gemmell

Taste of Fear is notable as the first of a long series of Jimmy Sangster-scripted psychological thrillers made for Hammer, most of which have one-word titles (*Nightmare, Paranoiac, Hysteria, Maniac*) and twisting narratives that owe a large debt to the estimable French thriller *Les Diaboliques*. More than a decade later, Sangster was still offering taut variations on the legendary Clouzot movie in the form of the underrated *Fear in the Night* (1972). All of these movies are efficient and worthy of at least one view, though *Taste of Fear* beats all of them in terms of atmosphere and tension. Arguably, it also has the most convincing of the troubled, damaged heroines that would be a recurring element of these dark thrillers.

Susan Strasberg (who deserves some kind of special Oscar for managing to keep a straight face throughout the astonishing *The Manitou*) has her best genre role as a neurotic American paraplegic staying with her stepmother on the French Riviera, while her ailing father (the unforgettable Fred Johnson) is away on business. Like so many of the protagonists in this subgenre, she is recovering from a recent personal trauma—her sister's mysterious drowning in Italy—and she is described by one character as being "afraid of everything."

Strasberg is surrounded by a supporting cast of apparently nice but potentially dubious older men, including a kindly chauffeur and Christopher Lee as a doctor with a comedic French accent that's almost as entertaining as the American one he sports in *The City of the Dead*. She also sees what appears to be the corpse of her father in and around the summer house—even though he's meant to be alive.

Sangster would later team up with director Seth Holt—arguably one of Hammer's most underrated craftsmen—for the bleakly impressive *The Nanny*, and they made fine collaborators. The Clouzot echoes, including disappearing cadavers in swimming pools and an apparent plot to drive the heroine insane, are deftly executed, and fans of *Les Diaboliques* will appreciate the way in which Sangster and Holt subvert the French movie's key moments when we least expect it. The recurring image of Johnson's ghoulish, motionless visage provides some of Hammer's creepiest scares, especially during the intense swimming pool sequence.

Holt was always good at building an escalating sense of unease, pulling off some unpredictable plot turns, notably a multiple-twisting finale with a cliff top demise for a key villain. Strasberg is a sympathetic central figure, credibly and unglamorously playing a vulnerable, unhinged heroine who turns out to be someone else entirely.

The film was shot beautifully in eerie, evocative black and white by esteemed cinematographer Douglas Slocombe, whose career included everything from *The Lion in Winter* to the Indiana Jones films. He returned to Hammer at the tail end of their filmmaking era with *The Lady Vanishes*, though far more worthy of attention is the work he did on the earlier genre efforts *Circus of Horrors* and, particularly, the gorgeous *Dance of the Vampires* [*Fearless Vampire Killers*]. In retrospect, while part of the initial success of Hammer horror was due to the ground-breaking use of garish Technicolor gore, so many of their best-looking films have no color at all.
—Steven West

Credits: Director: Seth Holt; Writer: Jimmy Sangster.
Leading Cast: Susan Strasberg, Ann Todd, Christopher Lee, Leonard Sachs, Anne Blake.

The Terror of the Tongs

After his daughter is murdered, a British sea captain (Geoffrey Toone) attempts to bring to justice the Hong Kong Red Dragon Tong organization in *The Terror of the Tongs*. This shoddy offering was commissioned by Hammer in order to make use of a big dockyard set constructed for an earlier film, *Visa to Canton*. *Tongs* is a follow-up to *The Stranglers of Bombay*, with several of the same supporting actors in similar roles and a comparable storyline in which an Englishman combats a bunch of foreign criminals who are terrifying the locals, in much the same way that Van Helsing saves the frightened Transylvanian villagers from the vampires. James Bernard's score, a slightly disguised version of his main *Dracula* music, the way the film was advertised and the relatively high level of violence on display make this more of a horror movie than anything else.

Also known as *Terror of the Hatchet Men*, it's pretty nasty for a film of this period, featuring various examples of the Tong use of hatchets to chop off their enemy's fingers, a high body count, and also a "notorious" incident in which Toone is tortured by having his bones scraped. (Don't worry, he recovers with no apparent ill effects a few minutes later.) The atrocities are presided over by Christopher Lee, playing the head of the Tong—his later Fu Manchu character in all but name. His scenes are virtually all confined to one set located in the Tong's gambling and prostitution den, in which he sits on a big red throne ob-

serving the proceedings and making snide remarks laced with Confucius-style aphorisms. Lee also displays an absurd form of Eastern fatalism in which he accepts all setbacks, including his ultimate demise, with what seems like a mere shrug of the shoulders.

With all of the Chinese speaking roles, except for Burt Kwouk, played by Hammer's stock repertory company wearing somewhat unconvincing "Oriental" eyelid makeup, the film now looks embarrassingly racist and anachronistic (*Stranglers* was shot in black and white, making the "blacking up" of the white actors less noticeable). Okay, it's fun spotting the likes of Roger Delgado, Ewen Solon and Charles Lloyd-Pack disguised under this makeup, but that doesn't negate the overall feeling of embarrassment. Mind you, Yvonne Monlaur playing a Chinese concubine with her usual heavy French accent is hilarious for all the wrong reasons. The script's key message—"You think we'll behave like English people; we don't and we never will"—is a typical "Eastern Peril" viewpoint of the period that all Asians are either evil incarnates bent on fiendish plots and gratuitous murder or fit only to be frightened slaves. The English may be nominally in charge of Hong Kong, but the natives are all still barbarians underneath and the Occidentals will never "convert" them. The film isn't overt in this regard—it's a disguised *Dracula* movie—but that's how it comes across.

Technically, despite good cinematography, this is sub-par for Hammer. Anthony Bushell's direction is, frankly, diabolical. Too many dialogue scenes feature characters staring blankly into space at an off-stage audience rather than the people they are addressing, and the choreography of the action scenes is limp and unconvincing with everything looking too constricted and taking place on obvious sets. Matters aren't helped by the numerous BBFC snips made to all existing prints, which render the assault on Toone's daughter nonsensical by an abrupt cut to her fainting—instead of including the footage of the Tong killers chopping off her fingers.
—Tim Rogerson

As a diehard Hammer fan, it's always a treat to catch up with one of the studio's rarer offerings, so you can imagine how delighted I was in 2001 when I finally viewed *The Terror of the Tongs*. To make it even better, it was on the big screen with two of the stars, Geoffrey Toone and Yvonne Monlaur, in attendance. Jimmy Sangster was also present (well, it was his book launch), but he was less than enamored with the film. Considering he wrote the script, you'd think he might have had some interesting comments to make. He certainly had something to say about it, and little of it was good. He did praise Christopher Lee's performance, but that was it. Prior to the screening, Jimmy actually left and advised the audience to do the same. No one took him up on the offer, and Toone and Monlaur looked less than pleased with his comments, to say the least. Quite a prologue to the movie, I think you'll agree. Anyway, the lights dimmed and *The Terror of the Tongs* began.

Did I agree with Sangster? Well, not really.

The film tells the story of the mysterious Red Dragon Tong, a secret society based in Hong Kong who deal in everything from extortion and racketeering to prostitution and murder. One of the very few Asian actors in the film—good old Burt Kwouk of *Pink Panther* fame—plays Mr. Ming, who possesses a book detailing all the Tong members' names. Unfortunately they are aware of this and wait for him as he sails into Hong Kong. Mr. Ming decides to hide the book inside a present, which he gives to the ship's captain (Geoffrey Toone). Needless to say, Mr. Ming doesn't survive for much longer, and the rest of the film deals with the Tong's efforts to trace the book at any cost.

Toone's Captain Sale is one of the most old-fashioned heroes ever to grace the screen for Hammer, and that's saying something. His performance isn't bad; he just seems out of place and time by about 20 years. His style and delivery would have been more at home in a '40s detective thriller. Then again, that's what this film resembles.

Yvonne Monlaur's acting leaves a lot to be desired, although she is extremely pleasant to look at even with her "Oriental" make up. She is far superior in *The Brides of Dracula*, in which her role perfectly suits her persona. *Tongs* is full of Bray and London locals wearing less than convincing makeup. Something that, thankfully, you'll never see now—well, at least I hope not.

Made prior to the Fu Manchu movies, *Tongs* gave Christopher Lee the chance to play an evil cult leader with his inimitable flair. Lee's makeup isn't bad, but it certainly looks uncomfortable, with his eyelids forced into what was considered an Asian angle. That aside, he does a pretty good job, undoubtedly saving the film from descending into pure melodrama. It takes an actor of Lee's caliber to carry off such a role and he does it with relish. It's a testament to him that, even now, you can enjoy his performance without cringing at how un-PC it is.

At heart this is a *Boy's Own* adventure that has dated badly. I tend to think it probably looked old fashioned even when it was made. There are moments to enjoy, such as the bone-scraping torture scene. Apparently Jimmy Sangster made this up, but it's played out in such a way that it's believable as a well-known and utilized torture device.

Did I enjoy the film? Yes, at the time. My opinion may have been clouded by a number of things. Firstly, Jimmy Sangster had set me up to think that it was one of the worst movies I would ever see. Secondly, I was seated near Toone and Monlaur at the time, and finally I was viewing an unseen Hammer movie on the big screen where it was meant to be shown. I mention these points to illustrate what a difference

time, place and context can make to one's viewing pleasure or otherwise.

The action is mostly studio bound, but the cinematography is worth mentioning as, once more, Hammer manages to convince you of the exotic locations, people and atmosphere that are pivotal to the story. Much has been said of the behind the scenes crew at Hammer, but I never get tired of marveling at their work. It's this kind of craftsmanship that kept them ahead of the game and is something that can too often be taken for granted.

My fondest memory of the movie is, as you might expect, something that happened after that London cinema screening. As we all left the theater and began chatting to fans and cast alike, Geoffrey Toone mentioned to Hazel Court that he had been annoyed regarding Jimmy Sangster's opinion of the film. Hazel smiled and said, "Well, that's Jimmy," to which the very elderly Toone replied, "That's Jimmy? I felt like punching him on the nose." They don't make heroes like that anymore, do they?
—Matt Gemmell

Credits: Director: Anthony Bushell; Writer: Jimmy Sangster. **Leading Cast:** Christopher Lee, Geoffrey Toone, Yvonne Monlaur, Burt Kwouk, Marne Maitland, Milton Reid.

What a Carve Up!

What a Carve Up! (aka *Carry On Killing*) is a 1961 comedy allegedly inspired by the same novel that spawned Karloff's classic *The Ghoul*. Yet the two films are nothing alike. *Carve Up* is a British take on the "Old Dark House" genre, complete with secret passageways and portraits with cut-out eyes. Quite honestly, if it doesn't provide you with a few chuckles, you should check that you didn't drop your sense of humor down a grid somewhere.

Because Kenneth Connor is still under 50 here, he gets to do his nervous, clumsy and hopeless-around-women shtick, as opposed to when he doubled his range and began playing old geezers with monocles and wandering hands. He plays Ernie Broughton, a down-at-heel proofreader of cheap horror paperbacks. Sharing his flat is Sid Butler (Sid James, who else?), a cackling rough diamond and bookie. So there's Sid stretching himself for once. When a sinister solicitor (Donald Pleasence) turns up to tell Ernie that his uncle Gabriel has "kicked the bucket," Ernie is certain he's about to assume his rightful place among the "landed gentry."

It's the homicide-splitting comedy of the year as the British take a sly look at the art of murder...and find it perfectly killing!

Together, he and Sid make their way to Blackshore Towers for the reading of the will, where they're introduced to Ernie's snooty and eccentric relatives (they're all quite mad). Among them are George Woodbridge, Dennis Price, dotty old Esma Cannon and *Revenge of Frankenstein* alumnus Michael Gwynn. Also turning up and adding a curvy blonde dollop of glamour to the proceedings is Gabriel's nurse (the stunning Shirley Eaton). Attending to everybody is Michael Gough as a Riff-Raff-style, limping butler. Upon seeing the motley collection of hangers-on, Sid says, "Ring up Madame Tussaud's; see if anyone's missin'!"

Predictably, it's not long before, one by one, the guests start getting bumped off, and suspicions run amok about the identity of the murderer. Ernie, fearful for his life, sticks close to his worldlier mate. This leads to the two sharing a bed in true Stan & Ollie fashion and results in some giggles. Little Ernie is lost in a voluminous Rip van Winkle-style nightgown and hat, while Sid must squeeze himself into his shorter pal's pajamas. When an uninvited guest comes between the pair, you realize that Talbot Rothwell must have recalled this scene when he came to write *Carry on Screaming!*

The treat for horror fans is to see Donald Pleasence and familiar Hammer faces Gwynn, George Woodbridge and Michael Gough spoofing their usual roles. The Plezz is supremely sinister in his usual soft-spoken and understated way. Gwynn is a po-faced treat as the organ-playing son who joins Connor for a rendition of "Chopsticks." Shirley Eaton, as the unattainable object of Ernie's bumbling affections, spends most of the film in her nightie and looks divine, as you'd expect. And Kenneth and Sid are perfect. In fact, it's impeccably cast all round. That is until Adam Faith turns up for a gratuitous cameo, probably to hook those "hep cat" kids, during the dying minutes. No, we don't want your love, "baby," now bugger off!

For its entire running time, *What a Carve Up!* maintains a jolly air of slightly spooky, *Cat and the Canary* comic cliché, more than capably performed. When the killer is revealed, though, it's a surprise. If they'd managed to squeeze Terry-Thomas in somewhere, this would be an outright classic. As it is, it comes close. It's well worth catching on a rainy afternoon or, preferably, a stormy evening, with the lights out, and a corpse hanging in the wardrobe.
—Jed Raven

Credits: Director: Pat Jackson; Writers: Ray Cooney, Tony Hilton.
Leading Cast: Kenneth Connor, Sidney James, Shirley Eaton, Donald Pleasence, Esma Cannon, Dennis Price, Michael Gough, Michael Gwynn, George Woodbridge.

Editor's note: Jonathan Coe's acclaimed 1994 novel *What A Carve Up!* about greed and corruption in 1980's Britain, lifted its title from this movie. What's more, Coe's main character, Michael Owen, is obsessed with the film, situations from which are mentioned or alluded to throughout the book.

1962

Captain Clegg (aka *Night Creatures*)

A swashbuckling adventure yarn, *Captain Clegg* is an oddity among Hammer's early 1960s output. There are no vampires, but don't let that put you off; besides, you do get the "Phantoms of Romney Marsh" as compensation. Don't worry, they have nothing to do with the footballer.

Closely based on Russell Thorndike's Doctor Syn stories, and the later George Arliss movie, this Hammer version changed the character's name to Blyss, under pressure from Disney, who'd secured the property for their own adaptation. As it couldn't be released in the U.S. under its original title, it's also known as *Night Creatures*, a title Hammer had intended for another, aborted project. All this confusion! Blimey, it's a good thing *Clegg* is one of Hammer's best!

Set in the late 1700s, the film follows Captain Collier (lantern-jawed Patrick Allen) as he and his sailors are sent by the Crown to investigate suspicions of smuggling in the English coastal town of Dymchurch. It seems anybody who gets close to exposing the town's secrets is frightened away by the mysterious "marsh phantoms," a band of cloaked, horse-riding skeletons. Collier soon comes to suspect that the seemingly benign Reverend Dr. Blyss (Peter Cushing, having a whale of a time) might know more than he lets on. Indeed he does: Blyss orchestrates a bootlegging operation at the premises of local coffin maker Jeremiah Mipps (ever-reliable Michael Ripper), in which it seems the whole town has a stake. But the operation is threatened when Collier's mulatto captive (Milton Reid) recognizes Blyss from an earlier time.

Captain Clegg is a cracking Hammer yarn, with action, scares, comedy and romance. Though everybody shines in what is very much an ensemble piece, it's the Cush who stands out, as usual, even if, in that wig and specs, he looks like an undernourished Barbara Woodhouse fronting The Damned. You just know he'd loved to have done more of this Errol Flynn-type stuff; he swings from a chandelier as well as anybody! Almost as good is the Ripper (Michael, not Jack) in a slightly more fleshed-out role than usual, though disturbingly, it seems he's been rummaging through his wife's makeup bag!

Running parallel to all the skulduggery is a nicely played out romance between squire's son Oliver Reed and the bounteously endowed Yvonne Romain (well, you have to keep the ladies entertained). She wears the same hairstyle as in their earlier Hammer collaboration, *The Curse of the Werewolf*, though you'll forgive her when you see her jugs. (Oh *please*, she's a barmaid!) Very nearly as pretty, if you like that kind of thing, is the young Ollie, who flutters his eyelashes almost as much as his gorgeous costar. No wonder her bosom heaves.

Peter Cushing as Captain Clegg

One of the more memorable roles goes to Milton Reid as the mulatto (that's un-PC lingo for "half-caste," sorry, "person of mixed race," sorry...). He was an ex-wrestler who popped up again and again in '60s and '70s Brit cinema whenever the role called for somebody fat, bald and a bit scary-looking.

If this wonderful production has a flaw, it's that it wallows in murky morality. The King's men are bullies while Blyss' gang of ne'er-do-wells are presented as roguish benefactors, having delivered their adopted town from poverty. This might be forgiven if we didn't see the same gang run an old man to his death in the early scenes. However, no ethical concerns should prevent you from enjoying this hugely enjoyable romp, which compares admirably to Hammer's better-known works.
—Jed Raven

Credits: Director: Peter Graham Scott; Writers: John Elder [Anthony Hinds], Barbara S. Harper.
Leading Cast: Peter Cushing, Oliver Reed, Yvonne Romain, Patrick Allen, Michael Ripper, Derek Francis, Milton Reid.

Editor's note: In the summer of 2009, Jesse Dayton put together a fictitious band named Captain Clegg and the Night Creatures to appear in Rob Zombie's film *Halloween II*. They later recorded an album and toured the Midwest.

The Day of the Triffids

Bill Masen wakes up in a world where everyone is blind and killer vegetation stalks the streets. John Wyndham's novel *The Day of the Triffids* cries out for film adaptation, containing everything a filmmaker could wish for, making it all the more strange that most of the book's ideas should be changed or

The Day of the Triffids

junked. This screen version is not totally without merit, since there are dramatic sequences unique to the film—for example, the more catastrophic fallout from the blinding includes planes in the air and ships at sea suddenly left without sighted crew.

The man-made Triffids have been turned into derivative alien invaders, reducing the movie to a place among the many "it came from outer space" films being churned out in the 1950s and 1960s. The Triffids have been on Earth long enough to have been documented, given a Latin name and stuck in Kew Gardens. Yet later radio reports state that it's an unknown plant on the rampage. Perhaps the Triffids have killed all the botanists?

The novel's everyman hero, Masen, has been changed to a bluff American sailor played by Howard Keel. Oddly he's denied the love interest, Josella Playton. Instead, a young girl, Susan (a great performance from a young Janina Faye), is introduced, to be cared for by Bill. Maybe the producers thought they could make this a more family-focused film by giving Keel a little sidekick. Masen does finally win some romance in the unconvincingly frosty form of the reactionary Miss Durrant (Nicole Maurey). In the tradition of movie ice maidens everywhere, all she needs is a strong bloke to get her metaphorically taking off her glasses and letting down her hair. Keep an eye out for Mervyn Johns (*Dead of Night*) as Coker, changed from a radical to a sweet old man, and Carole Ann Ford, a few years away from fame in *Doctor Who*.

Most of the novel's nasty undertones have been removed, apart from the idea of the blind using the sighted as guide dogs. Almost all the sociopolitical discussions and debates have been jettisoned, too. Some editing was perhaps wise, however, as Wyndham's debates continue for many pages.

Josella Playton's absence causes crucial structure problems. Half the novel is focused on Masen's search for her after they are separated. With no similar goal in the film, the plot drags as Masen and Susan meander around Europe visiting France and Spain.

When director Steven Sekeley delivered the finished film to his producers, they panicked, either because it was too short or not deemed good enough. They brought in Freddie Francis to shoot additional scenes with Kieron Moore and Janette Scott in a besieged lighthouse. Viewing the film now makes you wonder why they worried quite so much. Visually it's impressive, and the direction is imaginative. Watching Moore and Scott argue until they're reunited by a killer shrub is tedious stuff, though!

The Triffids are mediocre and unimaginative. The deadly plants' first appearance, when one stalks and kills a greenhouse attendant, is atmospheric stuff. The creature is kept in the shadows and we only see brief glimpses. But afterwards the attacks take place in the daytime with the Triffid in full view. In one such assault in a park, the tray at the prop's base and the root pulling it along obviously has a hand in it. They are noisy stalkers, too, and it's difficult to imagine them creeping up on anyone.

The ending, stolen from *The War of the Worlds*, is terrible. After coming all that way and subjugating us, the poor aliens always discover they're allergic to something. Whatever it is, after 90 minutes and huge loss of life, someone always suddenly discovers it. The aliens should have thought about it more before hopping into their spacecrafts. This time it's salt water. Even passing over the fact that all plants need water, it's a damn stupid Achilles heel.

Then Masen leads the local Triffids to their lemming-like doom in an ice cream truck. It rather makes a mockery of the invasion if they can be killed off so easily. Better luck next time.
—Gerald Lea

John Wyndham's apocalyptic 1951 classic received its first film treatment with Steve Sekely's adequate flick of over a decade later. A mysterious, luminous meteor shower lights up the skies all over the world, and the eager populace who watch it wake up the next morning blind as bats and at the mercy of carnivorous plants called Triffids. The few who found reasons not to watch the shower roam the world, banding together to reorganize human society and avoid becoming plant food. Chief among these are Bill Masen (Howard Keel), an American merchant seaman, Mme. Durrant (Nicole Maurey), a French landowner, Coker (Mervyn Johns), a vacationing

Briton, Susan (Janina Faye), a runaway schoolgirl, and Tom (Ktieron Moore) and Karen (Janette Scott), a bickering, vaguely alcoholic scientist duo.

They learn from fitful radio broadcasts of the world's predicament and swiftly realize the deadly threat the Triffids pose. Masen, Durrant and Susan eventually find themselves racing through the deserted Spanish countryside to escape the Triffids and make it to a promised rescue rendezvous as the scientists, surrounded by Triffids in their island lighthouse, struggle to find ways to combat the partially chlorophyll-dependent menace.

Triffids inevitably suffers from almost any comparison to David Maloney's superb 1981 BBC miniseries adaptation, but it also "boasts" a number of inarguable defects. The direction and camera work (it may simply be the DVD transfer, but the garish lighting and color frequently distract to a damaging degree) are rather undistinguished, something of a setback in a relatively epic movie. The scientists' subplot is both melodramatic and completely divorced from the story line, and the Triffids look and largely act like Audrey 2 in either film version of *The Little Shop of Horrors*. The Triffids in the novel and later series devour their victims over a long period of time—like actual saprophytes—but these act like classic "from *outer space!*" offenders, removing much of the realistic, cumulative horror from the story. (One poor sap at a botanical exhibit gets swallowed up as if he's just inconvenienced *The Blob*.) There's also a mildly wince-inducing "to hell with it" near-orgy sequence involving a gang of French convicts and Carole Ann Ford of *Doctor Who* fame. (It's not *nearly* as entertaining as it sounds).

Fortunately, though they're poorly served by the story, the actors are on the whole rather good, and make quite sympathetic heroes, especially Keel, an actor for whom *Triffids* doesn't seem such a natural fit at first. The "family" unit that he, Durrant and Susan eventually form really makes one want to root for the characters. There are also some memorable scenes of mass panic, the most noteworthy—and unnerving—of which takes place aboard a plane where the pilot and crew realize they're pretty certain to crash. While *Triffids* doesn't rank as a classic—certainly not next to its competition of two decades later—it has plenty of redeeming features.
—Wendell McKay

Credits: Directors: Steve Sekely, Freddie Francis [uncredited]; Writer: Philip Yordan.
Leading Cast: Howard Keel, Nicole Maurey, Janette Scott, Kieron Moore, Mervyn Johns, Janina Faye.

Don't Talk to Strange Men

"Samantha…what a beautiful name"—a seemingly innocent sentence, of the type one would expect to find in an old Gainsborough romantic comedy or drama, or a half-remembered wisp of some old *Children's Hour* production one vaguely remembers in the pub a decade or two later. But in the context of Pat Jackson's superlative thriller *Don't Talk to Strange Men*, it takes on a more sinister significance.

Anyone in the U.K. who has ever been off work, ill or just a late sleeper will have experienced at some point the delights of 1950s and 1960s black and white crime thrillers on TV. They vary in tone, subject matter and quality, my personal favorites being anything produced by Poverty Row maestros Butchers Film Distributors and featuring such a dizzying array of unknowns and also-rans that one often feels one has stepped into a parallel world. Filmed at long-lamented studios such as Merton Park, Walton and Teddington, they occupy a place in the hearts of television viewers of a certain age that they probably never gained during their cinematic life span. Most of them were B movies, anyway, sadly forgotten by the time the (often) American-made main feature had played and the public was wending its way home from its respective fleapits. Quite often the acting, plot and production values leave a lot to be desired. However, they share the same sense of accidental beauty, the same mixture of iciness and cosiness and downright olde worlde charm as any product of the monochrome era, and once one has developed a passing interest, it can turn into something of an obsession.

Now that I've whetted your appetites, I'll throw a spanner in the works by pointing out that *Don't Talk to Strange Men*, regardless of its low-budget status, is one of the few films of its kind not produced or distributed under the Butchers aegis. The party concerned this time was Bryanston Films; one wonders if they ever knew what a masterpiece (a minor one, but a masterpiece nonetheless) they had on their hands. In short (the film runs only 65 minutes, the very definition of a "quota quickie"), the story concerns, as these stories often do, a family living in a small village "somewhere" in the Home Counties and, as usual, there's something sinister lurking in them there suburbs.

The family are as "normal" as normal could have been back then, fittingly placed amid appropriate settings, all cosy firesides and oak beams juxtaposed with "modern" furniture and fashions. We have middle class, well spoken Mr. Painter (Cyril Raymond), his wife (Gillian Lind, one of those character actresses who seemed to crop up in practically everything at one time or another) and, most importantly, their two daughters: flighty, daydreaming, burgeoning adult in child's clothing Jean (Christina Gregg, who seems to have disappeared soon after the making of the film), and grounded, cynical and infinitely more sensible Ann (Janina Faye), who, despite being several years her sister's junior, seems to be of advanced intelligence, even to the point of writing anti-bloodsport letters to the local huntmaster, attempting to convert to Buddhism and berating her father for eating meat.

Seriously, if you want to hear dialogue way ahead of its time, you won't believe the conversations between father and daughter here. But, other than that, the girls are fairly conventional: They bicker like sisters, their walls are adorned with Cliff Richard and Tommy Steele posters (pre-Beatles, remember) and they collect small fluffy objects which bedeck their bedroom the way a young boy's room of the time would have been festooned with posters of Jimmy Greaves. So far, there's nothing out of the ordinary.

However, Jean, who has a part-time job in her dad's mate, Ron's, pub, is given to flights of fancy and wonderment way above her station. One of these is answering a telephone in an empty public call box and pretending, for some reason, to be called Samantha beginning a conversation with an unknown man she has never seen, who tells her what a lovely voice she has and how much he'd like to speak to her again at same time the following day.

Once we suspend our disbelief at Jean's outright naïveté (and, to be honest, Gregg is a convincing actress enough for this to work), we are hooked into the story until the very finish. Day by day, she returns to the phone box, each time revealing a little more about herself to the mysterious man she even refers to as her boyfriend. Her sister becomes increasingly worried at her behavior, as do her parents who believe she has a crush on Ron (especially as she is keen to work there, near to the box, as often as possible). Daily she relates more of her fanciful dreams concerning her mystery paramour to jaded bus conductress Molly (Dandy Nichols—was she *ever* young?), who, understandably, thinks her young charge is several hops short of a full pint.

As this develops, along with the expanding subtext of her father's increasing concern for his daughter's safety in light of the ever-changing world and "upsetting things he reads about in the local papers" (presumably referring to the pre-credits sequence in which children discover the body of a recently murdered woman), the previously innocuous telephone booth, merely a man-made invention of steel, paint and glass, becomes an almost portentous totem, a harbinger of evil. Every time it's shown, we become a little more disturbed. A purely accidental trick of the camera that reflects either Gregg or a member of the film crew makes it seem as if a human face can be seen visibly lingering in the window.

It's elements like these that have led some fans to elevate the film's status above mere crime thriller to that of horror movie: the effective use of wind, a chase through fields into a shed (where the heroine hears a number of characters' voices echoing in nightmare fashion), and a downright terrifying encounter with what is revealed to be nothing more than a local village tramp are all further grist to this mill. And that's to say nothing of the look of sheer terror on Jean's face when she recognizes the voice of her mystery lover as he approaches her, unaware, in a public place and asks her for change for the telephone. We don't see what's wrong with him, of course—like all the best mysteries, his face and identity are never revealed—but it's enough to spark the imagination.

To spoil it for those unlucky enough not to have seen the film by revealing the ending would just be unfair; but it races toward a climax quickly, in the way that all the best films of its kind do. Yes, there is a car chase and a punch up somewhere along the way, not to mention a genuine nail-biting moment

Don't Talk to Strange Men

involving Faye which leads to one of the best twists in a tale ever conceived. This, of course, was familiar territory for Janina, lately menaced by leering Felix Aylmer in Hammer's little-seen but highly recommended child-abuse drama *Never Take Sweets from a Stranger*. She also played a series of "victim" roles in both film and TV productions over the years, most recently alongside Ingrid Pitt and Robin Parkinson in Paul Cotgrove's *Green Fingers* (2000).

Don't Talk to Strange Men will never be regarded a classic, although it's high time someone credited it for the amount of influence it has had on the more Grand Guignol and contemporary horrors and thrillers of the past 40 years. From its opening shot of an unknown female waiting on a rainy street corner, being approached by "the" oncoming car, through its deconstruction of cosy suburbia, right up to its final reel of incredulity, it seems to have been the dry run for practically everything that Sidney Hayers, Pete Walker, Lindsay Shonteff and Alistair Reid excelled at a decade later. That's not bad for a film essentially made to fulfil the government subsidy quota for the Eady Levy.

—D.R. Shimon

Credits: Director: Pat Jackson; Writer: Gwen Cherrell.
Leading Cast: Christina Gregg, Cyril Raymond, Gillian Lind, Conrad Phillips, Janina Faye.

The Phantom of the Opera

Hammer's *The Phantom of the Opera* suffers from the same fate of all productions of the tale, in that the original source material just isn't that exciting. The story is not really horror but melodrama and, despite a few typical gory Hammer flourishes, that's all this film is, too. It's important to realize, though, that Hammer's *Phantom* shouldn't be dismissed outright. The film looks fantastic, and Michael Gough's performance more than makes up for the leaden pace—and he's not even playing the titular fiend.

After a classy start—the titles rolling over the Phantom's eye—we're treated to the beginning of Gough's full-on smirkathon, as he auditions young actresses for the lead role in the latest production based on work stolen from his supposedly dead friend. When he murmurs, "She's a *very* lovely girl," we know it's not just her arias he'll be admiring later on.

The film (like many Hammers) is absolutely bursting with interesting character study and Victorian clichés (see *Dr. Jekyll and Sister Hyde* for the ultimate in cobbled streets, grimy urchins and chim-chiminee sweeps). Michael Ripper appears at one point (under extreme makeup) as a cabby, and the old women in the theater's lost property section are a scream, female precursors of Harry Enfield's Old Gits 20 years before he'd even thought of teaming up with Paul Whitehouse (and stealing all his best mate's ideas).

There's also Patrick Troughton as the rat catcher ("They make a luvverly pie, y'know"), whose little cameo is cut drastically short by a knife in the eye. Herbert Lom, however, might as well not be in the film. His Phantom is pretty lackluster, skulking in shadows and letting an evil dwarf do all the dirty work. Cary Grant was reportedly interested in starring in a Hammer horror film, and, according to Anthony Hinds, the part of Harry Hunter in *Phantom* was scripted for the Hollywood legend. Sadly, the studio failed to lure their big-name target to Bray, with dependable Edward De Souza stepping in to take the romantic lead.
—Chris Wood

The Phantom of the Opera

Credits: Director: Terence Fisher; Writer: John Elder [Anthony Hinds].
Leading Cast: Herbert Lom, Michael Gough, Heather Sears, Edward de Souza, Thorley Walters, Michael Ripper, Miriam Karlin, Miles Malleson, Marne Maitland.

Vengeance (aka *The Brain*)

Curt Siodmak's novel *Donovan's Brain* had been filmed twice before Freddie Francis helmed the Anglo-German production *Vengeance*. Neither *The Lady and the Monster* (1944) nor *Donovan's Brain* (1953) is an outstanding adaptation, although the latter is fondly remembered as an entertaining schlocker.

Never having read the book nor seen any other version, I came to *Vengeance* without any preconceived ideas. In fact I was about 20 minutes into the film before I realized this was a story based on Siodmak's book. While the novel deals with a scientist being controlled by a malevolent, disembodied brain, Francis' version is more of a whodunit.

The brain in this case belongs to a millionaire who has been "murdered" in a plane crash. Among the many suspects are most of his family and business partners. Unlike the novel and previous film versions, *Vengeance* is concerned with a fight for justice in the Agatha Christie mold but, instead of Miss Marple, it offers a disembodied brain that controls the protagonist—an interesting premise and one that, at times, is reminiscent of *Frankenstein Created Woman*.

Freddie Francis began his film career as a director of photography and, although he directed many low-budget genre movies, he always considered himself a D.P. at heart, ultimately winning cinematography Oscars for *Sons and Lovers* and *Glory*. *Vengeance* gave him an early directorial outing, and he made

a decent attempt, guiding the story with an unobtrusive eye. He did use a large amount of close-up shots, which are absent from his later work. This may have been due to a combination of an extremely low budget and a particular style of filming that seemed popular in crime movies of the time. Whatever the reason, this becomes a bit tedious and has dated the film badly. Even though *Vengeance* is a series of talking heads, I wish Francis had pulled the camera back a little.

The horror elements are downplayed in favor of a murder mystery, which made me wonder, why bother with the disembodied brain plot at all? Yes, it serves as a unique contrivance, but the mind control exerted by the brain is so subtle that you could be forgiven for forgetting all about it as you try to unravel the mystery. Not that it's a difficult puzzle to solve.

Considering the outrageous plot, *Vengeance* strives to be something more than a sci-fi thriller, as it presents the viewer with a series of suspects for the main crime. The fact that the brain is controlling and guiding our protagonist is presented as almost secondary to the search for the murderer. Anyone looking for schlocky fun is going to be sorely disappointed by this. Similarly, fans of the traditional murder mysteries churned out during the 1960s will feel shortchanged. Francis should have made up his mind and settled for one or the other. As it is, we have a passable time-filler that could have been so much better if the script had brought the more horrific elements of the story to the fore.

As Dr. Corrie, Peter Van Eyck appears rather wooden in the main role. His attempts to show emotion (or indeed a lack of it) just don't come across, and I was acutely aware of an actor going through the motions. He's unlucky in that some of his co-stars are simply much better, in particular a young Bernard Lee as the alcohol swigging Dr. Shears. Character actors like Lee, Maxine Audley, Jack MacGowran and Miles Malleson help to lift *Vengeance* to a higher level than it probably deserves.

What is essentially a very silly sci-fi mystery is given an air of respectability by a fine cast who are definitely slumming it. Here we see, yet again, the main difference between low-budget Euro cinema and its American counterpart: a plethora of acting talent.

As a movie from a fledgling director, *Vengeance* could best be described as workmanlike. There's nothing particularly wrong in the way it's structured or presented, and the end result is competent if unremarkable. As a genre movie, either sci-fi or murder mystery, it fails to excite.

Vengeance is a difficult movie to track down. I'm currently unaware of any video or DVD release, which is a shame. Although I don't care for the movie, it does have its admirers, mainly due to the performances and the subject matter. It's an acquired taste but worth seeking out if you are a Freddie Francis completist or—and this is a long shot—a fan of Peter Van Eyck. —Matt Gemmell

Lucian Freud-style painting which dominates the room and gives him a huge presence of unworldly menace as it stares down at characters accusingly.

Some interest is created by he supporting cast, including Bernard Lee as Van Eyck's assistant—his constant imbibing of booze throughout the story mirrors his own real-life alcoholism. Alister Williamson, the disfigured Sir Edward of *The Oblong Box*, plays a policeman; Allan Cuthbertson appears uncredited as Max Holt's gopher, as do John Junkin and Bryan Pringle as hired thugs; and Jack MacGowran enlivens the proceedings as a blackmailing mortuary attendant who comes to a sticky end. MacGowran's eccentric performance is easily the most watchable aspect of the movie, although not up to the maniacal heights of his palaeontologist in *The Giant Behemoth*.

Unfortunately, after some build-up and a couple of murders, the ending is pathetically inconsequential. The brain itself is destroyed so casually that I wasn't aware it had happened until confirmed by later dialogue. Then, we get an impromptu left-field confession of murder, despite the fact that Van Eyck doesn't know "who done it" and hasn't any real evidence. This is followed by a limp conclusion in which he's told by another character that perhaps it would have been best if he hadn't kept the brain alive after all. This is good advice, because then we wouldn't have had to endure the entire affair. According to Francis, a different ending was filmed for the German market in which someone else is unmasked as the killer—although he didn't reveal the character's identity. —Tim Rogerson

A scientist (Peter Van Eyck) keeps alive the brain of a dead, megalomaniacal "international financier" in his country cottage laboratory. The brain exerts an influence over him, making him investigate the man's death, which leads to further killings before the murderer is unmasked in a bathetic ending.

This tedious little film was the third cinematic version of *Donovan's Brain* by Curt Siodmak. Here the subject is called Max Holt rather than Donovan. Its basic theme qualifies it as a horror-type film but, for most of its running time, this plays as a weak mystery. Van Eyck repeatedly interviews the same suspects in his attempt to get at the truth, and they all indulge him rather than just telling him to get stuffed.

Director Freddie Francis uses a variety of techniques in an attempt to enliven the proceedings, including subjective camera work that indicates Van Eyck's "possession" by the brain. In a sequence in which Van Eyck interrogates the chauffeur, who is then shot, the camera focuses unnervingly on a Western on TV, with the volume excessively loud. A subsequent chase sequence seems to be borrowed from *The Third Man*. All of this serves to create a sense of slight unease, although, unfortunately, it is all too apparent that these devices are a cover for mediocre material rather than stylistic touches inherent to the material. Holt's face is never seen—before his death he's photographed from the back only—and we see him via a large, alarming-looking

Credits: Director: Freddie Francis; Writers: Robert Stewart, Philip Mackie.
Leading Cast: Peter van Eyck, Bernard Lee, Anne Heywood, Cecil Parker, Allan Cuthbertson, Irene Richmond.

The Very Edge

With its title alluding more to the precarious emotional and mental states of several major characters, rather than to the high-rise rooftop setting of the climax, *The Very Edge* is a gripping early example of a post-Hitchcock, post-Powell psychological thriller. Jeremy Brett's lust-driven brute is presented in a similar clean-cut manner to *Peeping Tom*'s Mark or *Psycho*'s Norman, at least in dress and physical appearance—differing from his peers, however, in that his ability to disguise his "problem" is somewhat less accomplished. Brett pulls off the gibbering lunacy with some aplomb, mind you, and also anticipates the "unstoppable" nature of the mass-murdering fiends of the prolific stalk-and-slash movie boom, circa 1980.

The Very Edge aptly features its monstrous rapist as a peripheral figure, popping up on the outskirts of the main plot depicting the collapse of Anne Heywood's loveless marriage to Richard Todd. Heywood is pregnant as the story opens, but her closest confidant is not her hubby (to whom we are introduced as he self-absorbedly dashes off to work) but an annoyingly chatty little girl who lives next door. Heywood loses her baby following a savage attack by Brett, who has pursued her home from a nearby supermarket where we have been given an ominous glimpse of his distinctive pointy boots, a visual motif later echoed in *Blind Terror* (1971). The sex fiend is splashed with a face full of staining purple lotion, having to lie low while this tell-tale dye fades. One quirky detail typical of this period of Brit flicks depicts an investigating copper also being marked with the gunk, which is subsequently used by the crime team as a sort of human calendar. They realize that, once their colleague's skin becomes unmarked, so too will that of their at-liberty prey, limiting their opportunities for an early collar.

Much has been made by the film's few commentators of the screenplay's relationship between victim and assailant: Heywood, while terrified of the predatory Brett, seems to empathize with his compulsion, and oddly feels more at ease in her scenes with this disturbed figure than with anyone else. In *Flesh and Blood*, Kim Newman also points out that *The Very Edge* recognizes a peculiar postwar trait among the British people, particularly nine-to-five, business-suited types, such as Todd portrays, giving an inflated importance to status and possessions while letting emotions and relationships take second place. The married couple dwells on an estate similar to the bleak new-town setting of Frankel's earlier pedophile drama *Never Take Sweets from a Stranger*, a dull, stuffy, boxed-in existence where the sudden presence of a mauling, drooling madman has the impact of a volcanic eruption. It's no wonder Heywood leans ever so slightly in his direction while her spouse is pondering whether the embrace of his sexy French secretary might be worth tumbling into.

The Very Edge is a seething cauldron of a domestic drama, peppered with striking horror bits worthy of ITV's small-screen *Thriller* series of the '70s (which aped this type of lady-in-peril plot every other week). Frankel excels at the menacing fare, in particular two superb "reveals" which both feature animals: in one, a house-cat is brushed away from a window ledge, allowing us and the fuzz to spy a pile of back-issue fashion mags with covers adorned by our heroine; in the other, an

Foreign poster for *The Very Edge*

elephant idly wanders by during a lazy afternoon at the zoo, and is seen to have been concealing our antagonist, who looms toward us via a series of rapidly cut close-ups—an extremely effective sequence, despite being a theft from James Whale's *Frankenstein* (1931).

Just when you thought it couldn't get any better, the marvelous Patrick Magee turns up as a janitor for the final reel or two.
—Darrell Buxton

Credits: Director: Cyril Frankel; Writers: E. J. Howard, Leslie Bricusse, Vivian Cox.
Leading Cast: Anne Heywood, Richard Todd, Jack Hedley, Jeremy Brett, Barbara Mullen, Maurice Denham.

Editor's note: Here's where we need a cinema equivalent to "Rock Family Tree" maestro Pete Frame. *The Very Edge* and *Vengeance* are among a string of 1960s and 1970s films produced by Raymond Stross and starring his wife Anne Heywood. Meanwhile, Leslie Bricusse, co-writer of *The Very Edge* and renowned tunesmith of the era, was hitched to Brit horror starlet Yvonne Romain.

1963

Children of the Damned

At a London school, cohabiting psychologist Tom Llewellyn (Ian Hendry) and geneticist David Neville (Alan Badel) run a set of children through a series of intelligence tests, unsurprised to find super-gifted Paul (Clive Powell) trouncing the lot. Investigating his family background, they find that his mother Diana (Sheila Allen) is a blowzy harridan and that his father is nowhere to be found. After she threatens her son, Paul mentally forces Diana to walk in front of a lorry; her hospitalization doesn't prevent her, though, from revealing to the two scientists that she'd been a virgin when bearing Paul.

A few inquiries later, the two find five other super-intelligent children across the world with almost identical backgrounds. Brought to London as part of a UN research experiment, the children band together and occupy a deserted church, experimenting with hydrogen technology (!) and kidnapping Paul's cute yet spooky Aunt Susan (Barbara Ferris) to act as their mouthpiece, apparently with the rest of the world. After several deaths ensue under complicated circumstances, the authorities decide to wipe them out, with Llewellyn and Neville unexpectedly finding themselves on opposite sides. The film builds up to a horrific and bravura climax that poses more questions than answers.

Theoretically a sequel or companion piece to *Village of the Damned*, *Children*, while perhaps less of an enduring memory

in cinematic horror folklore, is in many ways a more gripping film. The action shifts from the bucolic English countryside to seedy, pre-Swinging London with the strangely Holmesian duo of Neville and Llewellyn taking center stage. Neville in particular is a marvelous creation and wonderfully rendered by Badel, whether he's hitting on every woman he encounters (perhaps to deflect questions about his living arrangements with Llewellyn?), bantering with creepy British "operative" Colin, attempting to connect with Paul, forgetting to offer Llewellyn his cigarette lighter after he's done with it, or suggesting a surprising course of action to deal with the children and then panicking when it all goes haywire. Hendry finds himself a little overshadowed as a result, but still does well as a more orthodox, Quatermass-style scientific type. There are few standouts among the supporting cast (although watch for Patrick Wymark and a young—okay, *younger*—Alan MacNaughtan as army officers) besides Ferris as Susan, with a husky yet babyish voice reminiscent of Judi Dench on helium.

Children is at once a less memorable and more thought-provoking film than *Village*, filled with nascent 1960s disillusionment. The moral ambiguity implicit in *Village* is made pretty obvious in *Children*, as their "evil" deeds are all clearly provoked by definite threats, and those entrusted with protecting humanity—intelligence people, army officers—have an almost palpable sleaze hanging over them, only dissipated by the downbeat finale. As with *Village*, we never really find out what motivates the children. A sequence with Susan and the children inside the church gives the kids (and Susan) depth and drive without really revealing what they're planning for the world (beyond the construction of a vague sort of transmitter). The screenplay scores a minor coup by splitting the audience's sympathies, with characters not acting the way viewers might expect in regard to the children. The inconsistent, *human* motivations of the human characters help to keep an audience off-kilter and more receptive to the drama, and the children manage to be both cute *and* inhuman without being cloying or sentimental.

The result is an engaging brew of Cold War paranoia and a warning of what happens when science becomes too heavily entwined in political machinations. *Children of the Damned* deserves a more respected place beside its more celebrated predecessor.
—Wendell McKay

Credits: Director: Anton M. Leader; Writer: Jack Briley. **Leading Cast:** Ian Hendry, Alan Badel, Barbara Ferris, Alfred Burke, Bessie Love.

The Damned (aka *These Are the Damned*)

Adapted from H.L. Lawrence's novel *The Children of Light*, this is probably the outstanding movie in a fascinating canon of offbeat, hard to classify, monochrome Hammer films made in the early 1960s and demonstrative of the studio's versatility. Along with *Never Take Sweets from a Stranger* and *The Stranglers of Bombay*, *The Damned* was ignored at the time of its original, low-key (and much delayed) release. Until a 2007 BBC showing, it ranked among Hammer's most rarely seen movies, though its sole U.K. home video release from the late '90s can still be found with a high price tag on Amazon Marketplace and other collector's outlets.

Substituting real, contemporary fears for traditional monsters and Arthur Grant's eerily beautiful black and white lensing of the Weymouth coastline for the studio-bound Technicolor ambience of the Gothic cycle, this bold departure for the company is a keynote British genre film of the 1960s. It's fascinating for all sorts of reasons, not the least being its place in the offbeat oeuvre of director Joseph Losey, whose McCarthy-era exile from Hollywood wound up producing a string of compelling, unique pictures like *The Servant* and *Accident*.

Though it ends as doom-laden, paranoid sci-fi, *The Damned* opens as something else entirely. In a surprising precursor to *A Clockwork Orange*, a gang of teddy boys led by Oliver Reed chirpily whistle the catchy tune "Black Leather Rock" while viciously beating up a middle-aged American tourist (MacDonald Carey) with an umbrella. Offering some compassion to the wounded outsider, Alexander Knox says bleakly, "You thought England was a country of old ladies knitting socks. The age of senseless violence has caught up with us, too." Subsequently focusing on the 20-year-old sister (Shirley Anne Field) of aggressively over-protective Reed as she attempts to escape the clutches of the gang, *The Damned* grabs our attention as a hard-hitting examination of rock 'n' roll youth culture out of control.

When Field, on the run from Reed and aided in her plight by Carey, stumbles across Knox's top-secret research site, the film shifts gears and genres. Knox oversees the study of a small group of 11-year olds at a cliff top base. The children, all unnaturally cold to the touch, are the mutated products of mothers accidentally exposed to radiation years earlier. (There are superficial parallels to the creepy kids of *The Midwich Cuckoos* and its 1960 movie adaptation.) Knox has kept them hidden away and under his control because he believes they represent the key to survival in the event of a seemingly imminent nuclear catastrophe. When the rest of humanity has been wiped out, he predicts these kids will inherit what remains of the Earth.

Losey's film isn't perfect, arguably devoting too much screen time to Reed's unhealthy, possibly sexually motivated, obsessive pursuit of his sister, and there's a distinct lack of chemistry between the leads. A weak Field and token "wooden American" Carey rank among Hammer's least charismatic central couples. Like the similarly timed *The Day the Earth Caught Fire* and *Never Take Sweets from a Stranger*, however, the film possesses both a haunting power and an impressively downbeat modern sensibility.

Cinematically, it is one of Hammer's finest black and white offerings, with Grant's camera achieving numerous visual coups as it roams subjectively or frames its imperiled

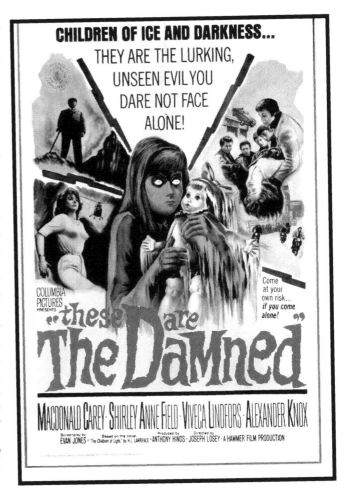

protagonists in appropriately oppressive ways, while James Bernard brings a subtler breed of menace to the proceedings than his usual, distinctively melodramatic Gothic scores.

Most remarkable is the pervasively grim tone of the second half and the pessimism of the resolution. Our seemingly doomed, radiation-exposed heroes are, in the closing shots, last seen with the ostensible villains literally looming over them, while the final sounds we hear are the pathetic "help me" cries of the children. As with so much dark sci-fi of this period, nuclear war is conveyed as an inevitability rather than a possibility, though this film, arguably Hammer's bleakest, depicts a human race barely worth saving in the first place.
—Steven West

Joseph Losey's remarkable, quasi-documentary style sci-fi drama utilizes a recognizably British seaside scenario as an integral part of the story, nicely summed up by the sleeve notes on the Trashville Films video release of *These are the Damned* (U.S. title): "An unusual and very interesting film. [Oliver] Reed plays a psychopathic leader of a gang of rockers who stumble on a weird scientific experiment [involving atomically irradiated children]. This Teds meet sci-fi movie is a great film and shows a slice of life in 1962 Britain."

Indeed, gangs of juvenile delinquents seemed to be a fixed feature of several British holiday resorts in the '60s and '70s, the Bank Holiday "rumbles" between Mods and Rockers in Brighton, as depicted in the film *Quadrophenia*, being especially notorious. Reed is excellent in his role and the Swedish actress Viveca Lindfors gives a fine performance as a holidaying sculptress and sometime mistress of the man in charge of the experiment. The scenes of her weird Easter Island-like stone sculptures atop the windswept cliffs overlooking the sea add greatly to the atmosphere of the film.

There's also a very otherworldly, though coldly clinical, feel to the scenes (surprisingly few) depicting the radioactive children in their lead-shielded laboratory home-cum-school, which serve as a kind of visual embodiment of society's contemporary fears over the misuse of atomic power at the time the CND movement was at its most active. The American publication *The Radio-Active Times* gave the film an enthusiastic thumbs up: "Not a 'B' movie at all. This quality film is well made and very atmospheric."

—Mike Hodges

Credits: Director: Joseph Losey; Writer: Evan Jones.
Leading Cast: MacDonald Carey, Shirley Anne Field, Viveca Lindfors, Alexander Knox, Oliver Reed, James Villiers.

The Haunting

"Hill House had stood for 90 years, and might stand for 90 more—whatever walked there, walked alone."

It's a sad fact that, these days, the turgid '90s remake of this wonderful film has probably (somehow) managed to outshine the original. There may even be people out there—sane, normal people in many ways—who don't even know that the Liam Neeson and Catherine Zeta-Jones farrago is actually a retread of what is possibly the most terrifying picture ever made.

There are some films which are crimes against cinema. *The Haunting* (1999), while not a dreadful movie in itself, is one of those: for besmirching the good name of the original in a welter of bad acting and CGI nonsense. In fact, I'm still of the opinion that whoever was responsible for the reprehensible idea of the remake had actually seen the similar *The Legend of Hell House* and decided to redo *that*.

But I digress. Let's not have an argument about who did what to whom, or why, or how. Let's just have a look at the original, brilliant and unsurpassable 1963 film, and not mention remakes again (much).

The Haunting is *the* scariest film ever made. I firmly believe this. It stands head and shoulders above every other horror movie as the perfect example of how less is more. There's no blood, no (seen) monsters, and hardly any special effects. A great deal of the dialogue is spoken in voiceover, there's no violence and, in fact, only the barest of stories. All this should add up to a disastrous entry into the horror genre but, of course, it doesn't. Perhaps that's the reason why the remake just doesn't work.

The real star of the film is the house, as our "hero," Dr. Markway (Richard Johnson), explains: "Scandal, murder, insanity, suicide—the history of Hill House had everything I wanted. It was an evil house from the beginning—a house that was born bad." Markway wants to conduct a paranormal investigation in the house, and after a brief history lesson explains to us that he hopes to find either "a few loose floorboards—or maybe the key to another world?"

He's assembled a rag-bag of seemingly unconnected strangers to help him: Eleanor (Julie Harris), a miserable spinster who spent most of her life looking after her sick mother and has a history of creating paranormal "happenings" (such as stones falling on her house when she was 10-years old, something she now refuses to believe actually happened); Theo (Claire Bloom), a psychic lesbian (but not necessarily in that order); Luke (Russ Tamblyn), the future owner of the house; and Markway himself, a self-appointed expert on the paranormal with a few woolly ideas on what is happening there and how it can be dealt with (plus a nice sensible cardigan).

Markway may be the catalyst for the story, but it's Eleanor who proves to be the driving force for the events that will unfold. She's a strange, fragile little woman, once abused by her now-dead mother, now abused by her sister and her family. Despite half owning the family car, she has to resort to stealing it to attend her appointment at Hill House—one which she hopes will lead to bigger and better things ("I hope, I hope, I hope this is what I have been waiting for all my life"). And it seems she has found what she's looking for, even as she drives up to the forbidding house, noting: "It's staring at me."

With little personality of her own, and no prior experience of larger than life characters like Markway and Theo, Eleanor immediately falls for both of them (though, in the case of Theo, her attraction appears to be purely non-sexual, despite Theo's predatory confidence). Theo immediately rechristens her "Nell," and on meeting Markway for the first time, Eleanor comments, "It's Theo who's wearing velvet, so I must be Eleanor in tweed."

But all this is just scene setting—although, as Markway has already stated, the presence of people like themselves should help stimulate some kind of activity in the house. (So perhaps he's more astute than his broom cupboard clowning around would lead us to believe? Never trust a man with a mustache, my old mum used to say.) Eleanor (egged on by Theo) is becoming more and more convinced that she belongs in the house, and after dinner, with everyone off to bed, the fun begins.

To list exactly what happens to the visitors would spoil it for those who haven't seen the film, but it's fair to say that anyone who's expecting sedate chills is in for a shock. The first night—from the moment Eleanor wakes to the sound of unearthly banging, mumbling, "All right, mother, all right," to the point where she realizes, "Now I've done it…it was looking for the room with someone inside!"—ranks as one of the scariest scenes in any film *ever* (as well as a testament to what can be achieved with a few *very loud* sound effects and some hysterical women).

From that moment on, the audience is experiencing the same terror that Eleanor and Theo are: What was behind the door? What happens if it gets in? And everything else that happens in the film—whether it's a bit of graffiti ("It's my name, and it belongs to me…it knows my name!"), an innocuous statue ("Haven't you noticed how nothing in this house seems to move—until you look away?"), a wonky bookcase, a shadowy "face" cast by moonlight hitting the raised pattern on the wallpaper ("Whose hand was I holding?"), or even just the fact that the nursery door is open (*believe* me)—becomes absolutely chilling.

Eleanor's already fragile psyche takes a bit of a bruising when she first realizes why Theo is taking such an interest (calling her one of "nature's mistakes"), and then she's introduced to Markway's wife, Grace (who, in a fit of pique, Eleanor puts in mortal danger—something she immediately regrets but can't undo). As the previous night's happenings prove to be nothing but an opening salvo, Eleanor finally realizes her destiny (and the audience is treated to a trapdoor-related shock which is guaranteed to get you every single time). "It's happening to you, Eleanor…at last, something is really, really happening to me."

The Haunting is quite rare, in that it not only delivers the goods from a horror point of view but it's also packed with interesting characters, psychological observations and dynamic cinematography (the disconcerting angles and the bizarre outdoor footage shot on infrared film to give the house an otherworldly quality). In other words, it's the kind of movie a clever film student can really get his teeth into (and indeed, many have). But, first and foremost, it should be watched, and enjoyed, as a brilliant horror film, which manages to deliver the chills right up until the final, haunting line: "We who walk here—walk alone…"
—Chris Wood

Robert Wise (1914-2005) directed more than his fair share of landmark films: *The Day the Earth Stood Still*, *The Sound of Music*, *The Andromeda Strain* and *The Haunting*, among others. All of these films (excepting the second) have either been remade or reimagined in some way. I consider all these fresh attempts failures when compared to not only the powerful versions directed by Wise, but their sources. *The Haunting* is based on the book *The Haunting of Hill House* by Shirley Jackson (1916-1965). The novel and film are remarkably similar. The only chunk of the story missing is a picnic scene, but I can understand why this was excluded, as any sunlit scene set outside would reduce the feeling of claustrophobia, dissipating all the tension that the film had been carefully building up.

Wise deliberately decided to film in black and white at a time when color stock was available to him. Black and white gives the filmmakers opportunities to misdirect the viewer with shadows, to conceal things and also focus the viewer's attention more directly. I think there may be even more to it than this—perhaps the intense contrast between light and darkness has something to do with the primordial parts of the human brain. Four people, Dr. Markway, a researcher, and his companions, Luke, Eleanor and Theodora, arrive separately at Hill House, a building with a horrible history. Admittedly, this sounds like a bunch of pale haunted house clichés, and doesn't do the film anywhere near the justice it deserves.

The Haunting is quite simply a cinematic gem. Every time scary movies crop up in conversation, I always name drop this one, and it is also my default recommendation for people wanting to watch an incredibly creepy film with no gore in it. Rarely does a film come along where you could make such a bold statement like, "Without a doubt, this is the best haunted house movie I have seen," but *The Haunting* set the benchmark for its subgenre and has yet to be bettered. It is also a film that I never once fail to spot something new in, or realize some other nuance whenever I revisit Hill House.
—Elliot Iles

Credits: Director: Robert Wise; Writer: Nelson Gidding.
Leading Cast: Julie Harris, Claire Bloom, Richard Johnson, Russ Tamblyn, Lois Maxwell, Rosalie Crutchley, Valentine Dyall.

A COLOSSUS OF ADVENTURE!

For the first time on the screen...the glory that was Greece...the legend that was Jason!

COLUMBIA PICTURES presents A CHARLES H. SCHNEER PRODUCTION

JASON AND THE ARGONAUTS

TODD ARMSTRONG · NANCY KOVACK · GARY RAYMOND · LAURENCE NAISMITH

as JASON   as MEDEA

Screenplay by IAN READ and BEVERLEY CROSS / Special Visual Effects RAY HARRYHAUSEN / Directed by DON CHAFFEY / A MORNINGSIDE WORLDWIDE FILM

EASTMAN COLOR

Jason and the Argonauts

Revenge is a dish best served with monsters and this take on the legend of the Golden Fleece is proof of that misquote. Jason, in a bid to reclaim his birthright from the man who killed his father, brings together a team of heroes who must face the undead, monsters and even betrayal to gain the fabled Golden Fleece and reunite his people. But will even love be enough to win through against the cruel gods?

To be honest, the film is a monster movie hung upon a Greek legend, and the real stars are Ray Harryhausen's creations, especially the skeleton warriors. In fact, these skeletons were so scary, the scenes of them screaming were cut by the British censor. For all the glory of Harryhausen's creatures, the beautiful blue skies from the Italian locations, and the string of British character actors, the budget is not great and at times it shows. Just watch the cast of 10s in the battle scenes; the indifferent mattes, especially the fat bloke and his wobbling rocks; and the unknown leads as proof. Still, these give moments of joy in their own way, and it also helps that the script has intelligence and humor to carry it through. While considering the script, points of note include the strong anti-religious stance and the posing of various philosophical questions. Surprisingly it all fits well within this sword and sandals epic, with Jason not believing in the gods until he meets them and later opining that one day man will no longer need them.

As befits a film based on Greek myth, the plot is convoluted as well as nonsensical. For instance, Pelias, who takes Jason's birthright and defiles Hera's temple by killing Jason's sister in it, not only has 20 years to rule but also is given the drop on Jason, who talks himself into going to the end of the world to get the fleece. Pelias must have really upset the gods!

Jason gets his ship and crew together with a strategy of appealing to greed and ego, in the process creating the Olympic Games, at which point the splendidly cast Nigel Green as Hercules appears. Sadly he exits the film all too soon. Once the "grunting men" montage is over, we are off sailing into high adventure. The mutinous, thirsty crew ends up on an island with the creaking bronze giant Talos, from there to fight the harpies and rescue the blind seer who gives them the key to get through those wobbling rocks — at which point Jason finds love before facing the cult of the Queen of Darkness, Hecate — and betrayal — finally to overcome the Hydra and stand against the screaming undead.

A good way to think of the film is looking at the Argo. It looks great and works wonderfully, except for the figurehead, which resembles a giant version of *Thunderbirds'* Lady Penelope, especially when possessed. The bits that work do so well, and the bits that don't are still fun, like Pelias' camp with 24-hour dancers and the super growing gods.

As the film ends, Zeus declares that the gods should continue their game another day. Sadly this promise of a sequel never happened; otherwise maybe further adventures would have told how they got back through the wobbling rocks! As for legend, Jason and Medea lived happily ever after until Jason dumped her for another woman, so Medea killed the rival with a burning (or poison-drenched) cloak, also bumping off the lover's father, and her own and Jason's children before setting fire to his palace and flying away by dragon-driven chariot while taunting Jason. I wonder why they never made that, or what Ray Harryhausen would have done with a decent budget?

—Wayne Mook

The ideal person to review this film would be Gary Gygax. Although sadly passed from this realm, I think the creator of Dungeons and Dragons would have something insightful to say about this film's cultural impact, not merely in terms of the genre of Sword and Sorcery, but also the formation of role-playing games (which occurred in the early 1970s).

The epic Greek poem *Argonautica* is this film's source material, and the film plays fast and loose with this, shifting encounters in time and omitting any family unfriendly aspect. I think we should overlook the fact that it is not true to the original simply because this film serves as such an astounding introduction to the world of myths and legends. As the narrative is a journey-based one, it is easy to remove events without damaging the whole story. (*The Odyssey* has been treated in a similar way, although the ending is difficult to "tame" for family audiences.)

Jason (our dubbed hero) wishes to reclaim his father's throne, and obtaining the Golden Fleece is the lynchpin of his plan. A boat is built by Argos (years before the catalog shop was a glint in his eye) to undertake the dangerous journey. The boat's figurehead is, at Jason's insistence, placed near the back of the boat, facing forwards in unorthodox fashion. The men accompanying Jason on his quest are called Argonauts in honor of the ship's builder.

The creatures really sell this film: Talos, with a wonderful patina across his bronze body; fluttering Harpies harassing Phineas (the always excellent Patrick Troughton); a giant Merman (Poseidon? I remember finding his silence particularly spooky when viewing as a child); and the Hydra. This latter creature is possibly the only disappointment, not because of the actors noticeably transforming into their stop-motion equivalents (which, although you can spot the change, is another moment where you again realize how good the effects are), but for

the fact you don't get the head cut off and two growing in its place—which is surely the reason for using a Hydra instead of a dragon or wyvern.

The crowning glory of this film is its final creatures, "The Children of the Hydra's Teeth." I'd bet that this breathtaking sequence is as amazing to modern youngsters as it was to me as a child. All the stop-motion critters are imbued with a real sense of character, which is something computer-generated imagery has yet to achieve (Nick Park's Wallace and Gromit being rare recent examples of character shining through in stop-motion).

Some good moral lessons are featured: not going back for an object (javelin/sewing needle) when it's dangerous to do so; not trusting people with curly beards (especially if they're lacking mustaches); and lateral thinking winning over brute strength. Seen now through adult eyes, the relationship between Olympus' gods and mortals is of more interest than the monsters (skeletons excluded!). Mere mortals being pawns in the gods' game is a great theme, worthy of deeper exploration than is granted here. The ending suggests a measure of jealousy from Hera, which is something I don't think younger viewers will notice (or care about), but shows a much-needed touch of humanity to the gods. Their domain, Olympus, is more subdued in this film than in its later appearance in *Clash of the Titans*.

Jason and the Argonauts is best discovered by accident on the telly schedules late during summer holidays, with the young viewer having no previous knowledge of the monsters and heroes it contains. How comforting it is to know that such a primer exists for future generations of budding fantasy film addicts.

—Elliot Iles

Credits: Director: Don Chaffey; Writers: Jan Read, Beverley Cross.

Leading Cast: Todd Armstrong, Nancy Kovack, Gary Raymond, Laurence Naismith, Niall MacGinnis, Michael Gwynn.

The Kiss of the Vampire

Taking its title from a throwaway comment by Peter Cushing in Hammer's previous foray into reinventing the vampire cinema, the opening sequence of *Kiss of the Vampire* is near perfect, with dynamic framing and a genuinely dismal atmosphere. It helps that the sequence was shot on one of those miserable days we get far too often in Britain, where all light seems to be absorbed by an invisible force.

Depicting a grim funeral taking place somewhere in Hammervania at the beginning of the last century, the holy rites are interrupted by Professor Zimmer (a furious Clifford Evans). The professor visits destruction upon the vampire lass feigning death in the coffin, much to the shock of the rest of the villagers as he plunges a spade bloodily into the casket.

The poor girl had been running with the wrong crowd, the local aristos, a Sadian bunch of libertines isolated from the village in the usual mountain Schloss. However, this family of God defilers has gone beyond a mere philosophy of the bedroom. They are, in fact, as the title promises, vampires, and in this picture they really are a sick bunch: a father, his daughter and his petulant, piano-bashing son, all lusting after fresh meat, with the youngest laddy acting as the honey trap for the ladies, and the daughter being a bit less proactive in luring the boys—she seems more interested in the girlies. This amounts to a still-shocking triangle of incestuous perversion.

Into this isolated, inward-looking, inbred bunch living in an ancient castle full of antiques, bumbles a thoroughly modern couple in a motor car when their newfangled contraption breaks down. The chap driving is the sort of jolly and resourceful Englishman usually played by Kenneth More, but here it's Edward de Souza doing a very good impersonation. His passenger is his new wife, Jennifer Daniel (arguably one of Hammer's least charismatic leading ladies).

They stay in a hotel, which is halfway between the modern world, with its picture of Otto Von Bismarck on the wall, and the ancient world of the vampire cult. Peter Madden plays Mein Host perfectly: He is such a charming and genuinely nice character that it makes his later betrayal of ze Englanders all the more shocking and disturbing. His wife (Vera Cook) spends most of her time bursting into floods of tears, much to everyone's discomfort.

The young pair are noticed by the head vampire, Dr. Ravna, spying on them through a telescope, and he promptly invites them to dinner. From this moment on, Jennifer Daniel's mortal soul is in deep trouble as she becomes ensnared by the creepy family, culminating in a fabulous Danse Macabre as scores of Dr. Ravna's acolytes descend en masse for *the* party of the season, *darlinks*. This masked vampire ball, which is a riot of color and scary masks, is fabulous stuff, the best thing director Don Sharp ever created, before landing the gig on the bonkers *Psychomania* nearly a decade later, and has obviously inspired many movies since, from *Dance of the Vampires* to the 1974 version of *Son of Dracula* (one of the worst films ever made). The vamps are only interested in Jennifer Daniel, however. Poor Eddy is chucked out un-ravished as an embarrassing drunk, with everyone denying ever having seen him with a wife—that is, all except the permanently soused Professor Zimmer.

There is a major and annoying problem with the script at this point. If only Zimmer, the film's vampire hunter, had spilled the beans to the honeymoon couple right at the start of the film, instead of staggering around drunk until it was too late, the whole mess would have been avoided. Then of course there wouldn't have been any story; but still you do watch the thing, internally shouting, "Tell them y' fool!"

In this film, Hammer, who had been adding on new bits of mythology to the Universal originals that inspired them, chucks in several new twists, most controversially to this film's climax. The dated special effects here do have to be watched with a kindly eye, but you can sense that the cumulative effect of the cartoon-generated onslaught still effectively generates a primal fear of being overwhelmed by (super) nature, and being utterly powerless in its face (see Hitchcock's *The Birds*, released the same year, for a bigger budget version). However, the seriousness of intent in editing, music, directing and cinematography all make the sequence still somehow work, whereas each passing year really should render it more absurd (lazy CGI effects creators take note!).

Before Hammer dragged Sir Chris kicking and screaming back into the old fangs 'n' scarlet contact lenses for *Dracula—*

Prince of Darkness, this film and *The Brides of Dracula* made a fascinating and superior Lee-less diptych. Yet Noel Willman, playing the vampire daddy, bore a striking resemblance to Lee, betraying where Hammer's allegiance *really* lay.
—John Rankin

Credits: Director: Don Sharp; Writer: John Elder [Anthony Hinds].
Leading Cast: Clifford Evans, Noel Willman, Jennifer Daniel, Edward de Souza, Isobel Black, Peter Madden.

Maniac

Slotting nicely into the Hammer psycho-thriller series, but also continuing the trend developed in *Taste of Fear* of "British horror films set in France," we find this directorial effort from the oft-maligned (and not without good reason) Michael Carreras scripted by the undisputed cinematic king of this stuff: Jimmy Sangster. All the requisite elements are there: an American beefcake leading man (Kerwin "Sinbad" Mathews), a pouting, doe-eyed heroine (Lilianne Brousse, yet another of those "where the hell did they disappear to?" women the studio was adept at casting in high-profile roles); a dodgy, duplicitous, slightly older female (Nadia Gray); a sinister looking nutter with a gun, sunglasses and a disability (Donald Houston); a ridiculous plot; and some beautiful monochrome cinematography. In short, Hammer had the winning formula down pat.

Maniac is one of the superior entries in the "mini-Hitchcock/ersatz Clouzot" canon that the studio mined from 1961 to 1972, a bloody impressive run by anyone's standards. It's more a suspense movie than anything else (as indeed are all of Hammer's films in this style); yet, on the other hand, it contains enough shocks, chills and psychosis to elevate it above standard thriller status.

The plot is fairly straightforward: One balmy, beautiful day in the Camargue, a young teenage girl (Brousse) is attacked and raped by the local nutter en route home from a hard day's berry picking. Daddy finds out, goes ballistic and, in what should be one of the all-time classic "name that scene" segments of a British horror movie, murders the culprit with his trusty blowtorch. Several years later, once recovered and out of the hospital, the young girl's affections are aroused by the appearance of a traveling American (Mathews) who just "happens" to be in the area. Before you know it, she and her equally alluring but definitely sinister mother (Gray) are engaged in an unspoken but blindingly obvious love tussle over his square jaw and healthy abs.

This would be hassle enough were it not for the fact that they've also hatched a plot to break out the incarcerated Dad (Houston), who obviously isn't going to take that kindly to this unrequited ménage-à-trois; and, having done so, it's not long before he's reaching for the weapons again and another series of "acetylene murders" is shattering the tranquil calm of the rural French shrublands. The police, particularly the grumpy and far from saintly Inspector Etienne (George Pastell), become interested and, before too long, one of those great "end of film"

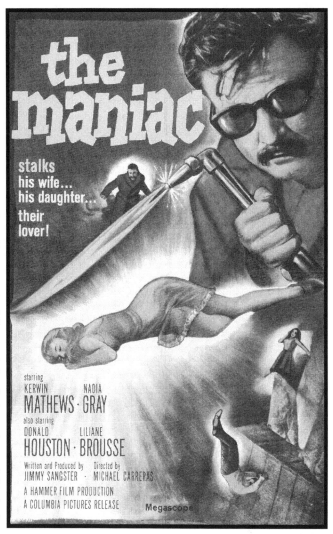

climaxes ensues in a stone quarry. (And why not? Hammer hadn't used one yet, to my knowledge, although the obviously influential Butchers' production *Painted Smile*, directed by Lance Comfort a couple of years earlier, had done so in a much bleaker manner.)

Of course there's a twist before the final reel (which I'm not going to be callous enough to reveal to you, save to say that it concerns the "identity" of one of our main protagonists). All in all, it's a film that does exactly what it promises on the tin, a far from workmanlike effort, and easy enough to follow despite its many plot layers. It's well worth a look, if only to see what Carreras could turn his hand to before he went completely tonto, or to get a glimpse of Houston, best known for his appearances in such televisual fluff as *Moonbase 3* and *Now, Take My Wife*, attempting a much meatier and darker role togged out in some decidedly camp getup.
—D.R. Shimon

Credits: Director: Michael Carreras; Writer: Jimmy Sangster.
Leading Cast: Kerwin Mathews, Nadia Gray, Donald Houston, Liliane Brousse, Norman Bird, George Pastell.

The Old Dark House

Both Hammer and William Castle had a reputation for producing entertaining horror films. What would happen when they came together? In short, the teaming produced a disaster—a horror comedy that's not frightening and is decidedly un-funny, which is rather a shame, as there was some real talent involved, including English eccentrics such as Robert Morley, Joyce Grenfell, Fenella Fielding and a terrific double turn from Peter Bull as twins Casper and Jasper. The film offers all this, plus Mervyn Johns building an ark in the garden. Although Hammer had long used American "stars" to boost the box-office take in the U.S., it was their very "Englishness" that enhanced their early success (despite the Mittel European flavor of the stories they adapted). The Transatlantic nature of this production may have spelt its doom. Castle's American films, with or despite their gimmicks, were great successes.

Tom Poston tries hard in the lead role, an American car salesman in England invited to the Femm household by his flatmate, Casper. He finds the Femm family not only barking mad (yes, all of 'em, despite appearances) but also somewhat murderous. Some of the deaths are pretty ingenious but still can't save the film. Not only does this fail as a horror film and as a comedy, but it's a pretty useless whodunit, too.

The Old Dark House was made in Eastman color but originally released in black and white (which may have improved the atmosphere, as the color version has none) with a host of Hammer regular back-room boys and girls. Screenwriter Robert Dillon has had a checkered career, including *X—The Man with the X-Ray Eyes*, made immediately prior to *Old Dark House*, and *Muscle Beach Party* soon afterwards. His peak was arguably *French Connection II*.

The Old Dark House also features possibly the worst animal attack in the history of cinema. An indeterminate, obviously stuffed creature is subjected to endless close-ups, with a faint snarling sound in the background. The special effects team somehow attempted to make the thing salivate. This interlude gives the viewer not only a chance to marvel at the taxidermists' art, but also a long, excruciatingly embarrassing time to question the wisdom of including a scene such as this in an already bad film. The bear in *Circus of Horrors* and Roger Dicken's bat in *Scars of Dracula* give far more effective performances. —Ryan Taylor

Credits: Director: William Castle; Writer: Robert Dillon.
Leading Cast: Tom Poston, Fenella Fielding, Janette Scott, Robert Morley, Joyce Grenfell, Mervyn Johns, Peter Bull, Danny Green.

Paranoiac

Ollie Reed: What a man—the very personification of everything both "chap" and "bloke"—fiercely intellectual yet with a burning urge for several pints and a damn good fight. Like his drinking buddies, Harris, Hemmings and O'Toole, only one of whom at time of writing remains with us, he trod that fine line 'twixt artist and hooligan, attempted often in modern times by lesser talents with far less convincing results. Lest we forget, he was also a damned good actor, whose career bestrode several fascinating phases—none more so than the years between 1960 and 1963 as Hammer's very own male lead, where he made three of their finest films: *The Curse of the Werewolf*, *The Damned* and *Paranoiac*.

Paranoiac was based on Josephine Tey's 20th-century Gothic novel *Brat Farrar*, which contains all the requisite elements of skulduggery and intrigue necessary for a good melodrama: murder, an inheritance, a lake, a faint whiff of incest, three siblings, one of whom is a nutter (but which?), and a mistaken identity.

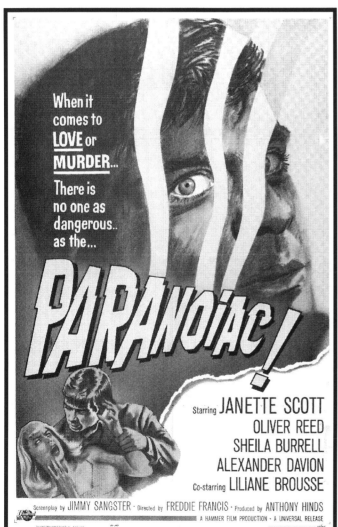

Reed plays Simon Ashby, a conniving wastrel of a young man whose family seems to own most of the local village. That is, what's left of the family: His parents died in a plane crash 11 years previously, and his brother, Tony, despondent over the incident, committed suicide three years afterwards. Or did he? Either way, the estate is currently in the hands of the dour, shrewish Aunt Harriet (Sheila Burrell) until "three weeks from now," when Simon and his supposedly "insane" sister Eleanor (Janette Scott), who feels guilt over her brother's death and receives a lot of "looking after" by her decidedly dodgy French nurse Françoise (Lilianne Brousse), come into their parental bequest of over half-a-million.

He seems quite pleased about this, especially as he's already pissed half of it up against the wall, saved from ignominy every time by the cachet his family name carries. The only thing that could put a spanner in the works right now would be for "Mr. Tony," as the butler calls him, to miraculously rise from the dead and claim his half of the loot—which is, of course, exactly what happens.

Saving Eleanor, who has been "seeing" visions of her departed brother right from the start, from another suicide attempt (this time by flinging herself from some rocks in the way he was supposed to have done), Tony carries her to the house as if he'd never left it, and then promptly buggers off, his air of nonchalance slightly broken by the fact that Reed, already completely loaded behind the wheel of his Triumph convertible (are we seeing art imitating life here?), spots him and subsequently drives straight into a hydrangea. Once he and Auntie know, we're in for a rollercoaster ride of suspense, scares and shenanigans, with the already unhinged Ollie getting progressively drunker, crazier and more violent—which is just how we like him.

Rather than the usual premise of "trying to drive someone mad," the plot of *Paranoiac* hinges instead on the Ashbys finding out what we already know, namely that "Tony" is merely an impostor after a share of the inheritance (something we see him discussing relatively early on with his co-conspirator, solicitor's son John Bonney), and that there's a reason at least one family member, if not two, shares this knowledge. The clever twist is that Tony (Alex Davion), whose real identity is never revealed (unlike in the book), actually turns out to be an all-around nice chap who tires of his fiendish purpose, and it's with him we are supposed to identify.

Unfortunately for Tony, Reed is so mesmerizing (even if one scene, which has him yelling unnecessarily at his butler, *is* slightly overcooked) that, even though he's a grade-A radio-rentalist with an attitude problem and several dodgy secrets, throws darts at people whose "pop-eyed faces" he dislikes, chats up sleazy tarts in pubs and victimizes random winos, we find ourselves rooting for him. On a simple level we've seen in a zillion previous horror films, thrillers and even Westerns, the baddie is more interesting than the goodie—and when it's Oliver Reed you're dealing with, you've got a baddie more interesting than most. Still young and devilishly handsome at this stage, you can see why the ladies, in particular Brousse, have a thing for him. It will prove her undoing; but, the minute you clap eyes on her, you know—as you know with all such characters—she's coffin fodder.

Janette Scott, on the other hand, has our sympathy from the start: As the frail, frightened Eleanor, whose "insanity" is clearly the work of others, she's the most beautiful she ever was. She may have slightly worried feelings toward her recently returned brother (the fact that he's an impostor justifies this to some extent, but I get the feeling that, in her mind, that's not the whole story), but she definitely doesn't deserve the kind of "bedside manner" Brousse dishes out: "He couldn't come back! There's no way! He's *dead*! His body must have been *crushed to pieces*!" If that's the kind of treatment private health care gets you, I'm glad I'm skint. Of the principal protagonists, a number of them could be the "paranoiac" (whatever one of those is), although ultimately I think we all know whom the term really applies to.

Paranoiac

Where *Paranoiac* succeeds against all odds is in its construction. The editing, even by Hammer's usual meticulous standards, is sharp, snappy and to the point, carrying the story swiftly from scene to scene with confidence and style, and the scares (at least one of which is enough to make the viewer jump readily out of his seat) are deftly positioned. In this respect it's a more powerful horror movie than *Hysteria*, *Fanatic* or *Maniac*, although it lacks the humor of the first film, the claustrophobic tension of the second, and the pastoral, rustic beauty of the third. Freddie Francis is no slouch here on the directorial front, either; and, quite unlike *Nightmare*, it seems like a team effort, with Francis and Jimmy Sangster working in tandem.

It's not perfect: There's never any *real* explanation given as to why one character has to go around wearing a mask that looks like a cross between a balloon and a Pink Pearl Light ad, nor where one gets vinyl recordings of one's offspring singing hymns slightly off key; and the vicar in the opening scene fluffs his lines quite noticeably to the point that you wonder why Francis left it in. And Davion, later to resurface as a similarly wet hero (a feature of these films, it seems) in *Incense for the Damned*, looks far too mature to be a young man of 21 or 22. But those minor hiccups are more than compensated for by the mixture of elegant poise and understated terror on display. There's also a dimly lit corridor, a skeleton and a church organ thrown in for good measure, and any combination of the above immediately gets my vote. Also commendable is its use of locations: Unlike many other Hammer films, which tended to be shot in and around the environs of Bray and Black Park, it features several sequences shot on the Isle of Purbeck in Dorset, one in particular relying on that very setting. Of course, I'm not suggesting for one minute that the makers of British horror films ever designed things purely for the purposes of plot expediency.

On balance, *Paranoiac* might just be the best in this particular series and sub-genre. Rather than retread old ground, and wear its influences on its sleeve, it spawned a few imitators of its own. To close on a humorous note, if that scene with the car dangling over the cliff *didn't* influence the makers of *Some Mothers Do 'Ave 'Em*, then *my* name's Tony Ashby.
—D.R. Shimon

Credits: Director: Freddie Francis; Writer: Jimmy Sangster.
Leading Cast: Janette Scott, Oliver Reed, Alexander Davion, Sheila Burrell, Liliane Brousse, Maurice Denham.

Unearthly Stranger

Overwrought, economical, sweaty and daft: These are the four words that came to me after watching *Unearthly Stranger*, a little-known sci-fi/horror film from the mid 1960s, full of paranoia and bizarre (and cheap) ideas of how aliens could appear in our midst. Imagine, if you will, that aliens are among us. They don't arrive by spaceship, as that would involve some kind of special effects. They don't look any different to us, as that would involve some kind of special effects. And they don't kill on screen, as that would—oh, you've got the picture. However, *Unearthly Stranger* is not as cheap and awful as it might sound. In fact, as paranoia inducing, stiff upper lipped British science fiction goes (which isn't very far), it's rather splendid, with enough twists and stupidity to entertain anyone who can't think of anything else to do for the 90 minutes.

A scientist finds out that his wife might be an alien. She is. How do we know this? Because she doesn't blink—much. That's about it. And, surprisingly, apart from the rather irritating point that you spend much of the film trying to see if the wife *is* actually blinking or not, *Unearthly Stranger* is a good example of its type. Lots of men smoking pipes wander around in tweed jackets expounding on the nature of the universe (they want to "harness the power of concentration" to travel through time and space, using "the force we call TP91"); the Stranger of the title is a definite saucepot (and handy in the kitchen as well—a far cry from Ridley Scott's *Alien*, who only succeeds in *ruining* a good meal), and the whole thing has a dour Cold War feel that's pure Brit.

It all starts with a sweaty man running away from a strange noise, past the Houses of Parliament (is there really no other landmark someone can run past to denote they're in London? It's becoming a bit wearing now, after 200-plus films) and straight into a space research center. He starts a tape and begins to recount his tale of woe: "John, in a little while, I expect to die—to be killed by something you and I know is here. Invisible— moving unseen amongst us all. Even if I had known what I know now, could I, or anyone, have held back—the terror?"

Blimey. So begins the flashback. Professor Munro (a Scottish Warren Mitchell) lasts approximately 30 seconds after discovering a new formula, an "explosion" having

taken place in his head. A similar thing has been happening to scientists in the United States and Russia, which is helping the Cold War to no end ("they suspect *us*…").

An investigation into the death is begun by Major Clarke (Patrick Newell, the bloke who played Mother in *The Avengers*), and Dr. Davidson (John Neville) is given the suddenly vacated job. Davidson is our sweaty friend from the beginning of the film. He takes on the role manfully, but his stiff upper lip is wilted somewhat by a number of strange occurrences. His predecessor's coffin turns out to be full of bricks, and then it disappears completely. A chemical usually only found in space capsules was discovered in the dead man's body (before it vanished, presumably), and many conclusions about the danger everyone is in are hastily jumped to by all.

Meanwhile, we are introduced to Julie (Gabriella Licudi), Davidson's new wife. She sleeps with her eyes open, has no pulse, picks up piping-hot ovenware without the aid of gloves, cries tears which burn the skin off her face, and can terrify entire playgrounds full of scarf-wearing children under 10 without so much as—blinking. And we are led to believe that our supposedly intelligent scientist hero put all this down to her coming from Switzerland. They didn't get out much in the 1960s, obviously.

Full of glaring plot holes (it takes an awful lot more evidence finally to convince Davidson that his wife is not all she seems), *Unearthly Stranger* succeeds, despite its limitations, on a number of levels. You can't knock a film that has people leaping to enormous conclusions after calculations done on the back of a cigarette pack. (She doesn't blink, therefore she's obviously an alien being who has been projected onto their world by the power of concentration to stop us Earthlings from perfecting the same kind of technology! Of course! The only question is why they didn't think of it sooner?) Julie is gorgeous, and the whole thing turns into a doomed love story ("I don't care where you have come from—you are what I love! I have only ever seen you as a woman, not as anything else!") with a great twist ending. Julie, as a supposed invader, confounds expectations as a being who actually seems upset about the job she has to do. But, even greater, full marks have to go to the scriptwriters for making a "casserole" (that most middle-class and British of meals) such a major plot device.

—Chris Wood

Credits: Director: John Krish; Writer: Rex Carlton.
Leading Cast: John Neville, Gabriella Licudi, Philip Stone, Patrick Newell, Jean Marsh, Warren Mitchell.

1964

The Black Torment

The Black Torment is almost a pure dose of Gothic horror, in the full meaning of that term, as it possesses many of the key elements that are associated with this currently unpopular subgenre, namely madness, secrets, suicides, cursed families, murders, ghosts, romance and melodrama, all given a period setting (here 1780).

Much of the joy to be had with this one is in watching events slowly unfold and trying to second guess where it's all heading, so I'll avoid a detailed full synopsis. Basically it's about Sir Richard Fordyce (a rather scary-looking John Turner who, with his black beard and hair and impressive build, seems to be half-pirate, half-grizzly bear), an 18th century aristocrat who has just married for the second time and is returning to his country manor in Devon with his new wife, Elizabeth (Heather Sears), to introduce her to his family. Things obviously don't go smoothly for this newlywed couple (although not in a way that any normal marriage guidance counselor would be familiar with, I trust). We quickly learn that Richard's hobby is shouting and being a bit dim (the latter is a plot requirement), and his wife is so amazingly understanding, although she does eventually reach a breaking point (it took far longer than I was expecting, mind you).

If you were going to convert a fan of costume historical dramas into the fun to be had from viewing horror films, this picture would be one of a number you'd use to brainwash, I mean acclimatize, him or her to the merits of the genre. It might even be placed near the top of the list. Although (please don't misjudge my above comment) this isn't a film solely geared toward the female audience (despite containing the modern telly and film dramatic requirement of a wife being more clever than the husband), there are elements a-plenty to interest us blokes. I'm thinking mostly of the superb sword fight, largely due to the look of rage on the duelist's faces as they attempt to plunge sharp bits of steel through each other in the time-honored fashion!

The film does rush its explanation, and I would have preferred less of the horse and coaches at the beginning so that more time could have been spent making major plot points crystal clear. The filmmakers might also have thrown in at least one secret passage, as this is a trope of Gothic horror that was extremely conspicuous by its absence. The use of firearms seems to fit uncomfortably within the film (shouldn't they have been sabotaged or removed like the family Bible?).

My outstanding memory is the ethereal image of the female in white who haunts this film, and rides through the forest on horseback shouting, "Murderer!" But having watched it and been entertained by it, I have a nagging feeling that I ought to know why it is called *The Black Torment*! Perhaps I wasn't playing close enough attention?
—Elliot Iles

If you've come looking for a proper, old-fashioned Brit horror yarn, one that pays no heed to the turning tide nor cinematic trends, and remains firmly within the traditions of good old-fashioned Gothic terror, country houses, sinister serfs and all, then you've found it in *The Black Torment*. From the opening scene, you know what you're in for, as a blonde "wench" pegs it through a forest somewhere between Slough, Staines and Shepperton, seemingly fleeing from some unknown assailant. Her fate is about as sealed as your own: hers, an immediate bloody death; yours, almost 90 minutes of utter cheese that should warm the cockles of one's heart on a cold winter night in front of a roaring log fire.

So, what's it all about? Put simply, something horrible is going on down on the homestead. Sir Richard (John Turner) has returned home to the family pile with his new wife, the bounteous yet frail Elizabeth (Heather Sears), and is therefore rather miffed when, instead of the usual prodigal's welcome, he receives the cold shoulder from all and sundry, especially his blacksmith (Francis De Wolff), a sullen type at the best of times, who won't talk politely to him, and seems to be under the impression that his master never left the area in the first place.

Allegedly, "Sir Richard" has been seen riding through the woods at night with his late wife's white-clad ghost in pursuit, crying, "Murderer!" at his mare's galloping heels. Which, of course, he swears he hasn't, and we are inclined to believe him. Oh, and, lest we forget (sort of key to the matter, really), some local girls have been murdered. Otherwise, riding around on horseback in the dark would, by itself, not exactly be a punishable offense.

Robert Hartford-Davis was a director of considerable skill, and though it's strange to see him working in Gothic melodrama here, as opposed to his usual urban/modernist metier, he takes what could easily have been formulaic, hoary old subject matter and manages to inject it with enough zing, venom and downright nastiness (not to mention some sterling cinematography from that stalwart of Britsploitation, Peter Newbrook, who manages to make even the day-for-night shots seem bearable) to keep us interested. The plot (the evil handiwork of Derek and Donald Ford, up to their usual mischief but without the smutty bits) may be more predictable than a Stenhousemuir away result, but to invoke the old adage, "It ain't what you do, it's the way that you do it."

Some may have chosen to cover the cracks with flashy camera work or cheesy special effects, but not in this case. Instead, *The Black Torment* makes up for whatever it may lack in originality or believability with a stellar ensemble cast. Just look at the names: Ann Lynn (stunning as ever), Peter Arne (shady and clandestine as usual), Norman Bird (always a pleasure), Raymond Huntley (I wonder if Compton-Tekli knew they were casting Britain's first Dracula?), Annette Whiteley (fresh from *Girl on Approval*, and definitely a contender for the "where the hell are you now?" files), the aforementioned De Wolff, Patrick Troughton (yes!), Derek Newark (double yes!) and, in his final role, Joseph Tomelty. There's even a bit part for future stalwart Edina Ronay, here seen hitting the trash trail early on in her career as the first victim (or at least the first we see) of the (not so) mysterious ghostly fiend. Bloody hellfire, with actors like that, and the directorial and scriptwriting talent involved, who *needs* a plausible plot?

Admittedly, the "stars" are probably the weaker links in the chain. Turner, a man obviously hired when Tenser and Klinger realized they couldn't afford Christopher Lee, and therefore instructed to shout and bellow as much as possible, was never the most prepossessing of leading men, and makes a less sympathetic hero than his better-known counterparts, although he does his best given the material he has to work with. Sears, on the other hand, makes a bit of a wet heroine, to the point where you're not really all that bothered what happens to her as long as there are plenty of bloody deaths and an exciting climax.

Despite its well-trodden subject matter (already dated in 1964), the film can still be viewed as a damn fine "rollicking romp." Sadly, this style of filmmaking has become known with hindsight as "high camp," a term which, as a horror fan, I find snobbish and disrespectful—but if one is honest, there *is* enough eye rolling, overacting, swashbuckling (the penultimate scene culminates in a sword fight atop the baronial staircase, complete with handily positioned axes) and general braggadocio to qualify that description.

Not that it's all as cozy or quaint as some may make out: There's a *genuinely* unpleasant and chilling death scene involving a disabled character and his wheelchair, which still engenders a slightly queasy feeling some 25 years after I first saw it; and one sequence which, if you're easily freaked out by the sight of hooded, faceless, sheety things in the dark, you won't be watching alone in a hurry.

For fans of a very particular type of horror, it's no less than the definite article; to others, merely nostalgia incarnate, perhaps of the type they've been trying to forget. For best results, view through a haze, as best achieved by several glasses of port and a plate of something savory, cigars optional.
—D.R. Shimon

Credits: Director: Robert Hartford-Davis; Writers: Donald Ford, Derek Ford.
Leading Cast: Heather Sears, John Turner, Ann Lynn, Peter Arne, Francis de Wolff, Edina Ronay, Raymond Huntley, Patrick Troughton.

Catacombs (aka *The Woman Who Wouldn't Die*)

For any fans of Hammer's psychological black and white thrillers of the early 1960s, I can report that you'd love this British Lion production, too—yet another Brit ripoff of *Les Diaboliques*, mainly shot on interior sets but with a couple of excursions to an airport and to Italy (which seems to be a mixture of a fake "exterior" and a bit of stock footage of an exploding car).

Georgina Cookson steals the show as a disabled, middle-aged, but still very sexually active and rich London-based businesswoman, whose husband (Gary Merrill) and young secretary (Neil McCallum) would both like to be rid of her, and so conspire to bump her off, hiding the fact by hiring an actress to play her for a short time. Into the mix arrives her young niece (Jane Merrow), a talented artist and sculptress, for whom Merrill (her uncle by marriage) falls big time. Bodies begin to pile up, the usual strange occurrences ensue, the film's odd title is explained away by the arrival of a not-quite-right postcard from Italy, and things take a few *Diaboliques* turns before the very clever final scene.

A few nifty scares pepper this one, bolstered with an excellent Carlo Martelli score conducted by Philip Martell, some fine performances (Cookson is especially good) and some really effective horror and murder scenes. Merrill's murder of Cookson, which sets the whole plot rolling, takes place in a bathroom sink, which may not be a first but is certainly rather offbeat!

Cookson's character is described early on as belonging to a religious sect, the Sophianists, who can read minds and believe strongly in life after death—another really bizarre addition to the script, but one that keeps you guessing as the revelations begin to unfurl later on.

The credits state that this is a "Parroch-McCallum Production," so maybe the juvenile lead had a financial stake in the proceedings—perhaps he invested his fee from *Dr. Terror's House of Horrors*? Parroch-McCallum had been responsible for the Dan Duryea kidnapping thriller *Do You Know This Voice?* earlier the same year. (Duryea also starred in the company's tense *Walk a Tightrope* [1965].)

Catacombs appears only to have been available for home viewing via an obscure Region 4 DVD release from Universal/Studio Canal. It's worth tracking down from Aussie retailers if you like *Hysteria*, *Paranoiac* and *Taste of Fear*.
—Darrell Buxton

Credits: Director: Gordon Hessler; Writer: Dan Mainwaring.
Leading Cast: Gary Merrill, Jane Merrow, Georgina Cookson, Neil McCallum.

The Curse of the Mummy's Tomb

The year is 1900, and an expedition to Egypt discovers the ancient tomb of the Pharaoh Ra-Antef. Despite the brutal murder of their chief archaeologist, Professor Dubois (Bernard

Rebel), and the usual dire warnings from the local naysayers, American entrepreneur Alexander King (Fred Clark) elects to take the mummified remains of Ra to London for the start of a planned world tour of exhibitions. Inevitably, the dischuffed mummy (Dickie Owen) is soon revived, courtesy of Egyptian prophet of doom Hashmi Bey (George Pastell in a role that is virtually a reprise of the part he played in Hammer's earlier mummy film) and the mysterious Adam Beauchamp (Terence Morgan), who is in fact Ra's immortal brother, Be-Antef, who seeks to use the marauding mummy for his own nefarious purposes.

Hammer's second mummy film is far less ambitious in scope than their 1959 "original," and marks a departure for the company in that it was shot, not at Bray, but at the much larger Elstree Studios as part of a recent financing deal with ABPC (Associated British Picture Corporation) which stipulated that they only use Bray when Elstree was unavailable. The irony here is that this is one of the most cramped and small-scale productions the company ever turned out.

Writer and director Michael Carreras elected (as usual) to shoot in the widescreen ratio (Techniscope), but the format is completely wasted on a production that is almost totally studio-bound, barring some poorly integrated stock footage during the desert prologue. Veteran cinematographer Otto Heller (who had previously shot films for such luminaries as Laurence Olivier and Michael Powell) will no doubt have felt his talents to have been criminally under used here. Also adding to the overall sense of cheapness is the re-use of existing musical cues taken from Franz Reizenstein's 1959 score for *The Mummy*.

However, in its own modest way, *The Curse of the Mummy's Tomb* is reasonably entertaining. Despite unfolding at a leisurely pace—the mummy only springs to life after two thirds of the running time has elapsed—it manages to maintain interest with some very good individual scenes, especially those featuring the revived mummy who, in typical fashion, seeks to punish and destroy all those who desecrated his tomb. Dickie Owen makes for a rather corpulent-looking revenant, but his appearances are well staged by Carreras, and very good use is made of sound effects, with the mummy's echoed breathing making him sound like an Egyptian counterpart to Darth Vader! Particularly effective is the scene in which the mummy stomps on the head of George Pastell's character, complete with sickening sound effects and the suitably horrified reaction shots of John (Ronald Howard) and Inspector Mackenzie (John Paul). The film is also bolstered by a couple of decent performances, particularly Fred Clark's barnstorming turn as the garrulous King, and also Terence Morgan who is suitably implacable as the villainous Adam Beauchamp/Be-Antef.

Released in October 1964 as the lower half of a double bill with Hammer's superior *The Gorgon*, the British quad poster artwork (based on an earlier draft of the script) misleadingly represents the mummy as a hulking 20-foot behemoth. Unsurprisingly, Hammer's budget fell approximately 14 feet short of their ambitions. Not

a classic by any means, *The Curse of the Mummy's Tomb* is nevertheless an efficient little shocker that occasionally rises above the mundane, and is comfortably better than Hammer's two subsequent mummy pictures, *The Mummy's Shroud* and *Blood from the Mummy's Tomb*.
—Stuart Hall

It took Hammer five years to follow up the success of 1959's *The Mummy*, and, despite producer-director Michael Carreras's enthusiasm for the project, *The Curse of the Mummy's Tomb* turns out to be something of a damp squib. The early treatment told of a 20-foot mummy rampaging through Cairo. And yes, that sounds—stupid. Thankfully, a lower than expected budget meant a re-jigged script courtesy of Carreras and Alvin Rakoff, but credited to "Henry Younger," an in-joke at the expense of Hammer writer Tony Hinds, who wrote as "John Elder." Well, we can assume *they* found it funny. (Rakoff's role in the "Henry Younger" subterfuge was first revealed by the man himself during a conversation with Jonathan Rigby for the *Death Ship* DVD commentary in 2007.) What we're left with is a retread of pretty much every previous mummy movie, with the bandaged one shuffling around and bumping off the desecrators of his tomb. There are a couple of new wrinkles in the formula, though, and they make it worth sticking with as the movie unravels.

It's 1900, and an archaeology professor is gruesomely murdered in the Egyptian desert (a totally unconvincing set at Elstree Studios), his hand being lopped off and delivered to his expedition party as a rather extreme way of saying, "sod off home." Having already plundered the tomb of Ra-Antef, the party is due to return to London. But Alexander King (Fred Clark), the "colorful American" sponsor of the expedition, dares to provoke the ire of everybody with his plans to tour the Pharaoh's treasures around like a cheap carnival sideshow. George Pastell, fetching as ever in a fez and virtually repeating his role from *The Mummy*, warns of the dangers of such sacrilege. Ooh, spooky—but does King listen? Of course he doesn't. What kind of horror film would this be if he did? I mean, *really*.

On the ship home, the dead professor's daughter is romanced away from under the nose of her intended by a mysterious stranger called Adam Beauchamp (Terence Morgan, looking like Robert Quarry), a man with a suspicious interest in Ra-Antef's treasures. Upon reaching London, Alexander King opens his great show to find his star has gone missing. Yes, the mummy's reign of terror has begun…

Unfortunately, it takes two-thirds of the movie before the "reign of terror" begins. Up to that point, we have to suffer the limp romantic coupling of Ronald Howard and Jeanne Roland, an Anglo-Burmese model whose career, surely to nobody's great surprise, turned out to be brief. Aside from Michael Ripper as an unlikely Egyptian (he's dead after 15 minutes), the most recognizable Hammer face is that of Pastell. Terence Morgan is passable, and the denouement revealing his real identity is the saving grace of the film. Otherwise, the shining star

here is Fred Clark as the brash Yank promoter. He plays King as loud, roguish and likable and provides a few laughs. There are humorous touches throughout, and also some surprisingly gruesome ones. Carreras goes crazy with the hand loppings, and George "Fruit" Pastell gets his head stomped on. Swap the fez for a crash helmet next time, Fruity!

Of course, the mummy himself is rather a letdown after Christopher Lee. This time it's Dickie Owen under the wrapping, like you should care. However, the simple addition of a Darth Vader-style asthmatic wheeze at least makes this mummy memorable. But when he meets his sudden end in a sewer under a shower of rubble, you're rather left scratching your head.

Though commercially successful, this is strictly B-grade Hammer. But it's short and provides mild entertainment for its length. And you can't say Pharaoh than that.
—Jed Raven

Credits: Director: Michael Carreras; Writer: Henry Younger [Michael Carreras].
Leading Cast: Terence Morgan, Ronald Howard, Fred Clark, Jeanne Roland, George Pastell, Michael Ripper.

Devil Doll

Let's be honest, ventriloquist's dummies are creepy. Imagine stumbling across one in a darkened room. See, I told you—creepy. And so *Devil Doll* doesn't have to try very hard to succeed in the creepy stakes, featuring as it does an evil hypnotist/ventriloquist and his all-too lifelike wooden sidekick, Hugo. But it succeeds nonetheless.

Bryant Haliday plays "The Great Vorelli," a sinister chap (you can tell he's sinister, he has a beard) and star of the variety circuit. It's a role you could imagine Christopher Lee in, if the film's budget had stretched to include his fee, but nobody else was considered for the part. Haliday had an association with producer Richard Gordon and his distribution company, Janus Films, formed in collaboration with business partner Cy Harvey. By the time of *Devil Doll*, Haliday had moved in front of the camera, and old buddy Gordon was happy to give him the first of four parts in his movies, climaxing with *Tower of Evil* in 1971.

William Sylvester plays Mark English, a journalist assigned to expose Vorelli as a fraud. He attends a show with his fiancée, beautiful socialite Marianne Horn (the luscious Yvonne Romain), where Vorelli hypnotizes her into being quite the little mover. Her partner, an "expert in modern dancing," certainly seems happy enough as Yvonne shakes her stuff. (And that's a lot of stuff. I think I'd be happy, too.) We know exactly what Vorelli's after as he stands in the wings, licking his lips, the dirty sod. Marianne later calls him "very attractive." That's when you *know* he's messed with her mind!

The high point of the show, however, is when Vorelli produces Hugo, the dummy. Hugo is just a tad too lifelike, especially when he shuffles to the front of the stage unaided. Duly impressed, Marianne invites the vent and dummy to a charity ball where they give another eerie performance and Vorelli pulls Marianne further under his thrall. Meanwhile, Mark investigates the walking, talking dummy to discover it's just that: a dummy. So what's Vorelli's secret?

Marianne is confined to bed (maybe she saw the wallpaper in her bedroom—it looks like somebody had a few spare rolls after decorating a synagogue) and Vorelli's assistant is murdered. The movie meanders slightly after this point, as Mark investigates Vorelli's past, having been given some vague clues by Hugo himself. I don't know about you, but if I woke to find a ventriloquist's dummy standing over me, I'd be too busy scrubbing the bedsheets to be flitting off to Berlin!

As the net tightens around Vorelli, the film picks up again to climax during the best scene, as Hugo confronts his "master." Their struggle is brilliantly edited and eerie as hell. Director Lindsay Shonteff also makes sparing use of negative inserts to unsettling effect. The "diabolical ending" seems predictable 40-odd years on, but doesn't detract from this much-underrated little movie.

Devil Doll is nowhere nearly as bad as you may have heard, after it was famously lampooned on *Mystery Science Theatre 3000*. It's an effective little shocker with memorable moments. Certainly, the sight of little Hugo's feet shuffling along the floor will stay with you. The film essentially updates a segment from *Dead of Night* and stretches it to feature length. You could argue the story doesn't support this, but the payoff is well worth your time. And Yvonne Romain, under a selection of enormous beehive hairdos and sporting some deadly eyelashes, looks phenomenal throughout. It's a neglected 1960s gem, ripe for rediscovery.
—Jed Raven

Credits: Director: Lindsay Shonteff; W: George Barclay, Lance Z Hargreaves.
Leading Cast: Bryant Haliday, William Sylvester, Yvonne Romain, Sandra Dorne, Francis de Wolff.

The Earth Dies Screaming

A brief glance at the synopsis of Terence Fisher's 1964 sci-fi quickie helps explain most critics' disdain (which Fisher himself shared). The pre-credits sequence shows the consequences of a low-budget alien gas attack. An out of control model train runs off the rails, an out of control car smashes into a brick wall at 5 mph, an out of control aircraft crashes to earth (off screen), a slightly too much in control commuter drops down dead on the station platform, taking care not to hurt himself in the fall.

A handful of survivors (rugged American pilot hero, pregnant woman, angry young man, pistol packing opportunist, pathetic alcoholic, etc.) congregate in the inevitable English village hotel and bicker among themselves in the time honored end of the world movie tradition. The dead are resurrected as cheap labor by the spacesuited (?) alien robots and shamble around menacingly. The group is finally besieged in the Territorial Army drill hall, as robots and zombies close in for the kill. In the nick of time, the hero blows up a radio mast, the robots collapse and the zombies are shot dead (?). Our heroes requisition a plane and take off to search for more survivors in an empty world— empty except for the cars that can be seen whizzing along the motorway beyond the airport perimeter fence!

Though made in 1964, *The Earth Dies Screaming* looks like it was made 10 years earlier thanks to the black and white cinematography, the illogical, pulp sci-fi plot, the rudimentary "special effects" and the perfunctory acting. The only inkling that the austere postwar decade is actually past comes during a scene in which the young man burns a haul of now useless bank notes: "That would have been for a car, that for a refrigerator, a television, a washing machine" is a reference in passing to the nation's growing prosperity and incipient consumer society.

Notwithstanding its potboiler reputation, two scenes in particular manage to elicit a shiver. The first comes as Willard Parker keeps a nocturnal vigil at the back of the hotel. The pregnant girl goes into the kitchen for a glass of milk. While she's pottering about inside, one of the robots appears around the corner of the building. Parker readies himself to take a pot shot, watching as the creature lumbers up to the kitchen window and looks in. The camera cuts back inside where the girl is blissfully unaware of the

impending danger. Elisabeth Lutyens' excellent eerie music crescendoes as the camera zooms in to a close-up of the thing's featureless "face" ensconced in a great glass helmet and made more unearthly by the underlit chiaroscuro lighting. Just when the tension is becoming unbearable, the girl simply walks out of the kitchen and switches off the light, causing the otherworldly visitor to lose interest and lumber away. The beauty of this type of scene is that, given just the right pacing, it makes us anticipate something far more horrible than anything that could be realized on screen, and Fisher was undoubtedly a past master at building suspense.

The second highlight is in a similar vein. A woman, fleeing from a pair of zombies, takes refuge inside a bedroom wardrobe. The camera adopts a subjective viewpoint as she peeps through the louvres and sees the bedroom door open. In comes a zombie, the lifeless blobs of dead tissue that once were eyes probing the room as it seeks out its prey. Fisher's direction here evokes the awful feeling of anguish and sheer terror, which permeates one of the most common and harrowing of nightmares. Who hasn't at one time or another experienced the dreadful dream of being trapped by some unspeakably monstrous abomination, the only chance of deliverance from an indescribably horrible fate being to remain undetected? Of course, she's snatched from the jaws of death by the arrival at the eleventh hour of Parker, who dispatches the undead with a blast of his shotgun.

No matter that the robots look like shambling geriatrics in oversized kiddies' playsuits and the zombies are scruffy extras with fried egg eyeballs, when viewed in context, with jarring violins on the soundtrack, atmospheric monochrome cinematography and Fisher's canny direction, they're every bit as frightening as those laughable papier-mâché monsters which were a regular feature of the contemporary *Doctor Who* and which, equally improbably, nevertheless managed to scare us out of our wits as kids. The above scenes still provoke a tingle of fear. After all, what could be more terrifying than the certain knowledge that "They're coming to get you?"

—Mike Hodges

Credits: Director: Terence Fisher; Writer: Henry Cross.

Leading Cast: Willard Parker, Virginia Field, Dennis Price, Thorley Walters, Vanda Godsell.

The Evil of Frankenstein

The first Frankenstein movie to be co-produced by Hammer and Universal Pictures, *The Evil of Frankenstein* is the least of the otherwise excellent series—not including the Cushing-less *The Horror of Frankenstein*—though it's by no means as bad as its reputation suggests. Present and correct is the reassuring sense of Hammer familiarity. All the elements we know and love are on display: gorgeous matte paintings, gratuitous zooms into heaving cleavage (we're really supposed to be looking at a necklace or something), a commanding performance from Peter Cushing and an angry mob climax leading to the usual fiery "death" for the Baron and his creation.

After an atmospheric body-snatching prologue, the persistent Baron removes a heart from a corpse under the opening titles, but the organ gets dropped during a struggle with a horrified authority figure. Frankenstein and assistant Sandor Elès flee to Karlstadt, one of those distinctive Hammer Eastern European towns.

Evil rewrites the series history to incorporate a Universal-approved creature: a square-headed, electrode-necked monster played by Kiwi Kingston that provides a visual echo of the iconic Karloff incarnation. To accommodate the Kingston character, the movie offers a 10-years-earlier flashback sequence that plays like a 10-minute distillation of both previous movies: monster created, escapes lab, brief rampage, authorities catch up, Baron arrested.

In Karlstadt, the Baron's work—and the typical movement of his staggering creations—are openly mocked by carny hypnotist Zoltan (Peter Woodthorpe), while an odd deaf-mute redhead (Katy Wild as one of Hammer's most feeble female leads) helps our anti-hero find his monster preserved in ice. When the traditional bolt of lightning fails to revive the creature, a concession to the changing face of modern horror results in Woodthorpe stimulating its brain with his hypnotic powers. The canny mesmerist, however, trains the monster to do bad things: steal gold, kill Frankenstein's enemies, etc.

The Evil of Frankenstein is directed with anonymous efficiency by the workmanlike Freddie Francis and suffers from arguably the most slack script of the series: the awkward plotting means that the monster isn't revived until almost an hour has passed. Even then, Universal's liberation of the formerly copyrighted makeup that even non-horror fans associate with the concept of the Frankenstein Monster results in a rather crummy-looking

central figure of fear. Kingston, a wrestler whose only other film credit appears to be a bit part in Francis' *Hysteria*, has the right imposing stature but manages none of Karloff's humanity and pathos. His creature is also, ironically, far less interesting than the "monsters" (Christopher Lee, Michael Gwynn) Hammer were forced to create in the preceding two Frankenstein movies to avoid any legal action from Universal Studios.

—Steven West

The Evil of Frankenstein is an odd, unsuccessful entry in Hammer's Frankenstein canon. Terence Fisher, who'd helmed the first two films, was supposedly in the company's bad books after the failure of *The Phantom of the Opera*, and so directorial duties were passed to the unsuitable Freddie Francis instead. Having secured £160,000 in funding and a distribution deal with Universal, for the first time Hammer was able to emulate aspects of Jack Pierce's classic (and copyrighted) Karloff makeup. Despite having produced almost 200 designs for the monster (played by all-in wrestler Kiwi Kingston), Hammer makeup supremo Roy Ashton was pressured into going with one of the worst. The result is terrible. The monster resembles nothing more than a papier-mâché kid's school project, with an egg-box head. It's not scary, and even if Kingston were any kind of actor (which he wasn't), he'd have been unable to emote through the mess anyway.

The plot also pilfers from its Universal predecessors and, as such, doesn't fit within the continuity as previously established. His experiments destroyed by an outraged priest, Baron Frankenstein (Peter Cushing, of course), together with latest assistant, Hans (Sandor Elès), returns to his chateau in the village of Karlstadt, from which he was chased years earlier. This prompts a flashback that contradicts the events as previously shown in *The Curse of Frankenstein*. The laboratory set is impressive, though, and is consciously reminiscent of that in James Whale's original. After seeing the monster shot we return to the present, where the Baron seeks revenge upon the

Burgomaster and the Chief of Police, the men responsible for scuppering his plans the first time around.

There are a couple of moments of sub-*Carry On* nonsense, with a shot to highlight the Baron's stolen cygnet ring, now on the finger of the Burgomaster. (It's not remotely intended to grab a crafty eyeful of the Burgomaster's wife's voluminous cleavage, honest.) Also, when Cushing escapes from the woman's bedroom you'd almost mistake him for Sid James in *Carry On Dick*. There's a snigger to be had when the Baron discovers the Burgomaster has raided his old wardrobe, exclaiming, "Convenient for you that we're both the same size!" Francis could at least have positioned them in frame so they look it!

Of course the Monster is rediscovered, thanks to an unfortunately deaf, dumb and ginger girl (Katy Wild), who offers the Baron and his assistant shelter. We're reminded of *Frankenstein Meets the Wolf Man*, as the creature is found suspended in ice. The plot takes a twist when, unable to revive the creature, Frankenstein enlists the aid of slimy mesmerist Zoltan (Peter Woodthorpe). Having also been expelled from Karlstadt, Zoltan double-crosses the Baron and, like Lugosi's Ygor in *Son of Frankenstein*, sends the monster out to punish his enemies. It all ends predictably enough, with the monster running amok in the lab and causing a fire. Oh, in the Universal tradition, the château blows up. Yawn. The ballyhoo at least means we see the Monster toss Cushing around and make his hair flap; that's always a treat. Ohhh, but then there's the horrific back-projection to deal with, when the Baron commandeers a horse and cart and rides it full pelt through Black Park, Buckinghamshire—sorry, deepest Karlstadt. It's so awful, it could almost sink the movie on its own!

This movie adds nothing to the Hammer Frankenstein series. In fact, it could be said to detract from it, as it muddies the waters of continuity. Unless you're a completist or have nothing else to watch, you can safely skip it.
—Jed Raven

Credits: Director: Freddie Francis; Writer: John Elder [Anthony Hinds].
Leading Cast: Peter Cushing, Peter Woodthorpe, Kiwi Kingston, Duncan Lamont, Sandor Elès, Katy Wild.

The Gorgon

Written by John Gilling—later to direct an equally interesting female monster in *The Reptile*—*The Gorgon* is a high-quality Hammer horror with a deliberate pace and an ultimately awkward-looking central creature. These are the two key factors that have led to its undeservedly mediocre reputation among keen Hammer fans and casual viewers alike. It *is* undeniably slow burning, but then so is the earlier, better-liked *The Curse of the Werewolf*, also directed with sensitivity by Fisher and dominated by a doomed love story that the director seemed to be most interested in.

The Gorgon is also notably lacking in many of the key Hammer selling points: You may look in vain for spectacular heaving bosoms and lashings of that delicious bright red Kensington gore. This neglected outing is more concerned with mood and ambience than gaudy horror and unsubtle sexuality, and it holds up remarkably well in that respect. James Bernard supplies one of his finest scores to usher in the main titles. The expected dramatic Hammer horror chords here disarmingly alternate with an eerily beautiful soprano (reflecting the gender of the all-new figure of fear) and the rarely heard early synthesizer, the Novachord.

The movie unfolds in the early 20th century in the village of Vandorf. Paranoia and superstition are rife, thanks to a local legend that dictates the ominous Castle Borski is home to one of three mythical "gorgon" sisters with the power to turn mortals to stone. The 2,000-year-old legend of Megaera lives on here, and everyone fears that the sister, who allegedly fled to Vandorf, her head crowned with living snakes, has taken human form. In a marvelously atmospheric opening, an artist's model (whose bare back provides the film's only titillation, unless you count Patrick Troughton's mustache) becomes the seventh unsolved murder victim in recent years, killed by a powerful off-screen presence in the woods.

Hammer's two biggest stars have fun playing against their established types. Cushing is stern and repressive as a sceptical, cold man of science, bemused when stony corpses start showing up and destined to be eternally miserable thanks to his obvious unfulfilled desire for downtrodden assistant Barbara Shelley. Lee, meanwhile, has a few brief scenes as a stuffy but unusually endearing professor. For once it's Lee who figures out who the "Gorgon" is and ultimately destroys her.

Seldom remembered among Fisher's classics—it followed his equally unloved, underrated *The Phantom of the Opera*—*The Gorgon* is a *beautifully* directed movie. The nocturnal exteriors have a wonderfully eerie, dark, fairy tale atmosphere, all luminous full moons, whistling winds and oddly romantic, heavy rain showers. The script is reliant on obviously doomed characters wandering around alone in the woods at night or foolishly deciding to take a late night trek to the castle (well, there was nothing on the telly and Vandorf seems bereft of chirpy Cockney hookers), but it matters not.

Fisher sustains a palpable sense of menace around an unusually downplayed Hammer monster, using some very modern fake scares to misdirect the audience and cannily depicting the Gorgon obscured by shadows or enigmatically reflected in pools of water. The film works particularly well when it offers only glimpses of its title monster, with the playful implication being that the filmmakers can't show her directly in case the regular Hammer audience gets turned to stone, too.

Hammer convention dictates the need for an all action, monster destroying climax but, despite the sight of Cushing leaping into an enthusiastic, if brief, sword fight with Richard Pasco, and Bernard's stirring music, Fisher is clearly more interested in the finale's tragic overtones than its horror and violence. Shelley's poignant portrayal of a woman trapped

The overall impact is sadly weakened by the goofy, brightly lit close-ups of the red-eyed Gorgon, complete with inept, twitchy rubber snakes. The big reveal, followed by an all too labored chance for us to study a terrible fake severed head, regrettably inspire unintended mirth during what is otherwise a satisfyingly bleak finale to a gorgeous Gothic piece. (The decision to deny Shelley's request that she also play the Gorgon for consistency also harms the movie as a whole. Prudence Hyman looks like some nutty panto character who has gate crashed the Hammer set.)

The Gorgon is still a film of many pleasures, including the fun spectacle of Lee and Cushing coming to blows, and an oddly moving sequence—again boldly uncharacteristic of Hammer—in which a dying Gorgon victim writes one final letter ("I am turning to stone"). Fisher's fascination with tragic characters and doomed romance would continue to find expression in the grimmest of his Frankenstein movies, *Frankenstein Created Woman* and *Frankenstein and the Monster from Hell*.

As an interesting postscript, *The Gorgon* (along with *The Black Scorpion*) was featured and referenced prominently in the indie gem *Teeth* (2008), a black comedy about a different kind of female "monster," a virginal teenage girl, who finds that being in possession of vaginal gnashers is an asset when dealing with horny jocks, perverse gynecologists and dirty old men.

—Steven West

Credits: Director: Terence Fisher; Writer: John Gilling.
Leading Cast: Peter Cushing, Christopher Lee, Richard Pasco, Barbara Shelley, Michael Goodliffe, Patrick Troughton, Jack Watson.

The Horror of It All

Released around the time that *The Addams Family* and *The Munsters* offered small-screen horror fans their choice of creepy clans, Robert Lippert's 1964 production *The Horror of It All* attempts a British take on the concept of the monster-filled household. Many see this frivolous movie as something of a comedown for its illustrious director, Terence Fisher, whose helming of many Hammer classics had steered the company into a position of dominance in the field of fright. Bear in mind, however, that Fisher's career did seem to have hit a slight lull at this point, and this fun little comedy then takes on a new sheen.

It's your basic old dark house plot: Jack Robinson (a personable Pat Boone, clad in natty driving cap and sheepskin coat) sees his car plunge into a ravine on his way to meeting his girlfriend Cynthia, and so completes his journey to her family pile on foot, eventually meeting the entire Marley family, a mixture of eccentrics, doom and gloom merchants, and semi-vampires and faux werewolves. Talk of a lost fortune, amounting to some £300,000, pricks up a few ears but also leads to the gradual bumping off of those who might have a claim to the cash.

by others *and* her alter ego (on a par with her fine work in a not dissimilar role in the subsequent *Dracula—Prince of Darkness*, also for Fisher) gives the final reel an added emotional dimension.

Ray Russell's screenplay is crammed with lame gags and puns, and the score has something of a cartoon-like quality to it, but the cast acquit themselves gamely and manage to cover up most of the cracks by keeping the dialogue and the comic interplay zipping along. There are stray moments of Fisher at his finest, too: Boone's flight from a tarantula discovered crawling in his bed, with his dash to the door scored with a heady rush of frantic strings, à la James Bernard; or, as Boone investigates a strange growling noise emitting from a closet, the sudden and unexpected cut to a shot of a bloody-mouthed Andrée Melly. Boone's confrontation with the escaped Muldoon Marley (Archie Duncan), a wild, hairy, lycanthropic man-beast, develops into an extended chase through the house and features inventive use of a telescope and some live-wire electrical lab equipment, worthy of the director at more glittering periods of his career.

Melly's sultry, sexy, yet oddly gloomy presence comes to dominate the film, her performance as Natalia—all glances, flinches and evil stares—rising well above the sub-standard script and taking on an iconic aspect worthy of Barbara Steele or Soledad Miranda. At one point, Natalia reveals that only she can control Muldoon, achieving this feat "with love… I am a woman, you see"—her delivery of the line bringing forth lewd and incestuous undertones probably not intended by the writer. Whether quoting Shakespeare while pounding out the Funeral March on the Marleys' piano, or acting part-seductress, part-predator to frequently unsettle our hero, Melly commands your attention whenever she is on screen.

It's nice to see radio legend Valentine Dyall for once—that all too recognizable voice is put to occasionally splendid use. Even while running through the breakfast menu, he manages to invest a line like "haddock, kippers, kidneys" with all the doom-laden, sepulchral intonation he can muster.

Even Boone's title song, strangely placed somewhere in the middle of the proceedings, is worth a mention—a not unpleasant little ditty with, in the main, rather better horror-themed gags than most of those found in the script. Sample verse: "When the spiders crawl, swift and hairy / through the shadows, tall, dark and scary / just one bite—and obituary"!
—Darrell Buxton

Credits: Director: Terence Fisher; Writer: Ray Russell.
Leading Cast: Pat Boone, Erica Rogers, Dennis Price, Andree Melly, Valentine Dyall.

The Masque of the Red Death

Of Roger Corman's highly regarded, early to mid-1960s "Poe cycle" movies, *The Masque of the Red Death* is arguably the best. Considering it's from a director remembered mainly for schlock, it's even more surprising that it's as good as it is. It could be Corman's best work.

The incomparable Vincent Price here enjoys one of his best roles as the wicked Prince Prospero. His character is clearly delineated from the beginning, as he lowers himself to appearing among the peasants over whom he holds sway. When two of the peasants (Nigel Green and David Weston) display a little too much in the way of disrespect for Prospero's liking, he casually commands his soldiers to "garrote them." When Green's teenage daughter Francesca (Jane Asher, then dating Paul McCartney) pleads for their mercy, Prospero gives her a stark choice: either her father or the man she loves must die, or they *both* will die. Who will she choose?

Needless to say, if Prospero were a stick of rock, he'd have the word "bastard" written right through him. There is no ham in Price's performance here, not even a wafer-thin slice. Only in the later *Witchfinder General* does the "Merchant of Menace" come close to rivaling this particular portrait of sheer, unadulterated evil. He's a sinful pleasure to behold.

Soon though, it becomes apparent that the village has fallen prey to the dreaded "Red Death," a plague that's swarming through the land. Packing up his entourage quick smart, Prospero takes all three peasants back to his castle, where he can decide their fates in relative safety, but not before giving the command, "burn the village to the ground." Nice.

Back at the castle, Prospero and his wife Juliana (Hazel Court) entertain their guests, rich layabouts who have taken refuge from the ravages outside. There are bizarre games of humiliation and a performance by the dwarf Hop-Toad and his tiny partner. As Prospero's chum Alfredo (Patrick Magee) leers at the girl, speculating, "I wonder…," Price retorts, "I'm sure you do, Alfredo." It's doubly icky when the dancer is clearly played by a child! Her voice is dubbed in later scenes by an adult woman, for a strangely unsettling effect.

When the girl spills Alfredo's wine, he slaps her to the ground and sets in motion a spectacular revenge on behalf of Hop-Toad that anybody who's read Poe's original "Hop-Frog" will recognize. Poe purists may balk at having two distinct stories interwoven into one narrative like this, but it works; and Poe purists probably aren't watching Roger Corman movies in the first place!

It soon becomes clear that Prospero, among all his other charming traits, worships "Satan, the Lord of Flies, the Fallen Angel, (whispered) the Devil." When a mysterious, red-hooded figure enters the party, he assumes it to be his master, but he's mistaken.

Asher is good (and very pretty) as the innocent Christian girl who finds her faith tested, and seems toward the end to have resigned herself to this casual onslaught of humanity's basest behavior. Court supplies somewhat more matronly glamour and meets an especially nasty end.

The Masque of the Red Death is a visually arresting movie, with lavish sets and lush costumes. It also benefits greatly from Nicolas Roeg's stunning cinematography, and plays many a novel trick with intensely colorful interiors that will root the film in the mind long after watching it. Even the title and credit sequences are a cut above par. It should be watched by anybody with an appreciation of good, classic horror.
—Jed Raven

There's nothing like a good treble act: Wilson, Keppel and Betty; Pip, Squeak and Wilfred; the Goodies. The triumvirate of Edgar Allan Poe, Roger Corman and Vincent Price also worked wonders, perhaps never better than in *The Masque of the Red Death*. Having been given color and a bigger budget to kick these off with *The Fall of the House of Usher*, Corman (no slouch in getting the best out of limited resources) had at last been able to give Hammer a run for their money.

Toward the end of their run, the AIP Poe squad turned up in Blighty itself. If you're looking for a good old fashioned horror film, the team's *Masque* offers some cherished clichés: creepy, cobwebby castle, aristocratic madman, witchcraft, shocks, blood and so much more!

Religion: Prince Prospero has given up on conventional Christian beliefs and embraced Satan as his master. His ancestors had tried twisting and controlling men's minds in attempts to open the door to their creator—unsuccessfully. (Doors of all kinds feature prominently in this film.) Prospero almost defines decadence: world-weary, reduced to pitiful "entertainments" (mostly involving humiliation, cruelty, torture and death) to sate his jaded palate. Another member of the Prospero family tree tortured more than 600 men, women and children in the name of the God of Love (i.e., the Inquisition, although *Masque* is set in Italy). Prospero is hell bent and determined to enjoy himself as much as possible on the way there, but it's becoming increasingly difficult to find suitable stimulation. He has literally been there, done that. Only the introduction of a simple peasant girl with "perfect faith" into his world of iniquity gives him pause and makes him think. This also acts as a catalyst to his woman, Juliana, who had been teetering on the brink of damnation. Prospero's interest in a wholesome lass tips Juliana over the edge.

The film opens with an elderly woman shambling across a blasted heath. She encounters a red-garbed "holy man" toying with a tarot deck. He transforms a white flower into a red one with a pass of the hand and a few drops of blood. She is to take this blossom to her village and tell the populace that their day of deliverance is at hand.

Prospero visits the village, almost running down a baby with his carriage, to inform the occupants that a feast is to be held. Opposition is shown to him, and his heavies arrest the would-be rabble rousers. They are the father and boyfriend of the peasant girl Francesca, who pleads for mercy. Prospero is rather taken with (the flame red hair of?) this miserable pleader, and has all three transported to his castle. A shock involving the elderly woman (now a victim of the Red Death, a virulent form of plague) sends them hurrying on their way.

Prospero (like his Shakespearean namesake in *The Tempest*) is cast away on an island—his castle, now surrounded by the Red Death. Two major themes of the film are now introduced:

Color: The castle is first seen through a blue-green haze. The colors are revealed to be a motif throughout the edifice, with some other non-reds thrown in. Prospero's suite of adjoining rooms, all decorated in different hues (yellow, purple, white, Stop! Forbidden!) are an example.

Animals: Prospero has a wall decorated with animal heads; he delights in making his upper-class guests act like pigs, worms, jackasses (they dare not refuse); dialogue often invokes animal parallels ("Where will the rabbit run?"; Prospero tells distraught villagers to make burrows like foxes, or hoard food like squirrels as they beg for shelter from the advancing Red Death); the Masque itself features many animal-masked revellers and an ill-fated gorilla. The gorilla is none other than Alfredo, a noble fascinated by innocence and Prospero's ability to corrupt it (although the Prince prefers the term "instruction").

So, it remains for the Satanic Prospero to invite his noble sycophants to join him for the Masque (no one wear red!) at midnight. When he spots a distant figure in crimson, he believes it to be his master and rushes to greet him, only to be faced with something quite different…

Corman had incredible good fortune with this production. Leftover sets from other Brit films were re-dressed by art director Daniel Haller. Aside from Vincent Price, who is in top form as Prince Prospero, there's Patrick Magee (Alfredo), Hazel Court (Juliana, unfortunately under used, but she does get to brand her bosom with an inverted cross and suffer one of Corman's delirious dream sequences) and Nigel Green. Even David Weston as the young male lead isn't too insipid. Jane Asher's hair is great. Charles Beaumont and R. Wright Campbell extend Poe's short story magnificently, and, as for Nicolas Roeg's photography, well, what future lay in store for him?
—Ryan Taylor

Credits: Director: Roger Corman; Writers: Charles Beaumont, R. Wright Campbell.

Leading Cast: Vincent Price, Hazel Court, Jane Asher, David Weston, Patrick Magee, Skip Martin.

Night Must Fall

The late 1960s and early 1970s included the introduction of a new kind of menace to the cinema screen: the pretty-boy psychopath. They were everywhere: *Twisted Nerve*, *Endless Night*, *The Night Digger*, *Straight on Till Morning*, *Blind Terror*, you name it; if it had a wide-eyed, long-haired, girlish-looking bloke in it, the chances are you'd found your murderer, pervert or murderous pervert. It was as if the sexual revolution had thrown up a new kind of bogeyman: the young lad who can get sex whenever he wants it, so sex has no longer become a goal. He's looking for a new kind of thrill, and he might be dating *your* daughter.

Night Must Fall is one of the first examples of the post-*Psycho*, post-kitchen sink combination, with Albert Finney taking his disaffected character from *Saturday Night and Sunday Morning* and tweaking his problems and neuroses up to 11. Without Finney's astonishing performance, *Night Must Fall* would be a much duller affair. His character Danny is an astonishing example of an eight-year-old boy trapped in a burly man's body, all nervous energy and violent mood swings, desperate to be the center of attention and determined not to let anyone spoil his fun.

But unlike the later films, there's no ambiguity here, no whodunit. In the first few minutes, as we see potential victim Olivia Bramson (Susan Hampshire) enjoying her soon to be disrupted idyllic life as she flounces around a sun-drenched garden in a floaty frock, while Danny (Finney) is busy bludgeoning an unseen someone to death and throwing the body into a nearby pond.

Olivia lives a strange, detached life with her disabled, wheelchair-bound mother, the pair of them looked after by the maid, Dora (a fragile performance by the wonderful Sheila Hancock). Danny is the unsuspecting Dora's boyfriend, and on a visit to see her he manages to inveigle his way into the Bramson home, charming the mother (or "Mrs. Jam-Spoon." as he christens her) into giving him a job as a live-in decorator. He arrives the next day on his scooter, the camera lingering on a hatbox he has strapped to the parcel carrier.

Danny, despite all his boasting, is rubbish at decorating, but Mrs. Jam-Spoon doesn't care. She's fallen for the boy, hook, line, sinker and copy of *Angling Times*, and he quickly becomes a permanent fixture. Mrs. Jam-Spoon may be in love with him ("You could call me mother," she tells him, her normally strident voice reduced to a simpering, almost orgasmic plea), but young Danny only has eyes for the gorgeous Olivia. Like Danny, Olivia is a child in an adult's body after a lifetime of being dominated by her mother, and she has watched, powerless to intervene, as the brash, bullying interloper has taken over the house.

But just as Danny seems to have conquered the entire household, the outside world arrives in the form of Olivia's boyfriend, Derek, a four square, tweed jacketed, cricket playing chap of the first order. Danny's good mood evaporates as he watches through his attic window, with Derek arriving in his sports car and instantly becoming the center of attention for the two women. Danny's composure evaporates and he flips out, ending up scratching at the walls of his bedroom with his fingernails, over and over again. He grabs the hatbox, opens it and mouths the word "hello" before retching and throwing it to one side.

But all is not well between Olivia and Derek, and he leaves. Danny begins his seduction of the newly single girl as, nearby, the police are seen conducting a search of the pond. Olivia is now falling for Danny's rough charms, and she wanders up to his bedroom to find out more about him, rifling through his possessions (which include a strangely spooky glove-makers' dummy hand and little else) to try and find out more about the new object of her affection. He arrives before she has the chance to look in the hatbox and reacts angrily to this intrusion (there's a remarkable ramping up of the tension as she tries to put the jigsaw-like dummy hand back together again), and things look like they're about to turn nasty, but in the next scene the pair of them are laughing and messing about as he teaches her to ride his scooter. Now Olivia, too, is enamoured with the boy ("I just wanted to know you. I love you, Danny."), putting him at the center of a bizarre *ménage à quatre*. And the police have now dragged the pond, and found the body and the murder weapon.

The police come to question Danny (the dead woman used to frequent a bar where he worked) and the scales begin to fall from Olivia's eyes as she sees that Danny has been playing everyone off against each other. Heartbroken, she tries to speak to Dora about her suspicions, but the maid has had enough and pushes her away. Back in the house, there is just Danny and Mrs. Jam-Spoon left, and they're having a game of hide and seek. But suddenly the game isn't funny any more.

Night Must Fall was based on a stage play by Emlyn Williams (previously filmed in the States in 1937), and the

Reisz movie occasionally shows its theatrical roots. It's more melodrama than outright horror, apart from the closing scenes of Mrs. Jam-Spoon wheeling her way around the house, the camera close-up on her face as she begins to panic ("Danny, we're not playing any more"). But there is much to recommend it. The crisp black and white cinematography is wonderful, and the performances are uniformly excellent. The tension is sustained well, and the feeling of powerlessness as Danny ruins everyone's lives is palpable. Finney is rightly regarded as a film icon but, when talking about his career, he seldom mentions *Night Must Fall*, which is a shame, as it really is one of his best performances. Much like Oliver Reed, his is a genuinely terrifying screen presence, and it is used to perfection here. —Chris Wood

Credits: Director: Karel Reisz; Writer: Clive Exton.
Leading Cast: Albert Finney, Mona Washbourne, Susan Hampshire, Sheila Hancock, Michael Medwin, Joe Gladwin.

Nightmare

A deserted courtyard, a grey, postwar, almost military building, and a green-tinted corridor lit by dim electric light, but still predominantly in darkness. As *Nightmare*'s credits sequence rolls, out of the shadows steps a figure: a girl in white, scared, terrified, troubled, yet drawn inexorably toward a room, where inside lurks another female, a mad, bedraggled, grinning, leering apparition. It is her mother. She laughs maniacally as the girl, realizing that the door is locked tight and there is no escape, opens her mouth and screams, a bloodcurdling shriek like you have never heard before. Then she wakes up.

The above constitutes the opening scene of one of Hammer's least known, underrated, chilling and yet at the same time frustratingly flawed and confusing films, almost as schizophrenic in some ways as the mental state of its heroine. *Nightmare* is, as one might tell by its single word, catch-all description title, another of the studio's Hitchcockian psychological efforts, but stands somewhat apart from the rest, firstly in that it eschews the suspense approach for forays into out and out terror, and secondly by taking an unusual approach in terms of character focus, which has been cited as either a mark of supreme individuality or its greatest flaw. Personally, after several viewings, I still can't make up my mind.

The troubled girl is Janet (Jennie Linden), and it's her plight on which the film initially focuses. Until recently, she has been under "special supervision" at her boarding school (which may be an institution for emotionally disturbed pupils, although this is never confirmed) due to recurring nightmares (so I suppose this time the title does have *something* to do with the plot), which stem, as her teacher and self-appointed care worker, Brenda Bruce, explains to housemaid Irene Richmond, from witnessing, at an early age, her mother stab her father to death.

Violent tendencies and a fear that she will inherit her mother's insanity have also added to her mounting

Albert Finney and Mona Washbourne play a make believe game until it turns into a feindish nightmare.
METRO-GOLDWYN-MAYER presents "NIGHT MUST FALL"

paranoia. But now she's home, being cared for, it would seem, primarily by her lawyer cousin (David Knight) whom she appears to favor with a more than fraternal love (although this is never really expanded and is ultimately irrelevant), a kindly chauffeur (George A. Cooper), the aforementioned maid and, to her surprise, a newly appointed "governess" (Moira Redmond). Bruce, compassionate in spite of her starchy authoritarianism, has also elected to stay around for a few days to help her charge ease back into everyday life. Except, of course, we know she's not going to.

Whereas some of Hammer's psychological thrillers (*Maniac* and *Hysteria* in particular) almost stretch the definition of "horror" to the breaking point, leaning further toward the conventions of the straight thriller and building up the storyline via studied references to "proper"

cinema, there is no doubt that *Nightmare* was intended as a full-on horror movie. The chills grow more with every sequence, as Linden is treated to a series of encounters with the gruesome apparitions of not only her deceased matriarch, whose knife-wielding antics appear more graphic each time, but a blank-faced woman in white (played by the wonderfully named Clytie Jessop, memorable as both the spectral Miss Jessel in *The Innocents* and the terrible statue in *Torture Garden*).

Every time Janet (and perhaps, the more gullible viewer) thinks she might be getting better, something happens which only ensures she gets a whole lot worse. Eventually she snaps, and upon being introduced to the same, raven-haired lady by her cousin in broad daylight, promptly stabs the terrible apparition through the heart and is immediately confined to an asylum. And there, she exits the film, never to be seen again—which is where things change.

Opinion is divided from here on in as to the subsequent direction of *Nightmare*. It's been pretty obvious from the get-go to anyone with a brain that none of these things are actually happening, the house is not haunted except in the *Scooby Doo* sense, and that a person or persons unknown is conspiring to drive Linden out of her wits, something even more apparent once we realize she is the sole heir of her gigantic house.

That much is expected, and therefore is not a disappointment. What *is* hard to stomach for some is the sudden shift in focus from Janet to her conspirators, who spend the remainder of the film becoming gradually more suspicious of one another and arguing until one of them meets a bloody and unpleasant demise. This is witnessed (and to a certain extent planned) by certain agencies with the heroine's best interests at heart, who have, unbeknownst to them, been secretly trying to catch them

at it from the very beginning—but one can't help wondering why they didn't intervene sooner.

So what started off as a gripping psychological horror story with nods to Dreyer and Franju effectively becomes a two-header interpersonal drama about an arguing couple. To some, this is a radical deconstruction of the established (at least by 1964) conventions of horror filmmaking, and all the more fascinating for it, especially if you're the type who delights in seeing the bad guys get their comeuppance. To others, it's just a gigantic pain in the arse.

At its most effective, it's incredible, leaving several icy, beautifully shot images firmly embedded in the brain which epitomize, maybe more than anywhere else with the exception of *What Ever Happened to Baby Jane?*, the concept of the "crazy madwoman" with which we now are so familiar. It's also a film with not only a few supporters, but a fair spectrum of influence. No less a genius than Brian Clemens seems to have copped several ideas directly for episodes of ITV's *Thriller*, particularly any involving shots of eerie corridors, staircases or women in floaty dresses. Coincidentally, two of its actresses starred in episodes of that same series less than a month apart: Linden in *Death to Sister Mary* and Redmond in *Sign It Death*, the latter of which plunges headlong into the bloody, knife-wielding violence that *Nightmare* presents so well, only this time in color. If it's good enough for The Clem, it's good enough for all of us.
—D.R. Shimon

Twenty minutes into *Nightmare*, Jennie Linden poses the question, "Where does the dream finish and reality begin?" It's a conundrum director Freddie Francis exploits to good effect in this worthwhile little Hammer chiller.

Lovely middle-class Janet (Linden) is sent home from her private girl's school after suffering nightmares of seeing her mother in a padded cell. It turns out mummy dearest redefines the term "cracker barrel," having stabbed her husband to death years earlier on Janet's birthday, with little Janet catching the bloody aftermath. She's been gripped by a morbid fear that she's heading the same way. And really, can you blame her?

Janet is placed in the care of her guardian and family lawyer, Henry Baxter (David Knight), and her house staff. Despite being assigned a nurse (Moira Redmond) to look after her, Janet's problems only escalate as she is tormented by apparitions of a scar-faced woman and a symbolic and strangely foreboding birthday cake. These persistent visions drive Janet around the bend in no time. She also screams a lot—I mean, a *lot*. You might want to watch this when the neighbors are out, unless you want the police bashing your door down!

Baxter refuses to have our sanity-challenged heroine committed, but later has no choice after Janet goes off the deep end at her birthday party. Let's just say she puts something of a damper on proceedings, and it's not the cake that gets sliced. All the Jimmy Sangster-scripted Hammer thrillers might be called *Psycho*-esque and that's nowhere more apparent than here, as a plot revelation suddenly shifts our focus from the blonde heroine to two secondary players. There's also the recurring motif of a kitchen knife featuring strongly, but, despite comparisons to Hitch's macabre masterpiece, the first half of *Nightmare* stands up well on its own terms.

The second half is slightly less successful: After all, our attention is now on two very unsympathetic characters, but you'll be more than happy to stick it out until the unexpected denouement. It would spoil the story to divulge too much more, but you're certainly kept entertained as cracks begin to show in the villains' seedy alliance. You'll even enjoy a guilty snigger as Redmond delivers the line, "You might have been all kinds of a gay boy before" to Knight. Oooh, and he looks so butch! *Nightmaare* is beautifully shot by frequent Francis collaborator John Wilcox, though it's hard to believe Francis had no input here. In the first half of the movie, Wilcox turns Janet's country house into a terrifying, shadowy labyrinth of wood-paneled doors and banisters. The opening sequence, in particular, is an eerie triumph of monochrome suspense. It wouldn't be half as gripping in color.

Of the cast, Jennie Linden is the standout. Her portrayal of the fragile, fearful heroine is spot on. It's a shame she's dispensed with halfway through. Viewers of a certain age will recognise *Grange Hill*'s hapless caretaker, Mr. Griffiths (George A. Cooper) in the cast, too. I bet Ziggy would have thought twice about raiding the tuck shop if he'd seen this!

Nightmare is a film you'll enjoy most the first time. On subsequent viewings, you'll be struck by niggling irregularities, mostly along the lines of "But if they're in on this, why are they talking like that?" The ending is grimly ironic, and the film as a whole paints an especially bleak portrait of humanity, but after the twists cease you'll be cackling up your sleeve nonetheless. This is one *Nightmare* you'll resent ending so quickly.
—Jed Raven

Credits: Director: Freddie Francis; Writer: Jimmy Sangster.
Leading Cast: David Knight, Moira Redmond, Jennie Linden, Brenda Bruce, George A. Cooper.

Seance on a Wet Afternoon

Bill and Myra Savage (Richard Attenborough and Kim Stanley) live a fairly humdrum, ordinary life in the London suburbs, the major exception being that Myra conducts séances in one of their rooms for interested parties. After these sundry details are quickly established, Bill and Myra carry on a conversation revealing their plan to kidnap a wealthy industrialist's daughter. Myra will then go to the distraught couple (Mark Eden and Nanette Newman) and offer her services as a medium, discovering the child's whereabouts, reuniting the family and establishing a wider reputation in her field.

A nervous Bill successfully swipes the girl from school, and the two wait for events to unfold. That's quite a twisted batch of plot already, and it comes as little surprise that (a) things don't go according to plan, and (b) there's a lot more to Bill and Myra's designs than a simple ransom scheme. It all comes to a magnificent head by the end of the movie, as Bill and Myra try to thwart the police investigation (conducted by Patrick Magee

and Gerald Sim) while attempting to maintain "normality" and figuring out what's really gone wrong with their lives.

Seance on a Wet Afternoon is a classic, a brilliant piece of psychological horror in which just about everything works: Bryan Forbes' intimate yet impartial direction; the black-and-white cinematography that renders almost every setting creepier, from suburban sitting rooms to roadside forests; the spooky score by the always good, usually great John Barry; the seedy atmosphere of a London in grimy pre-swing mode (at times it's like *Children of the Damned* by day); and especially the acting. The supporting players are predictably excellent, with seasoned old pros like Magee, but the film essentially belongs to Attenborough and especially Stanley. Bill could have fulfilled his role as a classic stereotype—the henpecked husband with a ruthless, chilly wife (*Seance* in some ways prefigures Pete Walker's 1974 masterpiece *Frightmare*)—but Attenborough turns him into something more empathetically human, particularly in his scenes with the little girl. It's quite obvious that Myra's in charge, but Bill doesn't just follow along because he's terrified; he genuinely loves her, and the scenes toward the end, when he has to face what they've both become, come close to heartbreaking.

It's hardly surprising, as Stanley's Myra starts out as a classic "psycho mom" type with memories of a dead son—and nails the delusional, manipulative middle-aged woman in a clear-eyed way few actresses have, before or since (the muted sibilance of her voice, which erupts into a yell without warning, can give one the chills)—but it becomes increasingly obvious that she's still capable of kindness or love. The fact that these qualities have been swallowed by madness becomes the scariest, saddest horror of all. Through the course of *Seance*, she's forced in one way or another to confront her own illusions and guilt (as is Bill), and the result is electrifying.
—Wendell McKay

Credits: Director and Writer: Bryan Forbes.
Leading Cast: Richard Attenborough, Kim Stanley, Mark Eden, Nanette Newman.

The Tomb of Ligeia

With extensive outdoor location shooting and a central conflict of wilful women reduced to animal avatars going at it tooth and claw over a man's soul, *The Tomb of Ligeia* is almost as far removed from the films preceding it in Roger Corman's Poe cycle as it is from the short story on which it was based. Following just months after the baroque feast of *The Masque of the Red Death*, many critics were a little too quick to dismiss it as a minor and too-often dull finale to the series. To some extent, perhaps the reason for this perception is the script by Robert Towne (who would go on to write *Chinatown*, *Shampoo*, *Greystoke* and *Tequila Sunrise*) that seeks to supplant overt Gothic melodrama with subtler psychological tensions, a worthy but not entirely successful ambition as the finished product often veers wildly between the two.

Edgar Allan Poe's short story "Ligeia" is simplicity itself: An opium addict is obsessed with his beautiful raven-haired wife, Ligeia, up to and beyond her death; he subsequently enters into a loveless marriage with the blonde Lady Rowena, only to see her die, too; but as he keeps vigil beside her corpse, she shows signs of both revival *and* physical transformation into Ligeia.

Towne jettisons most of these bare bones, instead concocting a power struggle waged from both sides of the grave for the love, sanity and soul of Verden Fell, played by Vincent Price with a fair degree of restraint. It's a conflict conducted mostly by implication and, well, by a cat and a fox.

The film opens with the funeral of Ligeia (Elizabeth Shepherd) in the grandiose ruins of Norfolk's Castle Acre Priory and wastes no time in clearly establishing the link between the cadaver, so wilful in life, and the black cat which haunts every frame of the titles and much of the film from then on. As the animal jumps onto her coffin, Ligeia's eyes flicker open in what Fell dismisses as merely "a nervous contraction, nothing more," although he can't resist baiting the sanctimonious, startled priest with "Has the cat got your tongue?"

No sooner has the cat established itself in the narrative than in scampers the fox, literally and figuratively as the beast is pursued by the red-headed (and often scarlet-garbed), feisty Lady Rowena Trevanion (Elizabeth Shepherd again) and her fellow hunters. It's the shape of things to come that her horse is spooked by the black cat and pitches her sprawling onto Ligeia's grave amid a riot of blooms mirroring her hunting red. She's even more alarmed by the sudden appearance of Fell in groovy tinted spectacles but, despite his pronouncement that they are "the flowers of death" and that his home turns out to be a crumbling, cobwebbed museum of eccentricities, she's evidently quite taken by him.

There's more ominous foreshadowing when her father (Derek Francis) and the conventionally solid Christopher (John Westbrook) turn up with the fruits of their hunt, an incredibly rare Egyptian fox (said by Fell to be a harbinger of bad marriages), which shortly after vanishes ("It appears the cat made off with the fox," muses Fell, as improbable and comical as such an abduction might be). A connection between the living and dead women in Fell's life is further reinforced when Lord Trevanion bluntly remarks of his spirited daughter, "Wilful little bitch, ain't she?"

Wilful she certainly is, and even Fell's attempt to strangle her when she shows up unannounced doesn't put her off matrimony (although it does leave her "shivering like a frightened kitten"), nor does the interruption of their first kiss by the jealous black cat leaping in to scratch her. She should have paid more attention to the signs and signifiers. No sooner has the happy couple returned from honeymooning in Rome when Fell slumps into his habitual cozy morbidity and Rowena starts finding ominous black hairs in her brush, saucers of milk on her balcony and bedside. She is reduced to infancy when Fell demonstrates his facility for mesmerism and awakes from a particularly harrowing and effective dream sequence to find a dead fox served up in a bouquet of flowers.

Christopher's discovery that Ligeia's corpse is really a wax dummy ushers in a frantic final act in which Rowena is panicked by the black cat and discovers Fell's secret nutty room where he keeps the remarkably well-preserved corpse of his first wife in a posture not so much suggesting necrophilia as scrawling it on the walls in ten-foot letters. It seems Ligeia's will has been taking possession of her widower to make him do her bidding, but Fell snaps out of it long enough to drop her body into a handy flame pit after Rowena hypnotizes him into remembering all that has occurred during his trances. With several of her nine lives left, though, she's soon back and Fell strangles her, only to pull a priceless double take and see it's Rowena he's really killed.

Finally, after spending most of the movie being pussy-whipped from beyond the grave, he turns the tables and snatches up a lash to flog the black cat (surely one of Price's most hilarious scenes ever), which in turn blinds him (literally this time, as well as metaphorically). Blundering about the place, he starts the traditional conflagration so beloved of Corman's Poe films, catches and at last kills the cat—so restoring life to Rowena—and lies down to die beside the body of Ligeia, now back in human form.

By no means the best of the Poe series, *The Tomb of Ligeia* nevertheless ends it on a worthy note, rich in animal antics, creditable performances and a sustained atmosphere of gloomy melancholy. And for those with a distaste of blood sports, it's always pleasing the see the fox ultimately elude its pursuers.
—Paul Newman

Roger Corman's final film adapted from the works of Edgar Allan Poe is a somewhat frustrating one. At times boldly experimental, *The Tomb of Ligeia* is also heavily steeped in tradition. The legendary director has spoken of being frustrated when running out of ideas for this series, and it's certainly no coincidence that, with AIP calling for more, he called it a day on this phase of his remarkable career. But, in my humble opinion, that was a shame.

Relocating the series to England in 1963 meant that AIP could take advantage of U.K. film industry incentives. At the time, this (relative) financial largesse resulted in a renewed enthusiasm for the series from Corman. And so, after filming *The Masque of the Red Death* in late 1963, he moved from Elstree to Shepperton in June 1964 for *The Tomb of Ligeia*.

It was always going to be difficult to film Poe's short story, first published in the Baltimore *American Museum* in 1838 and simply titled "Ligeia." An unnamed narrator tells of his obsession for his darkly beautiful and mysterious wife, the Lady Ligeia. Following her untimely death, the distraught, opium-addicted widower leaves their home on the Rhine for a crumbling abbey "in one of the wildest and least frequented portions of fair England." He fills the place with Egyptian artifacts and, "in a moment of mental alienation," marries the Lady Rowena Trevanion of Tremaine. Their unhappy marriage is overshadowed by the haunting memory of Ligeia. After only two months, Rowena dies. Keeping vigil over his deceased wife, the narrator is horrified when she rises up, now transformed into Ligeia.

Corman regarded the previous Poe adaptations as being studio-bound and dialogue heavy. To expand the atmosphere of this film, he shot on location as much as possible. He found the ideal principal location in a ruined abbey in Norfolk and made the Lady Rowena part of the fox hunting, landed gentry

so that expansive, picturesque scenes of the English countryside could be included. These scenes, gorgeously shot, enhance the film immeasurably.

Robert Towne's script sets the tone early on when Verden Fell (the now-named narrator) recites, as his beloved is lowered into her tomb, "Man need not kneel before the angels, nor lie in death forever, but for the weakness of his feeble will." (This is referred to repeatedly in the script. Unfortunately, although a bastardization of a quote from the story, it's not "genuine" Poe, as he was quoting 17th century scholar Joseph Glanvill.) Soon afterwards, the Lady Rowena strays into the ruins while fox hunting. Spotting the tomb, she reads out "Ligeia," whereupon a black cat suddenly appears, making her horse rear up. She is assisted by Fell, who carries her to his home in the imposing abbey, where he binds her injured foot.

This sequence introduces two key elements not found in the original story: the black cat and a perverse emphasis on sight. The cat, something of a calling card in works derived from Poe, is cleverly used to externalize the will and spirit of Ligeia, while sight manifests itself in a number of situations, from the wrap-around sunglasses Fell wears, due to his "painfully acute" vision, through the blank stare of an Egyptian bust to which he attributes "a mindless sort of malice," to the way in which the dying Ligeia hypnotized Fell to do her will. Adding to the perversity, Elizabeth Shepherd, who plays Rowena and Ligeia, provided the face cast for the Egyptian bust.

The character of Rowena is little more than a cipher in the original story. The film wisely fleshes her out, making her a wilful, spirited girl only too willing to upset the status quo. So, even when she returns unannounced to Fell's home, and he initially attacks her, mistaking her for Ligeia. Later the cat attacks her and scratches her cheek when she and Fell tentatively kiss, she positively encourages him. The couple are soon married. Leaving on their honeymoon, Fell is seen in daylight without his dark glasses and wearing light colored clothing. Ominously, an iris lens closes as the happy couple depart. When it reopens, as they are returning home, Fell's clothing is once again jet black and, as soon as they step inside the abbey, he reaches for the dark glasses.

Rowena eventually confides to Christopher, her friend (and suitor?), that she thinks Ligeia is still alive. One night, during a trademark Corman lightning storm (during which it doesn't rain!), Christopher digs up Ligeia's coffin while Rowena is "led" by the cat up a staircase hidden behind a mirror. Christopher discovers that Ligeia's corpse is a wax dummy, while Rowena finds her perfectly preserved body lying on a four poster bed, its arms reaching up as if in an embrace (adding the interesting possibility of necrophilia). Christopher arrives with Kenrick, a servant, who explains that, as Ligeia lay dying, she "held" Fell with her eyes, told him she would remain here for him and that he must be with her and care for her. During the day he was to recall nothing of this.

Rowena tries to break the spell by urging him to give over his will to her. However, she has cut herself badly on the broken mirror and collapses. Fell seems to come to his senses and, picking up Ligeia's body, throws it on the huge fire conveniently situated in the middle of the room. He asks to be left alone with Rowena, whom he places on the bed. The cat leaps on her and a shrouded figure rises up. It is Ligeia. Fell is strangling her as Christopher and Kenrick reappear. Christopher carries Rowena's body out as Fell hunts down the malevolent cat. Inevitably, as this is a "Corman Poe," a fire starts (and, equally inevitably, we get to see the Orange County barn from *House of Usher* in flames once again!). As the abbey burns down, Fell is seen lying

alongside Ligeia. Outside, Rowena regains consciousness and embraces Christopher. All appears well, although we don't rate Christopher's chances of having a truly successful relationship with Rowena!

One has to applaud Corman's efforts to widen out the story, but it is so slight and exposition heavy that it's no wonder that it seems at times rather drawn out, even at a scant 82 minutes. Its saving graces are a sumptuous look (Corman had the relative luxury of a five week shooting schedule, two weeks longer than he had been used to in the U.S.) and the excellent performances. Shepherd brings great maturity to her role, and one can easily believe how such a headstrong girl could see Fell as a challenge (early on, she confides to Christopher that it isn't necessary to be in love to get married). Unusually, for a period horror film, their relationship is that of equals. The true-life age gap between the leads—Shepherd was 27, Price was 53—is certainly not overly apparent. The leads are well supported by an array of fine character actors, including John Westbrook as Christopher, who plays Rowena's friend and confidant sympathetically, but never pathetically (in fact we are never sure he does want to be anything other than her friend).

It's a shame that the "abbey" is a two-storey country house on the outside and a huge medieval castle on the inside, although we do rather forgive this for the atmosphere of melancholy and decay the castle interior creates. Corman does do all he can to break the monotony of the dialogue exchanges by the use of a highly mobile camera and clever compositions. Overall, this is an entertaining companion to *The Masque of the Red Death*, making one wish that Corman had persevered at least a little longer with this series.

—Dave Simpson

Credits: Director: Roger Corman; Writer: Robert Towne.
Leading Cast: Vincent Price, Elizabeth Shepherd, John Westbrook, Oliver Johnston, Derek Francis, Richard Vernon.

Where Has Poor Mickey Gone?

Another of those curious British B movies, a brisk black and white quickie in which a *Clockwork Orange*-like gang get more than they bargain for when they torment an old Italian magician (Warren Mitchell). *Where Has Poor Mickey Gone?* was originally an hour long but is now most often viewed (if at all) in a truncated 37-minute version, which omits the Ottilie Patterson theme song and the first half of the movie, where the young hoodlums cause a bit of bother in a nightclub.

In the shortened version, we join the yobs soon after they have been thrown out of this establishment; looking for further thrills, they taunt and attack a

Monday, July 13, 1970

11:00 ⑨ Days of Our Lives	⑪ Merv Griffin
⑦ Meet Mullett	⑬ Tonight Show
⑪ Newlywed Game	10:00 ⑬ Ironside
11:25 ⑦ Double Exposure	10:30 ⑦ Memorandum On a
11:30 ⑨ Doctors	Frozen Ark
⑪ Dating Game	11:00 ⑦ News
11:35 ⑦ News	⑨ News
12:00 ⑦ Luncheon Date—Part 1	11:20 ⑦ News
⑬ Peyton Place	⑨ Stampede Go-Round
⑨ Another World:	11:30 ⑦ Movie: Break in the
Bay City	Circle
⑪ Secret Storm	12:00 ⑬ Edgar Wallace
12:30 ⑬ Uncle Bobby	1:00 ⑬ Today
⑨ One Life	1:30 ⑬ University of the Air
⑦ Cartoon Party	
⑨ Edge of Night	**Tuesday**
1:00 ⑦ Luncheon Date—Part 2	
⑬ The Boy	11:00 ⑨ Days of Our Lives
Cried Murder	⑬ Peyton Place
⑨ Gomer Pyle	⑪ Newlywed Game
⑪ Dark Shadows	⑦ Meet Mullett
1:30 ⑨ Mike Douglas	11:25 ⑦ Double Exposure
⑦ Movie: Where Has	11:30 ⑨ Doctors
Poor Mickey Gone	

Where Has Poor Mickey Gone? only appeared on TV in the U.S.

courting couple before discovering Mitchell, working late into the night. Before they can give him a beating, the quick-thinking conjuror suggests that he should put on an after hours display of his skills—and dispatches the gang one by one, using his disappearing cabinet to send them into some undisclosed netherworld. The unsettling closing shot reveals that their souls have been trapped for eternity, captured within the solid figures of a bar football game in a corner of Mitchell's workroom.

I have a real soft spot for these early 1960s "bottom half of a double bill" items. In his book *English Gothic*, Jonathan Rigby writes that *Where Has Poor Mickey Gone?* "warrants a seat-throwing response," but there's plenty to savor here, notably a splendid turn from a pre-"Alf Garnett" Mitchell (who is equally wonderful in his cameo role in *The Night Caller*, made a few months later) and that very effective surprise ending. Director Gerry Levy went on to make the Tigon sci-fi clunker *The Body Stealers*, another film about people mysteriously vanishing, but not half as much fun as this one.
—Darrell Buxton

Credits: Director: Gerry Levy; Writer: Peter Marcus.
Leading Cast: Warren Mitchell, John Malcolm, Raymond Armstrong, John Challis.

Witchcraft

"So what's *this* one about, then?" A bulldozer ploughs over a few old gravestones, to the consternation of a number of bystanders led by Morgan Whitlock (Lon Chaney, Jr, about as convincingly British as Jack Palance in *Craze* [1974]). Whitlock goes to see the man responsible, urban planner Bill Lanier (Jack Hedley), whose family has a feud with the Whitlocks improbably dating back to the Norman Conquest. Bill realizes that his partner Forrester (Barry Linehan, with a checked blazer and brylcreemed hair that comically mark him for the chop) is responsible for the headstone desecration, and the plot thickens as the latter is found dead in his bathtub with mysterious finger marks around his throat.

Bill's young wife Tracy (Jill Dixon) fails to see what all the fuss is about as comedy thunderclaps follow each new announcement of sinister wrongdoing, and his kid brother Todd (David Weston) makes no one happy by secretly dating Whitlock's cute niece Amy (Diane Clare). Another death convinces Bill that the evil surrounding his family can be laid at the door of—wait for it—*witchcraft*! As sundry Laniers fall victim to maleficent hallucinations, primarily of long-dead witch Vanessa Whitlock (Yvette Rees), and diabolical goings-on, Bill tries to maintain his sanity and protect what remains of his family's heritage at all costs.

Witchcraft is, in some ways, unfortunate. There are good ingredients, but they don't really add up to much in the end. The acting's decent if unremarkable: It's nice to see perpetual supporting face Hedley in a lead role for a change, and the characters are generally likeable and well played. Todd and Amy are especially sympathetic, and one really wants their relationship to work out in the end. Even Chaney isn't necessarily *bad*—he's just in the wrong movie. One scene shows him discovering Todd "making time" with his niece and, as he orders the former out of his house, it is almost a shame not to hear "This is *Michigan*! Where the hell do you think you are? *England*?"

Speaking of Michigan, there's a grimly amusing reference to Bill's experience with urban renewal in Detroit, three years before the riots (one can find a similar mordant frisson in John Davidson's song on the same subject in *The Happiest Millionaire* [1967]). Bill's clash with Morgan over a new housing project has probable echoes in any "Western" country (the reference also raises the question of how good he is at his job). The conflict between the Laniers and Whitlocks gains additional nuance with the revelation that the Laniers have been Catholic throughout history (a priest-hole figures prominently in the plot)—while the Whitlocks, as a horror-stricken Aunt Helen (Viola Keats) observes, follow "the old religion," so, according to the authorities of the time, did the Laniers.

There's pathos to be milked from these issues, but the filmmakers don't do much with them. *Witchcraft*'s shame really lies there. In the right hands, it could have been a fascinating horror commentary on the tensions between tradition and modernity, on differing forms of religious fanaticism, even on the proper aims and means of urban transformation and renewal, but it just amounts to a hokey scare flick. There's nothing wrong with this—scenes involving covens and crypts and so forth are well-handled from a visual standpoint—but raising the issues it does, *Witchcraft* misses an opportunity by letting them lie.
—Wendell McKay

Credits: Director: Don Sharp; Writer: Harry Spalding.
Leading Cast: Lon Chaney, Jr., Jack Hedley, Jill Dixon, Marie Ney, David Weston.

1965

Bunny Lake is Missing

In a London that barely swings, a young American mother (Carol Lynley) goes to pick up her four-year-old, illegitimate daughter at the end of the first day at nursery school, only to find she has vanished. Superintendent Newhouse (Laurence Olivier) investigates but finds that, not only has no one at the school ever seen her, there is no proof that she ever enrolled. Soon the question is not what became of Bunny but did she ever exist?

Yes it's an old, old story (dating back to 19th century Paris at least) but this taut psycho-thriller has a lot going for it. Firstly it's directed by Hollywood veteran Otto Preminger (of *Laura* fame), who brings a stranger's eye to the London of the mid 1960s. This city isn't the happening place of folk memory but a more uneasy realm, where the past (Martita Hunt brings echoes of her Miss Havisham as a slightly dotty old teacher hidden away in an attic; Finlay Currie's wheelchair-bound proprietor of an old doll's hospital) mingles with the dreary present of loud pop music (courtesy of The Zombies), unappealing bar meals taken in pubs with middle-aged drinkers, black and white television sets, endless traffic jams and talk of student demonstrations.

Preminger gathered an excellent cast. Olivier gives Newhouse a quirky air and makes what could easily be a dull role highly watchable, while Hunt and Currie add a Dickensian flavor. Noël Coward enjoys himself as a sadomasochistic, drunken landlord (he has a nice line in whips!), and even the smaller parts are filled by the likes of Anna Massey and Adrienne Corri. It's the two American leads who carry the movie, however. Keir Dullea is very convincing, both at playing the concerned brother and at showing the psychosis that lies behind his relationship with his sister. Carol Lynley is outstanding as the mother, starting out (understandably) hysterical and ultimately proving resourceful. It's a shame that her career petered out and she was reduced to playing the token Yank in episodes of Brian Clemens' *Thriller* and its ilk.

Unsung heroes of the film are Paul Glass, who provides a haunting, dreamlike score, while Denys Coop's camera work conveys menace equally during daylight (the school scenes) and at night (the hospital after dark has the sinister feel of a Val Lewton movie). The script, by John and Penelope Mortimer, has an eerie quality light years away from the more mechanical efforts of Jimmy Sangster's mini-Hitchcocks for Hammer (the closest in tone is *The Nanny*, not surprisingly since it also was based on a novel by Marryam Modell, aka Evelyn Piper).

Of course, there is a plot flaw, as the existence of Bunny could easily be established by contacting the States, but it's a mark of a good movie that this idea only occurs to you long after the movie has ended.
—David/ "Lot 249"

Credits: Director: Otto Preminger; Writers: John Mortimer, Penelope Mortimer.
Leading Cast: Laurence Olivier, Carol Lynley, Keir Dullea, Martita Hunt, Anna Massey.

The City Under the Sea (aka *War-Gods of the Deep*)

It's difficult to know what Jacques Tourneur, responsible for some of English-speaking cinema's pinnacles—*I Walked with a Zombie* (1943) and *Night of the Demon* (1957), among others—must have felt on making *The City Under the Sea* (released as *War Gods of the Deep* in the U.S.), maybe AIP's most unusual "Poe movie" (loosely based on the poem "The City in the Sea").

The craggy Cornish coast is the site of sinister doings afoot near the turn of the century, as American heiress Jill Tregellis (Susan Hart) is kidnapped in the middle of the night by a mysterious creature, with her friends—geologist Ben (Tab Hunter), artist Harold (David Tomlinson) and Harold's chicken, Herbert—in hot pursuit. Following her trail, the gang finds an underground cavern and whirlpool that somehow funnels them into the title location, probable inspiration for the lost kingdom of Lyonesse. Ruled over by the long-lost Sir Hugh (Vincent Price), the city's on its last legs, its life-giving Cyclopean

THE SEARCH FOR 'BUNNY LAKE' IS ON!

BUNNY LAKE IS MISSING

AN OTTO PREMINGER FILM

starring
LAURENCE OLIVIER · CAROL LYNLEY · KEIR DULLEA
MARTITA HUNT · THE ZOMBIES & NOEL COWARD
as Wilson
SCREENPLAY BY JOHN AND PENELOPE MORTIMER · FROM THE NOVEL BY
EVELYN PIPER · MUSIC BY PAUL GLASS · PHOTOGRAPHED IN PANAVISION®
A COLUMBIA RELEASE · PRODUCED AND DIRECTED BY OTTO PREMINGER

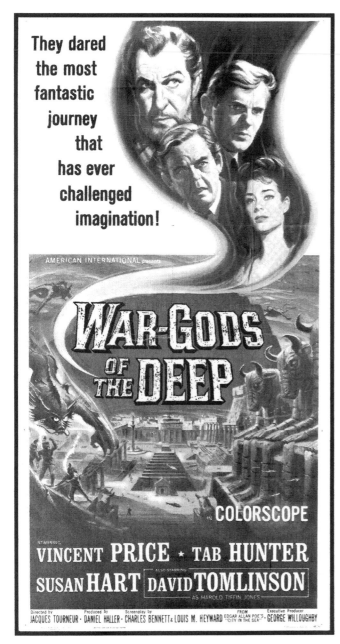

They dared the most fantastic journey that has ever challenged imagination!

AMERICAN INTERNATIONAL presents

WAR-GODS OF THE DEEP

IN COLORSCOPE

STARRING VINCENT PRICE ★ TAB HUNTER
ALSO STARRING SUSAN HART DAVID TOMLINSON
AS HAROLD TIFFIN JONES

Directed by JACQUES TOURNEUR · Produced by DANIEL HALLER · Screenplay by CHARLES BENNETT & LOUIS M. HEYWARD FROM EDGAR ALLAN POE'S "CITY IN THE SEA" · Executive Producer GEORGE WILLOUGHBY

a painfully weak attempt to match the success of the seal in *20,000 Leagues Under the Sea*, but it's responsible for at least one splendid joke.

The atmosphere (another Tourneur speciality) works well, with the set design particularly worthy of note. Presumably taking a cue from likely ancient Mediterranean contact with Cornwall and the Scilly Isles (the latter alleged remnants of Lyonesse), art director Frank White peppered the architecture with Egyptian statuary columns, Etruscan frescoes, Phoenician writing (misread by Harold as Babylonian) and Sumerian wall panels. The story quirk of Price and his henchmen being inter-lopers in this world, as opposed to its original inhabitants—a cynic might suggest this saved on costumes—is striking, adding a note of exploitation to their relations with the *Creature from the Black Lagoon*-like mermen. The latter are surprisingly well designed for a film of this sort, even if nothing much is really done with them in the end.

Sadly, the movie's many good qualities go for naught during the final third, largely because of that most difficult of film sequences to make exciting, the underwater chase (even the same year's *Thunderball* couldn't get it quite right), the only item of interest provided by occasional shots of Harold and Herbert sharing a diving helmet. Even so, the boring and confusing flail through Channel waters fails to dim the memory of the previous hour's entertainment. While Tourneur probably deserved a better coda to his career, *The City Under the Sea* is hardly a cause for shame.
—Wendell McKay

Credits: Director: Jacques Tourneur; Writers: Charles Bennett, Louis M. Heyward.
Leading Cast: Vincent Price, Tab Hunter, David Tomlinson, Susan Hart, John Le Mesurier.

The Collector

The Collector is a film about social conditioning, envy and death, adapted from a novel by John Fowles. It opens with an image of freedom, a man chasing a butterfly across an open field. But what does a butterfly collector know of freedom? He captures these quintessentially feminine creatures, and snuffs them out in a killing jar.

The man is Frederick Clegg (Terence Stamp), a bullied and repressed bank clerk, who is beginning a more ambitious project, the netting of a human specimen, a social butterfly named Miranda (Samantha Eggar), an aspiring art student. The abduction is played out in fashionable London (Hampstead, to be precise), where we observe Miranda walking the streets from Clegg's perspective. Impulsively he makes his move, and she is cornered, chloroformed and bundled into his pokey van. She wakes up in the naively decorated cellar of Clegg's country house, bought with his winnings in the football pools.

From here a blueprint for numerous realist ordeal horror films is formulated, there is resistance, an escape attempt and a prying visit from a blimpish neighbour. Finally a release date is negotiated, and she will be held captive for one month.

machinery threatened by a nearby seabed volcano. The popu-lation, including the always welcome John Le Mesurier and familiar British television faces like Derek Newark and Tony Selby, remain strangely ageless despite a century of residence. Hugh offers the trio their lives in exchange for assistance with the city's plight, but it's soon obvious that his plans for Jill are rather less pleasant, forcing Ben and Harold to risk everything in order to save their friend and return to the world above.

On one level, *The City Under the Sea* is great Saturday afternoon entertainment, with style to burn (hardly surpris-ing in a Tourneur flick) and an endearing goofiness coursing through its veins. The performances are decent, Hunter's occasional show of smarmy sarcasm making one realize John Waters didn't cast him in *Polyester* merely for the kitsch value (unlike almost everything else in his movies). He and Tomlin-son—square-jawed American and foppish Englishman—make an entertaining comic pair. Herbert's presence might seem

After Miranda is imprisoned, the scope of the film changes, the intimacy of the cellar is suited more to the stage than screen, something further emphasized by an unrealistic Hollywood set. The momentum and realism of the opening is lost, but is slowly superceded by a disciplined and astonishing character study. The direction by veteran William Wyler is visually static; his strength is a controlled rapport with the actors.

The Collector's only real flaw is its linear structure; with virtually no back story, a lot of expository dialogue is spoken. Two monochrome flashbacks and an introductory first person voiceover give a little information about Clegg, but they are clumsy and could have been used more strategically throughout the film.

Like Carl Boehm's character in *Peeping Tom*, Clegg is no charismatic psychopath, but something of an innocent, in love with Miranda, and believing she will love him back in the fullness of time. Terence Stamp is beautiful, but he is wholly asexual in this role. Eggar is unconventionally beautiful, her priggish upturned nose is perfect for the part, and her wide-apart eyes express both vulnerability and condescension. Her red hair is symbolic of her freedom, in direct comparison to Clegg's hand-flattened comb over.

There is a duality to the characters: Clegg is socially autistic, but by acting out his pathetic fantasy he has realized his potential to control. Conversely Miranda is a free spirit, who under duress becomes subservient and empathetic toward Clegg.

Superficially the main theme is the British class system: Clegg constantly refers to Miranda's "Posh School" and her "la di da" ways. Miranda represents a society where anyone can be elevated through education. However, her vision is limited only to what she is taught at art school; in reality she is no more intelligent than Clegg.

Clegg's stiltedness and ignorance is not evidence of his social class, but the poverty of vision and language brought about by a neglectful upbringing. He has seemingly sleepwalked through the 1960s, but in one context he is the embodiment of the times, representing the nihilism inherent in a generation raised in the shadow of the H-Bomb.

When the month is up, Clegg breaks his promise. Miranda uses her sexuality to try and lessen Clegg's mania, but this only acts as a catalyst, his shame and impotence sending him further into insanity. From here a true intensity is achieved as the heartbreaking final act begins.

—Sam Trafford

Credits: Director: William Wyler; Writers: Stanley Mann, John Kohn. **Leading Cast:** Terence Stamp, Sa-

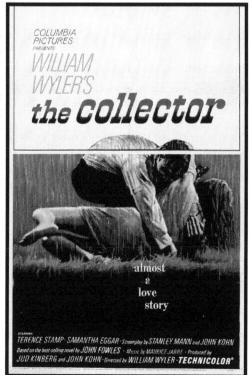

mantha Eggar, Mona Washbourne, Maurice Dallimore, Edina Ronay.

Editor's note: *The Collector* was primarily a U.S. production, with all interiors filmed in Hollywood and only the exteriors done in the U.K..

Curse of Simba (aka *Curse of the Voodoo*)

Curse of Simba: three words guaranteed to strike dread into the hearts of hardened horror fans. Before the film begins, we see a revolving globe with the superimposed words "France, Italy, Spain, U.S.S.R., Africa, China, Australia, Gala Film Distributors Limited cover the world." Let's just hope they had something better to cover the world with than this. The opening credits inform us that the screenplay was written by Tony O'Grady (according to the BFI, a pseudonym for Brian Clemens; it's unsurprising that he didn't want to be identified with this tosh), with "additional scenes and dialogue" by Leigh Vance. Never a good sign, and even with the extra input the film still struggles to fill its scant 75 (or, in the U.S. release version, 83) minute running time.

The plot is as hackneyed as it is ridiculous. White Hunter Mike Stacey (ever impassive Bryant Haliday, the Julian Sands of the 1960s) stalks a wounded lion while on safari in the Republic of South Africa, in turn being mauled by the animal. He finally kills the beast with a shot from his high powered rifle (it must have a long range, as Haliday is very obviously standing in the middle of Hampstead Heath, while the lion inhabits some African jungle stock footage). The Chief of the Simbaza tribe, who consider all lions sacred, puts a curse on Stacey. From then on, everything goes prickly pear shaped for Mr. Safari.

His wife, tired of him always being away on expeditions and/or drunk, gives him the big E, and heads back to Blighty, taking their son with her. He follows them, but his mother-in-law warns him to stay away. He's stalked by a spectral lion while walking through a park after spending a fruitless night (brewer's droop) with a prostitute. He sees a black man spying on him in the pub and is chased across Hampstead Heath (playing itself this time) by two "ghostly" tribesmen bearing spears. He sees visions of his faithful porter, held captive and tortured by the Simbazi back in Africa. Is he sliding into alcohol-induced insanity? Are the hallucinations due to his lion inflicted wounds turning septic? Is it all a question of auto suggestion caused by a guilty conscience? Or is it really the result of a juju?

The truth is, it's all so predictable, leaden paced, uninvolving and lacking in tension and suspense that this attempt to intrigue the audience with the "natural or

supernatural?" mystery angle is doomed to failure—as well as being a case of Clemens trying to have his cake and eat it, too, since a bombastic voiceover at the start of the film has already put us in the picture: "Africa! A country [sic] that for centuries was hidden from civilized man. Africa! Where primitive people still practice evil religions, which weave a dark web of death around all who sin against their gods...for any man who dares to kill a lion, the punishment is death!" The confirmation comes from an African expert on tribal Black Magic later consulted by Stacey's wife: "The only way is to return to the scene...find the man who placed the curse and kill him." As the woman leaves, he apologetically adds, "Sorry I can't be of more help" (!).

Director Lindsay Shonteff has a good eye for framing a shot, makes the most of light and shadow and is fairly skilful at moving his camera. He employs plenty of low angles, cross cuts and tight close-ups. Sadly, his efforts at visually conjuring up any sense of drama or menace are rendered totally ineffective thanks to other factors, the intrusive and overbearingly portentous "African Adventure" music, all blaring brass and rumbling kettle drums, foremost among them. Then there's the uneven pacing (many scenes drag on way too long) and seriously muddled editing. Stacey is dislikeable and Haliday unengaging and charisma-free as an actor. The wafer thin plot has to be augmented with a quantity of tiresome padding: stock footage of African fauna and tribal dancing, Beryl Cunningham's "sensual" nightclub dance to the strains of the Bobby Breen Quintet (that's 3:50 taken care of, mainly comprising medium close-ups of her trouser-clad bum), and previously seen sequences recycled as "hallucinations" or dreams.

The bottom line is that *Curse of Simba* is another of those films that look more impressive when viewed as a series of stills rather than as a (slooow) moving picture. And, by the way, reviewers who routinely describe this as Lewtonesque clearly need to take another look at Val Lewton's movies.
—Mike Hodges

Credits: Director: Lindsay Shonteff: Writers: Tony O'Grady, Leigh Vance.
Leading Cast: Bryant Haliday, Dennis Price, Lisa Daniely, Ronald Leigh Hunt.

The Curse of the Fly

So here we go again, with a further chapter in the unfortunate Delambre family saga. When will they learn?

The first thing to be aware of when you approach this movie is that there is no "Fly." Thankfully there are enough gruesome shenanigans going on that you don't notice that small fact much. It certainly starts on a high note, with a dreamlike sequence of a window shattering outwards toward the viewer, and the lovely Carole Gray emerging from it in her bra and panties. Well, it grabbed me. Gray, a dusky-eyed, brunette beauty in the Valerie Leon mold, plays Patricia Stanley, who for reasons unknown is hoofing it from the nuthouse. George Baker (as Martin Delambre) then experiences every guy's fantasy when he chances across the lingerie-clad lovely hiding out in the bushes. And before you know it, Bob's yer uncle, the pair is married. Why can't I get that lucky?

Martin has no idea his new wife is on the run, but then he has secrets of his own. Together with his brother and his father, Henri (Brian Donlevy), he is continuing the experiments in teleportation begun by his "grandfather" two films earlier. And if you've been paying attention, you'll know how they turned out (i.e., *not* good). Having recently teleported Henri to London from their native Quebec, Martin brings the old man home to the unexpected pleasure of meeting his new daughter-in-law. Henri's none too happy about having Patricia wandering around, believing she might jeopardize their research. When she comes close to discovering the human flotsam of their previous experiments kept captive in the stables, she's pacified with the notion that they're actually animals. "If Martin has to do it, I'm sure

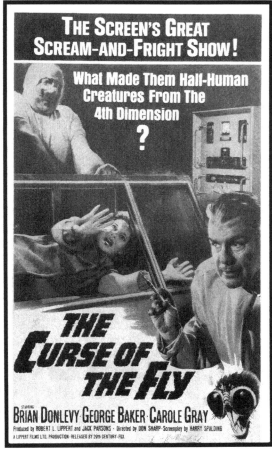

it's all right," she says. Yes, she's hot and she's *that* dumb. Seriously, she's the perfect woman!

Unfortunately for her, her blissful ignorance is shattered one night when the Chinese housemaid, Wan (Yvette Rees, looking about as Chinese as a bulldog and twice as mean), leaves one of the stable doors unlocked and Martin's former (and deformed) wife, Judith, escapes to have a Les Dawson-style tinkle on the old Joanna. This scene is quite effectively creepy, with the shuffling and mute Judith pursuing Gray through the house. Gray faints and the whole thing is hushed up, causing her to believe she's lapsing into her previous, fragile state. Eventually Delambre fills his wife in on the shady goings on at the house and things begin to unravel, especially when the second brother in London develops a conscience and just wants to be rid of the Delambre "curse" forever.

This is probably one too many outings for the Delambres. While a decent chiller in its own right, it misses the presence of Vincent Price and so rather pales in comparison to the previous episodes in the series. Also, it completely fudges continuity; even with the aid of a pencil and paper you'll be unable to work out who Henri is and how he's related to Andre Delambre, the originator of the teleportation device. But by 1965 it had been six years since *Return of the Fly*, and, without home video, it's doubtful anybody noticed such trifles. The absence of a fly-headed monster actually works in its favor, once you surmount the initial disappointment (after all, how many times can a mistake be repeated?), but the result is just not as memorable as its predecessors.

—Jed Raven

Credits: Director: Don Sharp; Writer: Harry Spalding.
Leading Cast: Brian Donlevy, George Baker, Carole Gray, Michael Graham.

Devils of Darkness

With a name like the Comte de Sinistre, it's unlikely that one would go into the gelato business and, sure enough, the Comte (Hubert Noel), also known as Armand du Moliere (!), becomes one of the world's most diabolical practitioners of black magic, enslaving saucy gypsy girl Tania (Carole Gray) in the film's first few minutes. A couple of centuries later (presumably), Sinistre's small Breton village with its charming folk rituals (particularly the traditional march on All Souls' Eve) plays host to a number of tourists—Paul (William Sylvester), Anne (Rona Anderson) and Madeleine (Diana Decker)—who runs into tragedy when Anne's brother dies in a potholing accident under mysterious circumstances. The likeable, attractive Anne soon turns up face down in a lake, and Paul starts to realize that things aren't really what they should be.

Returning to London, Paul arranges for the bodies to be flown back for a proper *British* autopsy, only for them to disappear. His scientist chum, Kelsey (Eddie Byrne), proves to be less help than he thought in countering the powers of superstition. Understandably depressed, Paul prepares to find solace in the arms of full-bosomed, super-pale artist's model Karen

(Tracy Reed), only for *her* to vanish as well, as he realizes that the Comte's, yes, *sinister* tentacles stretch into the heart of Chelsea itself. The film moves quite briskly and enjoyably to its explosive climax, as Paul is forced to question, as he never has before, who he can really trust.

Devils of Darkness begins rather unpromisingly but quickly turns into a proper hoot, diverting into soap opera and the hipster no-man's-land party world between the beatnik and hippie eras (a world that seems to be a full 50 percent lesbian). The plot plays quite a bit with the allegiances of some of the characters, ably juicing up the dreary good vs evil clichés these films often followed. Jealousy and mistrust play just as much havoc among the forces of evil as they do with the world's white hats, as Tania, the Comte's ostensible "bride," begins to worry that the eternal Gallic smoothie may finally be ready to throw her over. Gray's fiery performance is memorable and quite suitable for such a personality, especially as she was "snatched away" on her wedding night. Noel in particular is excellent, his charm (especially compared with his adversary) clearly masking a terrifying will to power.

Those who have encountered William Sylvester before (for instance, the same year's *Devil Doll* and the glorious *Mystery Science Theater 3000* subject, *Riding with Death*) will be

relieved to know that his unique, sub-Shatner charisma runs on all available pistons for *Devils of Darkness* (his reaction to the news of Anne's death is hilariously brusque). Watch for the scene (and it's hard to miss) when he uses, "I cook in a nonstick frying pan" as a pick-up line. Reed, given a largely Kewpie doll character as Karen, does more with her role than one might expect. The star of the show, though, is Decker, who somehow manages to evoke the spirit of pre-Swinging London despite looking and sounding like an American Rotary Club hostess, "dawling."
—Wendell McKay

Whether you find merit in this film is dependent on what you want from your horror pictures. There is no gore or nudity on display here, what little action there is seems tame by today's standards and the plot has more holes than a sieve. Many modern horror fans have mentioned the words slow, tedious, dull, and constipated in conjunction with this 88-minute curate's egg.

The precredits Gypsy dance is dire, as is the snake dance presented later in the proceedings. The latter slithery antics, I believe, earned this film its inflated 15 rating. Both sequences are padding in what is only a short film.

The party above the "Odd Spot" captures the decadent 1960s feeling (although I can't think of a firm reason for this impression). When another party occurs later on with all the assembled occultists/disciples (and the aforementioned snake who should get a better agent), it seems more restrained than the first gathering, which raises the question, "Are the youth decadent, or are these feeble occultists just not putting enough effort in?"

The more you examine *Devils of Darkness*, the more its internal logic seems to crumble away. For example, take the character of Karen. Much more could have been done with the plot if she'd been the hero's preexisting girlfriend. As the film stands, the hero doesn't have enough time to establish a realistic emotional bond before Karen is spirited away so the villain can offer to swap her for the Talisman.

Karen's main character traits seem to be the wearing of sunglasses indoors and being a redhead. Other major players including William Sylvester don't fare much better (character traits: American, writer), and the only sense of connection one makes with him is during the library scenes where he goes to do research, the most enjoyable part of the film. *Devils of Darkness* could have been improved if the focus was placed more on the hero. Jumping back and forth between different factions stifles the hero's place in the narrative, diminishing potential tension.

The villain, Count Sinistre, doesn't seem threatening enough when he needs to be. I wanted to see more evidence of the steel gauntlet beneath the velvet glove, particularly when this Count is so desperate to reclaim his McGuffin, the Talisman. Although it initially seems innovative to have a vampire who can walk around in sunlight, considering the movie's end this is probably a power either granted to him by his amulet or poor day for night filming. Moving his cult from Brittany to Blighty seemed a crazy idea. His cult (the devils of the title?) can't hide, conspire nor cover up their activities as effectively as they could on their native soil.

Who would be interested in this film? Perhaps someone doing a critical essay on horror cinema might find it a curious specimen to scrutinize. Its dissection, in skilled hands, could prove more interesting than the film itself.
—Elliot Iles

Credits: Director: Lance Comfort; Writer: Lyn Fairhurst.
Leading Cast: William Sylvester, Hubert Noel, Tracey Reed, Carole Gray, Diana Decker.

Dr. Terror's House of Horrors

The trendsetting debut of Amicus' portmanteau format, this breezy quintet of fun horror stories is probably the lightest of the studio's anthology cycle, and remains the only one to be afforded a PG certificate in this enlightened age! Although Roy Castle arguably overdoes the cheeky chappie comic relief shtick to the point where even Norris McWhirter might be seen reaching for a machete, this fondly remembered movie remains consistently amusing and is blessed with one of the subgenre's best ever wraparound stories.

Cushing, who later played another eccentric host character in *From Beyond the Grave*, is marvelously sinister as tarot card-reading Dr. Schreck, the last person with whom you'd want to share a train carriage, particularly if you have an aversion to scary eyebrows and German accents. He foretells the grim destinies of five travelers, with Christopher Lee immediately established as a snide, pompous arse who dismisses "the lunatic fringe" with the same kind of aloofness the actor would later convey toward many of his horror projects.

The film opens and closes with two simply titled, simply plotted stories featuring popular genre monsters. "Werewolf," a basic but atmospheric she-wolf chiller, is rich with dry ice and mysterious howls in the night. Neil McCallum travels to a remote island in the Hebrides to help renovate a house that once belonged to his ancestors. The uncovering of a 17th century coffin leads to a predictable but diverting finale.

"Vampire," the final story, offers another mild twist on a familiar genre monster, as Donald Sutherland's new French wife seems a tad over-enthused about sucking his finger after he cuts himself, while his patients begin developing anemia linked to suspicious puncture wounds. Amiable low-budget vampire bats figure in a tale that, like the later Amicus vampire episode in *The House That Dripped Blood*, ends on a comic note, as Max Adrian addresses the audience directly with a lament of "This town isn't big enough for two vampires!"

Arguably the most fun can be found in "Creeping Vine," a determinedly bizarre riff on *The Day of the Triffids* that plays its absurd yet apocalyptic premise straight despite casting disc jockey Alan Freeman as the hero. He and his family return from holidays to find an ugly vine snaking around the house and moving of its own accord. Attempts to cut it down are thwarted because it can knock the shears right out of your hand! Experts proclaim it to be a new species, a mutation that can protect itself. One dead dog later and the deadpan dialogue takes a turn for the ominous: "Plants like that could take over the world!" It's a brief but delicious combination of alarmist/hokey '50s sci-fi and unexplained nature-amok horror in the wake of *The Birds*.

Roy Castle does a 1970s sitcom style, prePC impersonation of a Jamaican native in the dated but oddly likeable "Voodoo," which delivers evocative moments despite the insulting portrayal of West Indian culture and a weak payoff. Castle is Biff Bailey, a jovial musician who tells mother-in-law jokes and gets a booking to play in the Windies, where Kenny Lynch teaches him the local sounds ("I dig that calypso music, man!"). While watching a ritual, Castle ends up noting down the

Illustration by Sam Trafford

music of a sacred voodoo god, theorizing. "If it's that old, it's out of copyright!" Slapstick mishaps turn a tad more serious as he receives his punishment for rejigging the sacred rhythms into his own muzak.

"Disembodied Hand" neatly punctures the pretentious world of art criticism and perfectly casts Lee as a snotty git fond of publicly lambasting the work of artist Michael Gough. His comeuppance begins with modest humiliation after lavishing praise on a work that turns out to be the haphazard daubings of a chimp. When Lee callously mows down Gough in his car, the story becomes a spry variant on the much-imitated *The Beast with Five Fingers*, complete with a persistent, living severed hand that survives being burned and dumped in the river. Lee gets his just deserts in a guessable but splendid EC Comics-like punch line.

All five episodes are worth revisiting, though it's the framing story that captures, more so than most of the subsequent anthologies, the eerily resonant impact of its inspiration, Ealing's *Dead of Night*. In a twist that would become *de rigueur* in post-*Sixth Sense* horror, the protagonists turn out to have been dead all along, marshaled by Cushing's Grim Reaper.
—Steven West

Credits: Director: Freddie Francis; Writer: Milton Subotsky.
Leading Cast: Peter Cushing, Neil McCallum, Ursula Howells, Alan Freeman, Roy Castle, Christopher Lee, Michael Gough, Isla Blair, Donald Sutherland.

Editor's note: A limited edition, 7-inch vinyl single from Trunk Records, featuring Tubby Hayes' much sought after music from *Dr. Terror's House of Horrors*, was released in 2009.

Dr. Who and the Daleks

Longtime fans of perennial British television staple *Doctor Who* may suffer feelings of disorientation on watching Amicus Films' pair of feature-length adventures starring Peter Cushing (*Daleks' Invasion Earth 2150 A.D.* came a year later). Remade by Milton Subotsky and company for an audience unfamiliar with the show, the title character loses his alien identity and becomes a dotty old inventor.

The film, based on the 1963-64 serial *The Daleks*, opens comically, with his granddaughters Susan (Roberta Tovey) and Barbara (Jennie Linden) reading weighty tomes on science, while Dr. Who (Cushing—*Who* fans might wince on hearing him introduce himself as such) is engrossed in the comic exploits of *The Eagle* magazine. Then Barbara's boyfriend Ian (Roy Castle) shows up and the pratfalls begin, one in particular accidentally triggering "Tardis" (no definite article), Who's time-and-space travel machine, which takes them to the mysterious and deadly planet of Skaro. Wandering about a bit, they find that almost the entire biota of the planet has been petrified or calcified by the results of a long-ago nuclear war. Everyone wants to leave, but Who's wish to explore the planet leads him to sabotage his own ship and pretend that the travelers need to find supplies of mercury before they can depart. Finding an ancient city nearby, they are captured by the merciless mechanical mutants known as the Daleks, whose xenophobic mania involves the travelers in a diabolical plan to wipe out their old foes, the Thals, and return to full biological efficiency.

The film is less a big-screen remake of the show than a typical Saturday afternoon matinée "shocker" (ironically enough, what British viewers might have gone to see had they not been at home watching the real *Doctor Who*), and doesn't fare *too* badly on those terms (although the sequel is marginally better). The characters, Daleks included, survive the transition to the big screen with little damage. Ian and Barbara (Susan's science and history teachers in the show) are a little less prepossessing than one might expect (Linden, later Ursula Brangwen in Ken Russell's *Women in Love*, and Castle are fine as far as performances go; one might blame the writing), but Tovey (substantially younger than her television counterpart, *The Day of the Triffids'* Carole Ann Ford) is an entertaining boffin in training (the first shot is highly amusing) and does all the "Grandfather, *look!*" lines proud.

Cushing delivers one of his more remarkable performances. Throughout his appearances, Cushing, despite his legendary charm and decency, could tend towards a "sameness" that's beautifully absent in the Dalek films. Playing about a decade and a half older than his actual age, he uses enough of William Hartnell's TV characterization to reassure fans but gives it a little more vitality, creating a genuinely new Doctor persona. The production's other aspects are a little more questionable. Malcolm Lockyer foregoes the mysterious Delia Derbyshire music of the original and substitutes something vaguely resembling the score for *From Russia with Love*. The alien planet is well realized, certainly for a film of this period (and for its relatively low budget and shooting time—under £200,000 and six weeks, respectively), but the Thals all look like they've escaped from a Seraglio. While a poor addition to the *Who* universe, the film makes a good if unusual fit among Amicus' more outré offerings.

—Wendell McKay

Credits: Director: Gordon Flemyng; Writer: Milton Subotsky. **Leading Cast:** Peter Cushing, Roy Castle, Jennie Linden, Roberta Tovey.

Dracula—Prince of Darkness

"If that man's master is anything like I think he's going to be, we're going to be entertained too!" So enthuses Frances Matthews at one particularly ironic moment in this direct sequel to *Horror of Dracula*, prior to leading a toast to the absent Count.

Matthews forms part of a quartet of almost parodic, stranded, middle-class English tourists who, although assured at the local garlic-encased pub that there is no bogeyman, are still warned in the genre tradition, "Steer well clear of the castle!" Matthews, his somewhat weak wife (Suzan Farmer), his doomed brother (Charles Tingwell) and his ever-complaining, killjoy sister-in-law (Barbara Shelley) find it

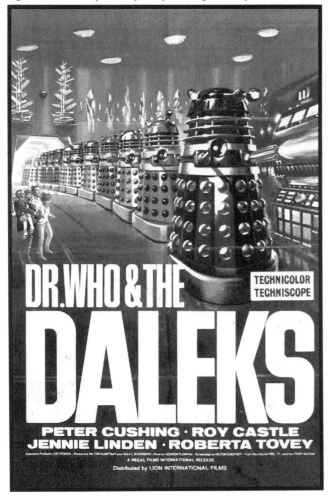

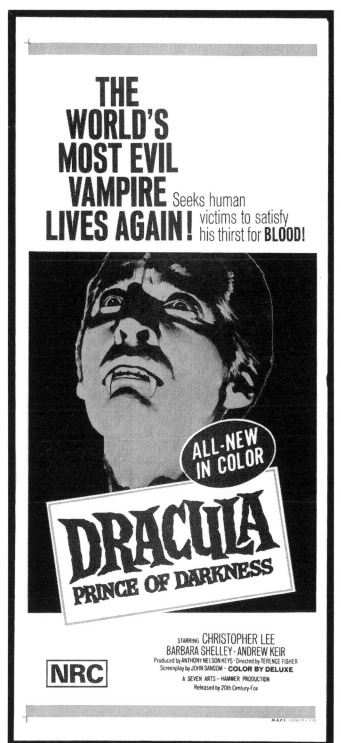

THE
WORLD'S
MOST EVIL
VAMPIRE Seeks human
LIVES AGAIN! victims to satisfy
his thirst for BLOOD!

ALL-NEW
IN COLOR

DRACULA
PRINCE OF DARKNESS

STARRING CHRISTOPHER LEE
BARBARA SHELLEY · ANDREW KEIR
Produced by ANTHONY NELSON KEYS · Directed by TERENCE FISHER
Screenplay by JOHN SANSOM · COLOR BY DELUXE
A SEVEN ARTS — HAMMER PRODUCTION
Released by 20th Century-Fox

NRC

build around his sporadic appearances? The build-up here is splendidly menacing and whets our appetite in fine style. A solemn narration accompanies a rousing reprise of the 1958 film's extraordinary climax before a funeral sequence conveys how the village of Carlsbad is eternally haunted by Dracula's evil, even 10 years after his death: paranoid villagers almost stake a non-vampiric dead girl.

The unsympathetic central characters are easily upstaged by Andrew Keir, taking the Peter Cushing role as a priest with sufficient knowledge of vampirism, and by Philip Latham as Drac's loyal servant, Klove, a subtly sinister fellow afforded a great entrance worthy of the Count himself. A fairly gruesome ritual—Tingwell is stabbed in the back, hung upside down and has his throat cut—revives the returning Christopher Lee at the halfway point. Lee's Dracula now sports a top of the range, red-lined cloak but, in the absence of any dialogue, is limited to bouts of snarling, woman pushing and thwarted seductions.

Although Lee is compelling as ever in his few scenes, the real pleasure of *Prince of Darkness*—Latham aside—is watching the transformation of Shelley's repressed, hysterical middle class wife from feeble emotional wreck to predatory, maliciously smiling vampiress. It's too bad that we don't get to see much of her in the latter guise before she becomes the victim of the story's sole staking. No such transition awaits Farmer, the kind of old-school genre heroine who faints at dramatic moments and saves the day only because she's crap with a rifle: Unwittingly missing Dracula by a good mile, she shoots the ice underneath him instead. The original, pared-down Hammer *Dracula* didn't have time for a Renfield figure, so an identical dotty, bug-eating character named Ludwig (played to the hilt by Thorley Walters) appears here for comic relief; subsequent sequels would also strive to incorporate unused elements of the Stoker novel.

This movie has survived less well than the two subsequent Dracula sequels, and lacks both the energy and genuine spookiness of its Fisher-directed predecessors. Still, however, it's a slice of vintage Hammer that's always fun to revisit.
—Steven West

Credits: Director: Terence Fisher; Writers: John Sansom [Jimmy Sangster], John Elder [Anthony Hinds]; Producer: Anthony Nelson Keys.
Leading Cast: Christopher Lee, Andrew Keir, Barbara Shelley, Francis Matthews, Suzan Farmer, Charles Tingwell, Thorley Walters, Philip Latham., Walter Brown, George Woodbridge, Jack Lambert.

The Face of Fu Manchu

When I was a child my mother used to own a cat, a seal point Siamese. Whenever he was found to have done something wrong—shredded my father's books, unraveled toilet rolls, shit in the washing basket—he would be carried out, glaring malevolently over my mother's shoulder with an expression that clearly said, "The world shall hear from me again." People

a bit queer that a driver-less coach spontaneously appears to drive them to Castle Dracula. And it's a tad odd that the deserted castle has four places set at the dinner table, isn't it? But it's a free meal, right?

Dracula—Prince of Darkness, Terence Fisher's final Dracula movie, faces the challenges that all the subsequent Hammer sequels met with varying degrees of success: How do we bring the Count back to life, and what story do we

Christopher Lee in *The Face of Fu Manchu*

short, when he's on screen, you watch him and only him, regardless of whoever else is present. The scene where he hypnotizes the elderly professor into obeying him is noteworthy. From the moment the professor realizes who is in the room, the outcome is not in doubt—there is no chance he can resist. In Lee's performance, Fu Manchu's power is obvious.

Sadly the same cannot be said for his minions. It seems likely that they came from the Death Cult Disciple equivalent of the local pound shop and make all the mistakes that one might expect. Standing around in an isolated area so someone can k.o. them and steal their robes? Check. Failing to notice that a couple of their colleagues have suddenly grown six inches and look decidedly Caucasian under their garments? Check. And then there's the scene where the portly, middle-aged Janssen (Joachim Fuchsberger) escapes captivity, thrashing a good dozen of his guards in the process. Clearly, lethally trained ninjas aren't what they used to be. I suppose the modern-day equivalent would be Heinz Wolff beating the proverbial shit out of an Al-Qaeda hit squad—and, to be fair, I'd pay good money to see that.

The heroes' main reaction to any situation in this film is to find a foreigner and hit him very hard indeed. The main exemplar of this is Assistant Commissioner Sir Denis Nayland Smith, played for the only time by Nigel Green, with Howard Marion-Crawford as a rather sidelined Dr. Petrie. The Smith-Petrie relationship owes something to the Holmes-Watson pairing in the Universal Sherlock Holmes films. Green in particular is physically reminiscent of Basil Rathbone—although a Rathbone dosed up on steroids and wearing an uncomfortably tight pair of pants. Visibly spoiling for a fight, he thumps, shouts and punches his way through the film, opening up by having an energetic fight with Janssen and destroying most of his laboratory in the process. Loudly expressing his disdain for such niceties as search warrants, Green brings an air of upper-class thuggishness to the role that disappeared from the next film when he was replaced by Douglas Wilmer. He is also a less sympathetic character than one might expect. This is a Nayland Smith one could imagine cheerfully supporting Oswald Mosley in a few years time. This brings a menace to the character, something decidedly absent from Wilmer's more subdued performance.

Director Don Sharp shows a talent for getting the most possible value out of a budget. Aside from the frequent energetic fights, there is an impressive underground lair for Fu, a nicely staged car chase brought to an end by an airplane pilot lobbing grenades at Smith's car, and the final,

who have seen the Christopher Lee *Fu Manchu* films may see the connection.

None of these films features Christopher Lee shitting in a washing basket. We can be reasonably sure that had this appeared in the script, he would have refused to do it. Or alternatively, he would still be complaining 40 years later about the fact, stating that it was not something that Sax Rohmer had ever written about and insisting that he had not appeared in a film featuring a laundry/feces interface since 1968, and why was it all that anyone ever asked him about?

The Face of Fu Manchu is the first of the depth-plumbing series of films and by some little distance the best. At this point, Lee looks interested in the role and any facial immobility is a performance choice rather than either a sign of boredom or the result of particularly rigid makeup. He brings to the film the same mixture of poised stillness and rapid motion as he did to his Dracula films, as well as a truly monolithic presence; in slightly hurried confrontation at a supposedly Tibetan monastery. All of which leads to the closing image of Fu's giant face apparently hanging in the air with its warning, "The world shall hear from me again." Given that Jesus Franco, with his unique approach to the filmmaking craft, was just around the corner, it was perhaps a promise to be regretted. —James Brough

Credits: Director: Don Sharp; Writer: Peter Welbeck [Harry Alan Towers].
Leading Cast: Christopher Lee, Nigel Green, James Robertson Justice, Howard Marion-Crawford, Karin Dor.

Fanatic (aka *Die! Die! My Darling!*)

Hammer's waning cycle of "mini-Hitchcock" thrillers was given a brief surge via the success of *What Ever Happened to Baby Jane?* Chiefly riffing on *Psycho* before, they now had a new source of inspiration, resulting in *The Nanny* and *Fanatic*, also known by the more lurid U.S. title *Die! Die! My Darling!* The script, by genre fave Richard Matheson, was derived from an Anne Blaisdell novel *Nightmare*. Of course, Hammer had used that title for a totally unrelated movie the previous year.

Fanatic stars a very young (and very lovely) Stefanie Powers as Patricia Carroll, in England to marry her fiancé (Maurice Kaufmann). Unfortunately for her, her conscience means she must first visit Mrs. Trefoile, the widowed mother of her previous lover, killed years earlier in a car accident. At first, Mrs. Trefoile (Tallulah Bankhead. in her final film role, also her first in 20 years) is all smiles, welcoming Patricia into the country home she shares with her housekeeper (Yootha Joyce), her housekeeper's husband (Peter Vaughan) and her mentally disabled handyman (Donald Sutherland, looking decidedly pasty). But when the old bag launches into her religious spiel, we know there's trouble ahead. She's outlawed mirrors and the wearing of red ("the Devil's color!") in the house, and spends every morning reading endless Bible verses. Despite all these subtle clues, it takes over a half hour until dopey Patricia catches on, muttering "she's insane." Maybe she'd been lulled into a false sense of security by the light, upbeat, jazzy score!

It soon becomes apparent it's Mrs. Trefoile's plan to reunite Patricia with her son in heaven, and this can only happen if Patricia, like her dead and presumably buried in a closet ex-fiancé, resists temptations of the flesh and remains an "unstained soul." Well, relatively unstained, as Patricia, in exasperation, has already confessed to not being a virgin (watch out for Bankhead's hilarious, chin-wobbling response). And so the lovely redhead is locked in the attic, bound, starved, slapped around and threatened with a gun by the rapidly deteriorating, would-be mother-in-law from Hell. If only Freeway the Dog had been around, he'd have saved the day.

Housekeeper Anna and her hubby Harry meanwhile, are sucked into the plot for reasons that are never adequately explained. Anna (Yootha Joyce, looking very different than she does in *George & Mildred*) mainly acts as muscle and Harry (Peter Vaughan) is seemingly kept around for no other reason than to provide a sexual threat. And he's quite menacing, though not as much as his Grouty in *Porridge*, obviously. Sutherland doesn't do much with an underwritten role but is convincing enough.

The undoubted highlight of this movie is the wildly OTT performance from Bankhead. She's a monstrous force of nature, barking out her garbled and often unintelligible lines through lips that never seem quite in sync. At this twilight point in her career, it's fair to assume Tallulah ("as pure as the driven slush") had consumed so much alcohol and cocaine that she was suffering some facial paralysis. But, blimey, it doesn't stop her trying! As her foil, Powers doesn't match up (who could?) but she's certainly into her part and is prepared to take her share of lumps! (Bankhead and Powers remained friendly until the former's death, surprisingly.)

Fanatic

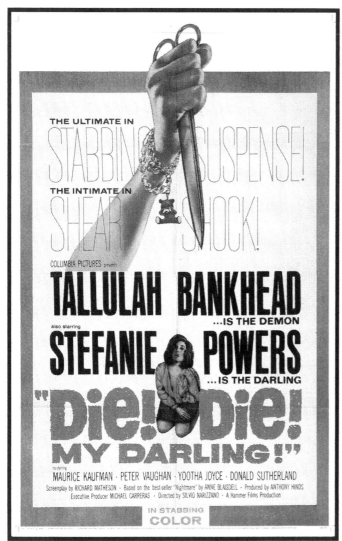

Viewed today, *Fanatic* is a piece of Grand Guignol high camp. It's not a great thriller. It's overly formulaic, and the climax is rushed and annoyingly ambiguous, but it's adequate. It's certainly entertaining! Honestly, I'm no "liiiaaarrrrrr!"
—Jed Raven

Sometimes the plot expediency in British horror films, even though we love them, beggars belief. I've heard of people walking right into things, but, if your former boyfriend had committed suicide and you were about to embark on a new relationship with the man you'd finally decided was the *true* love of your life, would you risk dropping yourself right in it by popping around to visit the dead ex's batty old actress mum, whom even *he* didn't care much for, at her crumbling country retreat somewhere on the outskirts of Letchmore Heath?

Like buggery you would. But, of course, this is Hammer, and plot expediency is the order of the day, so that's exactly what sultry redhead Pat Carroll (Stefanie Powers) does, setting the scene for 96 minutes of largely unbelievable yet somehow essentially enjoyable frippery from the man who gave us the dramatized works of "Saki" and would later bring you *Georgy*

Girl and *The Class of Miss MacMichael*. This may have been the studio's first psychothriller to be shot in color, but it wasn't anything the audiences hadn't seen before: a decaying mansion, spooky plants, some strategically placed staircases, a sinister handyman with a past (Peter Vaughan in this case, setting out a stall which he would work for at least another 10 years until finding his niche as Genial Harry Grout) and an endangered heroine. There are no cats this time, at least not in the actual film, but that doesn't stop director Silvio crowbarring them into the credit sequence, which has practically no relation to the storyline regardless of what title you saw it under.

Like all the best leading ladies (as opposed to heroines) in this particular subgenre, the scary old lady is a former star of the cakewalk and silver screen, played by someone from a similar real-life background. (See both previous and later entries in the canon such as *What Ever Happened to Baby Jane?*, *Whatever Happened to Aunt Alice?*, *Whoever Slew Auntie Roo?*, *Persecution* and *What's the Matter with Helen?* for further reference.) This time, it's Tallulah ("I was almost Scarlett O'Hara, you know") Bankhead's turn to play the nutter in question, Mrs. Trefoile, and a suitably hammy job she makes of it, too.

Never the most likeable of performers either on or offscreen (although fascinating for that very reason), her unpredictable behavior caused producer Anthony Hinds a few headaches, but she still managed to turn in what by her standards could be considered the performance of a lifetime. It's still not 100 percent—her trademark "daahling" is replaced by a grating overuse of "child" (but only when describing Powers or her increasingly put-upon maid, played by a surprisingly youthful Yootha Joyce), and there's a fair bit of eyeball-rolling, twitching and coughing, almost as if she thought this would be her last major performance and she had to express as many emotions as possible in one sitting—but it's engrossing enough to keep you wondering what she'll do next.

What she is doing is keeping Powers hostage in her home, first as a means of "purifying" and preventing the girl from slipping into the "errors of worldly evil" that killed her offspring, then eventually as a punishment when it is discovered how far from righteousness she actually hath strayed. Here the prisoner, like the house, is tended by Peter Vaughan, Joyce and mentally disabled gardener Joseph (a very young Donald Sutherland), but only the former, a cackling brute who thinks he will somehow inherit the house of the Trefoiles and is only staying on to claim his ill-deserved bequest, is a "bad un" in the true sense of the word. Joyce's only "crimes" are to be married to him and to face blackmail by her employer over some old debts. As for Sutherland, his presence is never suitably explained (presumably he lives with his family somewhere in the village, or maybe the Trefoiles adopted him) but he does provide several useful dodges and diversions for both Powers and, later on, her easily bemused fiancé (Maurice Kaufmann).

You get the feeling that, while *Fanatic* is in no way intended as any kind of send-up, Hammer had come so far by this stage that they were allowed to play with and parody their own formula. The tone *is* markedly different from that of its contemporary *The Nanny* or its successor *Crescendo* in that Powers, although no doubt in fear for her life from at least the middle of the film onward, takes everything, even every little criticism flung at her by Bankhead for such heinous crimes as wearing lipstick, smoking, eating meat, dressing in red and approving of the local vicar remarrying after bereavement (the old woman thus setting herself up as self-appointed rival arbiter of the village's religious welfare and subjecting her entire household, but particularly her American guest, to extended Biblical tracts), with the dismissive humor and sarcasm they deserve.

She even makes light of the interrogation she undergoes as to her supposed "virginal" status, and is quite rightly unimpressed when told that she has already consented to becoming the dead son's wife just by the simple act of going out with him—a marked improvement from the simperings of Wendy Craig's character in *The Nanny*, and one that perversely makes us sympathize with her more. An engaging heroine, she doesn't seem predisposed to taking things lying down—even after being repeatedly bitch slapped, donked on the head with blunt things and repeatedly flung down *those* staircases—she's still fighting, and not without the occasional well-aimed acid quip, either. You can see why Hammer used her again three years later in *Crescendo*.

Add a volatile eccentric like Bankhead, in full steam ahead mode, to the recipe, throw in a soupcon of chattering village gossips (Gwendolyn Watts, Robert Dorning, Diana King) and you have a film which is never in danger of being dull—although it is definitely overlong and, by the time we're an hour in, there is the occasional bit of watchgazing to be done as we see Narizzano and scriptwriter Richard Matheson struggling to find ingenious ways for Steffy to effect escape. To give the Canadian director his due, he does a pretty mean job of inserting suitably gruesome close-ups of bloodied corpses in sinks, zooms of worried and frightened eyes, POVs of hands turning locks on doors (even if the bracelets don't match from shot to shot!) and some suitably Bavaesque green and red lighting.

Elsewhere, Peter Proud, presumably not soon to be reincarnated, comes up with interesting production designs which seem to mirror the ramshackle state of Bankhead's addled mind ("She *is* barmy," quoth Vaughan almost an hour in, like we're supposed to believe he's worked there for 15 years and only just figured it out), while Mary Gibson excels with Tallulah's wardrobe (who I'm sure are a band featured on at least one Bam Caruso pop-psych compilation), creating a wonderfully raggedy world of old frocks, velvet drapes, chiffon scarves and general satin 'n' tat which matches perfectly the photos adorning the walls, taken from Bankhead's real life.

Miss Tallulah Bankhead, as she liked to be known, passed away in 1968, shortly after notching up two more noteworthy appearances, firstly in Jules Bass' *The Daydreamer* and finally in the role for which most people of my generation remember her, the Black Widow in *Batman*. It seems her fears that *Fanatic* would be her last performance were at least partially unfounded.

In the film, there's a somewhat unsatisfying if inventive (and almost incongruously supernatural) resolution, by which time two major players are dead; and, although Mrs. Trefoile *gets* her just deserts, she still avoids the kind of comeuppance you spend most of the movie waiting for. On the other hand, you'll be pleased to know that Joyce, who would sadly lose her own battle with the bottle 14 years later, and whose character seems like a genuinely good person who got unfairly roped into this situation, comes away at least physically unharmed.

There is a slight disappointment in that, by this stage, the film has traded the black humor which makes its first half so unusual (such as the cheery background music which plays as Powers accompanies her captor to the village church, almost aping her waddling walk, and the priceless delivery of the word "Mirror?" right on cue) for almost Slaughteresque melodrama, but even I have to admit, with those sets and costumes, it's tolerable. It would be wrong to call *Fanatic* (yet another title which has very little to do with the plot, unless it refers to the religious obsessions on display, and they seem more like delusion) an unqualified success, but it would be equally unfair to write it off as a failure, either. After repeated showings, even during the parts which *do* drag and make one shout, "Get on with it, Steff!" at the screen in wonder at how many drainpipes to shimmy down or windows to climb out there can be in one house, it still more or less does the job.

And, no, in case anyone who only knows it by its American title was wondering, it's *not* a film about a lovable but deaf Welshman.

—D.R. Shimon

Credits: Director: Silvio Narizzano; Writer: Richard Matheson. **Leading Cast:** Tallulah Bankhead, Stefanie Powers, Peter Vaughan, Maurice Kaufmann, Yootha Joyce, Donald Sutherland.

Hysteria

There are certain films for which you always feel a fondness, no matter how many people, both trusted colleagues and refusenik hacks, think of you as utterly bonkers for exactly that reason. Freddie Francis' *Hysteria*, the fifth in Hammer's popular series of Hitchcock-Clouzot homages, is without a doubt for me one of those.

The film marks a departure from its predecessors in several ways. For one thing, it's set mainly in London, and even its "French" segment was quite clearly filmed in Buckinghamshire (presumably the budget had all been spent on the obligatory American leading man, Robert Webber). Secondly, there's no spooky manor house involved, but a rather swish art deco apartment in Richmond, and both hero and heroine's origins are distinctly more rough and ready than usual. But more than anything else, the whole tone of the piece is undercut with a distinct current of wry humor, something the previous four films in the series distinctly lack. This humor is largely due to the performance of Webber—rather than hamming it up like Oliver

Reed in *Paranoiac*, or delivering a somewhat workmanlike performance à la Kerwin Mathews in *Maniac*, our man from *The Dirty Dozen* is incredibly easy to like.

After a remarkable, "swirly" credit sequence (replete with "car crash" inserts), Webber enters as Chris Smith, a man with no memory. He's in England for reasons unclear to everyone including himself, just about to be released from a (psychiatric?) hospital, and his therapist (the impeccably dubious Anthony Newlands) is at a loss as to what to do with him, except to impart the good news that the mysterious Magwitch-style "benefactor" who has been paying for his health care has not missed a single payment, and has gone to the trouble of setting up a flat, the previously mentioned Richmond Court residence, to be used upon his dismissal. I would say "jammy git," but this is a Hammer film, so, things aren't quite as rosy as one would hope.

The only thing he has to go on which *might* lead him unlock both his identity and his past is a half-burned photograph of a beautiful, Hepburnesque vamp who seems to be some sort of actress or model. Armed with nothing but this one artifact, some optimism and a complement of All-American muscles (which have already been put to good use in finagling

him into a relationship with his nurse, played by the ever-beautiful Jennifer Jayne), he must enter the outside world and begin looking for clues. So far, this is a fairly original premise, considering the derivative nature of the previous films in the series.

His first step is to employ a typically fleabitten, gabardine-clad private eye (Maurice Denham). Mozzer seems reticent to take the case at first, understandably believing our man to be several gloves short of a giallo, but we soon find out that this was merely subterfuge, as he is clearly seen lurking in the shadows as the story progresses. In the time honored "they're trying to drive me maaaaad" style expected from such films, it becomes obvious that someone is having a merry jape at Webber's expense—the allegedly dead (at least according to Peter Woodthorpe's wonderfully poncy fashion designer, whom he strongarms in the most jovial, casual and blasé manner) femme fatale begins to appear in various locations around South West London and, every time he goes home, he hears sinister arguments emanating from what appears to be the flat next door.

This causes him to reel around the corridors in a semi-hallucinogenic daze, stumbling as he comes upon such genre staples as a mysteriously swaying birdcage (check!), plants with large tendrils (check!) and eventually the inevitable body in a shower (match ball!). Cynics may well point out the formulaic predictability inherent in such things but, in a film as entertaining as this, they're rather welcome.

And clichéd or not, under the masterful camera of Freddie Francis and director of photography John Wilcox, every single one of those elements looks amazing. *Hysteria* may not be one of the greatest Brit horrors ever, or even one of the greatest Hammers (and in truth, of all their pychodramas, it's probably the closest to a straight thriller), but it's definitely one of the most beautifully filmed. Every single monochrome shot looks like some kind of photographic art, the architecture has the appearance of an advert for Frank Lloyd Wright, and the girls could have easily stepped off any catwalk after an hour posing for David Bailey or Terence Donovan. So, when the horror plot devices appear, they seem less like the work of a cynical Hitch impersonator (although the influence of William Castle is also writ large all over the shop) and more the product of an inspired mind painting a picture. All we need now is a wheelchair and a swimming pool.

It's not just the cinematic aspect that elevates the film above the mundane. Writer Jimmy Sangster (yes, him again) throws us a major curveball by deviating halfway through the narrative into an extended flashback (the aforementioned "French" sequence) with an almost comedic tone, which allows both us and "Chris" to unravel more of his past and manage to take in a sex thief (Sue Lloyd), a passing English do-gooder in a sports car (Sandra Boize, who appears to have been in no other films) and an amusing brute thug (Kiwi Kingston, which makes sense, as the film was shot soon after *The Evil of Frankenstein*).

Webber jumps out of windows into passing vehicles, smuggles himself in the boot of a car, drives through Lydd (as most people are wont to do should they find themselves in the area) and spins a Cary Grant-style web of good old fashioned charm and bullshit to get himself to the next step, until we arrive back at the car accident that led to his "amnesia." Both the vamp (Leila Goldoni, fresh from two very influential stints with John Cassavetes and, at the time of writing, still very much a fixture on American screens) and someone else central to the plot are in on whatever fiendish puppetry Smith/Webber has become slave to (or has he?), and the evil perpetrators get their comeuppance thanks to the diligence of Denham, who in this case is playing against type as a man not to be messed with unless you want several unfortunate bruises! There's obviously a twist or two in there as well, but you can have fun trying to figure those out for yourself.

—D.R. Shimon

Credits: Director: Freddie Francis; Writer: Jimmy Sangster.
Leading Cast: Robert Webber, Lelia Goldoni, Maurice Denham, Anthony Newlands, Peter Woodthorpe.

Invasion

Just when you thought you'd seen every Brit film about strange temperature meddling aliens and the sweaty antics of the stiff upper lipped twits within their range of influence, along comes another one. What was it with filmmakers in the 1960s and their desperation to get everyone as moist and wheezy as possible?

Like a particularly bad episode of *Doctor Who* (this one was even written by *Who* scribe Robert Holmes), something crashes in the woods, setting a few twigs on fire and making a nearby radar operator drop his novelization of *The G-String Murders* (complete with large photograph of tits on the front cover). "That's a bit odd," he underacts. "Much too small for a plane..."

Meanwhile, a couple (young woman in furs with a too old man) are busy mowing down a pedestrian in their car, with a typically stiff upper lipped reaction (or it could just be bad acting again). Little do they know they are being watched by strange figures in the woods.

At a nearby hospital, our hunky doctor (Edward Judd, from the very similar *Island of Terror*) is busy turning away a tramp who reckons he's been made blind by "lights in the sky," and, as the car crash victim is brought in, a couple of rubber-suited cuties are homing in on the place, too.

Finally, our doctor hero realizes that the crash victim isn't human—he has a plate in his head and dodgy blood. "Whoever he is and wherever he came from, he came prepared," he explains. The alien is prepared for everything except cars, obviously. Soon he's awakened and, after touching someone (and therefore learning English), he starts babbling on about coming from a planet called Lystria. The two cuties are escaped prisoners who went on the lam after his ship broke down.

Meanwhile, the army is investigating a crater nearby, and the local bobby mentions that a "foreign-looking bloke" has just been brought into the hospital. For some reason, a force field has been laid around the hospital, causing the temperature to rise and all the nurses to change out of their nylon slips (I kid you not).

Just when you're losing the will to live yourself (none of this has been particularly exciting), the hospital boss decides to jump in his car and leave, only to crash spectacularly into the invisible barrier created by the force field, his body shooting through the windscreen and burning up. In such a pedestrian movie, a simple little thing like this comes as quite a shock.

Realizing that the alien bloke seems to fear women, the feisty lady doctor carries on the interrogation and soon finds out that it's him who's the prisoner, and the women are his guards. As the male doctor makes his way under the force field through the sewer to recover the male alien's power pack (getting ridiculously dirty in the process), the alien women home in on their escapee, and the entire film ends very quickly indeed, in a storm of stock footage and namby-pamby liberalism, one character deadpanning, "Now we've got them killing each other—just like us..."

Invasion does actually play against the stereotypes of the time, with Chinese nurses and feisty lady doctors, but then it blows it big time by making the plot turn on the rather

Invasion was only shown in the U.S. on TV

offensive idea that "all Chinese people look the same." But, at the end of the day, it's as dull as its washed-out monochrome film stock. Yawn. The best thing you can say is that it's short, but it still outstays its welcome.
—Chris Wood

Credits: Director: Alan Bridges; Writer: Roger Marshall.
Leading Cast: Edward Judd, Valerie Gearon, Yoko Tani, Tsai Chin.

Boris Karloff in *Monster of Terror*

Monster of Terror (aka *Die, Monster, Die*)

Monster of Terror (released as *Die, Monster, Die* in the U.S.) is a very American film, and not just because it's (loosely) based on an H. P. Lovecraft tale. Although set in Britain, with a mainly British cast, somehow it has more in common with the drive-in movies being made across the pond at the time than anything by Hammer or Amicus. In fact, the town of Arkham could quite easily be in New England (apart from the "oo-arrr" accents which proliferate). The Yankee Doodle feel is furthered by the inclusion of a very American leading man (you can tell he's American, apparently, because his "clothes don't fit right") in Steve Reinhardt (Nick Adams).

Steve arrives in Arkham at the beginning of the film and immediately gets the cold shoulder from the locals; in fact, their reception is so frosty it borders on farce. On

mention of the word Witley, he's shunned in the streets, laughed at by drunken pubgoers, and can't even hire a bicycle.

"What will it cost me to get to the Witley place?" he asks the bike shop assistant. "More than you'd imagine!" is the reply. Well, at least he's *speaking* to him.

Steve makes his way there on foot, passing by an enormous crater in the ground and trees that have been turned to ash, and is watched by a mysterious veiled figure. On arrival at the Witley place (despite many "no trespassing" signs, they've neglected to lock the gate), he's welcomed by a wheelchair-bound Boris Karloff (if welcomed is the right word), who seems to appear out of nowhere.

Steve is actually there to see Karloff's daughter, Susan, whom he knows from college. He's been invited by Mrs. Witley. Unlike her dad, Susan's made up at his arrival, and gives Steve a quick tour of the family portraits ("That's my grandfather—he went insane," she chirpily explains). It looks like mum's going that way, too. She stays hidden behind her bed drapes and the maid got so fed up with her shenanigans that she's buggered off.

Meanwhile, Karloff's up to something in the cellar, darkly muttering things like "chains for devils" and saying about his father, "If there is evil, it's buried with him." In a cozy chat with his veiled wife, he adds, "I have uttered no incantations, nor called out to these so-called 'creatures of evil.' Whatever happened to my father will not happen to me!"

"It is already happening," she replies. But he hasn't finished yet. "The truth is that I see the future and all that I have planned for it will fill it with a richness we have never known!" To which his cheerful wife replies, "That's what you see. All I can see is horror, horror."

The night passes with strange screams coming from outside, the butler collapsing spectacularly at dinner (and later dying), and a very tense investigation of the darkened house by Steve and Susan, with clocks speeding up and fires spitting (well, it made *me* jump). After spotting Karloff walking around in the garden after dark and finding himself drawn to the strangely glowing greenhouse in the grounds, Steve decides to try and get some answers from the family quack, but is instead treated to a brief cameo from professional spooky doctor Patrick Magee (and learns nothing, of course).

Back at the Witley place, Steve takes Susan into the greenhouse and they discover enormous plants, strange stones in the soil, and (of less interest, apparently) a bunch of screaming (and extremely well realized, for the time) monsters in cages in the back room. "The room is being exposed to some kind of radiation," says Steve. "It looks like a zoo in hell!" As the storm-lashed ending approaches (those clichés are just piling up), we learn that a meteorite landed near the house and Boris discovered that it made things grow, so it might be good for the garden (Baby Bio being insufficient, clearly). There are deaths aplenty and a typically flaming climax, along with what looks like a stuntman in a Boris Karloff mask running around doused in silver paint (luckily much use of filters helps dilute this effect).

Monster of Terror is a pretty good little shocker, which also benefits from being mercifully short, although the two plot strands (mad family history, meteorite) don't actually appear to have anything to do with each other, which makes you wonder why they bothered shoehorning them both in. —Chris Wood

Credits: Director: Daniel Haller; Writer: Jerry Sohl.
Leading Cast: Boris Karloff, Nick Adams, Suzan Farmer, Freda Jackson, Terence de Marney, Patrick Magee.

The Nanny

Here's another of Hammer's several contributions to the "psycho" subgenre, and probably their best attempt at a Hitchcockian thriller since the original *Taste of Fear* (1961). Of course, this isn't just a Hammer, or even just a horror film—it's a Bette Davis film. No one played psychopathic matriarchs with quite the same mixture of panache and venom as our Bette, 'twas it would seem her natural calling in life. Both *What Ever Happened to Baby Jane?* and *Hush, Hush, Sweet Charlotte* had helped to cement this reputation. Naturally the Carreras dynasty seized upon it the way a starving man would seize a loaf of bread, and netted themselves a minor classic into the bargain, repeating the trick two years later with the non-horror but still decidedly sinister *The Anniversary*. One could suggest that these films led to Davis being typecast, but in all honesty the roles were never a million miles away from her off-screen persona anyway, and she was the best at them.

Davis, referred to simply as "Nanny" throughout, is in the employ of a typically starchy 1960s white upper-class London family: an austere James Villiers; a pill-addicted, emotionally and physically weak wife in the shape of Wendy Craig; and a sullen, troubled 10-year-old William Dix. There's also Auntie Pen (Jill Bennett), Craig's ineffectual sister with a dodgy heart condition and a propensity for Swinging '60s liberalism, but she lives far away and is only called upon when the family need her help.

It's between Dix and Davis that most of the tension in the film escalates, creating moments of incredible suspense. Recently returned from some form of corrective school, where even on his last day he plays cruel jokes, à la the later *Harold and Maude*, the boy is distrustful, not to say hateful, of his Nanny. In fact, he doesn't seem to get on with his father (a typically distant political diplomat type, always halfway across the world on some errand or other) or his mother. In short, he's a bit of a troubled young chap.

His two enjoyments in life seem to be primarily listening to loud, mod jazz 45s (great taste the preteens had back then!) on his Dansette, and talking to Bobbie (Pamela Franklin, in her second great horror role), the slightly rebellious and precocious teenage daughter of the doctor upstairs, who doesn't seem to mind hanging out with a younger boy, presumably as she has no little brother. I can't say I blame him. She's possibly the only positive and strong individual in the entire film, seemingly without any neuroses, hangups or detachments. Oh, and she's gorgeous.

During one of the conversations between Franklin and Dix in their bedrooms (separated only by a staircase and an insecure window—oh, those were the days), we find out the boy has reasonable grounds for distrusting Davis. She killed his baby sister. Or she may have. We're never too sure, until we've seen the ending, and even then there's a certain air of ambiguity.

But in psychological chillers, questions equal spooky flashbacks, not to mention the insertion of slow-burning sequences involving characters walking toward shower curtains, running water, and a doll. Yep, five years on, not only from *Taste of Fear* but *Psycho* itself, and they're still making with the Hitch stuff. The slight variation this time is that it's a *bath,* and in all honesty, damned creepy, too, but basically you know the drill.

Villiers buggers off quite early on in the proceedings, and Craig constantly drops in and out of the hospital, leaving most of the action to a quartet of Davis, Dix, Franklin and Bennett. Needless to say, one of these people isn't going to see out the full running time but, as for which one, I'll simply state that it's a particularly gruesome and unpleasant demise.

The Nanny is a bit of an oddity, even among the rest of the studio's tense thriller output: The horror is implied rather than supplied, and most of the suspense, save for one or two visual sections, is actually executed through conversation rather than action. Furthermore, while it may have a central (juvenile) male protagonist, who in turn has a close female ally, it has absolutely no hero or heroine. Rather, it relies on the simultaneous subtlety *and* immensity of Bette Davis' performance to carry the viewer through the film.

Hate her or not (and you will, which shows just what a bloody good actress she was), your eyes are never off Bette anytime she's on screen, wondering exactly what she will do, who she will do it to, if she will do it and whether or not she ever actually did it. A combination of falcon-like stare, suggested malevolence and implicit spite, topped off with that wonderful crack in the voice that was her trademark, she may have been an expensive and irksome folly for Hammer, but repaid the company's faith in her without a doubt.

Required winter viewing, I think—and, remember, once we've finished with Nanny, the Aunties are coming over.
—D.R. Shimon

Shot, like most of Hammer's psychological thrillers, in stark black and white, this reteaming of Sangster and Holt following the memorable *Taste of Fear* is a gripping adaptation of Evelyn Piper's novel. It exists somewhere between the 1960s British kitchen sink drama cycle and a typical Sangster murder mystery. As with most of Jimmy's thrillers, *Les Diaboliques* is a prominent influence, particularly reflected by a crucial weak-hearted female character and a catalytic bathtub death. Low key but driven by a gritty narrative featuring child death, mental breakdowns and back street abortions, *The Nanny* has aged remarkably well.

The flashback-laden script begins with the return home of young Dix, the son of stern, emotionless Queen's Messenger Villiers (always away on business or down at the "club" whenever his family needs him), and Craig, an emotional wreck since the bathtub drowning of her youngest child, for which Dix copped the blame. Dix has spent the past two years being treated at a special private school where those in charge concede to failure and refer to him routinely as a "monster."

Now he harbours a deep-seated antipathy toward middle-aged females, specifically the family Nanny, whom he insists was responsible for his sister's death. Attempting to expose the truth by "breaking" Nanny with cruel tricks (including face-down dolls in the bath) and apparently crafting a poisoned steak and kidney pie, Dix is just one messed-up character in a bleak study of grief and misery amongst the well to do.

The Nanny commendably avoids the kind of melodrama and campiness one might reasonably expect from a Hammer flick featuring such a grand, scenery-chewing veteran star. It cannily keeps the audience unsure as to who represents the main threat: Is the kindly, respected Nanny really capable of dark deeds or are the adults right to view the bratty Dix as a male, posh English equivalent of *The Bad Seed*? The uncertainty is reinforced both by the flashbacks depicting the same event from opposing perspectives and by the strength of the performances.

Davis, resisting the urge to ham it up, finds hidden layers and subtle menace within the doting, archetypal figure of the English nanny. A sympathetic, loyal supporting figure in the first half, it's only during the film's climax that the extent of her madness becomes apparent. Even then, the film refuses to make her a one-note "monster": The last time we see the ostensible "villain" of the piece is in a strangely moving sequence in which she openly sobs for the first time.

Introduced to us via a scene in which he fakes his own hanging, William Dix proves a remarkably unselfconscious juvenile performer. Effortlessly crafting a believably obnoxious yet intelligent prepubescent character, he helps evoke a palpable tension in his scenes with Davis. And there's a strong naturalistic quality to his interaction with rebellious, cigarette-puffing, boy-mad, 14-year-old neighbor Franklin (who grew up to be a minor genre icon, thanks to *The Legend of Hell House*, *And Soon the Darkness* and *The Food of the Gods*.).

Admittedly, Craig comes off as shrill and unsympathetic, as much due to the writing as her performance, with her character all but vanishing in the second half when the focus narrows to the more compelling stories of the Nanny and the boy. It remains a standout example of its type, with perfectly restrained use of music and style, and an unforgettably unsettling (albeit typically understated) depiction of young Susie's death. Four decades on, the image of the dead girl in the tub, and Davis' subsequent reaction to it, still has the power to haunt.
—Steven West

Credits: Director: Seth Holt; Writer: Jimmy Sangster.
Leading Cast: Bette Davis, Wendy Craig, Jill Bennett, James Villiers, William Dix, Pamela Franklin, Maurice Denham.

The Night Caller (aka *Blood Beast from Outer Space*)

The Night Caller begins in typical 1960s Cold War style, with a blonde at the radar screen noting that an object has appeared 100 miles up, heading straight for London. However, as the object should become visible to the naked eye in London, all is quiet (three cheers for Big Ben and the Houses of Parliament, once again making their presences felt). The next day the army is dispatched to the parkland where the object should have ended up, but they only find a glowing football and very little damage. What's more, "it's cold—freezing cold" (the ball, that is, not the weather). Top secret double A-cleared Professor Morley (Maurice Denham) also notes that it must have been "guided down with fantastic accuracy—inhuman accuracy!"

The football is taken back to his lab where the old Prof, along with his American helper, Dr. Jack Costain (John "*Enter the Dragon*" Saxon) and Ann (Patricia "*Virgin Witch*" and "Did you know I used to be married to Michael Caine? Not a lot of people do" Haines), the blonde from the opening scenes, begin their investigations. In between, Jack tries it on with Ann (and fails).

Ann is then left alone in the lab, when she notices a glow coming from the room where the football is stored. She becomes blurry eyed and sweaty, and is drawn toward the object by a strange force. She's then attacked by a less than terrifying rubbery claw and only just manages to raise the alarm.

The next morning, some poo is found on the floor (Ann must have been more scared than she let on) and a footprint can be seen on the ground outside the lab window. With the army dismissing Ann's ravings as "a practical joke," work continues on identifying the football and, in a huge leap to get the plot moving, it's quickly deduced that it's an "energy valve" which "receives matter" from another planet. "We've had a visitor from space, Ann," speculates the Prof, leading Jack to add, "What did it come for, and when will it return?"

A hugely unscientific further "test" involving Professor Morley being left alone in the room with the football follows. As it starts to glow again, he's at first delighted and then petrified, coming to a rather ignominious end as he loses his glasses and scrabbles around for them on the floor, Thelma (from *Scooby-Doo*)-style, and getting killed by an unseen foe. The foe then nicks the ball and makes his getaway in a handy Jag.

Back in London the billboards are all screaming, "Space Creature? New Development," but The Yard (as in New Scotland) is treating the whole thing with "incredulity." Yet another massive story jump informs us that the creature, whom they have dubbed "Smith," appears to be responsible for the disappearance of several girls in the city. The latest to vanish is called Jean. A quick chat with her parents reveals that she was visited by a strange man before she disappeared ("Ooh, he gave me the creeps, standing there in the shadow—did have a nice voice, though," explains the mum). He left a weird 3-D photo of the girl and, shortly afterwards, she vanished. The parents also reveal that she was always reading a magazine called *Bikini Girl*, because she wanted to be a model (but she found the articles interesting, too, one assumes).

The police pay a call to a dirty book emporium, which has apparently been passing on letters answering an ad in the back of *Bikini Girl* to a Mr. Medra, the slimy shop owner (Aubrey "unable to do anything *but* slimy" Morris), explaining, "Some people aren't normal, are they? I tell you something, he even gave me the creeps!"

Unknown to everyone else, Ann has applied to Medra's talent agency in a bid to get closer to the alien (whom they've deduced comes from Jupiter's third moon, Ganymede). There's a wonderful bit of film noir style as the police stake out the shop with Ann inside, but things don't quite go to plan. Yes, Ann gets to meet the alien, who gives her a lengthy

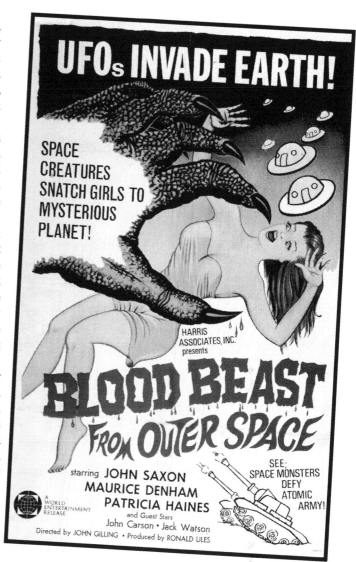

spiel about how tough it is to be an alien invader-cum-talent scout in 1960s London ("The problem of life is that there is always an enemy who will kill or be killed. I fear what I can't control, and I can't control a mind of equal intelligence to my own…"), and then he kills her. Bit of a shock, this, as not only does it come right out of the blue, but up until this point Ann has proved to be the heroine of the film. What's more, it's actually quite a graphic death (for the time).

As the scientists try to track down Medra using Jodrell Bank, the police are using more basic methods (they've found another girl who applied to Medra's agency and just follow her). The ending depicts everyone arriving at the same place at the same time, to hear Medra explain what he's been up to, the scamp.

The question with *The Night Caller* is, is it really science fiction, per se, or is it basically a typical 1960s sleazy, "call girl murdering psycho" story in the vein of *Cover Girl Killer* and *Night, After Night, After Night*, with some vague sci-fi trappings shoehorned in? In fact, that question doesn't really need to be asked. If Medra hadn't come from Ganymede, he could have been any other sad old perv. Judging by the state of the effects at the end of the film, there's a fair chance that he just *was* a sad old perv, and used a couple of arc lamps and a bit of dry ice to fool Scotland Yard into letting him go.

The film is also rather more entertaining than it ought to be, considering that very little happens and the budget is quite obviously tiny, even by British B-movie standards. The idea of an alien invader taking out an ad in the back of a rhythm magazine to lure young maidens back to Ganymede is barking mad (if he can travel through space, surely he could just zap into a few bedrooms and save a lot of time and fuss?), and there are a few nice touches: Ann's murder is quite shocking, and the 3-D photo effect actually succeeded in sending a chill down my spine the first time I saw it—which, after all, is the point.

—Chris Wood

Credits: Director: John Gilling; Writer: Jim O'Connolly.
Leading Cast: John Saxon, Maurice Denham, Patricia Haines, Alfred Burke, John Carson.

The Plague of the Zombies

The Plague of the Zombies stands at a crossroads in the subgenre of the walking dead, one moldering foot dragging from its far-flung exotic past even as the other lurches into a future of political and social metaphor. For my money, it's one of Hammer's finest films. Graced with John Gilling's crisp, no nonsense direction, Peter Bryan's intelligent script and Arthur Grant's striking cinematography, it exudes a ripe atmosphere of dread from every frame.

Plague of the Zombies

The frenzied native drumming and blood ritual of the opening voodoo ceremony take the viewer back to the Caribbean roots of zombie cinema, recalling such key colonialist cautionary films as *White Zombie* (1932) and *I Walked with a Zombie* (1943), in which innocent Caucasians abroad are seduced and "tainted" by exposure to libidinous—and therefore immoral—primitive foreign cultures.

In its original conception as "The Zombie" in 1963, the film was to have opened with a sequence in Haiti, and it's a masterful sleight of hand that this opening rite turns out to be taking place not in the lush jungles of the Greater Antilles but much closer to home, spreading its toxic influence from a previously abandoned Cornish tin mine like some foul tumor pulsing invisibly beneath the skin.

There's a similarly effective element of foreshadowing in the subsequent scene, as a typically pastoral English fox hunt cuts to the nearby village, and a somber funeral is brutally disrupted by a pack of huntsmen who roughly knock the cadaver from its casket; the bright traditional scarlet of their riding coats a violent, ominous splash of red amid the mournful palette of the community which anticipates the later puddle of blood in the graveyard dream sequence.

It's clear from the outset that something has gone dreadfully wrong with the natural social order in this place, and respected surgeon Sir James Forbes (a dependably warm and authoritative performance by André Morell) has come to help put it right, starting by scrutinizing the series of inexplicable and alarming deaths attributed to marsh fever and the incompetence of his former star student, now resident GP, Peter Thompson (Brook Williams). When Peter's wife Alice (Jacqueline Pearce) is taken, their investigations unearth the depraved design of Squire Clive Hamilton (John Carson) and his henchmen to kill off the local population and resurrect them as slaves for his condemned tin mines.

Hammer films are often tiered along lines of social hierarchy, but seldom has the studio been so explicit in its portrait of a traditional, ancestral ruling class which has become totally decadent and broken the ages old social contract requiring it to rule the lower orders with at least a modicum of paternal benevolence. Hamilton not only does not care for his charges, he actively preys on them, taking their lives and reducing them to a living death of miserable servitude; even the coarse hessian shrouds worn by the zombies recall medieval serfs.

But if the aristocracy is no longer prepared to face up to its civic responsibilities, upper-middle class professional Forbes is prepared to accept the burden and intervene to restore balance before the whole (literally) rotting culture comes crashing down. Although, being a decent sort, he does at least give Hamilton the opportunity to mend his ways and avoid the inevitable overthrow when he tells him, "I'm just trying to remember my manners. I wish I could say the same for you."

As if Hamilton had contracted some virulent contagion in Haiti, his disease spreads into this decaying microcosm to infect its women as well as its social status quo. In keeping with Victorian decorum, women in this world are most proper when infantilized. Casual reduction to the status of indulged children is their lot, as when Forbes variously remarks, "Excellent meal. You *girls* are to be congratulated," and "You *girls* run off to bed." But it's a different story after Hamilton has been in contact with them: They are poisoned by his insidious infection and reborn with a sexual wantonness that poses a direct threat to the patriarchy. Tragic Alice goes off to her premature grave the perfectly demure wife but rises from it charged with a lewd eroticism, a transformation to which the aghast Sir James can only respond by decapitating her with a shovel.

This theme of the seduction of the innocent is further underlined when Hamilton has abducted Forbes' prim, almost sexless daughter Sylvia (Diane Clare). Even as he lowers her to the sacrificial altar, her apparent sensual intoxication and tactile awakened sexuality is evident.

But above all of its sexual and social politics, *The Plague of the Zombies* is probably best remembered for its standout dream sequence. Bathed in writhing fog and a putrid greenish hue, the recently dead claw their way out of the moldering earth in a scene literally groundbreaking in zombie cinema, one that would be referenced again in films such as Amando De Ossorio's *Tombs of the Blind Dead* (1971) and Lucio Fulci's *Zombie Flesh Eaters* (1979).

And, although these zombies don't have a taste for human flesh, the final underground conflagration when they slip the leash and fall inexorably on their masters suggests it's only a matter of time before such appetites are acquired, and can't help but bring to mind the subsequent body of work of George Romero, which began with *Night of the Living Dead* (1968). —Paul Newman

Credits: Director: John Gilling; Writer: Peter Bryan.
Leading Cast: André Morell, Diane Clare, Jacqueline Pearce, John Carson, Michael Ripper

Repulsion

It's a hot, sweaty brace of summer weeks in London—as a hot, sweaty duo of French sisters, Carole and Hélène, uneasily share an Earl's Court flat. The dark haired one has a new boyfriend, in the shape of Ian Hendry. The other, blonde-haired one is a shrinking, monosyllabic, fretting enigma, disturbed by her sister's noisy sexuality. She lies awake at night listening

to her groans. During the day she is repelled by the objects the new boyfriend leaves lying about the house, particularly his straight razor. She is even more sulky and petulant when her sister prepares to go off on holiday to Italy, with Hendry leaving poor Carole home alone.

This abandonment by her sister leads to a gradual withdrawal from the world and a complete mental breakdown. Quite why this should happen is the film's big mystery. Catherine Deneuve's Carole is such a puzzle that everyone in the movie, dazzled by her superficial beauty, projects their most animalistic desires upon her. Everybody thinks she must be wildly sexually active, from the old woman at the beginning of the film who says, "I think you must be in love or something," to her hapless wannabe boyfriend (John Fraser) who asks, "Who's the lucky boy?" when stood up. From her friend Bridget, who asks her if "that smooth boy I've seen you with" is making her unhappy, to Hendry, who writes, "Don't make too much *Dolce Vita* while we're away" on the postcard from Italy. From the builder on the street (Mike Pratt) who asks, "'ow's about a bit of the other?" to even the anonymous voice on the telephone, which calls her a "filthy little tart." Her boss at the beauty salon where she works thinks she's been hard at it too, equating her peculiar behavior with an unwanted pregnancy. "You're not in any—trouble are you?"

Nothing could be further from the truth. The beautiful creature is in fact repulsed by the thought of sex and men in general. When Fraser clumsily kisses her, she flees to her bathroom and frantically washes her mouth. When she smells the discarded vest of Hendry, she vomits. Even the mention of her friend, Bridget's boyfriend, sends her from laughter to reacting as though slapped in the face. Once abandoned by her sister, her bizarre relationship with her own sexuality takes a turn for the worse, and she is visited every night by a shadowy, bit of rough rapist, conjured from her own peculiar imagination.

Repulsion was Roman Polanski's first English-language movie and his second as a refugee from behind the Iron Curtain. He arrived just as London started to swing, and Deneuve remains a true 1960s icon. In *Repulsion*, Polanski (who was born in Paris) is fixated upon her, like the rest of the men in the picture. She is in almost every single shot. The only brief moments not featuring her are when Fraser's unpleasant chums in the pub make crude comments about her imagined sexual appetite, and when Hendry remarks to sis Yvonne Furneaux that "she should see a doctor." At first she wanders around London with a nifty little jazzy flute tune accompanying her. However, roughly midway through the film, this changes and, following a demented stroll over Hammersmith Bridge, the rest of the film takes place entirely in Carole's flat, an audacious and confident feat of filmmaking, thanks partly to Gilbert Taylor's astounding cinematography (Taylor would shoot almost all of Polanski's British films).

Repulsion is the first of Polanski's quartet of paranoid apartment invasion thrillers, followed by *Rosemary's Baby*, *The Tenant* and *The Pianist*. All his sound obsessions are present: dripping taps, ticking clocks, a piano being practiced in another flat. In a typical ending, the flat is invaded by old age pensioners. His presentation of Deneuve is suitably queasy. She spends much of the film in a see-through nightie with no bra, yet she wears no makeup and her hair is a mess. A film of sickly sweat covers her face in the many close-ups, and you can almost smell the stink of her armpits. She is both the victim of the director's sexual gaze and the perpetrator of horrific murders, the first of which clearly mirrors an event in Polanski's own teenage life, when he was smacked on the skull and left for dead by a multiple murderer, his body stuffed into a sewer.

For all the voyeuristic gazing at Carole's exterior life, we must come to our own conclusions about her actions. Her interior obsessions are taken up with decay, disintegration, rape—and a dead, uncooked rabbit. The film even opens on a huge close-up of Deneuve's eye rolling around moistly in its socket. This window of the soul is giving nothing away, though. The film ends with another close-up of the same orb, this time in a photo of the pubescent Carol in a family photograph. That the source of all Carole's trouble is silently contained in this one image is all the more disturbing when Polanski's own history as a fugitive from U.S. justice is considered.

—John Rankin

Roman Polanski has a thing about apartments. Over the years, he's staged a series of tense, claustrophobic dramas in such enclosed spaces, notably *Rosemary's Baby*, set in New York's troubled Dakota Building adjacent to Central Park,

later the scene of John Lennon's murder; *The Tenant*, his terrifying adaptation of Roland Topor's novel *Le Locataire*, in which Polanski himself took the lead role of a stranger in Paris seemingly forced into insanity, transvestitism and attempted suicide; and the first half of his Oscar-winning *The Pianist*, with a distraught family confined to a handful of rooms as invading Nazis parade through the wartime streets below. Even open water fails to expand the director's horizons: his two boat-bound psychological character studies, *Knife in the Water* and *Bitter Moon*, having their battles of wits largely played out below decks in restrictive cabin locations.

Polanski's international success with *Knife in the Water* in 1962 led the talent-spotting heads of Britain's tiny but ambitious Compton-Tekli film company to hire the director. Producers Michael Klinger and Tony Tenser had a somewhat seedy background as the owners of a couple of strip clubs, but had achieved some success with a handful of exploitation and horror titles. Increasingly ambitious, they looked to Polanski to craft what Tenser described as "the first commercial art film." Communication breakdowns and budgetary problems were rife, and at one stage Tenser even threatened to fire Polanski and have the notorious nudie/glamour photographer, George Harrison Marks, step in to complete *Repulsion*! Ultimately, however, Polanski finished the movie to everyone's mutual satisfaction, although he later described it as his "shoddiest" work, "technically well below the standard I try to achieve."

This comment can easily be dismissed as the self-criticism of an obsessive perfectionist. A far more accurate assessment is given by British horror expert Jonathan Rigby, who calls *Repulsion* "the most mesmerising view of madness ever put on the screen." Carol, the young Belgian beautician whom we witness descending into bewildered derangement, was played by Catherine Deneuve, fresh from the bright, colorful, French musical *The Umbrellas of Cherbourg*, and rarely has any performer immersed herself into a role's dark depths so fully. As critic Ivan Butler pointed out, "it is quite unnerving to see her in some other film shortly afterwards." With Anthony Perkins and *Psycho* still current in audiences' minds, it would have been easy to turn Carol into a female equivalent of Norman Bates, but Deneuve's lost, haunted demeanor actually makes her this story's victim, despite the violence she almost unconsciously commits towards the film's close.

Note the careful use of sound as *Repulsion* unfolds: the minimalist score, with sparse percussion setting the empty, desolate tone; a simple but beautifully effective theme suggesting and illustrating Deneuve's downward spiral; the bashing drums and crashing cymbals accompanying her disturbing hallucinations; the echo of dripping water, one of Polanski's later trademarks; the too loud ticking of a clock. One sound heard through the walls was being permitted by Britain's censor for the first time ever in a movie—that of sexual ecstasy, as Carol's sister frolics with a lover in an adjacent room. Deneuve's revulsion during this scene may seem a little out of place on a first viewing, but the film's devastating final image, which requires your intense attention, might perhaps offer a few penetrating and explanatory insights into the psyche of our tortured subject.

One last word of warning, aimed mainly at the carnivorous members of the audience: You may never want to eat rabbit for dinner again. Prepare yourselves!
—Darrell Buxton

Credits: Director: Roman Polanski; Writers: Roman Polanski, Gerard Brach.
Leading Cast: Catherine Deneuve, Yvonne Furneaux, Ian Hendry, John Fraser, Patrick Wymark, James Villiers.

She

H. Rider Haggard's *She* was apparently a pioneering work of fiction in the "Lost World" fantasy subgenre and has spawned numerous film adaptations of which this, the Hammer version, was at least the eighth! Having not read the book, I can't confirm how faithful (or otherwise) it is, but there are worse ways to spend a lazy Sunday afternoon.

In Palestine in 1918, Cambridge archaeology professor Major Horace Holly (Peter Cushing), his valet Job (Bernard Cribbins) and younger companion Leo Vincey (*Black Sunday*'s John Richardson) are enjoying their post-military life like any good group of Englishmen would: by getting drunk and ogling belly dancers. To see both the Cush and the Crib up shaking their stuff is rather a hoot, let me tell you. Things descend into chaos and a Clint Eastwood-style bar brawl breaks out, but Leo is far too occupied working his twinkly, blue-eyed charm on a local girl called Ustane to get involved with fisticuffs. The girl (Rosenda Monteros) is but an exotic worm on a hook however, and Leo's clobbered on the head and ferried away. Upon waking, the first thing he sees is Ursula Andress (we've all been there) bathed in soft light (this from a time when she didn't need it) and accompanied by the ethereal plucking of harpsichord strings. "I am Ayesha, who some call 'She Who Waits'," she says in a tone flatter than Holland (and she's dubbed). Ah, well, she looks good.

Leo returns to Holly with a map and a ring, upon which Holly recognizes the insignia of Kallikrates, the High Priest of Isis, of the lost Egyptian city of Kuma. Could it be that the legends are true? Well, Holly thinks so, and so, before you can say "digestive biscuits," our three heroes are trekking across some very picturesque desertscapes in search of treasures galore.

Eventually, the trio find Kuma, an ancient city ruled over by Ayesha, "She Who Must Be Obeyed," aka "She Who Must Have A Half-Dozen Titles." Attending her is the High Priest Billali (unfortunately sans his Comets), played by Christopher Lee. Ayesha believes Leo to be the reincarnation of her long lost lover, the aforementioned Kallikrates, whom she stabbed to death in a jealous rage centuries earlier (though, this being Andress, don't expect much). Unfortunately, Leo has fallen for the servant girl Ustane. But the promise of eternal life with Andress proves too much of a temptation and, just like that, the fickle sod shifts his affections. Ah, well, Ustane ends up in an urn anyway, so it was probably for the best. Ayesha and Leo

will enter the "blue flame," the source of her immortality, and live together forever. Ah, but there's a twist: "Be careful what you wish for" and all that. Not to give anything away, but if you've seen Andress lately, you'll get the picture.

She is slow going in parts and a tad overlong, but it's not without a myriad of pleasures. Cushing's dignified performance holds this load of old tosh together, and the brief scenes he shares with Lee are a treat. Lee, though, is somewhat under used. Bernard Cribbins gets more screen time, and his deadpan quips are quite amusing. Richardson is lacking in personality and coasts through on his looks, not unlike Andress.

Hammer's costume department works overtime, the matte paintings used are ace, and it's a far more lavish looking production than most Hammers (it was the most expensive production yet for the studio at almost £325,000). *She* will provide old-time, adventurous fun for those not expecting *too* much.
—Jed Raven

Credits: Director: Robert Day; Writer: David T. Chantler. **Leading Cast:** Ursula Andress, Peter Cushing, Bernard Cribbins, Christopher Lee, John Richardson.

The Skull

The Skull begins with a cat's meow and screech of a graveyard's gate—clearly we're in horror film territory. Men are being paid to dig up a grave in what we later learn is an act of extreme phrenology by a Frenchman who wishes to obtain someone's head to study. This ultimately unfortunate figure takes the spade-severed bonce home and pours chemicals over it so he can examine the skull unhindered by decomposing tissue; he is then quickly dispatched by the very item he wished to scrutinize, and the opening titles begin.

The narrative jumps to the modern day, to an auction house in which sit, among others, Christopher Maitland (Peter Cushing) and Sir Matthew Phillips (Christopher Lee). Phillips, eyes wide, is compelled to buy four figurines, each imp representing one of the ranks from the hierarchy of devils. Maitland is also a collector of occult items, a hobby that helps his profession as a writer (convinced he will one day be able to "explain away" superstition).

Marco, a furtive dealer in Maitland's favored trinkets, turns up with an object for his prospective customer: a book bound in human skin—it's troubling to ponder what you might be expected to use as a bookmark with such a charming volume. This particular tome is about the Marquis de Sade, the deviant whose behavior gave the English language the term "sadist." Marco follows up this sale with a connected offering: the skull of the Marquis himself. Maitland hesitates and turns down the chance to purchase, and it's from here that the skulduggery begins in earnest, this having been the item disinterred in the opening sequence.

Maitland is warned off by Phillips, who reveals that he was under the influence of the skull when at the auction, also making it clear that it is dangerous and that he was glad when it was stolen from him—the suggestion, of course, being that people within the orbit of the skull may have a tendency to find themselves hideously and brutally murdered. After receiving another warning to leave well alone (delivered via the subtle method of kidnapping, including three rounds of Russian roulette), Maitland does what only characters in horror films can do, namely increases his efforts to possess the cranial liability. Reviewers of *The Skull* often describe the kidnapping sequence as an hallucination, but I dispute this, because Maitland is awake when "the police" call and then rouses in a different place. The conclusion I arrived at was that Maitland was fumbling at the fringes of a larger plot. A well-connected occult group clearly wants the skull. But I don't think the world's most lethal bone paperweight wants them.

Considerable differences exist between the film and the source material, a short story by Robert Bloch. Only the basic premise remains unchanged from the 13-page tale. Much has

been altered: Maitland isn't a professor in the story, and is more eager to add to his collection, while Marco is more disreputable and has a dog at his flat, which Maitland shoots. In addition, the Skull's teeth are described as deformed, thereby not having the typical grin of a death's head.

The silent sequence near the end is a triumph (making me wonder why more films don't dispense with dialogue). And such is the imposing nature of the skull prop itself, one almost wants to scan the credits to see who played an inanimate object, seemingly possessed of a personality all its own—and it's a spiteful and malevolent little bugger to boot!

The Satanism aspect is historically unfounded when applied to De Sade and, apart from the fact that the Marquis' skull was exhumed by a phrenologist, I can see no reason to choose him over a fictional cultist. An invented villain would have offered more room for the imagination to roam, but the Marquis is men-

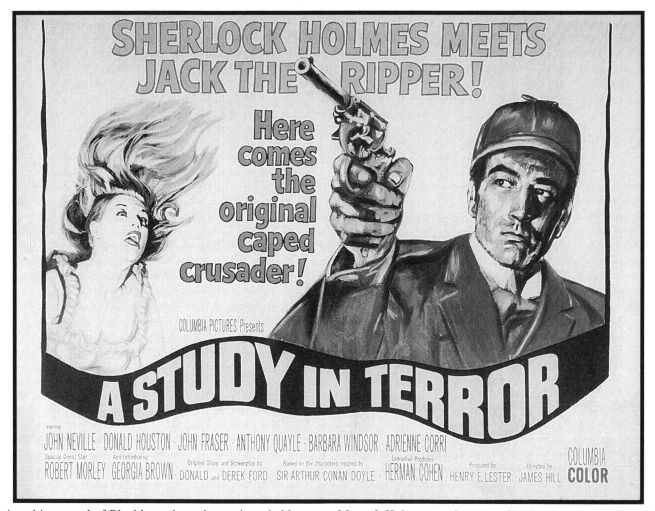

SHERLOCK HOLMES MEETS JACK THE RIPPER!

Here comes the original caped crusader!

COLUMBIA PICTURES Presents

A STUDY IN TERROR

starring
JOHN NEVILLE · DONALD HOUSTON · JOHN FRASER · ANTHONY QUAYLE · BARBARA WINDSOR · ADRIENNE CORRI
Special Guest Star · And Introducing
ROBERT MORLEY · GEORGIA BROWN · Original Story and Screenplay by DONALD and DEREK FORD · Based on the characters created by SIR ARTHUR CONAN DOYLE · Executive Producer HERMAN COHEN · Produced by HENRY E. LESTER · Directed by JAMES HILL · COLUMBIA COLOR

tioned in several of Bloch's works and must have held some significance for him.
—Elliot Iles

Credits: Director: Freddie Francis; Writer: Milton Subotsky.
Leading Cast: Peter Cushing, Christopher Lee, Jill Bennett, Patrick Wymark, Michael Gough, Nigel Green, George Coulouris, Patrick Magee.

A Study in Terror

How did Herman Cohen and Michael Klinger sell the doyen of detectives, trapped in an eternal netherworld of pea-souper London streets of a mythical 19th century, to the hepcat thrill seekers of the 1960s? Simple. They hired a poster artist who gave the film frenzied caption bubbles of "POW! BIFF! BANG! AIEEE!" and "CRUNCH!" then added the strapline, "Here comes the original caped crusader!" Yes, the portly specter of Adam West made himself felt firmly in the selling of *A Study in Terror*. Paradoxically, however, the actual film—while somewhat rough edged and sensationalistic—almost captures the pure essence of Holmes.

The key casting is superb. John Neville makes a surprisingly young but properly hawk-like Holmes, Donald Houston a convincingly dependable Watson, and Robert Morley *is* Mycroft Holmes, putting even Charles Gray's more famed performance to shame.

The story is another variant on that old fan fiction chestnut of "Holmes versus Jack the Ripper," overseen by such dependable trash-masters as Cohen and Klinger. And yet, perhaps through dealing with such a comparatively illustrious source, their usual blood and cleavage soaked fare is given a soupçon of style, a cutting of class and an input of intelligence. Certainly, there's unsubtle unpleasantness aplenty from the moment that a cameo-making Barbara Windsor (inevitably as a tart with a heart) becomes Jack's first victim in a welter of Kensington Gore, but the elegant sets, the restrained acting from all of the principal players and the sheer overall sense of a strange dignity make the whole enterprise surprisingly polished.

It would be a fool who called this film an edge of the seat exercise in thrilling suspense, but what it nevertheless remains is a solidly crafted, affectionately created halfway house between the assuredness of Rathbone and the intellect of Brett. It's an odd but highly enjoyable crossbreed—without a utility belt in sight.
—Ken Shinn

High heels echo on cobblestones, the sound of a male tread closes in and both begin to hurry. Only the feet are visible until the man catches up, and then the shot widens.

As expected with a low-budget "Sherlock Holmes against Jack the Ripper" picture, there are a number of clichés, but there is intelligence in the script and enough fine craft to balance these. The film's main drawback is the budget and the constraints of time and sets that this engenders. On the plus side, this does give the film a claustrophobic feeling that adds to the unease, lending the pace a hurried, desperate feeling; but it also ensures that *A Study in Terror* remains a minor effort, though a professional and highly enjoyable entry to be sure. The opening scene highlights some of the strengths: an understanding of the genre and a welcome thoughtfulness. When the woman is stopped, the knife doesn't fall as expected; instead we get a "Hello, darling" and, just as it feels like a false start, or a ratcheting up of tension with no payoff, our antagonist attacks.

As with many British horrors of the 1960s, the main strength of the film is the cast. Neville and Houston as Holmes and Watson hold everything together while surrounded by a strong British cast including Anthony Quayle and Robert Morley. Many of the cameos add value: Even Barbara Windsor performs effectively in a short turn, giving her character, a vulnerable and scared but hard-faced woman, a strength and humanity as she desperately tries to find somewhere to stay. What price a new hat now?

The direction and look of the film deliver some nice touches. The image of a bloody knife plunging into water with plumes of blood billowing around is a memorable sight. The whole thing looks more sumptuous than it should and the film has something to say about poverty and vested interest, while mixing in tension, horror and humor. Even toward the end the intelligence is not discarded, a good example being the question of why the last Ripper victim was killed indoors. The neat answer is that, being too scared to tout for business on the street, she picks a passing john she likes and calls him inside—simple, really.

The mystery is suitably Holmesian, with characters of more than one dimension that propel the story forward. Holmes actually enters the fray when a box is sent to him, a puzzle to whet his appetite. It sets him on a trail that brings in all the players who seem to have a link to a lost heir: a Duke and his other son, the suspicious surgeon in the charity hospital, the blackmailing landlord and the mysterious sender of the package. The coincidences fly and red herrings are played to the full until the questions are answered. What of the missing knife? Will the heir return? And what is the motive of the sender of the box?

Still, it's not a film for the Holmesian pedant or serious Ripperologist, but if you like to see an *EastEnders* star come to a nasty end, or experience the "Holmes meets the Ripper" fantasy staged in an enjoyable way, this is for you.

The movie is a well-crafted little gem, which slowly drifts out of the memory. It is the cinematic equivalent of having a good meal in front of a warm fire on a cold day; not earth shattering but proves a pleasant and satisfying diversion.
—Wayne Mook

Credits: Director: James Hill; Writer: Donald Ford, Derek Ford.

Leading Cast: John Neville, Donald Houston, John Fraser, Anthony Quayle, Barbara Windsor, Robert Morley, Adrienne Corri, Frank Finlay, Judi Dench.

Ten Little Indians

Ten people are lured to an isolated snowbound chateau on the top of a mountain where they are murdered one by one by an unknown person who is probably one of their party. This was legendary producer Harry Alan Towers' first crack at Agatha Christie's book *Ten Little Niggers*. He made two subsequent versions set respectively in the Iranian desert and on a safari (!). Unsurprisingly, no film version of the novel uses Christie's original racist title or the original rhyme on which the murders are based. In this version, "Indians" is the substitution, but in some reprints of the book the word "soldiers" has replaced the offensive original. It's now staggering to think that the word "nigger" seemed to be perfectly acceptable to use in this context in England as late as 1939 when the book was originally published. All film adaptations also change the original downbeat ending, which probably wouldn't work that well on screen anyway: Christie didn't use it in her own stage version.

Apart from the ending and the location (the novel is set on an island), the film is relatively faithful to its source. However,

some of the murders are changed slightly because the originals wouldn't work in the new locale. Therefore, the structural weaknesses of the film are basically those of the novel: The murderer is not a physically strong enough character to have been capable of committing the demanding acts of (off-screen) close-up personal violence required and, for a scheme clearly planned long in advance, too many of the murders seem to have been improvised on the spot and rely on the killer being extremely lucky or knowing exactly when other people will leave the house in the middle of the night.

Towers attempts to update his source material by using a contemporary jazz score, a romance between leads Hugh O'Brian and Shirley Eaton and a long, somewhat amusing fight scene about halfway through between O'Brian and Mario Adorf that looks quite punishing on the two actors, being filmed in several long takes without much use of stunt doubles. It's surprising that this was filmed in black and white rather than color, as that would have made it more "swinging," but presumably would have cost more money and made the snowy sets a little more obvious.

Leads O'Brian and Eaton are pretty weak. O'Brian, TV's *Wyatt Earp*, gives an irritatingly smug reading in which he remains unconcerned by anything as long as he can lech at Eaton and Daliah Lavi and show off the hairs on his chest to the audience at various points. Eaton can't really act, either, although she provides a few bikini scenes and manages to look positively smoldering and gasping for O'Brian in their sex scene. Both are thoroughly outclassed by the supporting cast of veterans Wilfrid Hyde-White, Stanley Holloway and Dennis Price, all of whom seem to be enjoying themselves (Price doubtless doubly enjoyed the numerous drinking scenes) and manage to provide much more rounded characterizations. Luckily Towers had the sense to keep these three all around until near the end, while stiffer performers like Leo Genn get bumped off earlier. However, he still contrived to make the diminishing cast sit down politely for black tie dinners each night, as if the day's murders were a spot of bother in some far away place.

The film was originally released with a hilarious "murder minute" break, in which the action is frozen at a key point near the end while the audience is given some brief time to reflect on events and try to guess the killer. The bombastic American voice that narrates this section is bound to result in some sniggers. Unfortunately, while this interlude was intact within the film when I originally saw it on TV, the U.K. DVD release confines it to the extras section. Trivia fans will also note that the voice of U. N. Owen, which can be heard on the tape recorder, is unmistakably that of Christopher Lee.
—Tim Rogerson

Agatha Christie's wicked novel *Ten Little Niggers* first made it onto cinema screens in the hands of a Frenchman shooting the shocking whodunit on a Hollywood sound stage. Despite this, René Clair's *And Then There Were None* (1945) comes across as one of the most quintessentially *British* of films. It is a relatively faithful adaptation with the characters unchanged and featuring the novel almost page by page until

Agatha Christie's original novel title seen today is shocking.

the closing episode. The book ends with an epilogue about a missive discovered in a bottle, of all things. Filmmakers have shied from the book's plot, where all 10 characters die and there is no romantic reprieve for a final couple. Lombard is shot and Vera Claythorne uses the noose. In Christie's output, it is, alongside the final case of Poirot (in which the Belgian detective is revealed to be the murderer), one of the sequences least likely to be realized.

Clair's film is so meticulous in its casting and delivery that it might have been expected to color all future productions. This, however, is difficult to assess, as producer Harry Alan Towers cannily picked up the film copyright on the property in the 1950s and retained it to the end of his life. Towers produced four versions of the film, three for the cinema and one for television, and so the real power to do something unusual with the story sat with one man. Towers was lazy with the adaptations, permitting the excellent Clair film to retain, and gain in, classic status.

The plot device of deaths fashioned by a one by one structure was not original to cinema, as previous horror films had turned dead men on their juries and greedy beneficiaries of a will against fellow family members, but Christie's novel was refreshingly unique and was the first film with an overt countdown through a trapped group. It is the forerunner of everything from *The Abominable Dr. Phibes* to the *Friday the*

13th films, via Bava and Argento. While the impact of the Clair film is little recognized today, it can be seen to have inspired a string of imitators.

In 1949 the BBC adapted the story. Outraged at the Hollywood scoop on a British property, the Corporation made a dangerous swat back by returning the original title, and it was telecast as *Ten Little Niggers*. Directed by Kevin Sheldon, it starred John Stuart as Dr. Armstrong, Arthur Wontner in the role of the General, Campbell Singer as Blore and John Bentley as Philip Lombard. Telecast live, it is now lost and more research would have to be undertaken to determine if the story also returned to the original grim ending, but the title exposes this country and its indigenous racism. The BBC rejected Hollywood's removal of the ugly epithet for the less derogatory "Indians" (though today, in new American editions of the novel, the word "Indian" has been replaced, too).

In the same year, the National Board of Canada made a public information film, *Ten Little Farmers*, which adopted silhouette cutout figures to warn the agricultural workers of dangers on the farm. Interestingly it was a theme to reappear more notoriously in the later British PIF (Public Information Film) *Apaches* (1975), directed by John Mackenzie. In 1959, the British public was warned again with *Crosses for Sale*, a road safety film shot two years earlier by Merlin Films and the Dagenham Borough Council that featured a rhymed parody of the original tune to accompany scenes of careless motorists, cyclists and pedestrians. Towers' first stab at the tale came in 1959 for American television, reputedly made in New York, safely recorded with the title *Ten Little Indians* for the first time.

For Towers' first cinematic outing of the Christie yarn, a limited company called Tenlit was set up, but the question for the producer was how significantly to change the story. Towers saved money and effort by recycling the original Hollywood script (with Dudley Nichols retaining a [posthumous] screenplay credit) that was now Tenlit property, crediting himself with co-authorship of the "new" screenplay under his common Peter Welbeck pseudonym. There was minimal attempt to change the dialogue now familiar from both the novel and the René Clair film. The film actually sports the title *Agatha Christie's Ten Little Indians*. The tie-in book would again stubbornly hold onto the "Niggers" epithet. By the end of the decade, the n-word would no longer be appropriate on a book cover.

One major alteration to Pollock's *Ten Little Indians* was the setting, with the houseguests relocated to the Swiss Alps and a remote schloss accessible only by a cable car. The dialogue hardly changes and the initial nips and tucks are in respect to the relocation. Given that barely any rewriting was needed, it is almost outrageous how little thought went into amending the script to reflect those few tweaks. Previously, the death of the butler had been proven in the discovery of his mutilated corpse but, in the Alps, his replacement, Joseph (Mario Adorf), is trying to escape by mountaineering down and his rope is cut, his body plummeting. The group can never see the corpse and yet it fails to occur to them, when they all agree the killer is one of the remaining group, that Joseph could still be at large.

Changes to a few professions and mentions of a colder climate and location complete the re-jig. The contemporary setting was unnecessary and done for the hell of it.

If I appear to return to the Clair film, that is because it is highly relevant. Not only is the 1945 script taken up in swathes, but a detailed study of the completed film had also been made, with scenes often reproduced very closely, particularly the spying through keyholes set pieces and the pool room exchange between Dr. Armstrong (Dennis Price) and Judge Cannon (Wilfrid Hyde-White), though whether Pollock or the scriptwriters should have claimed responsibility is difficult to surmise. If it was Pollock, it is odd that he could frame so approximately but failed to pick up accurately on Clair's effective pauses, unless he was absent at the editing stage.

When the group is asked who among them knows their absent mystery host, Mr. U. N. Owen (and what would that U stand for? Ulysses?), rather than the earlier film's steady exchange of looks, there is no pause, and Daliah Lavi (as Ilona, a beautiful actress, a glamorous replacement for the cold old maid played by Judith Anderson in 1945) jumps immediately to the next statement, as if having picked up in a millisecond the unspoken answer that none of the assembled knew Mr. Owen. This is one of several examples of sprinted dialogue losing something in the reading. When the accusatory tape recording is played, there are cutaways to each of the named, with each individual then reacting to their own name with a predictable turn of the head. In the original there are less pronounced acknowledgements; casual concession, bemusement and expectation. It shows little understanding of the characters by Pollock.

It is evident that several of the actors brought their own familiarity with the earlier film to their performances in the delivery and action. The film does not as successfully hide the identity of the killer, with Wilfrid Hyde-White playing it less insidiously, also failing to portray a faked fear at the stage that might successfully have hidden his secret (unlike the mock-fearful Barry Fitzgerald at the pool table in 1945). Dennis Price redresses the balance by more successfully bringing suspicion on his character in the later stages and is perhaps the most usefully cast.

The house is not the character that it is in the previous film, and we are not as certain of the architecture of the film as we were with René Clair. We understand the design of the house, the placement of the rooms and the geography of the surrounding land, and believe with Clair that the search of his island was thorough. Not here. The cinematography is poor, shoddy with shadows biting chunks out of the players. Leo Genn, Marianne Hoppe and Stanley Holloway fill out the supporting cast, while Fabian turns up as a pop star named Mike Raven, a moniker shortly to be adopted by a British radio DJ and would-be horror film star. None of the cast is a match for his/her 1945 predecessor and, but for an added sex scene (Shirley Eaton is twice reduced to her underthings), a more common familiarity and affectionate tone in the relationships between the characters is avoided. Guilt is black and white with no apologetic middle ground and no excuses. The innocent survive, the guilty die.

Towers, onto a good thing, would return to the story twice more, setting it on a Greek island in 1975 and in period Africa on a steam train in the 1989 version. The latter shoot was in defiance of an aversion to filming in South Africa during Apartheid, and the actors, including Oliver Reed, John Rhys-Davies, Herbert Lom and Brenda Vaccaro, would join a list of those sullied by such participation. The three Towers films are never more important than their landscapes, but as it is virtually impossible that the 1945 René Clair film will ever be improved upon, it is neither here nor there that the Towers films remain nothing more than weak pops at a fabulous story.
—Paul Higson

Credits: Director: George Pollock; Writer: Peter Welbeck [Harry Alan Towers]; Co-writer: Peter Yeldham
Leading Cast: Hugh O'Brian, Shirley Eaton, Fabian, Leo Genn, Stanley Holloway, Wilfrid Hyde-White, Daliah Lavi, Dennis Price.

The War Game (aka *After the Bomb*)

Peter Watkins came to the attention of the BBC thanks to two short films, *The Diary of an Unknown Soldier* (1959) and *Forgotten Faces* (1961). Both films were made with the help and assistance of Watkins' then-colleagues at the documentary film company World Wide Pictures, and both are early examples of a style of filmmaking now loosely called docudrama, a term which neither does adequate justice to Watkins' exceptional skill nor appropriately recognizes the scope of his vision.

Diary (about the experiences of soldiers in the trenches of World War I) and *Faces* (about the Hungarian uprising in 1956) acted as Watkins' calling card and, on the strength of both shorts, he was employed by the BBC in their documentary department, primarily as an editor under Huw Wheldon. It was Wheldon who gave Watkins the chance to direct a docudrama adaptation of John Prebble's examination of the battle of Culloden. Watkins' film version, *Culloden*, was an exceptionally affecting documentary drawing deliberate parallels between the sadistic actions of the Royal armies in the aftermath and the actions of American forces then extending the nature of their involvement in Vietnam. The film was a huge critical success for Watkins and the BBC. The fact that this undeniably political film was made by the supposedly independent BBC may have been easily forgotten because of this critical adulation. It wouldn't be the case with Watkins' next film.

The War Game begins with a series of "vox-pop" style interviews with the man and woman on the street. Brilliantly, some of these are staged interviews with "actors" and relate to the narrative (a fictional deterioration in East-West relations as a result of a Chinese invasion of South Vietnam), while others are genuine on the street interviews with the public about their (largely hopelessly unrealistic) expectations in the event of a nuclear attack. The film then unfolds in the same manner as popular TV current affairs programs like *Man Alive* (BBC) and *World in Action* (ITV), with Michael Aspel and Dick Gra-

ham providing the voiceover and asking the questions. Set in Rochester, Kent, *The War Game* continues to build tension as confrontation in Berlin brings the world closer to war, and officialdom continues to pontificate, in a hopelessly over-optimistic style, about how it would cope in the event of an attack.

When the attack does come, *The War Game* doggedly retains this docudrama style, resolutely refusing to editorialize or over sentimentalize the power of its imagery. We see the impact of radiation sickness and the inability of the governing to provide succor to the shattered governed. We see that most abiding symbol of British authority, the bobby on the beat, armed with Lee-Enfield rifles, executing looters and euthanizing the fatally injured. Image after shattering image follows and the impact is bludgeoning. Only 50 minutes long, as *The War Game* closes, its cumulative effect is harrowing.

Watkins brilliantly uses his trademark blend of documentary, drama and instinctive journalistic skill to ask a range of questions about reality in the media. We watch as "actors" playing civil defense managers, war strategists and, in one case, an Anglican Bishop make a range of pro-nuclear weapons comments. Because of the way these interviews are staged, one assumes they were scripted by Watkins. It then crosses the mind of the viewer that, if these elements were scripted, then the vox-pop interviews also must have been. In fact, neither were. Watkins' scripted interviews are actually direct quotes from real people and the interviews with the public are also the real thing. In this case, then, perhaps the images portrayed during and after the fact were based on reality too.

The presentation of *The War Game* in the style of *World in Action* and its ilk was deliberate. Thirty years before *The Truman Show* and *EDTV*, Watkins was asking extremely awkward questions about information, reality and how the relationship between the two changes on the basis of presentation in the media. This was an extraordinarily brave approach, given that the BBC was the funding organization and may help to explain at least in part why, when Watkins screened the finished film, the BBC took the action it did.

Interviewed in the aftermath of his TV nuclear war movie *The Day After* (1983), Nicholas Meyer said, "ABC gave me millions of dollars to go on primetime TV and call Ronald Reagan a liar." So it was with *The War Game*. Watkins' research was clearly painstaking and exhaustive, and the upshot was an inevitable recognition that civil defense, in so far as it went in the U.K., was designed primarily to ensure the continuation of government, regardless of the state of those who would be governed. This was clearly unpalatable for the British government, as was the depiction of the failure of their policy of safety through deterrence. These two elements together represented sustained criticism of British government policy and that made the BBC nervous.

By 1965, as Watkins completed *The War Game*, Huw Wheldon had been promoted from the BBC's documentary department to Controller of Programmes for BBC2 and, as a result, Watkins was not shielded by his former boss from the politics within and without the organization. Senior executives were shown *The War Game* prior to its proposed screening as part of *The Wednesday Play* series on BBC1 in 1966. Alarmed by what they had seen, they invited the Home Office (then responsible for Civil Defence in the U.K.), the Ministry of Defence and the GPO to view the film.

The Home Office was, in fact, already aware that Watkins was making a program on nuclear war. Watkins himself had contacted them while researching *The War Game* for details on health service provision in the aftermath of a nuclear strike. Both the government and the BBC were acutely aware of the need to insure that the independence of the Corporation was not brought into question. However, according to investigative journalist Duncan Campbell in his book *War Plan U.K.*, senior governors were aware of the problems they would face. In their statement in November 1965, in which they announced that *The War Game* would not be shown, the BBC stated that "the film was too horrifying for the medium of TV" and that the decision had "not been made as a result of outside pressure of any kind."

Given that the current Chairman of the Board of BBC Governors was Lord Normanbrook, who had previously been Cabinet Secretary, and given that Sir Burke Trend (his successor in the Cabinet Secretary post) and other senior civil servants did see the film prior to the BBC decision not to broadcast it, it is difficult to shake the feeling that pressure was put on the BBC by the government. According to Campbell, Normanbrook himself recognized that *The War Game* represented an implicit criticism of the government's deterrence policy. If this was Normanbrook's opinion, it is not a significant stretch to suggest that he would have been concerned about how the government would have reacted to the showing of the film and the questions they might raise with regard to the BBC's political independence. The whole episode is almost a dry run for the crisis which enveloped the BBC and the Labor government relating to the reporting of the "weapons of mass destruction" justification for the war in Iraq in 2003, which led to the Hutton Inquiry.

Whatever the reasons behind the BBC decision not to screen *The War Game*, Watkins was rightly furious, resigned from the BBC and, after the critically mauled, barely shown but eerily prescient theatrical release *Privilege* (1967), left the country. His subsequent films, particularly *The Gladiators* (1968) and the brilliant *Punishment Park* (1970) mix satirical science-fiction riffs on contemporary political themes (East-West relations in *The Gladiators*, and the U.S. counter-culture revolution and reaction of the forces of authority in *Punishment Park*) with Watkins' cinema verité method. A highly political filmmaker with a cleverly confrontational style, he continues to make strongly personal films and remains one of Britain's most visionary and underrated directors, even if his work is largely ignored in his country of birth.

And what of *The War Game*? The BBC eventually permitted a short theatrical run in 1966 (it subsequently won an Oscar for best documentary short in 1967). Thereafter it was unavailable on these shores until the Corporation screened it in 1985 as part of its 40th anniversary programming related to the dropping of the Hiroshima and Nagasaki atomic bombs. By this time, of course, a number of TV films dealing with the subject (*The Day After*, *Testament* and *Threads*) had already been broadcast, so the original argument about the horrifying nature of *The War Game* didn't hold much water.

Viewing *The War Game* with 40 years' worth of hindsight, you'd think it would be easy to distance oneself from the impact of some of the imagery. It may not have the scope of *The Day After*, or the poignancy of *Testament*, but it was a clear influence on Barry Hinds' script for *Threads* and retains an urgency and a power, even now, to shock in a way that virtually no other film in British broadcast history has done. The Cold War may be over, but 30,000 nuclear warheads still exist and government policy remains the same. It does the soul good to know that people like Watkins are still watching. *The War Game* remains that rare thing, a genuinely harrowing TV experience, one that may have aged but certainly hasn't dated.
—Neil Pike

Credits: Director and Writer: Peter Watkins.
Leading Cast: Michael Aspel, Peter Graham, Kathy Staff, Peter Watkins.

1966

The Brides of Fu Manchu

1966: a time for heroes. England wins the World Cup, the Beatles are bigger than Jesus, Captain Kirk commands the Enterprise, Patrick Troughton is at the controls of the *Tardis* and Raquel Welch is in a fur bikini. Connery was Bond, John Steed teamed with Emma Peel, Dylan released *Blonde on Blonde* and Pickles the dog *saved* the World Cup. Heroes all!

Now what has this to do with *The Brides of Fu Manchu*? I hear you sigh. Well, everything.

Brides is the second in the series of Fu Manchu movies made throughout the late 1960s by Harry Alan Towers' production company Towers of London and is probably the best of the lot. (If there is a court of appeal at the end of one's life, then the Jess Franco Fu Manchu movies are admissible in court as hours stolen from you. Claim them back, no win no fee.)

This film series has one of the great pulp antagonists of 20th century literature, and Christopher Lee delivers a great performance, carefully treading the fine line between evil and ridiculous, pulp and panto. But this film, and indeed the other Fu Manchus, is missing one vital ingredient: a decent hero.

To be fair to the film, the problem lies with the source material. Sax Rohmer told the tales of our Eastern antagonist, beginning in 1913, with the serialized *The Insidious Dr. Fu Manchu* and publishing the villainous Asian's final bow with *Emperor Fu Manchu* in 1959. It is clear that the heroes, Sir Denis Nayland Smith and Dr. Petrie, are cut from the Sherlock Holmes and Dr. Watson cloth, but sadly without all the things that make Holmes and Watson fascinating. While Holmes is obsessive and suffers from an addiction, Nayland Smith looks like he could be very happy in front of a roaring fire with a cup of Horlicks. And let's face it, Dr. Petrie is no Dr. John H. Watson. In *Brides*, they are bland and uninteresting, plodding their way through the evil machinations of Fu Manchu, never once giving any indication that they could be a suitable match for the "giant intellect" of the "Yellow Peril." When a villain cries out, "You are no match for my power!" the audience really shouldn't be agreeing with him.

Humor is a real problem in this film, which takes itself very seriously and could have done with a bit of light relief. I felt it was crying out for a John Steed and Emma Peel combo to inject a bit of British eccentricity and dry humor. Douglas Wilmer replaces Nigel Green as Nayland Smith and does a passable job (although you can't help but imagine Peter Cushing in the part). Burt Kwouk gets a raw deal, spending a good deal of the film as the major henchman, Feng, but being dumped halfway down the credits for his trouble.

While there is nothing drastically wrong with *The Brides of Fu Manchu*, there isn't anything special about it, either. The story meanders along and limps across the finish line with the standard "The world shall hear from me again" line to signal

another sequel. To be honest, I'm not sure if the world was particularly bothered.
—Adam J. Marsh

Credits: Director: Don Sharp; Writer: Harry Alan Towers. **Leading Cast:** Christopher Lee, Douglas Wilmer, Marie Versini, Howard Marion-Crawford, Tsai Chin.

Carry On Screaming!

Just as big a part of British cinema as Hammer was in the 1960s, the *Carry On* series is fondly remembered by those of a certain age, myself included. Derided in their day, they now attract the kind of respect and admiration which I think they always deserved.

The famous film critic Barry Norman listed *Carry On…Up the Khyber* and *Carry On Cleo* as his favorites. Since then, most critics and magazines have followed suit and declared both to be the high point of the series. For me, *Carry On Screaming!* beats both to the top spot. Maybe it's my fondness for British horror, and Hammer in particular, but this is one comedy shocker that's almost pitch perfect.

Before I go any further, I'd like to hark back to the pre-video days. You know, when taping the theme from *The Pro-*

fessionals or *The Sweeney* with your new tape recorder was pretty exciting stuff. I had a lovely new tape recorder with a microphone at the end of a very short cable. *Carry On Screaming!* was being shown, so I sat in front of the TV with my trusty machine and taped the whole thing, audio only, obviously. As a result, I had an appreciation for the title song that far exceeded normal expectations. The singer, credited as "Anon," is often thought to be the movie's star, Jim Dale, but was in fact prolific big band vocalist Ray Pilgrim. Ray was in fine form as he belted out "Carry on screamin', cause when you're screamin', I know that you're dreamin' of me." Great line, eh?

Anyway, when the music ends and the movie starts, you could almost be forgiven for thinking it's the beginning of a Hammer horror. The sets, costumes and music are spot on. The fact that it was made at the height of Hammer's powers also helps, as the film stock and color are the same.

Jim Dale is ideally suited to the role of the naïve young hero. His comic timing is masterful and his physical comedy is just as good as his delivery. He reminded me of a calmer version of Jerry Lewis in this film and I've often wondered if he could have made it big in Hollywood if he'd tried, minor accomplishments at Disney notwithstanding. As it was, he turned out to be extremely successful on the American stage, so I guess that's where he was destined to be.

It's also nice to have Harry H. Corbett of *Steptoe and Son* fame as a main character. As much as I love the *Carry On* family, it was always refreshing to see other leads, and Harry is by far the best. His fabulous turn as the bumbling Inspector is every bit as enjoyable as his TV rag and bone man, and I'm amazed he wasn't used in more *Carry On* adventures.

Unusually for a spoof, *Carry On Screaming!* includes an iconic monster, and an original one at that. Oddbod and his offspring are fantastic creations—strange enough to give you a start on a dark night but ridiculous enough to make you giggle. To be honest, they're better than a lot I've seen in "proper" horror movies.

As good as the sets, lighting and design are, the real delight of this film is the cast. From the regulars, such as Kenneth Williams, Charles Hawtrey (as Dan Dann the lavatory man) and Joan Sims, to the newcomers, Corbett and the wonderful Fenella Fielding, it's comic genius all the way. Fielding is terrific as the tantalizing, vampish

temptress who lures Corbett toward her cleavage. As they recline on the couch and she asks, "Do you mind if I smoke?" the audience can see it coming a mile away, but it's still funny when those fumes billow from every inch of her delectable frame.

It's not merely the comic set-ups that make this worthy of attention. When Dan is in his basement office at the public lavatories he spies a strange set of feet from the pavement above; they belong to Oddbod, who's there to do him harm. Dan's death in the next scene made a marked impression on me as a young lad. Yes, it was funny, but the set-up and the execution of the scene was done so well it would have worked as a serious horror without the jokes.

From Kenneth Williams shouting, "Frying tonight!" as he dips another body into his molten wax to the reanimation of his Egyptian mummy Rubba-Ti-Ti, it's vintage *Carry On*. Yes, the humor is base and obvious but it's bloody funny and, although it spoofs my beloved Hammer, it never feels like it's mocking the studio. By the way, the cinema poster was painted by Tom Chantrell, who provided artwork for countless movies—including many Hammers—during the 1960s.

Carry On Screaming! delivers the laughs even now, managing to do so with care and affection for the source material. There's more to a spoof than just ripping off and broadening everything from the original (take note, *Scary Movie* producers). You have to fit a story around the humor, and *Carry On Screaming!* does that with ease. The fact that it features some of Britain's best comedy actors at the top of their game certainly doesn't do any harm.

Around the same time, director Roman Polanski tried his hand at a Hammer spoof with *Dance of the Vampires*. While it has its moments, it's not a patch on *Carry On Screaming!*—which only goes to prove how something that looks so simple actually can be the exact opposite.

—Matt Gemmell

The 12th *Carry On* film was the last to be distributed by Anglo-Amalgamated, and definitely keeps its end up. Ooh, matron. Actually, there's precious little innuendo in this one. The great Talbot Rothwell's script instead is peppered with wordplay and in-jokes, some quite clever, most of it groan-inducingly corny.

It's also blessed with a great ensemble cast at the height of their powers. The notable absentee is Sid James, who had commitments elsewhere. And so Harry H. Corbett, fresh from *Steptoe and Son*, rose to the occasion (snigger). Of course, even though playing a role written for Sid, Harry's a bit typecast (a musical nod to his rag 'n' bone man alter ego confirms the fact). But he's better than Sid would have been. Sid would have pulled off (now, now) the henpecked husband part, but he'd have flopped as the coy lover, the object of Fenella Fielding's vampish attentions. Corbett is floored where Sid would have "phwoarrr-ed."

The abduction of Angela Douglas is the event that sets the plot rolling. Her frustrated, would-be lover Albert Potter (Jim Dale), Detective Sergeant Sidney Bung (Corbett) and the bungling Detective Constable Slobotham (Peter Butterworth) come to her rescue, their only clue being a finger found at the scene of the crime. The trail leads to a spooky manor house where, inside, undead brother and sister team Orlando and Valeria Watt make a buck transforming kidnapped women into mannequins. Helping them in their nefarious business are Frankenstein's monster knockoffs Oddbod and Junior, a big, hairy pair if ever I saw one!

The principals are all in top form: Kenneth Williams and Fenella Fielding especially stick out. Well, Fenella does. It's the clinging red dress, see. She's sexy and seductive, and it's certainly her most memorable role. Williams is somewhere near his nostril-flaring best as a dapper, electrically charged zombie. Peter Butterworth treats us to the inevitable cross-dressing and mucho proto-Les Dawson mugging. Joan Sims is Bung's large, and largely bed bound, screeching harridan of a wife; and if you can last the duration without wishing Corbett would just smother her with her own pillow, you're a better man than I. Bernie Bresslaw and Charlie Hawtrey, though, are relegated to cameos, as Lurch-alike butler Sockett and Dan Dann (the lavatory man), respectively. Bresslaw's role could have been filled by anybody over six feet two inches tall, but Hawtrey makes his few minutes count. It's ironic, as the role was actually written for *Carry On Cowboy* graduate Sydney Bromley.

Carry On Screaming! is a very affectionate (and quite accurate) pastiche of Hammer horror films, hence its inclusion in this book. In fact, it captures the Hammer house style better than some Hammer pictures did! The sets and costuming are surprisingly lush, but it's the lighting by Alan Hume that really sets the tone. Hume's cinematography had previously graced Amicus' *Dr. Terror's House of Horrors* and, more pertinently, Hammer's *The Kiss of the Vampire*, so they were in safe hands.

Oh, it's a *Carry On* film. You know what to expect. So stop messin' about and watch it!

—Jed Raven

Credits: Director: Gerald Thomas; Writer: Talbot Rothwell.
Leading Cast: Harry H. Corbett, Kenneth Williams, Fenella Fielding, Joan Sims, Jim Dale, Charles Hawtrey, Peter Butterworth, Bernard Bresslaw, Tom Clegg.

Daleks' Invasion Earth 2150 A.D.

The second of Amicus' big-screen adaptations of *Doctor Who* adventures, *Daleks' Invasion Earth 2150 A.D.* is a pretty straightforward adaptation of the 1964 TV story *The Dalek Invasion of Earth*. Bumbling policeman Tom (Bernard Cribbins) fails to stop a robbery and stumbles into a nearby police box—"Tardis." One balks at imagining a "casual viewer" for this film but, just in case, "Tardis" is the "time and space machine" of Dr. Who (Peter Cushing).

Along with his curvaceous "friend" Louise (Jill Curzon) and granddaughter Susan (the returning Roberta Tovey, who'd later fuse another interesting connection between the Brit horror universe and family television by appearing alongside Robin Askwith in the bizarre but not unappealing 1969 U.S. TV movie *Hans Brinker*, based on the children's classic by Mary Mapes Dodge), Dr. Who travels just about everywhere, and this time ends up nearly two centuries in the future, where his old enemies, the ruthless Daleks, grotesque mutants traveling about in equally grotesque pepper-pot machines, have conquered Earth and intend to strip mine the entire planet in search of the solution to their one weakness. Who and his friends find they have to stop the Daleks' evil plan if they want to save the Earth and preserve their admittedly unique lifestyle choices.

For some people, *Doctor Who* is the greatest TV show ever made, and watching Amicus kingpin Milton Subotsky attempt a cinematic makeover with all the glitz and glamour of, say, *The Day of the Triffids*, can be a surprisingly (and enjoyably) surreal experience. Composers Bill McGuffie and Barry Gray seem to have been under the impression that they were scoring *Godzilla vs. Megalon*, and some of the special effects look more ridiculous than on the actual show, for which one automatically makes allowances for the wizened budgets the BBC had in those days. Terry Nation's classic monster creations (designed by Raymond Cusick) spray dry ice at people to kill them (rather than the cool "negative" effect used on TV), the wires flying the spaceships stand out all the more in glorious color, and the action sequences are sometimes unnerving in quite the wrong way.

Flemyng's direction is rather uninspired—which seems all the more obnoxious when one thinks that frequent *Who* director Douglas Camfield never got the chance to direct a feature film—and the tone shifts wildly throughout the movie. There's a certain amount of jokiness that's amusing but doesn't quite fit with the relatively serious subject matter of enslavement and exploitation. Cribbins does have a classic comic bit that would have gone quite nicely in a silent film, masquerading as one of the Daleks' robotized servants, but it clashes with some of the grimmer moments.

The acting is all right if nothing special. Again, Cushing gives one of the most unusual, stylized performances of his career, fittingly halfway between his usual persona and William Hartnell's dotty old panjandrum from the TV show. Some familiar faces from both the show and other British horror films surface throughout the film—notably Andrew Keir and Ray Brooks ("the boy with *The Knack*," as he's hilariously termed in the vintage trailer)—but the acting standout is frequent *Who* actor Philip Madoc as a feline, untrustworthy spiv. Madoc played some of the great villains on the show—notably the War Lord in *The War Games* (1969) and Solon in *The Brain of Morbius* (1976)—and watching him chill his scenes makes one sad that he never got to threaten heroes on the big screen, perhaps ideally directed by Camfield.

—Wendell McKay

Credits: Director: Gordon Flemyng; Writesr: Milton Subotsky, Terry Nation (BBC series).
Leading Cast: Peter Cushing, Bernard Cribbins, Ray Brooks, Andrew Keir.

Eye of the Devil

Eye of the Devil may be crap and far too long, and it may be black and white even though there's no reason for it to be, but it is a veritable roll call of Brit horror alumni and half-forgotten TV faces. For a start, not only does it have David Niven, Donald Pleasence, John Le Mesurier, David (*Blowup*) Hemmings and even Devon from *Knight Rider* in it, but it also features top '60s bird Sharon Tate. *And* it's also practically a

dry run for *The Wicker Man*. So there are a few reasons for digging it out.

Philippe de Montfaucon (Niven) is a French aristo without a hint of a French accent who has to return to the family pile when his grapes start failing (which as we all know is a painful business). He's followed there by his wife Catherine (also French and sans accent), who slowly deduces that things aren't what they should be and soon drops herself right in the merde.

There are Satanic rituals aplenty going on, and Philippe is in up to his neck. So is the local vicar (Pleasence), the doctor (Le Mesurier) and assorted mustachioed French peasants (both male and female). There are a couple of good bits: Catherine is chased though a forest by a gang of cowled figures at one point and later suffers a nightmare in which she relives this and any other vaguely scary bit from the film, with a few new scenes chucked in for good measure. Hemmings and Tate also wander around with a bow and arrow trying to get kids to jump off ramparts and turning toads into doves (like you do), but not even a bizarre scene where Niven gives Tate a good flogging (which she looks like she's enjoying just a bit *too* much for 1966) can save this one from being anything more than average.

—Chris Wood

Credits: Director: J. Lee Thompson; Writers: Robin Estridge, Dennis Murphy.
Leading Cast: Deborah Kerr, David Niven, Donald Pleasence, Flora Robson, Emlyn Williams, Sharon Tate, David Hemmings

The Frozen Dead

Nazis on ice? Well, stored in the refrigerator, at any rate. *The Frozen Dead* formed one half of a particularly paltry pairing from Goldstar Films in the mid 1960s, with director Herbert J. Leder also being responsible for *It!* starring Roddy McDowall, both titles being filmed at the Merton Park studios so beloved of fans of this type of material.

Leder's imported fading star for this earlier picture was Dana Andrews, playing a German scientist hidden away in the English countryside, having kept a number of military personnel in cryogenic stasis since World War II, waiting for the day when he can thaw them out in a bid to revive the glory days of the Third Reich. Unexpectedly, his young niece and her best friend turn up at his mansion (isn't that always the way—mad scientists?) and begin poking around in places they shouldn't, resulting in the lopping off of one unfortunate girl's head.

Cheap-looking, slow-moving and very, very silly— "unusually insane" is how Jonathan Rigby describes both this and its companion piece in *English Gothic—The Frozen Dead* is nevertheless memorable for the frequent scenes depicting the uniformed corpse-popsicles, the horde of failed zombie experiments huddled in the basement, and the wall of severed, electronically controlled arms (about as far removed from the poetry of Cocteau's *La Belle et la Bete* as possible, despite the visual similarities!).

As for the disembodied head, shot in an eerie blue-green light and with perspex-encased pulsating brain on display, this proves to be remarkably affecting, a real testament to the performance of Kathleen Breck who manages to convey the desperation, hopelessness and tragedy of her predicament to genuine effect. Deservedly taking center stage during the film's climax, Breck uses the power of her mind to control the adjacent row of dangling, strangling limbs before being featured in a quite stunning closing shot, mouthing the words, "Bury me" over and over again into the fade-out.

—Darrell Buxton

Credits: Director and Writer: Herbert J. Leder.
Leading Cast: Dana Andrews, Anna Palk, Philip Gilbert, Karel Stepanek.

The Hand of Night

The Hand of Night is one of the more offbeat British horrors of the 1960s, a rare and intriguing venture into the world of North African vampires. The Moroccan locations set the film apart from Hammer's standard Middle Europe ambience, and the film is pervaded by a fatalistic obsession with death, making it a virtual horror noir.

The film has its problems. The pace meanders, the Francophone accents make some of the dialogue hard to follow, and it has the most rubbish mechanical bat in a British horror film until *Scars of Dracula* claimed the title. However it's still a very interesting one-off, with medieval Moorish castles,

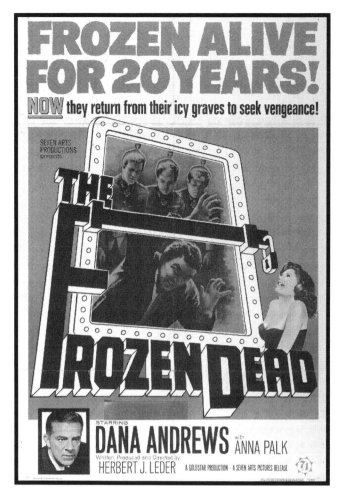

stark desert scenes, shadowy back streets and a background of African folklore creating a unique atmosphere.

Arguably not an outright horror, the film centers on bereaved architect Paul Carver (William Sylvester), who travels to Morocco on a whim after his wife and family are killed in an auto accident. Carver was driving the car and blames himself, believing that he is a "harbinger of death and desolation." He may well have a point, as the doctor he has arranged to meet on his arrival in Morocco turns out to have died the previous day.

In a vaguely amusing scene, he gets plastered in a local bar, feeling thoroughly sorry for himself and boring an unfortunate barman with a series of slurred existentialist banalities. Wandering the streets at night, he comes across sinister old man Omar who, in between bouts of overly theatrical cackling, says things like "The creatures of the day are one sort and the creatures of the night are others" and "Between light and darkness each must choose his side." Omar leads Carver to the sinister and alluring Marisa (ex-Miss Israel Alizia Gur), a vampiric siren who tells him, "The darkness isn't strange to those who dwell in it" (do you get an idea where this film is coming from yet?). Marisa is not your usual pointy-toothed, blood-sucking vamp, though. Her aim is seemingly to drain the life force out of the vulnerable and depressed such as Paul and pull them to the dark side.

Blonde Diane Clare (contrasting with "evil" nocturnal brunette Gur) plays Chantal, the assistant of archaeologist Gunther. She represents Sylvester's potential salvation, though one of the film's enjoyably offbeat touches is that her character is almost as ghoulish as Carver. Rather than offering sympathy when he tells her his family is dead, her first question is "Did you kill them?"

The film is boosted by a nice orchestral score from Joan Shakespeare, which sounds quite Morriconeesque in the vaguely psychedelic opening dream sequence of Carver at the funeral/wedding. It also makes an enjoyable travelogue of the period, and there is a nice contrast between the ancient and modern Morocco with scenes featuring a brand new airport and hotels that sprang up with the country's mid-1960s tourist trade.

The Hand of Night's leading man, William Sylvester was a decent supporting actor, whose career high point was playing one of the scientists in Kubrick's *2001: A Space Odyssey*. He also appears in three other 1960s Brit horrors: *Gorgo*, *Devils of Darkness* and *Devil Doll*. He's okay here, but you can't help wonder what someone like Peter Cushing might have done with the role in portraying Carver's inner turmoil and attraction to the night. The film's ending is especially bleak for the era, with seemingly little hope for Carver and Chantal to have a happy future together. Overall, *The Hand of Night* is no classic, but it is one of those interesting "little horrors" that crept out virtually unnoticed at the time and can now be enjoyed for its quirky and unique charm.
—Liam McLoughlin

I confess to an unfettered fondness for Frederic Goode's 1966 vampire film *The Hand of Night* (aka *The Beast of Morocco*). It sours opinion in most viewers early in its running time with a succession of simple but failed effects that many may consider should have been consigned to redundancy during the era of Georges Méliès. The camera cuts away from a body only to cut back to find it replaced by bleached bones. Fake bats flap, a square of linen "supernaturally" directs our protagonist but is clearly on a wire, and the first part of the film is a mess of day for night shots captured at dawn and dusk, nudging

the natural light up and down in reckless shades of blue. The blundering is so apparent in the first act that it is commonly overlooked that the film improves on its continuity during the remainder of the action.

The Hand of Night is unique. No other British horror uses Morocco as a backdrop and so no British horror shares *The Hand of Night*'s landscape or architecture. In the postwar period, development agencies were set up to improve the lot of the impoverished countries, and in the 1960s, the World Bank saw that a sensible answer to this lay in the financing of tourism in those countries through soft loans. By the mid-1960s, a new-look Europe coincided with the appearance of original resorts in more exotic locations. Morocco benefited well, and the mix of new hotels on the coast and the charm of the old perfected the range of attractions in the country.

One might have expected canny film producers to latch on to this and attempt to tap into that funding, on the basis that by filming on location in these countries they were promoting the new holiday resorts, though I have yet to identify a living producer from the era who can verify that this ever occurred. Genre films, particularly modern thrillers, heist capers, comedies and horrors, seized upon the new landscapes across Europe and into Africa and the Middle East in the 1950s, but it was in the 1960s, with the rise in color film production that a more vibrant flavor came of it.[1] Genre movies acted as travelogues and, for the British public who could now afford travel, helped to determine where their first holiday destination might be.

The Hand of Night is careful never to reveal actual locations. The airport is unnamed, and the action takes place on neat new roads in a city, in an old medina, in a deserted casbah (passed off as a palace), on the beachfront and in the desert. To name Rabat or Fez or Marrakesh or Essaouria would be to send the tourists in a single direction and the authorities would want the visitors to seek out all quarters. When Michael J. Murphy shot *Insights* in 1975, it was funded by the Greek tourist board and the arrangement was for the production to fulfil a demand to shoot in a set number of cities; the plot of the film was painfully aligned to that. In *The Hand of Night*, even the street signs are fake, a game tied to the film's theme of vampirism. The archaeologist Otto Gunther (Edward Underdown) lives on the Rue Eliakim, which translates as the street of those "whom God will raise up," and it is to this location that a group of survivors flock.

William Sylvester plays Steve Carver, an architect using whisky and relocation as a means of distancing himself from a recent tragedy in which his wife and two children were killed, whereas he escaped with barely a scratch. Only two months have passed, and he brands himself a harbinger of death, when on arrival he discovers that his new client, a doctor, has passed away overnight. In his pocket is a card with the name and address of Otto Gunther, whom he had met on the plane, having dreamt of him and a fellow archaeologist, Leclerq (William Dexter). He visits Gunther's home in the old quarter and finds a party in full flow, celebrating the discovery of a new tomb. A beautiful woman in traditional dress passes between him and a mirror, and an in-camera effect (in a technique borrowed from the 1931 *Dr. Jekyll and Mr. Hyde*) reveals that she has no reflection, though Carver is too transfixed on her person to notice this.

Gunther's assistant is a young French woman, Chantal (Diane Clare), who is unusually brusque when inquiring of the fate of Carver's wife and family. "Did you kill them?" she asks him with what at first seems to be an intense morbidity. Forthright and bold as she may immediately appear, she too is the victim of a tragedy. She has no family and her great love (Gunther's son) was killed while serving in the army. The film is a criss-cross of opposites, the lost and the found, life and death, light and dark, and just as Carver's occupation preempts construction, his new acquaintances' existences are in the aftermath of civilizations and fallen architecture. What they all have in common is an obsession with the dead, to which the dead respond.

The vampires arrive in the form of Marisa (former Israeli beauty queen Alizia Gur), a long dead Princess entombed alive by her jealous husband along with faithful servant Omar (Terence de Marney).[2] She is essentially a lamia, though scriptwriter Bruce Stewart is as unwilling to commit himself to any precise area of the occult as the makers are to a location. Following the death of his family, Carver sought to join them in darkness, and a desire to be one of the dead is the wish Marisa wants to grant him. Marisa has the looks but she is less interesting than Diane Clare's Chantal.

Clare has unfairly become a figure of derision, cast in dislikable supporting roles or wearing mannerisms that are out of time in a handful of 1960s horrors. In *The Hand of Night*, however, despite playing the most conflicted and contradictory character in her career, Clare is at her most likeable and intriguing. At first remote yet buoyant, then a touch callous, abrupt and sarcastic, she follows this with romanticism, affection, concern, tears, churlishness and playfulness, as the film allows her a broad arc. It is unfortunate then that the story reduces her to the role of damsel in distress before it reaches its end, watering down her character somewhat but at least allowing her to portray trepidation, fear and horror. In the cruel twist close, Carver, on whom hope had been revisited, appears to be removed from society again, a jabbering, prayer-dispensing lost soul upon whom Chantal can only look in desperation.

The small cast is well employed and several of the players would become favorites of the director and production company, appearing in other productions: de Marney and Dexter would appear in *Pop Gear* (1965) and *Death is a Woman* (1966); Underdown in *The Great Pony Raid* (1967); and Sylvester in *The Syndicate* (1968). Frederic Goode first filmed in the Middle East in 1961 for *Journey of a Lifetime*, and Associated British, the production company, would return several times during the 1960s, often for religious-themed work.

Terence de Marney had a string of early genre titles to his credit, including *Eyes of Fate* (1933), *The Unholy Quest* (1934), *The Mystery of the Mary Celeste* (1935) and *House of Silence* (1937). His Omar is a grubby role, harassing Carver

and capable of any wickedness. His death scene is the horror highlight of the film, not unlike the scorching of the vampires in open sunlight in Kathryn Bigelow's *Near Dark* 20 years later. Caught in the sun, he tries to outrun it and his desperation is tangible, his skin flaking and his eye bulbous. The sequence is topped by Omar stopping, forlorn; resigned to his destruction, he turns on his heels and then, following another cut, collapses into a pile of rags and bones.

William Dexter is playful, a personable adventurer always one step removed from the core action, and shielding himself from the painful, babbling company of an unoccupied American wife, Mrs. Perry (Sylvia Marriott). His character is well established by the dialogue: "In such extraordinary circumstances, madam, there is only one thing to do — en avant!" The characters are alive, the utterances occasionally surprising and real. Listening to Gunther talk with some credulity about vampirism, a frustrated Chantal snaps, "But you are talking like an idiot!" and the delivery is like a rocket, the final word hitting like a thunderbolt.

Joan Shakespeare's score soars and swoons thrillingly and provides a secure tempo for the proceedings. Bruce Stewart, no stranger to the unusual, anticipated the beauty of the Moroccan locations with an uncommonly romantic script. *The Hand of Night* reminds you of jigsaw box covers, comprised of rich colors and clean landscapes and capturing a time that would have been otherwise lost.

—Paul Higson

[1]The Moroccans have only recently produced their first populist home-grown horror feature, *Kandisha* (2008).

[2]An earlier nudie cutie exists, titled *The Vampire of Marrakesh*, possibly an American production; the vamp of the title is possibly more a temptress than a supernatural entity.

Credits: Director: Frederic Goode; Writer: Bruce Stewart.
Leading Cast: William Sylvester, Alizia Gur, Diane Clare, Terence de Marney, William Dexter.

Island of Terror

We've all seen those TV adverts in the middle of the afternoon for the Cancer Research Society. You know the ones: "Who can see a time when we've beaten cancer? We can." Of course, what they're failing to tell us is that when this happy time comes about, we won't be celebrating. Oh, no, we'll be cowering in fear from an onslaught of bone-eating carpets. That's the premise of *Island of Terror*, a great little sci-fi horror in the best tradition of "science runs amok on a small British island" flicks (see also *The Deadly Bees* and *Night of the Big Heat*). In fact, I'm going to go out on a limb here and state for the record that *Island of Terror* is one of the best of this mini-genre, if not the best. It's got everything: nasty effects, Peter Cushing, a fast-moving plot and the greatest radioactive cow massacre you've ever (not) seen.

There's a group of scientists hard at work off the British mainland, looking for a cure for cancer. Unfortunately, some-

Island of Terror

thing goes wrong in their laboratory, and it's not long before a duffel coat wearing chap goes to investigate a strange sound emanating from a nearby cave and dies horribly (well, it *sounds* horrible). The local bobby comes across the unfortunate man's body, and after much mugging into the camera, pokes it with his truncheon. It's gone soft. He rushes to tell the local doctor about his find, explaining, "His body is all like jelly. It's like nothing I've ever seen. There was no face—just a horrible mush with eyes sitting in it!"

The doctor goes to have a gander at this. His prognosis? The man's had his bones sucked out, probably due to some disease. He gets in touch with his mate Dr. Brian Stanley (Cushing), a pathologist, who in turn brings in *his* mate—a bone expert David West (the ever dependable, and always angry, Edward Judd). Stanley, West and West's latest girl Toni take her dad's helicopter and fly to the island (the helicopter must have cost the filmmakers a fortune—it gets far more screen time that it deserves).

Once on the island, we get our first look at the filleted body, which is reasonably effective, although nowhere near as gruesome as the policeman's enthusiastic description would have had us believe. After much fannying about with microscopes, Stanley and West decide they need better facilities, so they make their way to the laboratory seen at the beginning of the film (oh-oh). They discover more bodies, but still don't know what's causing the deaths. And now local farmers are finding their fields strewn with deflated horses. As one islander puts it, "There's some peculiar goings-on going on on this island…"

Finally, Toni is attacked by something as she sits in a car, but slightly unhelpfully, she can only describe it as "grayish." Cheers, love. Suddenly everyone's talking about "all those things running around," which is a bit rich considering that no one has actually seen them properly and lived to tell the tale! Back at the lab, our heroes finally get to see what they're up against: a bunch of slithering rugs with periscopes sticking out

of the front of them. Hitting them with an axe is a bad idea (as the unfortunate village doctor discovers to his cost) and they realize that, once they have fed on the bones of their victims, these "silicates" become inactive and then split in two. Although this gives the rest of the gang a chance to escape, it does pose another problem: within a week, there'll be over a million of the buggers on the island.

After discovering that guns, petrol bombs and dynamite don't work on the pesky things, it's finally made clear that radiation will work (hurrah for Strontium 90!). The only problem is, how do they permeate the silicates with the deadly energy? Why, by irradiating an entire herd of cows and sending them to be eaten, of course. In one of the most amazing scenes in 1960s sci-fi horror, we see Judd injecting cow after cow with lethal radiation, and the islanders packing the herd off toward the advancing silicates. The entire massacre is then relayed to us by a bored-looking Stanley and two villagers, who watch it through binoculars (we don't actually get to see it ourselves, as they'd obviously overspent on that helicopter at the beginning):

"Well, this is it."

"It's a nightmare."

"It's all over."

But as the silicates continue to advance on the villagers, will the offbeat defense mechanism work in time? And just what was Stanley going to do to Toni with that syringe? *Island of Terror* has a fantastic ending (despite the budget-saving off-screen cow massacre) which is genuinely exciting. Despite their looks, the silicates are extremely menacing; after all, they actually manage to severely disable Peter Cushing, so they must be capable of anything! And it's refreshing to see a 1960s science fiction film in which radiation isn't the threat, but the cure. (It's also great to see that wearing an enormous condom over your head will protect you from the ravages of Strontium 90. You don't believe me? Watch the film.)
—Chris Wood

Credits: Director: Terence Fisher; Writers: Alan Ramsen, Edward Andrew Mann.
Leading Cast: Peter Cushing, Edward Judd, Carole Gray, Sam Kydd, Niall MacGinnis.

It!

The only feature-length British movie to be based on the Eastern European legend of the Golem, *It!* is a peculiarly ambitious yet ultimately unsuccessful effort. Roddy McDowall plays Arthur Pimm, assistant curator at a musty, relic-filled museum, who discovers the ancient, eight-foot clay figure after a fire at a nearby warehouse. While Pimm's attentions are elsewhere, the impressive, imposing Golem appears to murder his boss (Ernest Clark at his most dapper and urbane), and Arthur starts to get ideas. Before long, he's controlling the gigantic stone man to do his bidding, corpses begin piling up, and the police take as much interest in Pimm as he has shown toward alluring museum employee Jill Haworth (paucity of budget allows for a modish hairdo for our fetching female lead, but unfortunately very little in the way of trendy accompanying outfits).

The addition of a would-be Norman Bates angle, with the nervous McDowall keeping his late mother's decayed body around the house for conversation purposes, over-eggs the pudding somewhat since Roddy's manic performance not only imitates that of *Psycho*'s Anthony Perkins, but at times anticipates the twitchy sarcasm of Jeffrey Combs in the later *Re-Animator*. As the film lumbers, much in the manner of its title character, to a close, the Golem manages to demolish Hammersmith Bridge before eventually being nuked by the armed forces; but, on an outlay of about one-and-ninepence, [$1.98 U.S.] I'll leave it to you to rate just how spectacular the achieved effects of these mediocre "highlights" really are. It probably all sounded great in the script.

—Darrell Buxton

Credits: Director: Herbert J Leder; Writer: Herbert J. Leder.
Leading Cast: Roddy McDowall, Jill Haworth, Paul Maxwell, Noel Trevarthen, Ernest Clark.

Naked Evil

"It's not just *evil*, it's…" Life in an unnamed British city seems pretty straightforward: Sleazy West Indian-run juke joints and Commonwealth students' hostels are both rigidly segregated. Or *are* they? A series of weird incidents and deaths convinces the local police and Inspector Hollis (Richard Coleman) that there's some connection between voodoo-related disturbances at "Spady's" (!) and the increasing malevolence that seems to affect both the nearby university and the church run by Reverend Goodman (Olaf Pooley). The gangs understandably clam up, while hostel rector Benson (Basil Dignam) and his assistant Alderson (Anthony Ainley) don't see how their prize pupils—many of whom are nascent scientists—could have anything to do with this literal mumbo jumbo.

Gang members, hostel staff and students begin to find obi (tokens of death or menace) crashing through nightclub windows and peppering their hallowed halls, not to mention all the bloodstained, sacrificed cockerels strung up in the surrounding trees. Not surprisingly, more than a few go a little batty as people start turning up either possessed or dead. As the craziness escalates, Hollis learns that star student Danny ("George A. Saunders," aka John Ashley Hamilton) and wizened old caretaker Amizen (Brylo Forde) may have more to do with the titular menace than he first imagined. Can he find who's been leaving the obi scattered around the city and stop them from causing more deaths?

Naked Evil, based on Jon Manchip White's play *The Obi*, is a bit of a mess, but an intriguing and fascinating one that yields both a few moments of genuine suspense and an interesting picture of how the British establishment saw the postwar immigration that permanently changed the face of their country. The convoluted plot mishmashes a variety of supernatural folkways, hinting at possible scientific influences on orthodox magical practices (including both voodoo and Goodman's Christianity), but disappointingly reverts to a rather traditional explanation and ending.

The West Indian (largely Jamaican, from the script's description) population alternately scorns and worships the old ways. (This is a lot more *Live and Let Die* than *I Walked with a Zombie*.) Their relationship with white authority figures is portrayed with a surprising degree of nuance (assuming it wasn't simply the direct, unthinking result of the filmmakers' own attitudes). Benson and Olverson want to "help" their students, but their assistance comes tinged with an authentic mid-1960s paternalism that frequently tends towards outright racism, especially in Benson's case, as he becomes more of a lush throughout the film. Jokes about "winds of change" and dancing abilities come and go, but it's worth watching simply to see Ainley "get down" in a way that makes *Scream and Scream Again*'s Julian Holloway look like Bootsy Collins. Goodman, on the other hand, is more of a Hammer period protagonist lost in *Naked Evil*'s quasi-swinging world and behaves accordingly ("It's really cool, man," he sarcastically smirks at one point).

Interestingly, the least objectionable character from such a perspective is the inspector: His scenes with gangster Lloyd

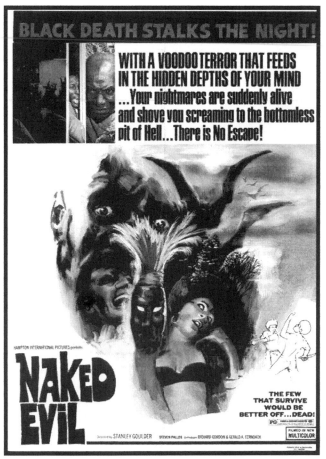

(Dan Jackson) have a natural, laid-back feel that makes one think that there are two different movies on offer here. That the script itself doesn't share their views (at least not entirely) is arguably proven through the sympathetic treatment of young lovers Danny and Spady's former "hostess" Beverley (future OBE Carmen Munroe), both well-acted and likeable characters who find themselves trapped between the harshness of gang life and the atavistic terrors of the voodoo world. While *Naked Evil* isn't exactly *good*, it's well worth a look for a few decent scares and some possibly unintentional social commentary.
—Wendell McKay

Credits: Director: Stanley Goulder; Writer: Stanley Goulder. **Leading Cast:** Anthony Ainley, Basil Dignam, Brylo Ford, Richard Coleman, Suzanne Neve.

Editor's note: The 2002 Region 1 DVD release from Image Entertainment includes *Exorcism at Midnight*, the 1973 American re-edit of the movie overseen by Sam Sherman, featuring several minutes of new color scenes starring Lawrence Tierney.

One Million Years B.C.

One Million Years B.C. is an iconic movie. How many boys at the time plastered their bedroom walls with images of its sexy star Raquel Welch and indulged in nights of hairy-handed, under the duvet shenanigans? And you can't blame them; she wears a fur bikini!

For once, Hammer supremo Michael Carreras loosened the purse strings for what was advertized as their 100th production, shipping cast and crew out to the Canary Islands under the guidance of *Jason and the Argonauts* director Don Chaffey. He was rewarded when the film went on to become Hammer's biggest smash. Ah, but does that mean it's any good? No, it's rubbish but, who cares, Raquel wears a fur bikini!

The film opens with swirling mists, stock footage and volcanoes puking porridge (yes, really). A portentous voiceover introduces us to a world "early in the morning of time." We meet Tumak (John Richardson), a member of the Rock Tribe. He wrestles a fake warthog, then pisses off his dad and is sent packing, only to be molested by a giant iguana with a rubber tongue. Oh, and we're only 27 minutes in; but, never fear, it's Raquel in… (Well, you get the picture.)

As cavegirl Loana, Raquel in her prime insures this film needs very little else. That we have the equally gorgeous Martine Beswick on top is a bonus. (Did I say "on top"? Maybe I should rephrase that, or I'll never get this finished.)

Soon a giant turtle appears, the work of stop-motion special effects genius Ray Harryhausen. Loana dramatically rolls away from the turtle very slowly, probably so as to not mess up her hair, and takes Tumak back to her tribe. They're not keen 'on him at first (he's got rotten table manners), but he proves himself by saving a little 'un from a raging Allosaurus attack, so that's okay. However, Loana's would-be suitor gets jealous of his bird sniffing around this newbie, and kicks him out of the tribe. So, Tumak ends up wandering the wastelands with Loana in tow, like it's some sort of punishment. He eventually gets her back to his cave, the lucky bastard. As far as plot goes, that's about it.

Throughout the movie, the cast babbles an unintelligible language consisting of about three words, most often "akita." But what does it mean? As Elton might croon, "Oh, akita, you will never know."

As you may have guessed, it's impossible to take *One Million Years B.C.* seriously. Quite frankly, it's stupid. For the

most part, however, it entertains, not least due to the rampaging dinosaurs. Oh, the dinosaurs! Next to Raquel's legs, they're the saving grace of this film, and Harryhausen delights with his creations throughout. Best of all is a triceratops in deadly combat with a ceratosaur. Indicative of Harryhausen's skill is when the ceratosaur lies in its death throes, its belly rising and falling. Now that's attention to detail. If that titanic clash wasn't enough, we also get Loana going head to head with the dark-haired Nupondi (Beswick) in a sweaty cavegirl on cavegirl brawl. It makes you feel you want to get your club out and have a bash yourself.

As crap as it is, *One Million Years B.C.* kicked off a short cycle of such films, and is a masterpiece next to *Slave Girls*, made the following year on the same sets. It was also prescient in introducing 1960s audiences to the concept of smelly, long-haired layabouts; the following summer, London would be crawling with them. It's all Hammer's fault—it really is.
—Jed Raven

Credits: Director: Don Chaffey; Writer: Michael Carreras.
Leading Cast: Raquel Welch, John Richardson, Percy Herbert, Robert Brown, Martine Beswick.

The Projected Man

There are those who shudder at the words "Tony" and "Tenser" on a film's opening titles, the very name heralding the prospect of cheap movies with rubbish production values and no moral worth, which rip off any passing cinematic genre in a desperate bid to generate quick box-office profits. And then there's sensible folk like you and I who respond to this opinion with a quick "Yeah, and your *point*?" and settle down for the ride 'cause we know that cheap movies with rubbish production values are pretty gear and even, I might venture, where it's at.

And *The Projected Man* is where it's at indeed. Really, there's a lot to like.

The film opens with two scientists fiddling around in a research foundation laboratory, doing that scientist thing where one of them says something like "laser pre-heat" and the other repeats it while twiddling a few knobs and turning some disco lights on and off. These scientists are *faux* sandy-haired Professor Paul Steiner (craggy—okay, pock-marked—Bryant Haliday, who played the ventriloquist Vorelli in *The Devil Doll* [1964] to great effect) and Dr. Mitchel (Ronald Allen, infamous for his role as the camp as a row of tents motel manager, David Hunter, in the popular 1960s and 1970s soap *Crossroads*).

Steiner and Mitchel are carrying out experiments in matter transportation—the projection of solid objects over long distances using laser technology—does any of this sound familiar? Well the original story for the film, by Frank Quattrocchi, dates back to the 1950s, so I leave you to draw your own conclusions about influences.

Anyway, where was I? Oh, yes, the experiments. Well, flashy and noisy they may be in execution, but the results—not so much. In the course of three "projection" demonstrations, they manage to kill a guinea pig, set someone's watch running

backwards, and nearly put someone's eye out when they lose control of the laser projector in a big lab explosion. Steiner ropes in Doctor Hill, a pathologist with a past romantic attachment to Steiner (Hill's a *she*, if you're wondering), but evil deeds are afoot.

It turns out that the lab explosion was a bit of planned subterfuge, and that this ground-breaking knob twiddling project is the subject of much internal politics within the research facility. Bow tie wearing Foundation Director Doctor Blanchard, manipulated by two ministry "puppet masters" (who are often seen in smoking jackets, swilling brandy, and directing the action from the comfort of their club), attempts to put the kibosh on Steiner's breakthrough, thus discrediting him. The pressure's on, though: Failure to achieve said discreditation will result in the ministry types releasing certain, er, details about Blanchard's life into the public domain—all very fraught.

Blanchard's sabotage has the desired effect, and Steiner's project is shut down. Back at the lab, an enraged Steiner, desperate to prove the machine's potential, enlists Blanchard's dopey secretary, Sheila (later her clothes will fall off), to do the knob twiddling and disco light operating while he shows the powers that be a thing or two and—you guessed it—successfully projects himself. Actually, make that just "projects himself." I suppose the word "successful" should only be employed if, as part of the experiment, you *intended* to refashion your face to look like it's permanently wearing an all-day breakfast. Yes, the projection's a failure (Sheila twiddled the knobs in the wrong order) and Steiner emerges looking none too hot.

From here the film moves firmly but somewhat disappointingly into monster on the loose territory. Steiner's half messed-up fizzog, complete with an eggs over easy eyeball, isn't his only post-projection adjustment. He also carries a lethal charge of electricity from one of his equally messed-up hands. Now all this could have been quite frightening, and while Bryant Haliday's makeup is inventive (apparently about a quarter of the film's budget was spent on special effects), sadly its facial coverage lends his speaking voice an unusual quality, muffling his post-projection diction to the point where it resembles that dog who used to say nothing but "sausages" on *That's Life*!

Anyway, hell-bent on revenge and flash frying his enemies, Steiner wanders the suburban streets of London despatching various ne'er-do-wells like Blanchard and one of the ministry puppet masters, but sparing dopey Sheila (whose clothes don't really fall off—she just gets undressed and then forgets to put anything back on—but, as the actress involved was a former model, and it *was* the 1960s, I don't *think* it was gratuitous), Dr. Mitchel and his new love interest Dr. Hill (oh, I forgot to mention that they'd become an item during all the carnage; and, yes, Hill's *still* a she, if you're wondering). Finally, after a bit more wandering around, during which Steiner attempts to top up his power by plugging himself into the Battersea station—and, no, we never get to see how that would have been achieved—we all end up back in the lab where Steiner, in a last self-sacrificial act driven by his professional and emotional defeat, destroys all the lab equipment, turning the laser machine on himself and getting vaporized in the process.

Cobblers? You betcha. Exciting? Not particularly, but worth an hour and one-half of your time if you are in any way interested in cut-price British science fiction and horror.
—David Dent

After having his key presentation to a leading scientific expert sabotaged, a scientist (Bryant Haliday) makes the mistake of using his dumb secretary (Tracey Crisp) to help him in an ambitious matter transportation experiment and ends up as (one character helpfully describes him) *The Projected Man*.

This derivation of *The Fly* was taken from an old script by Frank Quattrocchi, rejected by AIP, and subsequently considered by expatriate producer and wheeler-dealer Richard Gordon to make the perfect double-bill filler to accompany *Island of Terror* when he sold the U.S. distribution rights. In the U.K. market, since Tony Tenser's Compton company had the rights, it was an A picture and double-billed with *Passport to Hell*. Classified as a B feature in the States, it was cut from 90 to 78 minutes, and U.S. audiences still haven't seen the full-length British version. They have also had to suffer a chaste take of the scene in a mortuary in which a naked female corpse is uncovered for our pleasure.

Apparently, novice director Ian Curteis found it all too difficult, was fired toward the end of the shoot and replaced by production supervisor John Croydon. These production problems aren't apparent on screen, where most of the action unfolds in stiflingly long takes, many of which are in excess of one minute. No wonder these films use a lot of stage actors in the supporting roles, as at times we seem to be watching a filmed play.

Mary Peach gets top billing over Haliday for, frankly, a disposable role as his fellow scientist and ex-girlfriend who annoys him by taking up with his other assistant, future *Crossroads* star Ronald Allen. This didn't help Peach's declining career at all and, by playing the role too straight-laced, she manages to get totally upstaged by Tracey Crisp, who can't act at all but does provide several gratuitous bikini scenes. Meanwhile, an odd group of villains proves the main adversary for Haliday, comprising a short Andrew Keir look-alike who always wears a bow tie, a civil servant who is shaking so visibly, even when he's supposed to be dead, that he seems to be suffering from Parkinson's disease, and an unnamed and unaccredited chief villain who strokes a cat like Blofeld in the James Bond films.

And what of the Projected Man himself? Well, he kills by electrocution with one touch, is impervious to bullets, and is horribly disfigured with a big white sightless eye and some big buck teeth. However, the other side seems normal and he appears in total control of his faculties. These logical inconsistencies are brushed off with an "anything could have happened when the process was interrupted" excuse. The horror makeup itself, though, is pretty good for this kind of cheese, although alarmingly inconsistent in application from scene to scene; sometimes it's grey-ish, in other shots it has a red glow with pulsating veins.

If I'd popped down to see this at the flicks in 1966, I'd probably have had quite a good time. The title monster is sufficiently different in appearance to anything I had seen before, the laboratory actually look like a proper laboratory and equipment rather than the contents of someone's garage. There's some explosions at the end, a brief view of some bare breasts and more than a few unintentional laughs.
—Tim Rogerson

Credits: Director: Ian Curteis; Writers: John C Cooper, Peter Bryan.
Leading Cast: Bryant Haliday, Mary Peach, Norman Woolland, Ronald Allen.

The Psychopath

Appropriately for a book titled *The Shrieking Sixties*, we come to a film made midway in that decade which was promoted with the tagline "A New Peak in Shriek!" But this Freddie Francis picture, his first color psycho-thriller after a run of similar black and white subjects made for Hammer, in fact contains very little to shriek about. Though not exactly a *bad* film, it's more like "A New Apogee in Apathy" thanks to some very listless and half-hearted performances (with the honorable exception of Patrick Wymark as Inspector Holloway), poorly paced murders which fail to generate any tension or suspense, and some inappropriately sedate soundtrack music which totally dilutes the dramatic impact certain key scenes should deliver.

Particularly wooden are the awful, female romantic lead Judy Huxtable (cast because her father was one of the financial backers) and the inevitable token Yank, Don Borisenko, as her boyfriend. The plot (script by Robert Bloch from his own story) is another version of the old thriller favorite "ex-members of Allied War Crimes Commission get knocked off one by one," supposedly spiced up by the addition of another hackneyed genre cliché, "Crazy Old Dame in Wheelchair who Talks to Dolls." This is embittered war widow Mrs. Von Sturm, played with hammy relish by Margaret Johnston. "Zey are my children," she says, surveying her parlor packed full of creepy toy figures, enough to supply the cast of the entire *Puppet Master* franchise.

After preview screenings of the final product, the ever interfering Milton Subotsky altered the denouement, which he thought too obvious: "We changed the whole last scene with post-synched dialogue, and that way we changed the murderer!" He needn't have bothered since, despite the contrived and often incoherent plot (including some feeble attempts to fob us off with several red herrings; the doctor's assertion that the old girl's paralysis is psychological rather than physical being a particularly desperate ploy to explain how she is able to wheel herself all the way across town and gain entry to a locked house, unaided and unseen) and notwithstanding Subotsky's meddling, it's *still* patently obvious all along who's behind the vendetta.

To be fair, the film does have some points of interest. The opening murder is fairly gripping. A man is repeatedly run over by a car (nothing graphic, but the violin he was carrying being reduced to matchwood under the wheels is a nice visual metaphor). There

are a couple of other interesting touches: the automatic doors of the crippled woman's house swinging open—and menacingly shut—make for an eerie update of the traditional self-closing portals in countless Old Dark Houses and Gothic castles, and the shot of Prime Suspect (no names, no pack drill) being crushed in thick coils of heavy anchor chain which cuts to a pile of spaghetti bolognese being twisted round a fork is a nice, sick detail.

Unfortunately, that's as good as it gets. Francis does his usual competent directing job, with a number of subtle traveling shots, lengthy single takes, eye catching framing and multiple camera set ups, and it's to his credit that he manages to make at least a sow's ear out of the load of offal he's given to work with. But you know a film has a problem when the best acting comes from secondary characters. "Personally I wouldn't want to sell anything you couldn't cuddle," says the slightly camp and disaffected toy shop owner, in a great little cameo by Harold Lang (Roy Castle's agent in *Dr. Terror's House of Horrors*); and, as the sour ever disgruntled doctor, Colin Gordon effortlessly gives a better performance than any of the "stars."

The next few Amicus films (*The Deadly Bees*, *The Terrornauts* and *They Came from Beyond Space*) were far worse. Thanks to Wymark's solid central performance, Francis' professional direction and a certain amount of eye-catching cinematography, *The Psychopath* never quite sinks to the putrid depths of those stinkers.
—Mike Hodges

Milton Subotsky's Vulcan Films achieved synchronicity with the shock structure of the film version of *Psycho* in their *The City of the Dead*, directed by John Llewellyn Moxey. The same producer's Amicus company then courted the original novel's author, Robert Bloch, through the adaptation of his short story "The Skull of the Marquis De Sade" into the feature-length *The Skull*.

Bloch had followed up his initial big screen success by writing scripts for low-budget horrors in the United States (*The Night Walker*, *Strait-Jacket*, *The Cabinet of Caligari*). They were not greatly received. Amicus had three successful horrors in the bag (the aforementioned two

The Psychopath

and *Dr. Terror's House of Horrors*) including the Bloch story, and the author probably saw the British-based company as the substantive alternative worth clamping onto. It was a cruel irony, then, that Amicus' three-picture deal with Paramount and its fantastic run with the horror film genre concluded with two poor movies supported by Bloch scripts.

Bloch conceded that the script for *The Psychopath* was below par. The film fails to excite as much on the visual level as it does on the spoken. There is a mild attempt at the infusion of some potentially controversial historical context, as the film places the cause for the series of murders on the actions of a corrupt allied commission. The prime suspects are the surviving Von Sturms, the widow, Ilsa (Margaret Johnston), now in a wheelchair and in a rapidly crumbling mental state, and a son Mark (John Standing). The family abbreviated by injustice is extended again by a large collection of dolls that Ilsa refers to as "mein kinder." Bloch appears to lightly amuse himself with a Teutonic theme (a poisoning using prussic acid, for instance) but is never committedly engaged in this as a thread. Mark is not overshadowed by his plastic siblings and remains his mother's "liebling," the gentle son; however, his leather jacket, dyed blond hair and uber cool demeanor scream of dangerous camp.

The killer's modus operandi shifts for the benefit of audience interest from automobile to poison to blowtorch and rope, but at each murder a doll is left behind. The heads are modeled in wax to close facsimiles of the victims, the clothes and accessories (a noose in one case) are also authentically reproduced to scale. When Frank Saville is poisoned, the killer even has the perspicacity to anticipate his dressing gown. Ilsa, a dollmaker, has her wheelchair act as an alibi, and Inspector Holloway (Patrick Wymark) visits Mark at the boatyard where he is employed, somewhat undemandingly, as security. Mark's private library of "abnormal psychology" indicates that, during the writing of *The Psychopath*, Bloch was not that greatly removed from the Bates Motel (in the novel, Bates collected similar literature). Though, in his short fiction, Bloch commonly explored fantasy and comedy, the novels predominantly acted as psychopathological studies, as if these were the only tales worthy of lengthy exploration. His short fiction is fun but never overly descriptive, and his screenplays often followed suit.

The budget for *The Psychopath* insured that the sets were as sparse in the decoration as the screenplay was in its detail. Scenic curtains or painted backdrops might be expected outside of doors and windows, but such fake exteriors look onto impenetrable night instead. Rooms are oversized but underdecorated. Johnston's doll collection is chucked together without finesse and her character's lifestyle is unbelievable. Reality is remote and any claim to affectation in the film's appearance would be dishonest.

Yet there are fizzes of promise. The waxen effigies sculpted by Irene Blair Hickman are impressive. The opening murder is a hypnotically drawn out sequence in which there is continuous gentle movement, be it by the camera or within the frame, in pans to the right, in static shots of a car window winding up and a tire going down, all of this beautifully pointed and paced by cinematographer John Wilcox. The car prowls the victim Klemer just as later the noose will stalk Ledoux (Robert Crewdson) through the junkyard. Patrick Wymark is, as ever, a solid presence as Holloway, and there are some strong supporting performances (Johnston, Standing, Crewdson, Knox and Thorley Walters) but the lead couple are bland. Don Borisenko is forgettable as the American boyfriend and Judy Huxtable is no more than a beautiful zombie; she is not so much wooden as positively balsa.

The dialogue rarely goes anywhere interesting, but an effete doll seller does have one great line when assessing the changing tastes in the toy market: "All bombs and rockets—aggressive plastic in rather vindictive colors—personally, I'd never want to sell anything you couldn't cuddle." The film also has some structural eccentricity as it takes a slow buildup between deaths one and two before the culpable quartet are finished off in one fell swoop with a double kill, leaving the film having to find a new direction with considerable time to run. There is an additional victim, which begins to account for the illogical number of doll bodies originally purchased. This refresh button, though, is reputedly not all by design, and the substantial third act is in part serendipitous, the result of a short-falling script. A certain running time had to be met, and there was a need to complete it with some ad hoc additional scenes drawing on the remaining cast and locations, knocking square pegs into round holes. Indeed, without them, *The Psychopath* could have been even duller.

—Paul Higson

Credits: Director: Freddie Francis; Writer: Robert Bloch.
Leading Cast: Patrick Wymark, Margaret Johnston, John Standing, Alexander Knox, Thorley Walters.

Rasputin — The Mad Monk

Mad? He was bloody furious, I can tell you. Hammer's overwrought entry into the almost-straight historical drama-cum-horror genre is actually a bit of a masterpiece, despite being saddled with crap production values and a galloping lack of actual historical accuracy. It's also Christopher Lee's finest Hammer hour, as he finally gets the chance to cut loose and be what he is, a larger than life ham.

Lee's turn as the original hairy krishna is actually what makes the film so good. From his overpowering entrance into the bar at the beginning (he looks *huge*) to his eventual over the top murder, he overshadows everyone else (literally, at some points). It's the part he was born to play, and he knows it. Whether he's out-drinking an entire pub, seducing and then abandoning Barbara Shelley, or plotting the murder of the Tsarina, he's never less than brilliant.

Unfortunately, Lee's powerhouse performance is pretty much the whole film. Produced back to back with *Dracula — Prince of Darkness*, *Rasputin* shares identical sets, the same cast and even the same wardrobe (by the look of it), which tends to detract from the proceedings slightly. When our villain eventually does get thrown from the castle walls, you half expect him to land on Dracula as he frantically scrabbles to stay afloat on his ice floe. They're that similar.

And as Russia's greatest love machine hypno-murders, acid chucks and hand lops his way through the cast, you tend to find yourself on the side of the far more interesting and less cardboard-like Lee. All the other characters are just there to be mutilated, driven insane or chucked off the battlements. The final scenes are fantastic, though, as everyone finally decides they've had enough of the by-now bonkers (never mind just mad) monk, who, in best Jason Voorhees-style, refuses to lie down when poisoned, etc.

Rasputin — The Mad Monk may be mild compared with the excesses of the other stuff Hammer was churning out at the time (there's no throat cutting, heart staking, zombie beheadings, or hideous snakebites to contend with), but where it scores is in its (shaky) basis in historical fact, Lee's tremendous presence, and the fact that 1970s silver-clad funksters Boney M wrote a song about it. It doesn't get better than that.
—Chris Wood

Credits: Director: Don Sharp; Writer: John Elder [Anthony Hinds].
Leading Cast: Christopher Lee, Barbara Shelley, Richard Pasco, Francis Matthews, Dinsdale Landen, Suzan Farmer.

The Reptile

Ever watchful of their budgets, Hammer began filming *The Reptile* just five days after *The Plague of the Zombies* wrapped, utilizing the same sets, the same director (John Gilling) and some of the same cast. It's from the brief mid-1960s period when the studio was attempting to diversify beyond their Frankenstein and Dracula franchises. *The Reptile* is a great little movie with an intriguing (if silly) new monster, a fine example of Hammer's oeuvre.

A newlywed couple, Harry and Valerie Spalding (Ray Barrett and Jennifer Daniel), inherit the Cornish home of his brother after he dies in mysterious circumstances. The locals, including "Mad" Peter (John "*Dad's Army*" Laurie), ascribe the brother's fate — and that of other previous victims — to the "Black Death." "He won't be the last. You'll see," he remarks to cuddly landlord Tom Bailey (Michael Ripper). What a ray of sunshine he is. He'll be saying, "We're all *doooomed*" next…

The locals are hostile to the newcomers, but Bailey takes them under his wing. "They don't like strangers in these parts," he says, a line you *imagine* Ripper says in every film; he doesn't, it's just this one. Other villagers soon make themselves known, such as the brusque Dr. Franklyn (Noel Willman), who lives nearby and seems to be hiding something. When confronted with the body of the unfortunate Mad Peter, Franklyn unconvincingly dismisses his black face and foam-flecked chin as being down to a simple fit. Oh, yeah, and spontaneous human combustion is just a spot of heartburn, mate.

One afternoon, Franklyn's daughter Anna (Jacqueline Pearce looking fragile and lovely) appears uninvited at the Spaldings' home and makes Valerie's acquaintance. However, Anna's visit is cut short by Franklyn's manservant (Hammer regular Marne Maitland). He's been popping up everywhere being all sinister and Indian, the cad. Franklyn subsequently arrives and wills the girl to return home, but not before she's invited the couple to dinner. That night Anna impresses all with her dynamite sitar playing, but when the doctor goes all Pete Townshend and busts up her instrument, he rather puts a damper on the proceedings. I'd understand if it was bagpipes! Meanwhile Harry and Bailey have taken to digging up coffins in an attempt to get to the heart of the mystery and realize all the victims have suffered a mysterious bite to the throat.

The Reptile is a mystery that unfolds at a leisurely pace, but is no less interesting for that. Unfortunately, the DVD case all but gives away that mystery, so it doesn't seem unfair to talk about the titular "snake woman," the perpetrator of the attacks. Roy Ashton's makeup job is certainly memorable and striking (no pun intended). The point at which she emerges from darkness to put the bite on Barrett still packs a punch.

The cast is good. Barrett and Daniel are engaging and attractive; Pearce is suitably tragic; Willman effectively plays a man beaten into a corner, unable to save his daughter from a fate

she doesn't deserve; and Maitland is creepy as he doesn't blink for minutes on end. Maybe he has no eyelids, unlike the snake woman! And there's a nice, if brief, comic turn from Laurie. But Michael Ripper's the star here. He's given a meatier role than usual and makes the most of it. And, what do you know, it ends with a big fire. What more do you want from a Hammer movie, Peter Cushing?
—Jed Raven

A spiritual companion piece to Hammer's other keynote femme-monster movie *The Gorgon*, this was also the second of John Gilling's exquisitely realized Cornish chillers, following the haunting *The Plague of the Zombies*. Whereas *The Gorgon* is remembered chiefly for its clunky monster makeup, this movie is able to make the most of Roy Ashton's work. Afforded a juicy red-eyed/fanged close-up an hour in, *The Reptile* is one of the studio's most horrific original creatures.

In a typically atmospheric, eerie prologue, a hapless Victorian gent, pursued by an unseen monster, winds up looking like a forgotten star of *The Black and White Minstrel Show*, albeit with an additional "foaming at the mouth" party piece for the viewers at home. Inheriting the victim's cottage in a quaint Cornish village, his brother (Ray Barrett) and sister-in-law (Jennifer Daniel) soon realize something funny is going on.

Frightened publican Michael Ripper, in an unusually prominent role, mutters ominously, "They don't like strangers in these parts." John Laurie's "Mad" Peter ("not mad, just a little vague!"), a local nutter for local people, displays questionable table manners in between doom-laden warnings ("This is an evil place"). And stern doctor Noel Willman tries to unconvincingly pass off the increasing number of bizarre fatalities, referred to by the villagers as "the black death," as being the result of epileptic fits (!).

We know, however, that his unfortunate daughter (the excellent Jacqueline Pearce) is the reptile-woman whose fate was sealed when her dad pissed off a snake-worshiping cult during his travels in the East. Jacqueline is a pretty young woman, with a good sense of humor, nice hair, a fondness for biting people and a mildly irritating habit of shedding her skin every winter.

Muted in terms of on-screen action and horror, and ending conventionally with a cathartic fire, this movie may lack the blood and cleavage of Hammer's better known works, but fine performances and beautifully nuanced direction mark it as a quality production all around. The effectively rainy, ambient backdrop proves perfect for a steadily unfolding plot full of strange deaths and gloomy exhumations.
—Steven West

The Reptile

Credits: Director: John Gilling; Writer: John Elder [Anthony Hinds].

Leading Cast: Noel Willman, Jacqueline Pearce, Jennifer Daniel, Ray Barrett, Michael Ripper, Marne Maitland.

Theatre of Death (aka Blood Fiend)

Theatre of Death is cursed by association, really. I know I can't be the *only* person ever to have taped it expecting to see Vincent Price, Diana Rigg and assorted violent Shakespeare-related deaths. Unfortunately, what you get (instead of the awesome and similarly titled *Theatre of Blood*) is one and one-half hours of un-gory melodramatics, saddled with a bland and derivative Christopher Lee performance. The titles won't do anything to impair your false sense of security, either, featuring, as they do, lots of photographs of skulls with eyeballs popping out of them etc (à la those Dennis Wheatley novels of the mid-1970s).

"This building, located in the back streets of Paris... its speciality is horror," Julian Glover's sonorous voiceover tells us, after we're treated to an unconvincing guillotining, "together with murder, mystery and mayhem make up the principal ingredients of... the *Theatre of Death*." Oh, if only. Anyway, on with the "plot."

Charles (Glover—why are they always called Charles?) is our square-jawed, stiff upper-lipped, What's he doing in Paris?- English hero. His girlfriend Dani works at the Théâtre de Mort, which is run by a bloke called Darvas (Lee). At a "swinging" party, we find out that Darvas enjoys spying on his guests through eyeholes in paintings (one of the few actual times *that* old clunker appears in a Brit horror, by my reckoning). Darvas makes his grand entrance to the party after a spot of fortune telling goes wrong for Dani's roommate Nicole and immediately starts barking orders at people, showing off his very hairy knuckles and scaring small children with his Noel Gallagher eyebrow and bad hair combination.

Poor Nicole appears to be under the influence of Darvas, and nearly kills her friend Dani during rehearsals for a witch-burning segment in the theater's new show. Meanwhile, Charles (who, it turns out, is a pathologist) has been called in to investigate three murders, in which a strange-shaped blade has been used to stab the victims in the neck and drain them of all blood. As another tramp is offed (the action freeze-framing before anything of interest happens) and Nicole moves in with Darvas and his amazing hypno-ray eyes, Charles comes to the conclusion that the murders are the work of a "haemotagiac" or, to put it another way, a vampire.

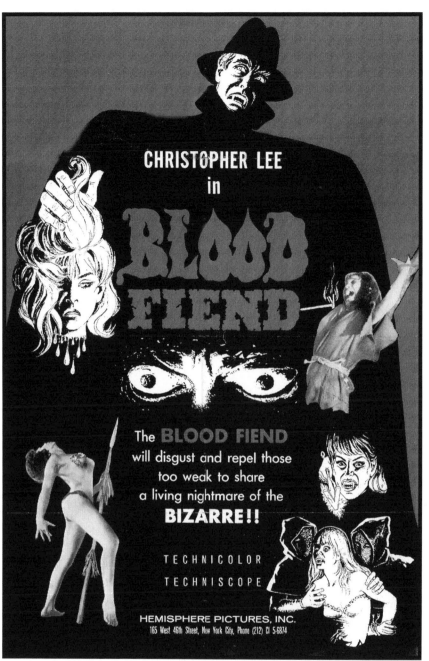

The plot muddles along, with mucho kettledrums and bongos on the soundtrack for some late-1960s reason, with everyone (including Charles) suspected of being the murderer before Darvas goes missing. But is he the murderer, or has he already been killed?

To be fair to the film, it does turn on a rather spectacular twist towards the end, only to ruin it with a huge and pointless chase. *Theatre of Death* is an okay way to spend 90 minutes, but it just isn't hugely exciting. For a vampire flick, there's a shortage of actual vampires, very little blood, and not enough of the awful women in it (particularly the whinging Dani) actually get killed. I'd suggest you make the effort to watch *Theatre of Blood* instead.
—Chris Wood

Gwen threatens to tell all, and someone, probably a lazy stagehand, plants the same tribal props from the opening sequence in her bedroom, inducing a breakdown. She's packed off to a home for a long while until the drama has reached a decent duration (or until Gwen "regains her memory"). She returns in time for some of that old black magic at the coven's performance dance contest.

Of course it's blindingly obvious who's leading the coven. The film tries misdirecting the viewer by including Granny Rigg (Gwen Ffrangcon Davies), a traditional sinister wise woman, but it comes as very little surprise when Kay Walsh steps into the center ring. She gives such a barnstorming performance it's almost worth the 70-minute lull preceding it ("Give me a skin for dancing in").

Apparently Fontaine brought the novel *The Devil's Own* to Hammer, which could explain why, with its cheery parochial tone, it's so out of synch with the studio's late 1960s output. If it had been made in the 1950s, the mock tribal dancing and the teenage girl writhing on an altar might have seemed exciting. Fontaine delivers a passable performance, but her presence fails to fill the screen like other "Baby Jane" actresses (Tallulah Bankhead, Bette Davis). She seems to sleepwalk through the film; in the scenes when she's sedated, it's impossible to tell the difference. Maybe she was pissed off knowing Kay Walsh was stealing the film from underneath her.

The unimpressive script surprisingly came from the pen of the legendary Nigel Kneale (creator of Quatermass). Maybe his roof needed repairing, or perhaps the screenplay was heavily edited by others behind his back. Still, some Kneale-like references remain intact, for example, comparing the force of witchcraft to an H-bomb.

There is one bold idea for 1966, presumably intentional: Before it's explained why the villagers want Linda and Ronnie kept apart, your imagination begins working overtime wondering exactly what the pair of mature-acting children are doing. Then there's the rabbit scene, which probably got this film its X certificate. Gwen is in the butchers listening to cheery Bob. He gets out a rabbit and removes its skin on camera. Horrible as it sounds (and is—even Fontaine grimaces), maybe viewers back then would've found it more acceptable, and it does make you wonder if we are too squeamish about the origins of the food we eat.

The supporting cast is full of familiar faces. Schoolboy Ronnie is played by Martin Stephens, former child star of *The Innocents* and *Village of the Damned*, in his final film role. Also visible are Michelle Dotrice, Leonard Rossiter, Duncan Lamont (the original Victor Caroon) and Bryan Marshall.
—Gerald Lea

Credits: Director: Cyril Frankel; Writer: Nigel Kneale.
Leading Cast: Joan Fontaine, Kay Walsh, Alec McCowen, Martin Stephens, Duncan Lamont, Leonard Rossiter.

Credits: Director: Samuel Gallu; Writer: Ellis Kadison, Roger Marshall.
Leading Cast: Christopher Lee, Lelia Goldoni, Jenny Till, Julian Glover, Ivor Dean.

The Witches (aka *The Devil's Own*)

It's Africa and the natives are getting very restless. In a tense opening scene, teacher Gwen Mayfield (Joan Fontaine) is in the school hut alone, abandoned by her helpers. Drums sound in the distance and before she can leave, the Witch Doctors, in massive masks, storm the hut and the camera cuts outside as we hear her scream. Back in Blighty, a recuperating Gwen gets a job as headmistress at a village school. The locals seem eager to keep two students, Ronnie and Linda, apart for some unknown reason. One of them becomes sick, and a doll full of pins is discovered. That's not an awful lot to go on, but Gwen has already deduced there's witchcraft afoot. Of course she's right (as the title proves).

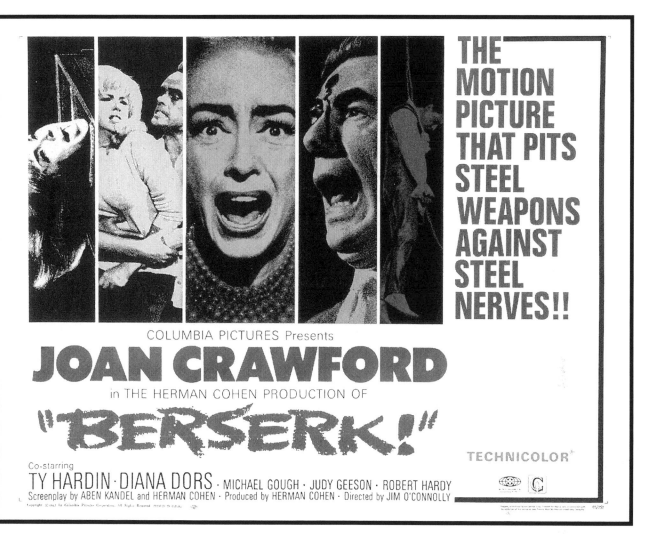

1967

Berserk

When noted high-wire act Gaspar the Great is fatally hanged during his patented show, cold-hearted, box-office focused Joan Crawford correctly assumes that the tragic incident will reignite public interest in her traveling jamboree as it tours the U.K.. ("We're running a circus, not a charm school!") While Joan chews the scenery and flirts with men half her age (including vapid new star performer Ty Hardin), her associates are bumped off at regular intervals by a mysterious gloved killer.

This typically gaudy Herman Cohen production, helmed by future *Tower of Evil* director Jim O'Connolly, follows a pre-slasher movie, creative death narrative similar to Herman's earlier *Horrors of the Black Museum*. The big top backdrop, cribbed from the superior *Circus of Horrors*, is employed liberally to pad the running time with extended footage from the novelty acts. The combination of police procedural and gruesome deaths, plus the presence of Gough as Crawford's business partner, all echo *Museum* (itself a possible influence

on *Blood Feast* and other 1960s splatter epics). The murders are, inevitably, the most fun aspect of the film, though Crawford's fan base gets its money's worth by way of a game performance confirming her late entry into genre roles (alas, *Trog* was next). Twenty minutes in, potential suspect Gough has a tent spike rammed into his head. Hardin is impaled on multiple steel bayonets. Diana Dors, typecast as a brassy tart ("attractive in a common sort of way," bitches Crawford), and prone to hair-pulling cat fights, is bisected by a rotating saw.

Away from the mounting body count, we're treated to the bizarre jump-rope antics of the marvellously named Phyllis Allen and Her Intelligent Poodles, an incongruous musical number and a hilarious scene in which the nervous surviving carny folk express their fears and suspicions. The Strong Man admits, "I am stronger than two horses…but even I cannot fight what I cannot see!," while the Bearded Lady is quick to shift any suspicion pointing her way ("You see my beard before you see me!"). In a suitably offbeat cast, Geoffrey Keen shows up, predictably enough, as a bit of a miserable bastard, while the emergence of perky Judy Geeson as Crawford's daughter helps make the mystery more obvious. This meandering but endearing flick perks up considerably during her climactic wig-out ("Kill, kill, kill! It's all I feel inside me!") before a bit of divine intervention (aka lightning) strikes her down in a final scene, cheekily cribbed from *The Bad Seed*.

—Steven West

Credits: Director: Jim O'Connolly; Writer: Herman Cohen, Aben Kandel.

Leading Cast: Joan Crawford, Ty Hardin, Diana Dors, Michael Gough, Judy Geeson, Robert Hardy, Geoffrey Keen.

Corruption

"*Corruption* is a super shock film" screamed the ads, literally, as shots of a terrified female face featured heavily in the film's campaign. With a storyline that combines Jack the Ripper style murders, a teenage gang running wild and a mad doctor storing a severed head in his fridge, *Corruption* certainly proved a super shock to many critics of the day. One of them, so appalled by the perceived amorality and degeneracy of the film, suggested any fitting review of *Corruption* should be written in blood rather than ink. Kinder appraisals tend to write the film up as a sort of British version of Georges Franju's *Les Yeux Sans Visage* [*Eyes without a Face*] (1959), both films concerning guilt ridden doctors driven to murderous ends to restore the facial disfigurement of a loved one. Here, it's top medico and laser surgery pioneer Sir John Rowan (Peter Cushing), who, after accidentally causing his model fiancée to be facially scarred at an impromptu photo shoot, goes on to murder several women for their pituitary glands which, with a little help from his laser drill, appears to restore his companion's features temporarily.

The hauntingly poetic, monochrome world of *Les Yeux* has little in common with the gaudy color one of *Corruption*, which at times resembles an episode of an ITC show, no doubt due in part to many of the supporting cast being familiar from walk-ons in series like *The Saint*. With 1967 being perhaps the key year when the world looked to London as a Mecca for fashion, style and music, *Corruption* is quick to play out the atmosphere of a hip and swinging capital, an approach that would make the film look dated just a few years down the line, but also gives it a unique identity beyond that of its French cousin.

Scratch beneath the surface, and *Corruption* is surprisingly true to some of the concepts its writer

Derek Ford would later develop as a British sex film director, his big theme in films like *The Wife Swappers* being affluent middle class types indulging in weekend sexual activities that eventually scandalize and destroy them socially. With the murder and mayhem in *Corruption* seemingly acting as a stand-in for swinging, Sir John suffers a similar downward spiral. At the outset of the film, he's the epitome of the English gentleman (this is Peter Cushing we're talking about, after all) but, as events progress, Sir John's search for murder victims leads him to trail blondes at train stations, visit a prostitute and team up with his wife to lure a teenage girl back to their country home, to such a degree that even the girl in question misinterprets his actions: "I thought first there isn't going to be any wife, and second lunch is going to be served in bed."

Bizarrely Ford even remade one of *Corruption's* murder scenes—in which the doctor nervously eyes up a blonde in a train compartment—as a sex scene for the opening of his 1977 comedy *What's Up Nurse?* Tony Booth pops up to deliver a highly animated performance as Mike, a flashy and loud fashion photographer. Obnoxious shutterbugs were stock characters in Ford's work, with similar examples featured in *Scream...and Die!*, *Suburban Wives* and *Don't Open 'til Christmas*.

Former colleagues generally remember Ford as a socially quiet man of letters, albeit one with a few skeletons in his closet, which would suggest he identified the most with the Peter Cushing figure here. Such is *Corruption*'s hyper style, though, that it could have been directed by Tony Booth's character. It's not difficult to imagine the film's director, Robert Hartford-Davis, using Booth's lines like, "All right, gimme the pretty girl bit, that's it—freak out, baby" on the actresses. In contrast to Ford, Hartford-Davis was a known quantity as a domineering, extrovert director who would occasionally suffer on-set panic attacks after giving too much for his art. Fiery energy that rubs off on the film itself, with murder scenes that give the impression they were directed by someone in the midst of a seizure, and the climax—with women screaming, the laser drill going berserk and the men melodramatically punching each other out—emerging as a dazzling piece of hysteria-pitched horror.

Corruption also demonstrates Hartford-Davis' peculiar talent for anti-typecasting, especially when it comes to the youth gang that shows up at the

end. Actress/puppeteer Alexandra Dane usually plays barmaids or busty comedy roles in the *Carry On* films, but there is little trace of that in her performance as the gang's sole female member. Complete with leather jacket and put-on husky voice, gleefully trashing Cushing's house, she's every bit as mean and nasty as the men. Even more remarkable is the transformation of David Lodge, another comedy player, into the menacing Groper, the odd one out of the mob. In fact, "odd" pretty much defines Groper, a punch-drunk aging heavy the gang has seemingly adopted and dressed like a grotesque mock-up of John Lennon, circa *Sgt. Pepper*. Hands down, Groper is by far the most memorable character to ever have stumbled into a Robert Hartford-Davis film, or arguably any 1960s British horror film, for that matter.

According to Cushing, *Corruption* made Hartford-Davis a small fortune, especially from its release in the Japanese market, but, despite (or perhaps because of) this success, Hartford-Davis continued making films for the next few years at workaholic speed, shooting an ill-fated adaptation of Simon Raven's "Doctors Wear Scarlet," released years later as *Incense for the Damned*, and then, in 1971, making a final stab at British horror with *The Fiend*. He died prematurely from a heart attack in 1977, having spent the last few years working quietly in American TV. His eclectic body of work (who else can claim to have produced or directed star vehicles for Peter Cushing, Norman Wisdom, Jim Brown and Lulu?) has, however, developed a cult following in the years since his death, with *Corruption* standing as the most fully realized and fondly remembered of his horror efforts.
—Gavin Whitaker

A film that has taken a bit of a hammering (npi) from critics over the years is this gritty horror thriller starring the late, great Peter Cushing in probably his most sordid role. As plastic surgeon Sir John Rowan, he is emotionally blackmailed by his facially disfigured fiancée Lynn into stalking, murdering and decapitating young women in order to supply human tissue for the skin graft operations she needs to restore her beauty, following a terrible accident inadvertently brought about by Rowan himself.

The first part of the film attempts to reflect the contemporary "Swinging '60s" ethos with an embarrassingly (in retrospect, at least) "hip" party scene where Rowan is discomfited by the stoned swingers and humiliated as a brash young fashion photographer eggs Lynn into adopting provocative poses for an impromptu session. In the ensuing struggle, Rowan accidentally knocks over an arc lamp that comes crashing down on top of Lynn, scorching the flesh off her face. The second half of the film is set on the south coast near Brighton, where Rowan has a seaside retreat in which he and Lynn seek refuge after the eventual failure of the first operation. The serenity of the cozy cliff top cottage and its neatly tended garden overlooking the sea, the epitome of the traditional genteel middle-class lifestyle, is contrasted with the mindless violence perpetrated by a gang of Beatniks who break in looking for their female stooge who had been sent to "case the joint" for cash and jewelery. Real-

life nastiness carried out by social malcontents, a phenomenon which many law-abiding citizens perceived to be sharply on the increase as the "Permissive Society" gathered pace during the 1960s, is paralleled by the hideous and amoral acts committed upon innocent victims by an originally well-intentioned man.

Corruption is in some ways a rather nasty and distasteful film. The scene in which Cushing is abused and man-handled by the gang of thugs with the complicity of his beloved fiancée is strangely upsetting. It's like having to watch your own grandfather being beaten up by football hooligans, a far cry from Cushing's usual innocuous escapist fantasies, once described by latter Hammer boss Roy Skeggs as being like "Walt Disney with a bit of blood."

Moreover, the version released in Europe includes an undignified scene of Peter Cushing grappling with a topless prostitute and mauling her breasts with his bloodied hands (in the U.K. release the woman is fully clothed). The spectacle of the First Gentleman of Horror enacting such a sordid and tasteless scene as might be encountered in one of Pete Walker's low-brow sleaze extravaganzas (still a few years in the future) is most unsettling, something like watching the once majestic King of the Jungle reduced to jumping through hoops in some tatty two-bit provincial circus. However, it's fair to say that *Corruption* draws much of its power precisely from the moral dilemma of a good man forced to carry out hideous acts for the furtherance of what he perceives to be a righteous cause, while at the same time despising himself for doing what "noblesse oblige." There's an obvious parallel to be drawn between Sir John Rowan, surgeon and gentleman, and Peter Cushing, actor and gentleman, who once lamented, "*Corruption* was gratuitously violent, fearfully sick."
—Mike Hodges

Credits: Director: Robert Hartford-Davis; Writers: Donald Ford, Derek Ford.
Leading Cast: Peter Cushing, Sue Lloyd, Noel Trevarthen, Kate O'Mara, Vanessa Howard, David Lodge, Anthony Booth.

Dance of the Vampires (aka *The Fearless Vampire Killers*)

Let me begin by saying that *Dance of the Vampires*, aka *The Fearless Vampire Killers (or Pardon Me, But Your Teeth are in My Neck)*, is my favorite film of all time! That probably means this won't be the most balanced and objective film review ever, but I'll do my best.

So, this being my favorite film, I've always been slightly dismayed that it's so poorly received by most other viewers. I think it's partly a matter of expectations. *Dance* was misleadingly promoted as a knock-about comedy, and so perhaps people come to it expecting something along the lines of a "Carry On Staking." On the other hand, the film is also said to be a spoof of the Hammer cycle of vampire films, so perhaps fans expect some more obvious blood and scares? Again, if that's what viewers are after, they're likely to come away disappointed.

The opening sequence gives us a good flavor of what's to follow, as the familiar MGM lion transforms into a green-

Who says Vampires are no laughing matter?

METRO-GOLDWYN-MAYER presents A MARTIN RANSOHOFF-ROMAN POLANSKI PRODUCTION

THE Fearless Vampire Killers OR: Pardon me, But Your Teeth are in My NECK

starring JACK MacGOWRAN · SHARON TATE · ALFIE BASS · co-starring FERDY MAYNE

Story and Screenplay by GERARD BRACH and ROMAN POLANSKI Produced by GENE GUTOWSKI Directed by ROMAN POLANSKI

A CADRE FILMS-FILMWAYS PRODUCTION In PANAVISION and METROCOLOR MGM

The first act of the film is perhaps where some audience members have their patience tested. It's quite a while before any vampires make an appearance, and most of the first 30 minutes are concerned with domestic farce. The vampire killers mistake a randy Shagal for a vampire, and Shagal's wife mistakes the Professor for her husband as she bashes him on the head with an enormous sausage. Sarah talks Alfred into letting her use the bathroom, while he thinks she's after something else altogether.

This section of the film is crammed with wonderfully observed details and bits of business that establish the setting, the characters and the tone very effectively. The inn and the village are clearly built on a soundstage, but the wonderful painted backdrops and the theatricality of it all lends the film a deliciously artificial, fairy-tale quality.

But eventually the vampires do turn up, and we have the wonderfully absurd sequence where Count von Krolock floats down through an open skylight, attacks Sarah in the bath and whisks her off to the castle. Then her father falls afoul of the vampires in attempting to rescue her, and, once a member of the undead himself, leads our vampire-hunting duo up to the castle, where we find out how the other half lives. Or should that be un-dies?

Like the inn, the castle is a triumph of production design and set construction. While it's built on a soundstage, it still manages to feel like a real place.

The film is said to have been inspired by the Hammer films of the mid- to late 1960s, especially *The Brides of Dracula* and *The Kiss of the Vampire*. But Polanski had access to a budget and resources that Hammer could only dream of. This is a very lavish production, with richly textured production design by Wilfrid Shingleton and lush widescreen cinematography by Douglas Slocombe. Krzysztof Komeda provided the music score, a melodic, haunting and playful one that complements and enhances the film beautifully.

Not only does the film look and sound exquisite, but it's crammed with excellent performances, too. Jack MacGowran is amazing as the Professor, presenting the ultimate caricature of a quacking, daft old academic. Whether one finds the film funny or not probably hinges on how one reacts to MacGowran. To call it a broad display of acting would be an understatement, but it seems to form the centerpiece of the film. By contrast, Polanski's performance as Alfred is much less overstated, but he's perfectly adequate as the slightly gormless but well-intentioned bungler.

Again contrasting with MacGowran is Ferdy Mayne's Count. He gives a wonderfully stately performance, and his dialogue positively drips with the centuries-old ennui of the immortal undead.

Back at the broader end of the acting spectrum, we have Alfie Bass as the caricatured Jewish innkeeper. His "Oy, have you got the wrong vampire!" moment is one often cited by the "it's not funny" brigade as one of the few effective moments of

skinned cartoon vampire, whose fangs disgorge a drop of animated blood that drips through the opening credits, accompanied by a flitting cartoon bat. Then we see a sleigh making its way through a moonlit, mountainous snowscape.

Ferdy Mayne's sepulchral narration informs us that Professor Abronsius and his faithful disciple, Alfred, are on a mission in deepest Transylvania, on a quest that has earned the Professor the alternative title of "The Nut." The sleigh is attacked by wolves, but only Alfred notices. The Professor is seemingly asleep and won't awaken, and the sleigh driver is oblivious to the danger. Alfred has to fend off the attacking canines with the help of an umbrella, which he loses in the struggle. And when they arrive at the village, it becomes clear the Professor failed to react to the wolf attack because he is frozen stiff. He is carried into the inn, where he thaws out and begins inquiring about the vast amount of garlic that hangs everywhere, and whether or not there's a castle in the district.

humor in the film. And then there's Ian Quarrier as the mincing gay son, dubbed with the fey tones of Vladek Sheybal. Former boxing champion Terry Downes makes a very impressive club-footed hunchback.

The female roles are a little under cooked. Sharon Tate does the best she can with the role of a shallow young woman whose main interest in life is to bathe as often as possible, and she looks absolutely stunning. The fact that shortly after making this film she was murdered by the Manson Family adds a melancholy tone to proceedings. It's just a shame that Sarah Shagal isn't a more interesting character.

And what of Polanski? What does he have to add to the vampire subgenre? He brings us one thing that has rarely been seen in other vampire films, and that's snow—plenty of it. Somehow it feels right for the tale to play out against a backdrop of a winter landscape. The land itself is frozen in a death-like sleep, just as the vampire clan of the Von Krolocks lie cold in their tombs. On the surface, the film might seem like a bit of a departure for Polanski, but all his usual themes and preoccupations are present and correct.

There's a definite whiff of Kafka to it all. Our vampire killers are continually being sidetracked, confounded and hampered by their own bungling. In the end, their efforts are futile and self-defeating. In a traditional vampire film, Abronsius would be a kindly savant, the ethical center of the piece. But Abronsius is an eccentric old duffer who seems to have no real moral interest in exterminating vampires, merely seeing them as a subject of scientific curiosity, and needs to be reminded that human lives (and, presumably, immortal souls) are at risk. Ultimately, he dooms mankind because he has no idea what's happening right under his nose. Or, in this case, just behind his back. Alfred seems completely disinterested in his mentor's quest, and his actions throughout the film are mainly motivated by his desire for Sarah. He wants to save her but he's too inept to carry it off.

All of this might suggest that Polanski was sneering at the vampire genre, but the film is so obviously a labor of love that I can't believe that. I think that the trouble is that his sense of humor is just a little too off-center for most people's tastes.

The downbeat ending may be another reason for the film's poor reception. It's a very Polanski touch, but it is quite a bit ahead of its time. It's the sort of ending John Carpenter would give his films over a decade later, but it may have been the final nail in the coffin for those expecting a more lighthearted denouement.

In the end, the film is incredibly rewarding if approached in the right spirit. Don't come to it expecting anything as pedestrian as a horror spoof. Instead, come to it expecting a deliciously subversive, absurdist, Kafkaesque fairy tale—then you won't be disappointed.
—Paul Mudie

How does that line go, "Imitation is the sincerest form of flattery?" Well, much like the Dukes of Stratosphear's loving imitations of British psychedelia on the equally enthralling *25*

O' Clock album, Polanski's love letter to Hammer, *Dance of the Vampires*, almost outdoes the very subject it is parodying.

The film immediately evokes the correct mood with the haunting music of Krzysztof Komeda (a good friend of Polanski's, who would go on to record the soundtrack for *Rosemary's Baby*) and the superb exterior shots of the (Italian) Alps. This is a fairy tale for sure, but it's one with a dark undercurrent. The story rolls along fairly conventional vampiric lines with the superstitious villagers, the castle no one wants to talk about, the esteemed professor/vampire hunter Abronsius (Jack MacGowran) and Alfred, his loyal sidekick (Polanski himself), but the charms of this film are in the details. There are pleasing twists to the genre conventions: a Jewish inn keeper, which leads to interesting problems for our valiant duo when he eventually joins the undead; the Count's gay vampire son (cinema's first?); and the "sting in the tail" ending (more about that later).

But one of the greatest things about this film is how it looks: The scenery is breathtaking and the sets are fantastic (I'm sure Hammer would have given anything to boast such lavish creations); designed by Wilfrid Shingleton and lensed by Douglas Slocombe, they manage to capture a mythical Mittel Europe that both enchants and chills in equal measure. The section where Polanski and MacGowran follow the Count's hunchbacked henchman (Terry Downes) to the castle is like a sinister re-shoot of the Alpine scene in the Beatles movie *Help!* It is these parts of the film (including the castle rooftop scenes) that surpass Hammer's own efforts (the Alps or Black Park? Which would *you* prefer?). Sure, this movie plays for the laughs, but there are moments during the Hammer Dracula cycle that evoke similar mirth—for all the *wrong* reasons.

Dance looks great, is sassy and humorous and not a little disturbing. This film also marks the first point in horror cinema where the bad guys win, something that Hammer (and most other companies) shied away from during all of their bloodsucker movies. Not bad going for a comedy. Throw in the gorgeous Sharon Tate (who did a semi-nude, on-set shoot for the March 1967 *Playboy*) and it just goes to show that imitation can occasionally transcend its source material. Considered an aberration in Polanski's canon by some, the time is right to re-evaluate this as the classic it arguably is.
—Adam Easterbrook

Credits: Director: Roman Polanski; Writers: Roman Polanski, Gerard Brach.
Leading Cast: Jack MacGowran, Roman Polanski, Sharon Tate, Alfie Bass, Ferdy Mayne, Ronald Lacey.

The Deadly Bees

Probably cinema's only murder mystery hinging upon two suspicious beekeepers and resolved via a copy of the book *Practical Beekeeping*, this Amicus production is also notable for pre-empting the 1970s American fad for (mostly dull) movies about hostile swarms of bees. The central setting (one

hives
of horror!

Excited by the smell of fear
they inflict their
fatal stings!

PARAMOUNT PICTURES
PRESENTS

THE
DEADLY
BEES

STARRING SUZANNA LEIGH
FRANK FINLAY · GUY DOLEMAN

SCREENPLAY BY ROBERT BLOCH AND ANTHONY MARRIOTT · PRODUCED BY MAX J. ROSENBERG AND MILTON SUBOTSKY · DIRECTED BY FREDDIE FRANCIS · AN AMICUS PRODUCTION · TECHNICOLOR®

camp agent to spend two weeks of recuperation on the aforementioned idyllic island. Staying with bee farmer Guy Doleman and his permanently hacked-off wife (Catherine Finn), Leigh is convinced by rival beekeeper and butterfly collector Finlay that Doleman is working on an adrenaline formula devised to drive his bees into attacking humans. A series of serious assaults on people close to Doleman seems to confirm this, but can Frank Finlay *ever* be trusted?

Leigh is an unsympathetic heroine (though Francis relishes a suspense sequence showcasing her fashionable 1960s undies), with more fun to be found in the supporting cast. Katy Wild, quite memorable in *The Evil of Frankenstein*, is sexier and spunkier as the victimized daughter of local landlord Michael Ripper (who else?), and part-time seductive home help for the unhappy bee farm couple. Finlay hams it up in an amusing role that requires him to look and act like a Peter Cook comedy caricature, and Finn is a standout as the ill-fated, effectively embittered wife.

Like most killer bee movies, the film struggles to find sufficient menace in its eponymous threat. Unconvincing superimposed swarms of real bees combine awkwardly with evidently plastic insects stuck on actor's faces and close-ups of genuine hand-stinging action. Still, if you can overlook the phoney FX and Bloch's struggle to pad a short story idea to feature length, the movie has some decent enough scenes: Finn's death sequence and Wild's non-fatal ordeal in the woods generate bona fide tension.
—Steven West

Credits: Director: Freddie Francis; Writers: Robert Bloch, Anthony Marriott.
Leading Cast: Suzanna Leigh, Frank Finlay, Guy Doleman, Michael Ripper, Katy Wild.

"Seagull Island"), an imperiled and somewhat aloof blonde heroine with a penchant for silly hats, and the presence of a naff pop group named The Birds all suggest that a then-recent Hitchcock chiller was a prominent source of inspiration.

Robert Bloch, in one of his blander movie credits, cowrote this adaptation of H.F. Heard's "A Taste for Honey" as a genre piece for Hammer-Amicus genre regular Freddie Francis. Recurring scenes of dismissive authority figures in Whitehall cheerfully ignoring threats made by an anonymous "fruitcake" threatening to unleash killer bees on the public amount to little more than a setup for a throwaway final scene. The focus is on the wooden Suzanna Leigh, proud owner of two facial expressions, as a fur-clad pop star with Elkie Brooks' singing voice. Leigh, best known for snogging Elvis in *Paradise, Hawaiian Style* and for being Sharon Tate's best friend, would subsequently be upstaged by Dana Gillespie's magnificent breasts in Hammer's marvellously wacky *The Lost Continent*, among assorted other genre appearances.

Collapsing from exhaustion during a suitably cheesy sub-*Top of the Pops* 1960s music show, Leigh is ordered by her

Editor's note: The 1999 compilation CD *The Collector's Guide to Rare British Birds* features, as a hidden track, snippets of The Birds' "That's All I Need," seemingly lifted from the *Deadly Bees* soundtrack.

Doctor Faustus

Based on Marlowe, Richard Burton's *Doctor Faustus* (made in collaboration with his former Oxford tutor) plays out pretty much as a vanity project. Dick is on screen for virtually the entire thing, as well as co-producing and co-directing the movie, and he has plenty of opportunity for emoting and overacting (depending on your opinion of the man's talents).

Visually it's superb, with skulls, skeletons, dusty old books, weird laboratory equipment and the like abounding. Burton gets to wear a pair of specs that Elton John would kill for, Liz Taylor pops up as the seductive Helen of Troy, there's a great pre-Python scene where Burton makes himself invisible to disrupt a meeting of the Pope's Privy Council (leading to fart gags and custard pies in faces galore), and a great climax where he spends the last hour of his life ranting at the heavens and pleading with God to save his soul (don't want to spoil the ending, but I don't think it's giving much away to reveal that such pleas are in vain). It would make a great double bill with *The Passion of the Christ*, and is highly recommended for those of you who like something a little adventurous or different in your British horror. The more literary-minded movie buff may know whether Burton took many liberties with Marlowe's text. Not being an expert myself, I wouldn't know, but much of the dialogue sounds as though it could have been lifted verbatim.

The Region One DVD also contains a trailer for that other totally bonkers semi-British, semi-horror film starring Liz Taylor, *Suddenly Last Summer*!
—Darrell Buxton

Credits: Directors: Richard Burton, Nevill Coghill; Writer: Nevill Coghill.
Leading Cast: Richard Burton, Elizabeth Taylor, Andreas Teuber, Ian Marter.

Frankenstein Created Woman

In a typically mature and intelligent entry in the outstanding Terence Fisher-directed Frankenstein cycle, the emphasis is on tragic inevitability rather than gaudy horrors. The strain of melancholy apparent in the fate of Michael Gwynn in *The Revenge of Frankenstein* resurfaced to an even greater degree here and in the subsequent *Frankenstein Must Be Destroyed*. The beautifully elegiac theme James Bernard composed for the central "monster" in *Frankenstein Created Woman* reinforces the desperately sad nature of the title character in one of Hammer's most emotionally affecting films.

At the outset, a drunken killer goes to the guillotine in front of his young son, a boy who grows up to be Robert Morris, an amiable assistant to Baron Frankenstein. The Baron, no longer able to use his crippled hands and fighting against a bad reputation, is first seen revived after an hour of being dead. It's all part of a fresh, insanely ambitious attempt to discover if the soul can survive the demise of the body (in a subtle echo of more melodramatic earlier Frankenstein movies, one of the Baron's assistants greets his revival with a quietly enthusiastic "He's alive!").

The Baron, eager as ever to play God ("We have conquered death!"), is much more sympathetic than the film's true villains, a group of heartless young upper class gits who cruelly mock disfigured landlord's daughter Susan Denberg, the object of Morris' affections. When her stern father is beaten to death by the loutish toffs, Morris is wrongly convicted of his murder and executed. Hurling herself off a bridge after seeing her lover guillotined like his father, Denberg is revived as an unscarred blonde by the Baron—accompanied by the vengeful soul of Morris.

Within an exemplary cast—even usually OTT comic relief Thorley Walters underplays nicely—Cushing inevitably steals the show with a performance that's as charismatic and quick-witted as ever. It's the Baron's dry sense of humor and irony that provides this unrelentingly grim film with its only levity. In the courtroom, when accused of witchcraft, Frankenstein defends himself: "To my knowledge, doctorates are not awarded for witchcraft," adding self-deprecatingly, "but if they were, no doubt I'd qualify!" His deadpan delivery also raises a chuckle in a later throwaway moment in which a copper rhetorically asks, "Do you take us for fools?" to which the stoic reply is a droll "Yes!"

Austrian-born model and actress Denberg, whose own tragic "death" was widely misreported by certain sources in the late 1960s, can't quite pull off the schizophrenic nature of her later incarnation, but shines in the first half as the mousy, doomed Christina. Brown hair hanging over the scarred side of her face and overwhelmed by the desire to be merely "ordinary," Denberg's Christina is a haunting presence. When she returns from the grave, clever juxtapositions convey the brutality of her retribution without recourse to fake blood, and an intrinsically perverse element involves the vengeful, dead Morris seducing the men responsible for his death via the body of the equally vengeful Denberg.

In an understated but powerful movie full of striking imagery, it's the non-horrific, abrupt ending that packs the biggest punch. For once bereft of angry mobs and a fiery resolution, the film culminates with a scene as tragic as *Bride of Frankenstein*'s immortal "We belong dead" climax. The Baron, more humane here than ever before and almost irrelevant in the latter stages of the movie, fails to stop Christina from leaping to her death for a second, final time. At the end of a movie in which revenge leaves only emptiness, justice is elusive and death is the only escape from a miserable existence, her last words are a simple, heartbreaking "Please forgive me…"
—Steven West

After the creative (if not commercial) dud that was *The Evil of Frankenstein*, Terence Fisher returned for the fourth

be gofer for Peter Cushing's Baron Frankenstein. Many years later, the Baron is engaged in experiments to determine whether the "soul" leaves the body upon death. His assistant, Hertz (Thorley Walters), a self-confessed "muddle-head," brings the Baron back from an hour's worth of frozen death. The success of this experiment convinces the Baron that the soul in fact lingers on for a time in the physical frame. It's a good job this is only Hammer; in the case of a power cut, there'd be murder at Iceland's.

Hans (Robert Morris) is quietly seeing tavern keeper Kleve's daughter Christina (*Playboy* model Susan Denberg), who is disfigured and crippled. When three foppish ne'er-do-wells enter the tavern and put Christina through their usual ritual of cruel mockery, Hans yells, "Come on then!" and kicks their toffee-nosed arses. And, by God, they deserve it; their petty taunting of Christina is hard to watch and is somehow more cruel than any number of blockbuster, celluloid terrorist acts. Creeping back into the tavern after hours, the trio of bruised Lord Snootys are disturbed by Kleve and proceed to bludgeon him to death with their canes. Hans, who was actually sharing Christina's bed at the time, is found guilty of the crime and, like his father before him, is sentenced to the chop. Upon finding out, Christina jumps eight feet into the river for a paddle, sorry, to top herself.

Quick to exploit an opportunity, Frankenstein isolates Hans' soul, transferring it to Christina's body, now fixed up and looking shipshape (though she never appears in the film as she does in the famous publicity stills). Guided by Hans' vengeful spirit, Christina sets about seducing our three villains and dispatching the loathsome snots in various gory ways. When she carries on a conversation with Hans' head, impaled on the bedpost, it's a shocking and gleefully macabre touch.

Here, Frankenstein is not the obvious villain. He is a more benevolent figure than usual, and his Holmesian relationship with Walters' Dr. Watson-like Hertz imbues him with a humanity that is utterly absent in the next installment. (Cushing

installment in Hammer's franchise. It's an improvement on Freddie Francis's misfire, but simultaneously the least of Fisher's Frankensteins. Inspired as a joke following Roger Vadim's *And God Created Woman* (1957), Hammer originally planned "And Then Frankenstein Created Woman" as the third film in the series. But it was years later before they got around to turning out their own, sexier spin on *Bride of Frankenstein*.

The pre-title sequence gets the ball rolling as a drunken killer is dragged to the guillotine on a gray and somber day. His gruesome adieu is witnessed by his son Hans, who grows up to

and Walters, of course, would portray Holmes and Watson respectively, albeit in different productions.) The film seems to follow on from *The Evil of Frankenstein*, with the Baron's burned hands, but is considered part of the official canon, unlike its predecessor. Denberg is better than you'd assume, but was dubbed in post-production. The film looks cheap; the lab is nothing more than a basement. Yet Fisher makes a good, but not great, movie out of a potentially silly premise. Presumably, the metaphysical questions posed were right up his alley.
—Jed Raven

Credits: Director: Terence Fisher; Writer: John Elder [Anthony Hinds].
Leading Cast: Peter Cushing, Susan Denberg, Thorley Walters, Duncan Lamont, Robert Morris.

Editor's note: Asked to select a number of his favorite films for a 1987 season at London's National Film Theatre, Martin Scorsese included *Frankenstein Created Woman* among his choices. Scorsese was quoted in the NFT programme as follows: "If I single this one out it's because here they actually isolate the soul. The implied metaphysics are close to something sublime."

The Mummy's Shroud

Hammer's cycle of four Egyptian horror-themed pictures can be easily be put into order. The best two are the dramatic *Blood from the Mummy's Tomb* (1971) and the satisfying *The Mummy* (1959); the worst is the lackluster *The Curse of the Mummy's Tomb* (1964) with its damp-squib ending and ineffectual policemen. Sandwiched between these two extremes is *The Mummy's Shroud*, which has some fine sequences but is held back from true greatness by some of its faults.

Considering *Shroud*'s bad points first, we come to its most obvious failing, one it shares with most mummy outings, namely the flashback sequences to ancient Egypt. These are often overlong, and *Shroud*'s 8:30 of masochistic history drags interminably. Positioning these scenes at the beginning handicaps the film before it's even off the starting line. This dull segment also seems racially confused (compare Kah-to-Bey to his parents, and note Prem being played by a blacked-up white man whose shade seems to magically darken), but then I'm no anthropologist!

Claire de Sangre (expedition linguist) never looks quite right in the 1920s clothes and this, coupled with what I humorously presume to be a touch of Deep One taint showing around her mouth, gives her, in my view, an unconventional appearance for a lead female.

Kah-to-Bey's tomb is a bland cave, and its guardian, Hasmid (Roger Delgado), is not given enough to do, which is a shame because he's an actor capable of exuding menace from every pore. Here he mumbles gibberish from the sidelines while sulking in the shadows (and exposes his bottom teeth, curiously revealing what must be a serious liquorice addiction). A lot of the minor roles are well defined (Inspector Barrani, Harry, Sir Basil, Barbara) and competently acted, but this does contribute to suffocating the character of Paul, making him seem rather bland and ineffectual for a hero.

Good and bad simultaneously is the death of Longbarrow (Hammer stalwart Michael Ripper), a harassed, fawning, ever-apologetic figure. Notice how Longbarrow appears browbeaten even *before* he meets Mr. Preston for the first time during this film. Ripper is a delight to watch, playing a long-suffering character of this nature. His demise is therefore invested with true horror. He's one of those ill-fated innocents who act as collateral damage; when he dies it's as if a shard of the film's spirit departs with him. I suppose as a shortsighted person myself, I find his farcical and tragic moments a stark warning about spectacle care.

Good bits include the darkroom tussle; Haiti, the drooling fortune teller (a couple of pharaohs short of a dynasty); and the film's ending, a minor triumph. I don't want to spoil or over-hype this finale for those who've not seen it, but I've christened it "the Oxo Cube ending." It's worth sitting through the entire movie just to witness the occurrence which follows a brief but well choreographed climactic fight sequence. Ian Scoones (special effects) contributed magical work on that day's filming, because, for me, it is the standout sequence from *any* mummy movie, past or present.

Some fun questions remain. Who narrated the opening? (many sources erroneously claim Peter Cushing). Who (badly) mummified Prem? Why does Claire only predict the future when in the desert? Did Mr. Preston have Basil moved to the asylum? What happened in Longbarrow's past to make him so twitchy? How does Paul keep his shoes so white? Why does the Inspector only keep three bullets in his revolver at a time when he has a full compliment of six on his person? Did Hammer get a discount on shoe polish?
—Elliot Iles

Credits: Director and Writer: John Gilling.
Leading Cast: André Morell, John Phillips, David Buck, Elizabeth Sellars, Michael Ripper, Roger Delgado, Catherine Lacey.

Night of the Big Heat
(aka *Island of the Burning Damned*)

Remember those conversations we used to have in the playground during the atom bomb 1980s, when everyone seriously expected that we'd all end our days with just four minutes to do whatever we could? Usually our schoolmates would venture ideas about stealing a Porsche (none of us could drive, or knew how to hot wire a car; also, living as I did in rural South Cheshire, we'd have probably only been able to find a tractor within four minutes, or if luck was on our side, a Ford Capri) or getting legless (perhaps the most realistic claim, as half a can of Top Deck shandy would have done the trick!).

In the 1960s, there were no thoughts of car theft when it came to the end of the world. But getting pissed did feature

quite heavily. In films like *The Deadly Bees*, *The Earth Dies Screaming* and, of course, *Night of the Big Heat*, huge natural disasters mean only one thing: a trip to the local pub.

Not that there's much wrong with that, of course; and it also gives such films a believable stage on which to tell their unlikely stories. Take, for example, this one. The temperature on a small island off the British coast climbs incessantly, despite the fact that it's winter and bloody freezing on the mainland. But is anyone worried? Nah. They're just a bit hot and sweaty, that's all.

Of course, the mainland knows all about the freak weather conditions, but have they sent anyone to investigate? Not a bit of it. There's just Christopher Lee, wandering around and bothering the sheep, by all accounts—a strange man.

He's the only one who concerned about the heat, yet everyone thinks he's the odd one. I ask you—anyway, there are a number of deaths, the mercury keeps on rising and Peter Cushing refuses to take off his jacket. Chris Lee deduces that there are extraterrestrial powers at work, most of the cast gets fried, and then it rains and the "aliens" (which look like castoffs from 1960s *Star Trek*) all die. Crap, really.

The film often resembles a tepid domestic drama rather than the sci-fi invasion extravaganza it is supposed to be,

with that bloke out of the Barratt Homes ads trying his best to ignore the sultry shenanigans of his sweaty secretary, and the pub interior becoming so scorching that all the bottles of Pilsner explode. Is that likely? I think not. And if the monsters' temperatures are so high, how come humans can survive so long in their presence? No sizzle, all drizzle.
—Chris Wood

Credits: Director: Terence Fisher; Writers: Ronald Liles, Pip Baker, Jane Baker.
Leading Cast: Christopher Lee, Peter Cushing, Patrick Allen, Sarah Lawson, Jane Merrow.

Our Mother's House

There are films whose inclusion within the boundaries of the horror genre seems more *de facto* than strictly justified, nudged in by a macabre episode or supernatural twist that's parenthetical to the whole. *Our Mother's House* could be casually dismissed among such miscellany; indeed, its commercial failure during the Summer of Love of 1967 probably owes something to the incongruous blend of whimsy with its morbid premise. Yet as with director Jack Clayton's more celebrated work *The Innocents*, it absorbs the viewer in a private Gothic fantasy that explores the loss and corruption of childish things with beguiling effectiveness.

Adapted from the 1963 novel by Julian Gloag, it centers on the closely knit Hook children—four brothers and three sisters, age four to 13—who are left orphaned when their bedridden mother dies in the opening minutes. After discovering a handwritten will bequeathing them the house, and faced with the prospect of being put into care if they inform an adult, they instead decide to bury her in the back garden.

Informed by their pious yet evidently deeply affectionate upbringing, the children spend the first half of the film adapting to their new circumstances. There are clear allegorical overtones in the schism between the more tolerant sensibilities of the eldest child Elsa (Margaret Brooks) and the Puritanism of some of her siblings in the struggle for control. Of particular note is the "tabernacle," a ramshackle shed in the garden in which another daughter Diana (Pamela Franklin) channels the spirit of their dead mother for guidance during their nightly séances at "Mothertime."

The unexpected (as much as any star billing can be) entrance of their "father," Charlie Hook (Dirk Bogarde), shortly after the halfway mark, introduces a new dynamic. In a role comparable with Bogarde's more celebrated turn as *The Servant* four years earlier, the amiable chancer wastes no time settling in and winning the children's confidence (Elsa notwithstanding). Before long, however, Charlie's seedy lifestyle brings a dose of reality into the house and their discovery of the full extent of his betrayal hastens events to a shocking denouement.

Our Mother's House is not a place all viewers feel at home in, though curiously many of the criticisms tend to be based on the belief it was intended as a naturalistic drama. True, the screenplay by Jeremy Brooks and Haya Harareet trims away some of the excesses of Gloag's original (in which the youngest daughter, Gerty, also dies) but by and large this only serves to enrich its fable-like quality. The gloomy old house and its occupants live in an eerily timeless world, sealed off from the neophilia of Swinging London. Shot in a vivid Metrocolor palette suggestive of a child's eye view and complemented by Georges Delerue's charming score, Clayton achieves at times a dreamy lyricism. A rare exterior interlude when Charlie takes the kids to see Benjamin Waterhouse Hawkins' dinosaur sculptures at Crystal Palace is among the most sublime in any British film of the period. It's also a cute choice; the sculptures are quaint Victorian anachronisms not unlike the Hooks themselves, and even Charlie is a caricature of the duplicitous Dickensian villain.

One could be tempted into thinking this strays too readily into mawkishness; however, like much of Clayton's work before (*Room at the Top*, *The Innocents*) and after (*The Great Gatsby*, *Something Wicked This Way Comes*), it shares the common trait of characters seduced by naive fantasy to their eventual cost. The director's penchant for adapting successful novels and stories often overshadowed his subtle skills, so that he's perhaps unfairly regarded as a skilled craftsman rather than a bona-fide auteur. That's a debate for another time and place. Let's summarise by saying that *Our Mother's House* may be an atypical entry in the British horror canon, but it's also a very good one.

—Richard Halfhide

A multilayered, complex, subtle and beautifully autumnal film dealing with several simultaneous concepts, but most of all the idea of an alternative reality, *Our Mother's House* is the kind of work that shows British mainstream cinema (it was distributed by MGM) at its most daring and experimental. It's also further proof of the underrated talent of director Jack Clayton, the man who chilled us all with *The Innocents* (1961), taken from Henry James' Gothic classic "The Turn of the Screw," and would later even manage to redeem the corporate evils of Walt Disney with his atmospheric reading of Ray Bradbury's *Something Wicked This Way Comes* (1983).

Whether or not he chose these novels to film or was simply hired by coincidence on each occasion (you know as well as I do how these things happen in the film industry) is irrelevant, but you'd have to be blind to miss the recurrent themes of lost innocence, progression from child to adult, and an unerring belief in the supernatural in all three. In *Our Mother's House*, we approach the subject matter from an ambiguous perspective, as eight recently orphaned children of a supposedly devoutly religious, physically frail mother (whose death is never fully explained or ascribed to any illness, thus allowing yet more scope for imagination and interpretation) choose to, in their words, "carry on like before," burying her in a self-constructed "tabernacle" in the back garden, sacking nosey home help Mrs. Quayle (Yootha Joyce) and constructing a series of elaborate lies for the benefit of their teachers and neighbors.

The idea that Mother's physical death on Earth would separate her from her offspring is never even mentioned, and

as if it were the most natural thing in the world, the second eldest daughter Diana (Pamela Franklin, further refining her role as a "haunted child" from *The Innocents*), uses herself as a "channel" through which she and the others communicate with their deceased parent nightly during a specially designated period referred to as "Mothertime." Once a reverent, communal display of respect, this has now transformed since her passing into an eerie, ritualistic series of seances: During one such event, the older children chastise, supposedly at the behest of "Mother," their younger sibling Gerty (Phoebe Nicholls, then still called Sarah, in her first role), for the heinous crime of allowing a stranger to bring her home on his motorcycle, thus potentially exposing the family unit to public scrutiny. The suggested punishment is for the girl to have her long locks forcibly cut off, and the screams that echo around the ghostly shrine as they carry out her bidding are as chilling as anything heard in the bleakest Pete Walker.

It's moments like this, where Clayton changes the tone—from quaintly charming melodrama to unrelenting fear, from sweetness to trauma—in that his controlled power as a filmmaker is illustrated. It's also these elements that help confirm the film's status as a psychological horror movie, something often disputed by self-appointed cinematic arbiters who would not like to admit to enjoying such an item. Yet, in a perfect illustration of the difference between society, then and now, not

one mention is made of the suggestion of pedophilia or perversion on the adult's part: In a more disturbing reversal, the others refer to their sister, who cannot be older than seven at most, as a "harlot" and lay the blame, not that anything has actually happened, at her door (*You allowed him to touch you!*"). The fact that the child told the adult nothing is of no consequence; in the private universe, where the morés of society are nonexistent, rules must be obeyed or else. However, despite the brutality of the deed, what emerges is an overriding feeling not of malice, but of fraternal love, and the desire to protect one's nearest and dearest from a real world which is ultimately more threatening.

Eldest daughter Elsa (Margaret Brooks, daughter of screenwriter Jeremy Brooks) assumes the role of guardian, although she vies constantly for power with the equally determined Hubert (Louis Sheldon Williams), and it is this struggle that will prove the undoing of the family unit. Against his sister's better judgement, he has written to the man believed to be their father, Charlie Hook (Dirk Bogarde), and for a while it looks like a good idea, as his entrance (literally, through the door of the rambling Victorian mansion) comes at an opportune moment and saves the group from an interfering schoolteacher (who they seem on the verge of frightening to death with harmonized, monk-like chants of "Go away") looking for an "abducted" schoolmate Louie (Parnum Wallace). And it's this sudden destruction of the previous dynamic that shifts the story to its next level.

Some have complained that Bogarde's arrival, almost precisely 50 minutes in, changes the timbre of the picture to the point where it becomes almost another film. True, the dreamlike trance of the first half is now tinged with a gritty realism, but every second of the production is so unified by the captivating browns, greys and greens of Clayton's superb photography and the drifting textures of Georges Delerue's evocative soundtrack, that any join is nearly invisible. The well-chosen suburban London locations (Croydon, Chessington), also used by Clayton to great effect in *The Pumpkin Eater*, add to this effect, the end result almost the British Horror equivalent of a Ray Davies or Al Stewart lyric, and despite the decaying house looking like it probably hasn't been cleaned in over a decade, you find yourself strangely drawn to such a place.

Bogarde *owns* the film from the moment he first sets foot on-screen, and Charlie Hook is one of his most fascinating, perplexing creations. Even though his biological parentage of them is always in question (and later revealed to be practically nonexistent), his joy and contentment at being reunited with his children, and the pleasure he appears to derive from spending time with them, is clearly visible. Yet, underneath, we discover him to be exactly the wastrel their mother's writings had described, a fly by night confidence trickster who wants little more than to defraud them out of their will and house. We are already aware of the talent the youngest boy Jiminee (a pre-*Oliver!* Mark Lester) possesses for forging the signature on Mother's fortnightly welfare cheque: Dastardly Dirky soon has him embezzling her savings book, the resulting cash frittered away on loose women (not something Bogarde would have done in real life, but if anything, further proof of his acting skills), booze and cars.

He also destroys the "tabernacle," sells off his late wife's furniture and reinstates Joyce, who has her own agendas, but it's impossible to see him as merely a "bad lot": His own revelations about the children's "sainted" mother, who in truth rebelled against her own religious upbringing by becoming little more than a common prostitute, seem less like the declamations of a scheming opportunist and more those of a saddened, crushed man who, for reasons known only to himself, chose to remain in a relationship with such a woman and give each of her offspring his name. Undeniably, Charlie is not, for want of a better word, "nice," and, indeed, he turns unnecessarily on the children with a display of verbal venom as only the actor at the peak of his powers (following on from similar tours de force in *Victim* and *Accident*) could deliver. Yet he is not strictly "a nasty piece of work," either: Although he cares little for anyone except himself, one wonders if it were always this way or if we are witnessing a man at the end of his tether.

Furthermore, his rejection of Franklin (who is becoming a woman, and by now has developed a hopeless crush on the man she believes to be her father), which leads the film to its admittedly predictable but no less effective conclusion, is actually not an aggressive act but an almost noble gesture. During a game of rough and tumble in the garden, he recognizes her burgeoning feelings for him but clearly refuses to encourage them, even when she catches him in bed with local floozie Edina Ronay; and her love, which she retains long after the others have seen his true colors, is compromised. Admittedly, he could have chosen more tactful words than "Get away from me, you give me the bloody creeps" before throwing her to the floor, but at least his intent remains honorable.

The film may belong to Bogarde, but begins and ends with the children, and their contribution cannot be undermined. Clayton manages to coax flawless performances from all of them, most of whom had never acted before and did little after (Franklin, a scream queen in waiting, remains to this day a cult icon, but is mainly retired). It may be *about* childhood, but *Our Mother's House* is most definitely *not* a kids' film, and we can only wonder what effect (a la the stories oft told of Bob Ezrin's recording of "The Kids" on Lou Reed's *Berlin*) the experience may have had on them.
—D.R. Shimon

Credits: Director: Jack Clayton; Writers: Jeremy Brooks, Haya Harareet.
Leading Cast: Dirk Bogarde, Margaret Brooks, Pamela Franklin, Louis Sheldon Williams.

The Penthouse

Bruce (Terence Morgan) is a married estate agent engaged in an affair with young shop assistant Barbara (Suzy Kendall) in the penthouse flat of one of Bruce's clients. In the middle of a discussion about the possibility of Bruce leaving his wife,

Tom (Tony Beckley) and Dick (Norman Rodway) gain entrance to the flat diguised as meter readers. Once inside, the pair then subject Bruce and Barbara to an escalating cycle of abuse and humiliation aimed at stripping away the confidence of the debonair and self-centered Bruce, before taking some items and leaving. It takes the arrival of Harry (Martine Beswick) to demolish the final layers of Bruce's facade and leave Barbara to recognize what he really is.

Although *The Penthouse* shares some superficial similarities with the home invasion thriller that would briefly become the vogue in the 1970s, the film owes more to the "kitchen sink' drama and the work of confrontational 1960s playwrights like Harold Pinter. In fact, the film unfolds as an anti-kitchen sink piece, taking a central figure typical of the genre and deconstructing him to expose the hypocrisy and self-centered egotism that this style of drama appeared to idolize. While the most base of the humiliation is heaped upon Barbara, it's key that at the end of the film it is Bruce who runs in panic from the penthouse, and she who walks away from him at the end. While *The Penthouse*, in dismantling the traditional kitchen sink protagonist, positions itself as an antidote to the form, Bruce's exposure as a self-obsessed coward and Barbara's liberation do isolate and identify an important theme that would run through subsequent home invasion horror films, from Sam Peckinpah's *Straw Dogs* to John Trent's *Sunday in the Country*: the idea that the antagonists function as an external force for change.

In *Straw Dogs*, the dribbling locals represent an onslaught that disassembles David Sumner's carefully constructed wall of scientific emotional detachment in order to expose the savage reality of his subconscious. In *The Penthouse*, Tom, Dick and Harry (and there's a clue in the names) deliberately, through their actions, shatter Bruce's carefully constructed lies and expose them for Barbara to see, in turn giving her the tools to recognize the true nature of her manipulative lover.

The Penthouse is both served by, and appears a victim of, its theatrical origin. The action is almost entirely confined to a single set, generating a very real sense of claustrophobia. It also forces Collinson to be creative with his camera, which prowls and moves through *The Penthouse* like an animal. That said, the dialogue is at times ponderous and unsubtle, and the pace is horribly uneven. It feels like a filmed play (which is what it is), with all the strengths and weaknesses that status suggests. Performances vary; Beckley and Rodway in particular might have better suited the stage rather than the confines of a filmed set. Morgan is excellent as the unattractive Bruce, and Kendall gives Barbara an ethereal strength that anchors the film. Beswick is entertaining in what is basically a cameo role, but one crucial in helping the scales fall from Barbara's eyes.

The Penthouse was the first film from director Peter Collinson, who, in too short a career, demonstrated an ability effortlessly to jump between genres. He would return to similar territory on several occasions, initially with the 1971 thriller *Fright,* in which psychotic Ian Bannen lays siege to an isolated house containing babysitter Susan George, and later with *Open Season* (1974) starring Peter Fonda and *Tomorrow Never Comes* (1977) with Oliver Reed. Whilst *Fright* carries more straight suspense and is a more effective piece of horror cinema than *The Penthouse*, it is also less cerebral and contains fewer ideas. It is perhaps *Open Season* that expands most on the concepts presented in *The Penthouse*, though flawed to some degree by its Western trappings. Collinson also directed *The Italian Job*, but died in 1980, aged just 44.

Interesting rather than fully engaging, *The Penthouse* lacks sufficient scope and suffers too much from an uneven pace to be a really effective piece of horror (it's a label that doesn't sit comfortably with the film); however, it remains a fascinating counterpoint to the swinging '60s mentality which had crept into British cinema by this point. It is also a queasy, cynical and introspective introduction to a subgenre that would really find its teeth in the decade that would follow.
—Neil Pike

Credits: Director and Writer: Peter Collinson.
Leading Cast: Suzy Kendall, Terence Morgan, Tony Beckley, Norman Rodway, Martine Beswick.

Quatermass and the Pit
(aka *Five Million Years to Earth*)

In a disused section of the London Underground, construction workers unearth a series of skulls, immediately investigated by Dr. Roney (James Donald) and his statuesque, flame-haired goddess of a lab assistant, Ms. Judd (Barbara Shelley). The subsequent discovery of a large mystery object buried at the site leads to the arrival of the bomb squad, everyone assuming the artifact to be unexploded German ordnance from the Blitz. In charge is the ornery, sneering Colonel Breen (the great Julian Glover). Breen, in the middle of commandeering Prof. Bernard Quatermass' rocket research for military uses, invites Quatermass (Andrew Keir) along to the site, where the latter instantly recognises Roney and Judd as kindred spirits.

Breen thinks the unfamiliar shape of the salvaged item, and the strange phenomena that begin to affect the soldiers, are all the result of a German propaganda misfire, but Roney, Judd, and Quatermass aren't so certain. The latter eventually discovers the object to be an insectoid alien wreck, millions of years old, part of an attempt at genetic improvement of the human species. The psychic phenomena surrounding the spaceship's "reawakening" (in a misguided publicity stunt) spirals out of control, resulting in the possession of large numbers of Londoners and the need for Roney to make the most fateful decision of his life in order to save the human race.

The performances are almost uniformly excellent. Julian Glover, much smoother in most of his villainous roles (one thinks of the glorious Count Scarlioni in the 1979 *Doctor Who* story "City of Death"), perfectly embodies the blinkered, unreasoning side of "the military mind," but it's also easy to see how he arrives at his decisions, even if one doesn't agree with him. Andrew Keir and Barbara Shelley, no strangers to more orthodox Hammer horror productions, acquit themselves well as scientists whose open-mindedness and problem-solving abilities set them apart from the likes of Breen (the most telling moment comes with Quatermass' answer to Breen's accusation that his "imagination is running wild": "Isn't yours?"). Minor performers shine, too: Peter Copley's colorless bureaucrat made flesh, Duncan Lamont's wisecracking safecracker (whose possession scene is one of the film's highlights), and Bryan Marshall's befuddled Captain Potter.

The standout, though, is James Donald, whose roles as rather glum military types in *The Bridge on the River Kwai* (1957), *The Great Escape* (1963) and *King Rat* (1965) suggest he was cleverly cast against type. Enthusiastic, scrappy and brilliant, his Roney proves the perfect foil not only for obtuse bureaucratic and military blundering, but also for the terrifying (and kindred) forces unleashed by humanity's tampering with its own history.

History in many ways is the key to *Quatermass and the Pit*. The film's main thesis is that the aliens' genetic advancements were a success; that, as Barbara Shelley observes, "we're the Martians now." We've *already* been taken over by aliens, and the chief "improvement" is a fundamental xenophobia, the subconscious fear of "the Other" so beloved of post-modern scholarship. Kneale was hardly a post-modernist, but the idea of murderous, even genocidal racism was hardly new, and received added currency in 1960s British science fiction with the Daleks' popularity (!) in *Doctor Who*. The Quatermass twist lies in how this discovered difference visibly affects the characters' behavior. Even Quatermass is easy prey for alien takeover when the time comes, only to be talked out of it by Roney. Almost anyone can succumb to these dark powers, not supernatural but scientific, a vulnerability Kneale brilliantly employs to create a modern horror fable par excellence.

—Wendell McKay

French poster for *Quatermass and the Pit*

Credits: Director: Roy Ward Baker; Writer: Nigel Kneale.

Leading Cast: James Donald, Andrew Keir, Barbara Shelley, Julian Glover, Duncan Lamont.

The Return of Dracula

Sitting before the TV one dark night in late 2005, I was tempted for no reason whatsoever into a bit of channel flicking and suddenly found myself watching an 8mm Dracula—good colors, no sound, quality a bit grainy—what on earth! It was the Halloween edition of the BBC's *See Hear* and an interview with Stephen Pink, who between 1965 and '67 made an amateur vampire movie on 8mm at feature length, calling it *The Return of Dracula*, with Pink taking the starring role and even then looking like the Oldest Swinger in town. Forget *Deafula*, this is the first deaf Dracula movie (in fact, some people seemingly call it "Deaf Dracula"). I was flabbergasted at encountering this seemingly largely unknown British vampire picture.

The film runs 89 minutes and its date of release/completion is put at 1967. The film had its premiere at the Brixton Deaf Club in the late 1960s and was a wow among those attending, so it went on a tour of the deaf clubs with some 20 screenings. Pink even allowed close-ups of his books, showing dates and venues, and details of box office; one of the screenings took place on October 27, 1969, suggesting that this was a popular Halloween deaf community treat and there was significant word of mouth. It also played at deaf clubs in Torquay, Leeds and Coventry, among others, over the next few years, at least until 1971.

Pink, now into his 80s, got up into his original Dracula gear for the interview. I took some scant words down: "The cemetery we filmed in was an actual cemetery...we found a hole in the fence...we got power for our lighting from a car battery!" One of the intertitles explains, "Dracula turns into a bat!" just in case the audience fail to work it out. It is pretty lame in truth. But the images are relatively fresh, and the color is vivid, so the cemetery at least looks impressive. Some of the box office was donated to the deaf clubs of the time.

This is not the only British deaf horror feature. Wayne Hargood's 1995 werewolf film, *Night Stalkers* is another specialist item aimed at hearing-impaired audiences.

Recent additional research has revealed that Stephen Pink was interviewed again on the Community Channel for the Deaf programme *Wicked!* The episode containing Stephen's interview was screened originally in May 2009 and was made available to Internet viewers at www.communitychannel. org—they seem to have done a 30-second crunch-down of the film for the program. Close-ups of Stephen's notebook show details of the takings from Lewisham and Acton Deaf Clubs in November and December 1967 (£11.00 and £16.00, respectively, were not bad for 1967). Pink made the films with his brother, Tony, and there is a nice shot of a poster publicizing the film. He also reveals that he and Tony had considered a further film, to have been titled *Wolfman*, but had to pull out of the idea because of his own poor health. To think, there could have been a spate of BSL horrors long before *Deafula* and *Night Stalkers*.
—Paul Higson

Here is some information on a rare screening from 2004, posted by "Beverley" at www.deafforum.co.uk:

For Deaf people who love going to the cinema, Saturday night is usually frustrating, cinemas hardly ever show anything that is accessible to them.

On Saturday 27th November, the 9th Deaf/Sign Language Film and Television Festival will change all that. Not just one, but two feature films accessible to Deaf people will be shown at the same time at Wolverhampton's Light House. One is in British Sign Language (BSL), the other is subtitled.

The two films picked for screening are a complete contrast. Cinema One will be showing the new British film, *Dear Frankie*, which has not been released yet.

But for many Deaf people, the real treat will be in Light House's Studio Cinema. Here, for the first time in nearly forty years, they can enjoy the first feature-length film ever made in BSL—and it's a real thriller.

The Return of Dracula was written and directed by Stephen Pink, who also starred as Dracula. It was shot on 8-millimetre film between 1965 and 1967. The actors and crew were Stephen's family and friends—all of them Deaf people who used Sign Language.

When the film was completed, Stephen showed it in Deaf clubs, with a total of over two thousand people coming to see it. The biggest audience was a massive turnout of three hundred at Coventry Deaf Club on October 18th, 1969.

Stephen never dreamed his film would be shown in a real cinema, although his inspiration came from the Hammer Horror films starring Christopher Lee. For nearly thirty years the film sat in his house, gathering dust.

Then in 1995, Joseph Collins, a Deaf researcher for the Channel 4 programme "Sign On," learned about it when researching a programme on Deaf culture. It was shown once in 1996 at the second Deaf Film and Television Festival in Newcastle, but at a time when most Deaf people could not make it.

For Joseph Collins, "Stephen Pink is an unsung hero as a Deaf filmmaker." Bob Duncan, who was the producer of "Sign On" in 1995, agrees. He believes this is the kind of screening *The Return of Dracula* deserves.

"I think this film will be seen one day as a silent Sign Language classic," he says. "It uses a few captions, like the old silent films, but the dialogue is all in BSL. It's obvious that, if Stephen had been hearing, he really could have had a great career in films. The aim of the Festival is to make sure that Deaf filmmakers in future do have the opportunity to make films for cinema and TV."

It's hoped that Stephen Pink, now 80, will be present for the screening of his film. Shona Auerbach, the director of *Dear Frankie*, will definitely attend.

Credits: Director and Writer: Stephen Pink.
Leading Cast: Stephen Pink.

Ruddigore

A Halas-Batchelor animated version of the Gilbert and Sullivan operetta, *Ruddigore* brings a taste of culture to the 1960s British genre scene. Prior to reviewing the movie for this book, I hadn't seen this since, oh, 4:05 p.m. on Saturday, September 15, 1984. How can I be so precise? Well, blame Robin Askwith. A pal of mine, aware of my Askwith obsession, bought me an old copy of *TV Times* featuring Robin on its cover as a Christmas gift—and, lo and behold, in the same issue, *Ruddigore* is mentioned in the film pages and on the Saturday evening schedules. Call it fate! Anyhow, let's move on to the film. Every reference I've seen lists this as a 1967 production, but genre researcher extraordinaire Paul Higson claims it's from 1964, and indeed that date is mentioned during the extras on the DVD release. However, I'd guess that production may well have commenced then, and was likely completed two to three years later. One of the animators is interviewed on the DVD and points out that the crew was very small: just himself, John Halas, Joy Batchelor and a couple of others. I confess to being an utter dunce when it comes to "classical" music (are G. and S./D'Oyly Carte "classical," anyway? Or are they rather too late in the day to be termed thus?), so the songs in this production are all a little over-dramatic and top-heavy for my tastes.

The animation is a different matter, however, somewhat limited due to budgetary constraints, but working in that stylized manner popularized by UPA in the 1950s with stuff such as *Gerald McBoing-Boing* and taken up by Friz Freleng at Warner Bros. for many of his cartoons in the early 1960s. The opening scene features a caricatured scary witch being executed, managing to croak out a curse just before she dies: The Murgatroyds, the family ruling the area of Ruddigore, must commit a crime every day or suffer unspeakable agonies and torments, and the witch's spirit takes up residence in a gargoyle atop the family pile to

Top: John Halas and Joy Batchelor
Middle and Bottom: Scenes from *Ruddigore*

keep an eye on them. Those of you who know your Gilbert and Sullivan will know the rest of the plot, involving a thwarted romance, various sibling rivalries, a hidden identity and the eventual clever way in which the curse is beaten (I assume Halas and Batchelor remained faithful to the storyline; apparently they were ordered not to change a word or rewrite any of the lyrics, despite having to compress the telling of the tale into a 52-minute running time, so it seems they simply had to prune out a lot of superfluous material, to the chagrin of the G. and S. aficionados!).

The second half of this production is loaded with macabre horror imagery: the ghosts of previous generations of Murgatroyds looming out of family portraits to put the current nobleman on trial, turning him into a frog, a duck and a worm when they find him guilty of not adhering to the witch's terms; a night-time skeleton dance in a spooky graveyard; Robin Oakapple turning from clean-cut hero in the first half to Byronic/vampiric semi-villainous presence in the second. This is very entertaining indeed, even for a philistine like me. And one of the very, very few British horror films to be directed by a woman, something that has changed a little in the past decade or so; prior to the late 1990s, you could probably count 'em on the fingers of one hand (one-third of *Three Cases of Murder*, *Red*, *The Godsend* and not much else that I can call to mind without additional in-depth research). A couple of further made for TV and video versions of *Ruddigore* followed, but I'd imagine this is the one to see.
—Darrell Buxton

Credits: Director and Writer: Joy Batchelor.
Leading Cast (voices): John Reed, David Palmer, Kenneth Sandford, Ann Hood.

The Shuttered Room

Here's a film that could be so easily overlooked as a British horror classic. It's set in the United States, everyone has American accents and one of the stars is a whacking great big American car of the type only ever seen in films like *Grease*. But it's British through and through, the main clue being the sight of several well-known English character actors struggling to deliver their lines in broad New England accents. As with every attempt to do this, they have a roughly 50 per cent success rate and constantly have to readjust before their RADA-trained slip shows too much.

But dodgy dialects aside, *The Shuttered Room* is a fine film, making good use of its meager budget to deliver a few chills and some memorable scenes (although the non-supernatural ending is a bit of a let down). It begins with a young girl being menaced in bed by an unseen foe, before the mystery assailant is beaten back by her dad. The film shifts to the present day and the girl, Susannah (Carol Lynley), has returned, all grown up and looking pretty saucy. She's brought along her new husband Mike (Gig Young) and is determined to put her demons behind her by returning to her parents' mill. The locals consist of a real bunch of misfits: Oliver Reed (reprising his terrifying bully-boy role from *The Damned*) and his gang, a one-eyed bloke who delights in informing the couple that he lost his binocular vision when "the hot breath of hell" blew on his face up at the old mill ("There's nothing but demons live there..."), and Flora Robson, who spends her days sitting in a lighthouse gazing meaningfully out to sea.

Despite living on an island (and hence surrounded by water, you'd suppose), not-so jolly Ollie and his cronies appear to spend their time pretend waterskiing (which consists of some hapless berk being dragged behind a truck on a packing crate until he flies off into a barbed wire fence). Reed is also deeply concerned when he learns that Susannah is the heir to the old mill, as he was under the impression it would come to him.

As Susannah and Mike finally arrive at their new home, it becomes obvious (through the power of point of view camera work) that *something* is watching them from the attic of the building. Despite very unveiled threats by all and sundry that something horrible will happen if they stay there, Mike buggers off to let Susannah clean the place, but it's not long before she's fed up and goes for a walk along the beach. Narrowly missing out on what looks like a consensual gang bang involving Reed, his mates and a local girl, Susannah then gets chased and almost caught by the half-wits. Luckily Mike arrives in time to save her and beats the crap out of Reed (hooray!). Despite having possibly the worst first day in their new home in the history of moving, the couple endeavour to stay, and the way is clear for them to find out exactly what it is that lurks in the shuttered room at the top of the mill.

The Shuttered Room is very enjoyable, right up until the derivative climax. It has a gorgeous heroine, a cool as ice hero, a terrifying baddie in Oliver Reed and enough plot twists and turns to keep you guessing up to (almost) the end. It is also extremely brutal, with near-rapes, vicious attacks and some great set pieces. Keep an eye out for Reed's improvised torch (no children's toy would burn that easily or well these days) and make sure you shudder when Susannah tells us how terrified she was that someone—or something—used to watch her from the windows of her doll's house during the night. —Chris Wood

Credits: Director: David Greene; Writers: D. B. Ledrov, Nathaniel Tanchuck.

Leading Cast: Carol Lynley, Gig Young, Flora Robson, Oliver Reed, William Devlin.

The Sorcerers

Before his premature death, Michael Reeves located hidden depths of darkness within both the handsome romantic lead (Ian Ogilvy) and that renowned camp genre showman Vincent Price in his historical horror masterpiece *Witchfinder General*. Earlier in his short career, Reeves pulled off a similar feat within a smaller-scale horror story tinged with sci-fi: *The Sorcerers*, which casts Ogilvy as an arrogant player who becomes an unwitting murderer and genre legend Boris Karloff, at the end of his life, as an involuntary accomplice in the evil actions of an unlikely villain.

Although the four Mexican movies that represent his final screen work remain borderline unwatchable, Karloff made some of his finest movies in the last decade of his life. Sandwiched between the terrifying *Wurdalak* segment of Mario Bava's *Black Sabbath* and Peter Bogdanovich's *Targets*, a bleak study of the chasm between real horror and the passé cinematic kind, *The Sorcerers* casts him as Dr. Monserrat, a self-proclaimed practitioner of "medical hypnosis." The careers of Monserrat and his wife (Catherine Lacey) were blighted 30 years earlier by a tabloid-provoked scandal surrounding their business. In their old age, however, they continue "curing" patients of various afflictions while operating in their own home.

Karloff and Lacey also have a personal mission requiring the use of a willing stranger. The film acts initially as a darkly comic culture-clash piece in which the couple plan to set up a foundation so that old people like themselves, trapped within uncooperative, aged bodies, can experience the kind of sensations being enjoyed by thrill-seeking 1960s youth. As their guinea pig, they choose Ogilvy, who's bored of the clubbing lifestyle (which involves grooving along to Lee Grant and the Capitols) and his girlfriend ("bloody artistic temperament"), and is approached by Karloff with the promise of "intoxication with no hangover, ecstasy with no consequence." A very young man himself, Reeves has fun with the concept of elderly folk (the kind who would typically be disapproving of the "youth of today") yearning to experience everything their 20-something counterparts are relishing.

Karloff and his wife have developed the means with which they can reclaim their youth by living vicariously through Ogilvy, whose actions they can control, while he lapses into fugues. It starts innocently enough: Via Ogilvy, the couple enjoy a late night swim and high speeds, but Lacey's will is stronger than her husband's (Reeves' amusing comment on the age-old battle of the sexes) and her desires run into darker realms than Karloff's. Hence Ogilvy is steered on a downward spiral into petty crime—stealing a tiger skin from "Exquisite Furs"—and ultimately to violence.

Although one of the most novel Brit horrors of its period, *The Sorcerers* falls broadly into the post-*Baby Jane*

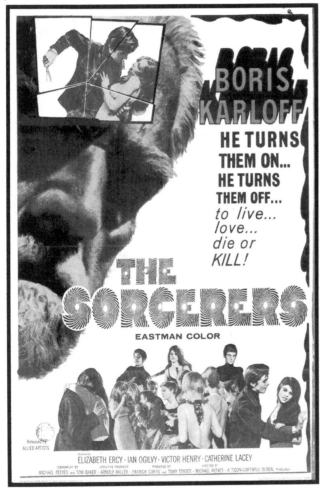

subgenre of films in which the central threat is a controlling, heartless old woman played by a veteran actress relishing the opportunity. Reeves twists audience expectations by making Karloff the one with a conscience, a genteel pensioner who wants the thrill of living through Ogilvy but is horrified by the extremes to which his more adventurous (or dangerous)

wife is willing to go. The two veteran actors have roles that consist almost entirely of sitting at a table projecting thoughts and actions onto another character, but they are never less than riveting.

It's a tidy, flab-less picture with a multilayered, unusually thoughtful theme and a surprisingly perceptive insight into the plight of the elderly, especially considering the director's tender years (ironically, Reeves would die just days after Karloff in February 1969). "Wish I were your age," laments mechanic Alf Joint when he catches a glimpse of the girl hanging around his young apprentice, neatly summing up the movie's central notion of older characters wishing they were savouring the 1960s as their younger selves or, more likely, as the more enlightened, turned-on, tuned-in youths of the era. Like *Targets*, the film offers a poignant evocation of the difficulty of coming to terms with the fact that the world has moved on and left you behind.

Unglamorous, non-touristy location shooting in London and brief but gritty fight scenes give Reeves' second feature a contemporary edge, as do the murders that Ogilvy (who's convincing as a cold-blooded killer) eventually commits. These include the alleyway throttling of a miniskirted pop singer and a fashionable post-*Psycho* fast-cut stabbing (of a young, brunette Susan George, in only one scene as Ogilvy's old flame).

Reeves' nihilistic world view, which permeates the whole of *Witchfinder General*, is apparent for this film's most impressive element: a typically bleak and grimly ironic late-1960s resolution in which the villain and two unfortunate innocents die horribly in the same way. Karloff wins one final battle of wills, but all this means is that he, Ogilvy and Lacey, who has gotten them caught up in a high-speed police chase, get to enjoy the shared experience of burning to death in a car wreck.

—Steven West

Credits: Director: Michael Reeves; Writers: Michael Reeves, Tom Baker.
Leading Cast: Boris Karloff, Catherine Lacey, Ian Ogilvy, Elisabeth Ercy, Victor Henry, Susan George.

The Terrornauts

Where to begin? Well, possibly with the fact that this film clocks in at a lean 75 minutes, meaning that, whatever else, it never drags on you. And that it was adapted from "The Wailing Asteroid" by well-known sci-fi writer Murray Leinster, with a screenplay courtesy of even more well-known sci-fi writer John Brunner. And that it boasts the unlikeliest band of galactic heroes that you're ever likely to see.

A group of scientists at a radio telescope observatory, plus their inquisitive tea lady, are swept off into space to a remote space station by a bizarre alien robot bearing a slight resemblance to obscure Euro-animation favorite Ludwig, and run through a series of intelligence tests before being sent into battle against the evil, empire-building aliens called (presumably, we never are told for certain) the Terrornauts. On a near-by planet, after shenanigans in the obligatory sand pit with green-skinned aliens (who, to confuse matters further, may or may not be the said Terrornauts), they pit their mental abilities, which they use to reactivate the space station's weaponry, against an armada of invading (ah, presumably Terrornaut) spacecraft.

What has this got? It's got the lot, in the most endearingly childish manner that you're likely to see: the sort of effects work that makes the 1930's *Flash Gordon* serials look like *Attack of the Clones* by comparison, a plot that doesn't really make a hill of beans of sense in this crazy (alien) world, and a cast of eccentric individuality for any science fiction adventure. In no particular order: Simon (Ridge) Oates! Patricia (Gran) Hayes! Max (Ludicrus Sextus) Adrian! André (SPECTRE #10) Maranne! Richard (yes, the writer of *Catweazle*) Carpenter! Frank (Asylum Gatehouse Keeper) Forsyth! Charles (Widdle) Hawtrey! And, in a non-typecast move, Robert (Leader Dalek Operator) Jewell as the Robot Operator.

The sheer joy of this one is that, probably via the very lowness of its budget, it becomes the perfect celluloid encapsulation of getting out your Nuxleys toy space helmet and plastic, spark-firing space gun and playing Spacemen and Aliens (presumably before going home for space buns for tea) as a sprog. There's an innocent spirit of adventure and imagination to it that makes it all great fun—best of all in "You don't understand, officer. We're from Surrey. We've just saved the World" (paraphrased, but you get the idea)—it has a closing speech of which Arthur Dent himself would surely have been proud. Blast off!
—Ken Shinn

The imaginatively named Project Star Talk is searching for alien radio transmissions. Lack of success means the project is in danger of being shut down. An accountant is already eyeballing their expenditure. Luckily aliens begin sending signals and turn up in a spaceship to abduct the team, their hut, the accountant and the tea lady.

On the aliens' ship, they meet a robot that looks like a rubbish bin with knitting needles jutting out. It puts them through a series of Krypton Factor-style tests, which they pass. As they finish they are told that Earth is about to be invaded! Using information absorbed from the alien knowledge cubes, they must harness the power of the ship and save Mother Earth!

One word that describes this film is "cheap." When the hut is taken into space, the backdrop doesn't change. A quarry stands in for both an alien planet and a French archaeological dig. For a Stone Age painting, a flower power style doodle has been painted on a rock. The aliens wear shower caps. Their food units are bath cubes. The alien ship is a pipe bracket, and under attack it just wobbles lamely.

The script is based on a short story by Murray Leinster (the pen name of writer William Fitzgerald Jenkins), and I hope he

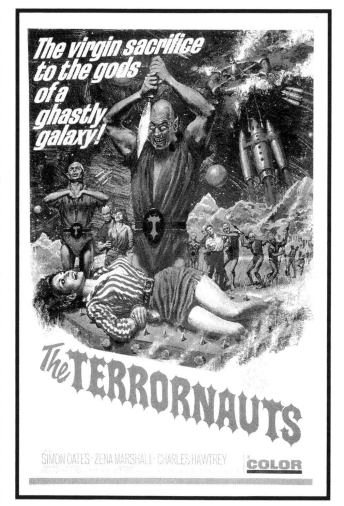

never saw the finished product. The ideas are still there but are practically invisible behind the general shoddiness. There's a lovely moment near the end when the team lands in France and is surprised to find a newspaper in French!

The Project Star Talk team—Simon Oates (Dr. Joe Burke), Stanley Meadows (Ben Keller) and Zena Marshall (Sandy Lund)—are a wooden bunch. Poor Zena, in her final film role, suffers the indignity of being dubbed by a very bored-sounding actress. It's left up to the supporting players to entertain.

Carry On regular Charles Hawtrey is wonderful as accountant Joshua Yellowlees. He might be pissed. He's definitely having a bad wig day. But he's still wonderful. Watching him bring a spark of joy to the drab proceedings makes it all the more puzzling why he wasn't offered more roles in horror and fantasy films. Maybe stories about his alcoholism had leaked out or he was too closely identified with the *Carry On*s.

Patricia Hayes is great fun as Mrs. Jones, the chirpy Cockney tea lady. She does overdo it sometimes with an endless stream of quips reminiscent of Acorn Antiques' Mrs. Overall. She makes a good double act with Hawtrey. She clings to him like she's hoping *Carry On* producer Peter Rogers will soon be on the phone. Maybe she is holding Charlie up.

Look out for Max Adrian as the campy, sinister site manager Dr. Shore, Frank Forsyth popping up to collect his

paycheck, and André Maranne, Britain's favorite Frenchman, as a gendarme. The rubbish robot is operated by 1960s Dalek operator Robert Jewell. He appeared alongside William Hartnell, Patrick Troughton and Peter Cushing before returning to Australia and working on *Prisoner in Cell Block H*.
—Gerald Lea

Credits: Director: Montgomery Tully; Writer: John Brunner.
Leading Cast: Simon Oates, Zena Marshall, Charles Hawtrey, Patricia Hayes.

They Came from Beyond Space

We begin with some groovy swirls against the credits, along with a score suggesting among other things that a sinister and abusive striptease is about to begin. Instead, there's a freak meteor shower in Cornwall, one whose perfect landing in a "V" formation sparks understandable alarm bells at (one would imagine) the highest levels of the British government. Arden (Bernard Kay), a space-specializing bureaucrat, heads on

down with Lee Mason (Jennifer Jayne), a scientist and squeeze of more important boffin Curtis Temple (Robert Hutton), the latter forced to remain behind due to health complications from a recent car crash. News from the site of mysterious financial dealings (million-pound bank withdrawals from Lloyd's) and larger than usual requisitions of material (machine guns?) arouse Temple's suspicions, so he drives down to the site to find out what's happening.

Before anyone can say, "*Quatermass 2*," Temple discovers myriad cases of possession by some sort of alien intelligence, as well as a disfiguring plague in the local bucolic village that keeps nosey visitors well away from the affected site. Forced to take drastic action, Temple joins forces with Lee and his colleague Farge (Zia Mohyeddin) in a daring plan to reveal the mysterious intelligence and destroy its nefarious project to alter the destiny of Earth.

They Came from Beyond Space is really something of an object lesson in the enduring value of cult science-fiction television (particularly the British variety). Elements from the basic plot would have made (and eventually did make) for terrific material in the hands of those behind *Doctor Who*, the *Quatermass* serials (it really is somewhat jarring to see the similarities to *Quatermass 2*) and *The Avengers*, but they suffer greatly when paired with an uncharismatic scientist "hero," clunky dialogue and special effects that forget to be charmingly, budget appropriately quaint instead of flat-out goofy.

They Came from Beyond Space has a fair number of interesting ideas, but most of them had already been used very well in other productions, and it's hard to see why this even *exists* alongside, once again, *Quatermass 2*. There are a few good scenes and some genuine shocks, but the music in particular is a sore thumb, defeating most of the attempts to build tension. The acting is all right but wholly unspectacular. Fortunately, for most of the actors, they're supposed to be possessed by aliens and therefore don't have to do much in the way of emoting (Jennifer Jayne, in particular; in fact, her own possession actually seems to *give* her a personality where she had none before). The bright spot is Zia Mohyeddin (Tafas in *Lawrence of Arabia*) as Farge, who gives the movie a zing and spark where none would otherwise occur: His expression when Temple decides to melt down his silver racing trophies (long story) delivers a classic moment you wouldn't expect in this movie. One might say that there's a treat for horror fans in the appearance of Michael Gough, but he doesn't really get much screen time (although his wardrobe is hilarious, as is that of his fellows). All in all, *They Came from Beyond Space* is a worthwhile enough diversion for an afternoon in which one has absolutely nothing else to do, but rather disappointing as a Freddie Francis film, and easily replaceable with other films or television productions of the same variety.
—Wendell McKay

Credits: Director: Freddie Francis; Writer: Milton Subotsky.
Leading Cast: Robert Hutton, Jennifer Jayne, Zia Mohyeddin, Michael Gough.

Torture Garden

Robert Bloch's screenwriting work for Amicus was a diverse mixture of the sublime (*Asylum*, *The House that Dripped Blood*) and the likeably ridiculous (*The Deadly Bees*, *The Skull*). Usually dismissed in overviews of the studio's cycle of portmanteau movies, *Torture Garden* falls somewhere in between. Certainly notable as the only movie in which *Dracula Has Risen from the Grave*'s excellent Barbara Ewing is chased by a malevolent grand piano, this anthology lacks the edge and wit of many of Amicus' multi-story chillers.

The quartet of stories is framed by a storyteller overly reminiscent of Peter Cushing's superior Dr. Schreck in the earlier *Dr. Terror's House of Horrors*. Burgess Meredith hams it to the hilt as Dr. Diabolo, a showy carnival barker who foretells the inevitably grim fates of a series of sceptical customers.

In "Enoch," jobless, selfish Michael Bryant visits his obscenely rich, dying uncle (Maurice Denham) to beg for a loan. When the old goat refuses, Bryant kills him and subsequently falls under the influence of Denham's possessed cat, which drives him to commit a sequence of murders while securing his own demise. Of the four, this enjoyable opener is the most indebted to EC horror comics, with its greedy protagonist destined for a telegraphed comeuppance.

Bloch's oft-apparent dark sense of humor makes the second story, "Terror Over Hollywood," an amusing satire of the movie industry's fixation on youth and glamour. Determined starlet Beverly Adams bids to sleep and deceive her way to the top of the showbiz pile but, in the process, discovers that the movie stars we know and idolize are, in fact, robots engineered by an L.A. scientist tasked with sustaining eternally good looking and youthful celebs. At least now we know the origins of Morgan Fairchild.

Despite the gleefully absurd premise, "Mr. Steinway" is the dullest of the selection: a plodding story of a famous but deranged pianist (John Standing) whose piano, inhabited by the soul of his overbearing dead mother, becomes murderously jealous when any woman (step forward, Barbara Ewing) shows romantic interest in him.

The standout episode is the last, "The Man Who Collected Poe," a neat, original addition to the vast array of Poe-inspired genre flicks of the 1960s, given a major boost by two charismatic stars. Eccentric, obsessive Poe fan Jack Palance (with English accent) kills the world's biggest Poe collector (Peter Cushing) only to realize that he has resurrected the dead author, who wants Palance to figure in one final, gruesome work.

All of the British horror anthologies of the 1960s and 1970s are worth seeing—even *Tales that Witness Madness* has considerable charm if you catch it in the right frame of mind—and *Torture Garden* is no exception. Relatively speaking, however, it borders on the bland, and Meredith's host (whose true identity in the twist ending won't surprise

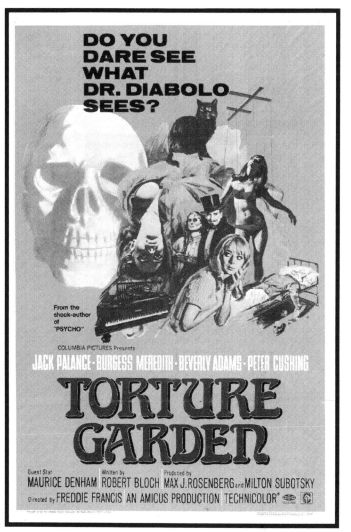

anyone with half a brain) is the least engaging of Amicus' deliciously bizarre range of wrap-around storytellers.
—Steven West

Credits: Director: Freddie Francis; Writer: Robert Bloch.
Leading Cast: Burgess Meredith, Jack Palance, Peter Cushing, Michael Bryant, Maurice Denham, Robert Hutton, Michael Ripper, Beverly Adams.

The Vengeance of Fu Manchu

This is the third in a series from producer Harry Alan Towers that began well and terminated with some of the crappiest movies Christopher Lee ever crawled out of his coffin to make. So it should be reasonable, middling entertainment, then. And it is.

The Chinese arch fiend of the title (Lee, in the familiar droopy eyelids and droopier 'tache) is understandably pretty bored sitting around in his remote, mountain hideout and so hatches another diabolical plot to take over the world by replacing police commissioners with surgically altered, murderous doppelgangers, and—oh, well, it's too fiendishly diabolical to

German poster for *The Vengeance of Fu Manchu*

Director Jeremy Summers replaced original series director Don Sharp for this installment (Jess Franco loomed on the horizon), and does an adequate job keeping the story moving. Some will carp about missing Sharp's "light touch," which for me translates as "slightly dull touch," and this changeover results in a more entertaining flick. There are a couple of scenes you'd imagine Sharp shying away from, but Summers is happy to include a beheading and a branding scene, the latter of which might be a step too far for some, even if the victim (Suzanne Roquette) is visibly not burned! All this helps push the movie further down the exploitation u-bend that would be the series' ultimate fate.

Fu's plot would never work, of course. If one respected police commissioner turns murderous maniac, that's unfortunate; two might be written off as a ghoulish coincidence, but dozens around the globe? Wouldn't somebody smell a big, yellow rat? The subplot about an American syndicate leader traveling across the world to strike a deal with the Asian genius seems tagged on to help pad out the running time.

The long-nosed Wilmer has a pretty easy ride in this, as for most of his time onscreen he's playing a hypnotized Smith look-alike who utters not a word. Still, he's a likeable presence. Lee's not around much, but perhaps more than in the previous movies. If you've seen them, it's more of the same. Tsai Chin makes her mark as Fu's loyal daughter, Lin Tang.

One thing: The last we see of poor old Dr. Petrie, he's under the impression that Nayland Smith has been executed. The film's ending is rushed and there's no scene at the end showing them being reunited and reaffirming what is, I dare say, a latent homosexual coupling with so much as a brisk handshake! I say, chaps, that's not cricket!
—Jed Raven

Credits: Director: Jeremy Summers; Writer: Peter Welbeck [Harry Alan Towers].
Leading Cast: Christopher Lee, Douglas Wilmer, Tsai Chin, Horst Frank, Maria Rohm.

The Vulture

This is a frankly amazing film: a jaw-droppingly bizarre idea coupled with a relentlessly slow plot and wooden acting. In a slightly effective opening sequence, it's a "dark and stormy night" as a bus slows up at the stop. A passenger announces she's going to cut across a graveyard at night. "Ahh, ya wouldn't get me in that place after dark!" warns the bus driver. And as she crosses the yard a gravestone wobbles and the ground bulges as something leaves the grave. The woman screams and collapses as something flaps away.

What is it that flaps, you ask? Well, in olden times, the local squire had a man buried alive with his pet vulture because

explain here. But, trust me, it's diabolical—and quite possibly fiendish. And if Mr. Manchu can have revenge on our hero, Assistant Commissioner Nayland Smith of Scotland Yard (Douglas Wilmer), at the same time, then the job's a good 'un.

And so, under duress, a kidnapped surgeon transforms a rebel prisoner into a dead ringer for our Nayland by referencing just two photographs. Talk about working miracles. Leslie Ash wants his number.

The real Smith is abducted, to be offed by the Yellow Peril in his own time. Meanwhile, the doppelganger (Wilmer again), ashen-faced, perpetually sweating and looking like he's going to pebbledash your shoes, subsequently throttles Smith's maid and is put on trial for murder. Of course, it's an open and shut case, and Smith (or his doppelganger—is this getting complicated?) is sentenced to hang! Dr. Petrie (Howard Marion-Crawford), Watson to Smith's Holmes, is understandably pretty gutted. Who'll make him look slightly slow and buffoonish now? Pretty much everybody, probably. Of course, Smith has already managed to survive two films in the series, and so shouldn't be counted out, just yet.

he was supposed to be a witch. Now some "unknown scientific brain" tinkering with a nuclear whatsit has produced a "monstrous creature, half bird, half man."

And Big Bird is after the descendants of that squire, "from the oldest to the youngest." Luckily the youngest, Trudy (Diane Clare, whose most memorable role was as André Morell's daughter in Hammer's *The Plague of the Zombies*), is married to scientist Eric (American import Robert Hutton, who's old enough to be her father). He deduces the existence of this nuclear budgie out of thin air with no proof apart from a dead sheep and some feathers.

No one believes him except for his wife and kindly Germanic scientist Professor Hans (Akim Tamiroff). Who is behind it? Is it the slightly disturbed Sexton wandering around uttering vague threats? Or could it be the kindly Germanic scientist or the kindly Germanic scientist or the kindly Germanic scientist or…

This is a truly painful film to watch. Everything unfolds at a snail's pace. The only let-up is the unbelievably hilarious dialogue Eric comes out with when explaining the creation of the Vulture. Using "nuclear transmutation," someone was transferred through the "ether" into the grave. And this man is supposed to be working for the U.S. government!

It takes Eric forever to work out that the only "scientific brain" in the area belongs to Professor Hans. He even has to phone the local electricity board before the penny drops.

The acting is poor. When Eric, Trudy's Uncle Brian and the local improbably American-accented Superintendent share a scene, it's like a forest because there's so much wood on the screen.

The Vulture itself is just hilarious. It's like something out of a Dave Allen sketch. When it attacks, two yellow feet descend from the air and the victim, now wearing a wire, is winched into the sky. Finally the creature is fully revealed and it's just poor Akim Tamiroff in a bird costume. And this is what is supposed to have frightened one woman so much her hair turned white—lucky she didn't die laughing.
—Gerald Lea

The Vulture is a turkey. And that facile, clichéd, throwaway statement bears as much relation to reasoned film critique as this potboiler does to entertaining popular cinema. Slow, talky and ludicrous are just three appropriate adjectives. Boring and inept are two more. Which is a shame, because the opening scene of a woman who disregards a bus driver's warning about spooks in the cemetery and crosses a rural Cornish graveyard at night is rather creepy.

But that's as good as it gets. In the next scene, the now white-haired woman tells an unbelieving policeman about her encounter with a "huge bird with a horrible human head" (guess we've all been on a date with one of those, eh, lads?). Cut to an interminable (and exasperatingly static) expository scene in which the copper learns of a local legend about the descendant of a Spanish survivor of the Great Armada and

his monstrous pet bird, his cache of gold coins buried with him and his curse upon the future generations of his persecutors, and it looks like we're in for a Poverty Row rip-off of *The Hound of the Baskervilles*.

The remaining running time is full of illogical red herrings (a white-haired creep in a black raincoat pops up from time to time and delivers a few lines in the manner of someone attempting to remember the conjugations of irregular verbs in a language unknown to him), and non sequiturs follow in succession as a holidaying American nuclear physicist (the ever awful Robert Hutton) waffles around, fruitlessly investigating the strange events (45 minutes into the film, the Scotland Yard man fittingly echoes the audience's exasperation by bursting out, "This is getting us nowhere!"), until the "climax," when his wife (the ever awful Diane Clare) is briefly abducted by the titular monstrosity, portrayed with effects which make *The Giant Claw* seem like *Jurassic Park* by comparison.

There's no mystery: When you have weird Akim Tamiroff playing an old codger limping around an English village in floppy black hat and cloak and speaking all his dialogue with a cod Mittel European accent, not even Bunny Bruce's Doc Watson would be hard pushed to add zwei und zwei [2 plus 2] and guess the identity of the birdman. Worst of all, in this listlessly directed stinker (take a bow, Lawrence Huntington) that purports to be a horror movie, there's absolutely no suspense, no thrills, no shocks, nor anything remotely scary. And though made in the swinging '60s, there's nothing (apart from the odd fleetingly glimpsed Morris Minor) to suggest that this rubbish wasn't made three decades previously.
—Mike Hodges

Credits: Director: Lawrence Huntington; Writer: Lawrence Huntington.

Leading Cast: Robert Hutton, Akim Tamiroff, Broderick Crawford, Diane Clare, Philip Friend.

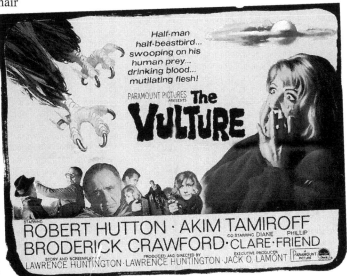

1968

The Blood Beast Terror
(aka *The Vampire Beast Craves Blood*)

While many—all right, *some*—British horror films can be regarded as "presents" to the audience, Tigon's nifty yet berserk *The Blood Beast Terror* is more of a "stocking stuffer," even with its ridiculous title (at times, "What the *hell*?" seems more appropriate). It's occasionally hard to see how it all fits together (if it even does), but it's a lot of fun.

After a brief moth-hunting prologue along an African river (any "Monkey's Paw"-style "empire strikes back" nuances really end there), a coachman in Victorian England happens upon a dead body, clawed almost beyond recognition. Dr. Mallinger (Robert Flemyng), in the midst of delivering an entomology slideshow to his students, finds an unwelcome surprise in the person of Inspector Quennell (Peter Cushing), who has come to ask him about some recent murders which have taken place near his house, all in the manner seen earlier. Another fatality is discovered in a nearby coach, and the viewer quickly discovers that Dr. Mallinger's up to no good.

Following the clues, some unwittingly provided by Mallinger's scarred and sneering butler (Kevin Stoney), as well as smirking dope Britewell (William Wilde), Quennell traces the murders to Mallinger and his alluring daughter Claire (Wanda Ventham), only to find the house nearly deserted and the Mallingers escaped. No slouch, Quennell tracks down the Mallingers at a country retreat and, in a ridiculous but enjoyable plot twist, brings along his *own* daughter Meg (Vanessa Howard of *Mumsy, Nanny, Sonny and Girly* fame). As Quennell draws nearer his quarry, the Mallingers grow increasingly desperate in their attempt to evade justice and protect the terrifying secret behind the murders.

The plot seems rather simple and straightforward, but there's just so much else *The Blood Beast Terror* has to offer. Only the most reticent and gentlemanly of plot synopses can disguise the fact that a giant, blood-drinking moth figures in the proceedings, and while the creature itself is unintentionally hilarious, some of the surrounding special effects (or camera tricks to *avoid* special effects) are unexpectedly clever, the film effectively serves as a cross between a classic Hammer and a 1950's American monster flick. The no-frills direction and camera work work in the story's favour: There's a loose, low-key cool to this story that few other Gothic-flavored British horror films ever achieved. There's always *something* going on, even such unfortunate bits as the "comic relief morgue attendant" eating his dinner get a sinister musical flourish (courtesy of *Witchfinder General*'s Paul Ferris), probably to disguise the fact that the scene is otherwise unremarkable (there's a near minute-long take of the guy talking!).

The acting is by and large superb. Cushing's in top gear and his quiet yet tenacious cop offers an interesting change from his usual roles (although not *that* much; at one point, his supervisor comes close to taking him off the case, and Cushing essentially replies, "Oh, I'd rather you didn't"). Flemyng's a bit of a bland villain, but his cronies are excellent: Ventham's dismissive and mysterious, and the great Kevin Stoney makes the most of his limited screen time, taunting raptors (!) and lounging around Flemyng's house like Dirk Bogarde in *The Servant*. Even toward the dodgy end, Howard's memorably sweet as young Meg, and her meet-cute romance with young lepidopterist William (David Griffin) strikes an interesting note that subtly contrasts with Ventham's increasingly obvious loneliness—*and* she's a good screamer to boot.

While hardly a patch on later Tigon "historicals" like *Witchfinder General* or *Blood on Satan's Claw*, *The Blood Beast Terror* offers a wonderfully entertaining example of what their more run of the mill output could deliver.

—Wendell McKay

In Victorian London a deadly flapper is killing young men and draining them of blood in this delirious horror from Tigon. Straight from the false start we know we are in the low-budget mad-lands, for a few tall grasses and plenty of stock footage does not make the Thames on a dull day into Africa. Even if the charade does set up a later "too much sun while up the Limpopo" line and helps to explain why men in pith hats put green knobbly things in boxes, it is a misjudgment.

Quickly we are back in Blighty proper and in olden times, for a horse-drawn coach is being driven recklessly into the night (note: the speed denotes the genre; sedate for romance; reckless for horror; and backward for Will Hay), when a scream rings out in the forest. The open carriage stops and the driver then finds the poor victim with blood everywhere (of course, later every drop of red will be drained from the body and puzzled authorities will wonder where it all went), but wait, something is returning—cue scream!

No sooner has the viewer been hooked than logic is thrown out of the window, as the dying man is taken to police Inspector Quennell. Despite a handful of diverting scenes including more of the demented driver and a search with bobbing bobbies, we remain largely in the company of the professor, his daughter and the Inspector. Are they hiding something? Is the play a clue? Which is funnier, Roy Hudd or his hair? Will we get the answers? Well we do, but that does not terminate the craziness. Meanwhile the main culprit (can you tell who it is yet?) escapes by train with a lot of boxes, and tips big. Luckily the wily old inspector has deduced the villain's bolthole and goes in pursuit with only his daughter as cover, just the sort of backup you need when tracking a mass murderer.

This second part of the film is a real treat. It's complete with "homages," outrageous plot and underlying themes that lend life to this type of pulp. For the psychiatrist there are three motherless young leads with differing paternal types: the jealous father, the indulgent father and the loving but standoffish father. We also have the beloved Euro-Gothic plot twist of hypnotism with a doomed sleepwalker, experiments with that evil and newfangled electricity, transforming clothes and a fiery end or three.

The film feels like a British version of a European period exploiter, and as with that particular strain, its biggest problem is with the budget (or lack of) and the problems inherent. Sets are stretched in use and isolated from each other (note the smallest major train station in London). The cast is minimal but in the main excellent, and "spot the British character actor" is happily in place as it should be with all British horror. The special effects are weak, from a splodge on the negative to a Japanese style be-suited person playing a mad monster, but what a unique and marvelous creature! You will not have seen anything like it. Scenes commence and then evaporate, for no other reason than to add atmosphere and to entertain. To complete the Euro feel, it even has various other titles like *Blood Beast from Hell*, *The Deathshead Vampire* and (in the U.S.) *The Vampire-Beast Craves Blood*. It also has early product placement: Fancy a Madeira sherry, anyone?

The film belts along. Cushing is wonderful, as always (his asides about tea are splendid), and, apart from the monster and odd stock shots, it looks good. It's a low-budget joy that makes you glad it was autumn.
—Wayne Mook

Credits: Director: Vernon Sewell; Writer: Peter Bryan.
Leading Cast: Peter Cushing, Robert Flemyng, Wanda Ventham, Vanessa Howard, Roy Hudd.

The Blood of Fu Manchu

In the midst of a suitably exotic location, several blindfolded women are hustled, in various states of undress, into a cavern where they find themselves confronted by a dastardly Chinese villainess (Tsai Chin), and the viewer becomes horribly aware that another installment of the soporific misbehaviors of Fu Manchu (Christopher Lee) is about to begin. Fu, using his unique intellect and boundless talent for intrigue, is about to implement another moronic plan for the subjugation of the entire world to his unthinkable pleasures. In the meantime, an expedition led by Carl Jansen (Götz George) is underway to find the lost city where Fu's holed up. The intrepid explorers naturally run into trouble, and Jansen finds the annoying and pointless local government unable or unwilling to help.

Meanwhile, Scotland Yard's Nayland Smith (Richard Greene) and stalwart chum Dr. Petrie (Howard Marion-Crawford, again demonstrating his astonishing talent for gruffly repeating the main ideas in others' sentences) discover through seemingly pleasant means the gist of Fu's depraved plot. Ten women will travel to selected locations around the world and polish off Fu's deadliest enemies by kissing them with poisoned lipstick. After that, nothing else is really of any importance to tell or watch. There's a Frito Bandito type whose compañeros carry out a wretchedly filmed "attack" on a village, Jansen's doctor friend Ursula (Maria Rohm), displaying a predilection for tight pants, gunplay and a big waterfall.

It's *awful*. What the film really makes one want to do is take a tire iron to the screen. *Blood*'s stupidity and boredom are compounded by a number of "arty" touches (presumably courtesy of Mr. Franco) that only serve to underline how pointless and excruciating the whole thing is. Nobody's of any real interest or sympathy, and the usual pleasures of watching a bad movie somehow get leeched away by a defiant listlessness that pervades throughout.

As a result, the accompanying DVD documentary, *The Rise of Fu Manchu*, featuring interviews with Lee, Chin, Franco, and producer (and screenwriter) Harry Alan Towers, is both of more interest and outrage than the actual movie. Whatever one's opinion of the effective deification of Terence Fisher's

contemporary classic *The Devil Rides Out*, Franco's condemnation of directors like Fisher—that they "didn't understand horror"—will render speechless those who've seen his own two monumentally embarrassing *Fu Manchu* entries (although he's on better and shrewder ground discussing his star's ambivalence towards the genre). Lee starts off with "What I wanted to do with the character," and the rest is a dreary rehash of his battles with Hammer and Towers' comparatively refreshing take on his latest villain.

The most interesting stuff comes from the lively Chin, talking about the racial politics surrounding the main character and her own mixed feelings in taking her role (issues that, for this viewer, were rendered null and void by the movie's fatal anomie). One almost wishes the movie had starred Chin and been about Fu's daughter—it might have actually been worth watching.

—Wendell McKay

Credits: Director: Jesus Franco; Writers: Jesus Franco, Peter Welbeck [Harry Alan Towers].
Leading Cast: Christopher Lee, Richard Greene, Howard Marion-Crawford, Tsai Chin, Maria Rohm, Shirley Eaton.

Curse of the Crimson Altar (aka *The Crimson Cult*)

Curse of the Crimson Altar begins its garish little tale the way it means to go on: mint green writing on a fuchsia pink-lit background of stone gargoyles. Nice. We then get a lovely little made-up quote from a made-up book—"and drugs of this group can produce the most complex hallucinations and under their influence it is possible by hypnosis to induce the subject to perform actions he would not normally commit" (Extract from medical journal)—superimposed over a kaleidoscope image.

Woo, groovy, man. Apparently, this was bunged in at the last moment to capitalize on the late 1960s drugs boom, even though the rest of the film has nothing whatsoever to do with hallucinogenics at all, even during the "swinging" party scenes.

Cut to naked woman writhing on an altar, watched by the She-Hulk (sorry, Barbara Steele in green makeup as the witch, Lavinia), a priest (?), some cowled servant-types, a burly bloke in leather underpants and a horned helmet, and a completely normal fella in a tweed jacket. Normal signs something. Steele: "Enter our world of darkness. You know what you have to do." Tweed jacket man stabs the girl on the altar, and then gets branded by Leatherpants. Cut to hefty and almost-naked bird (cries of "Get 'em on!") brandishing a whip, with bits of black plastic covering her nipples. They obviously eat well, these Satanists, even if they can't afford decent clothes.

Then we're whisked off to a 1960s antiques shop, where we get a handy explanation of the old "spring-loaded bodkin" trick (which is more boring than it sounds; it's a knife used to "expose" witches by making it look like they don't bleed when stabbed). The shop owner Bob gets a letter from his brother Peter saying he's been staying at Craxted Lodge, near the old family seat. But when Bob tries to phone Peter, they've *never*

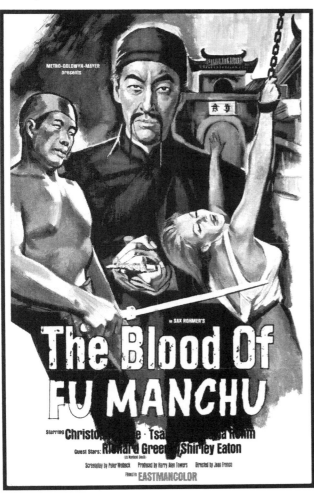

METRO-GOLDWYN-MAYER
presents

in SAX ROHMER'S

The Blood Of Fu Manchu

Starring Christopher Lee · Tsai Chin · Maria Rohm
Guest Stars: Richard Greene (as Nayland Smith) · Shirley Eaton

Screenplay by Peter Welbeck · Produced by Harry Alan Towers · Directed by Jess Franco

Filmed in EASTMANCOLOR

heard of him. Bob decides to visit this Craxted Lodge in his trusty white MGB. The unusually helpful petrol attendant seems happy to furnish our hero with lots of local knowledge about "witches night" in the village, but clams up when the lodge is mentioned.

After witnessing a bizarre game of hide and seek involving a catsuit-clad girl and four cars, Bob arrives at the Lodge to find a party in full swing. In an horrific example of what happens when middle-aged men imagine what "youth" gets up to, we have artistic blokes painting women's breasts, adults playing kids' games, people smoking enormous cigarettes and rubbish cat fights. Eve Morley (Virginia Wetherell, wearing a hideous yellow outfit) welcomes Bob with a snog, and then directs him to her uncle, the owner of the lodge (Christopher Lee). Lee fobs the letter off as a practical joke (it is hilarious, after all) and invites Bob to stay.

We are then treated to a bit of pre-post modern post modernism, as on the way to Bob's room, Eve remarks, "It's a bit like one of those houses in horror films," to which Bob replies, "I know what you mean—as if Boris Karloff is going to pop up at any moment." Of course he does, about one minute later, as Professor Marsh. It could be an incredibly clever attempt to deconstruct the idea of film, or it could be just a crap joke. Come to think of it, it's probably the latter.

Regarding his accommodation, Bob asks, "I wonder why they call it the gray room?" (because the walls are painted gray, you arse) and then spots a candlestick exactly like one his brother sent him. Shock, gasp! Enter Boris as the brandy-swilling Marsh, the acknowledged occult expert in this part of the world, "Past, present—and future" (eh?). He reckons brandy is completely wasted on women, that there's "good reason to rue the day they burned Lavinia" and that "we shall meet again" (much eyebrow acting). Perhaps Professor Obvious Red Herring would have been a better name for the character.

At the Burning, the villagers display a distinct lack of knowledge of the Firework Code, and then, acting on a tipoff from the butler Elder (Michael Gough, also doing a nice line in eyebrow acting), Bob visits the graveyard for no apparent reason. By the way, Elder appears to communicate with Lavinia through the power of the spinning standard lamp.

Bob then has a dream where we discover that the branded bloke at the beginning of the film was his brother, and he gets to meet Lavinia, who's now added to her entourage with a "supposed to be naked but obviously still got her pants on" long-haired woman and several farmyard animals. I believe there is an uncut European version of this film somewhere out there—could be interesting (although I doubt it).

After surviving being shot at by Professor Marsh's groovy manservant (who's never going to hit his target with those sunglasses on), Bob discovers that his brother *did* stay

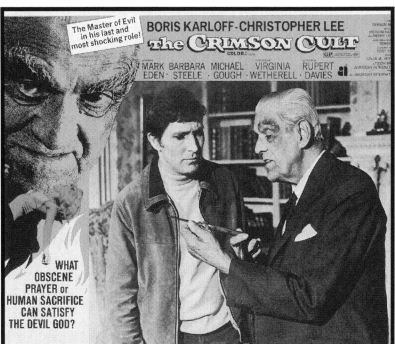

at the lodge, but used his *nom de plume* (which Bob has failed to mention up until now, the berk). Eve ventures the idea that "He's gone off with some bird."

Of course, Peter won't be doing any knobbing where he's gone: he's dead. After telling Lee that he's going to the police (always a big horror no-no), Bob nearly ends up killing himself during another dream while sleepwalking into a nearby pond. Luckily he's saved by a passing policeman, and when he gets back to the lodge he falls into the arms of the considerably undressed Eve (there certainly doesn't seem to be a great deal of point to her see-through dressing gown; I hope she doesn't go down to breakfast in it, her uncle wouldn't know where to look). The next morning, Bob finds a secret door that leads to the room in his dreams, but is fobbed off when he reports the strange occurrences to his policeman friend. Probably because he can't get his lines right: "I know there's something wrong going up on that lodge."

Bob then finds out that he is the linear descendant of one of the people who put Lavinia to death centuries ago, and after much unnecessary fact finding at the nearby church (as if we hadn't sussed it all out already), Lee tries to sacrifice Eve (why?) and sets fire to his own house (why?), eventually turning into Lavinia before burning to death on his roof.

Curse of the Crimson Altar (released as *The Crimson Cult* in the U.S. in 1970) might not make much sense but, as a product of its time, it's great. Lee as the moustachioed Morley might as well be one of the filmmakers, a middle-aged square totally unaware of what the young folk are getting up to all around him while he carries on doing what his ancestors have been doing for years. It's crap, but I have a sneaking feeling that it knows it's crap. And where else are you going to find Christopher Lee, Barbara Steele, Michael Gough and Boris Karloff all in the same picture?

—Chris Wood

Credits: Director: Vernon Sewell; Writers: Mervyn Haisman, Henry Lincoln, Gerry Levy.
Leading Cast: Boris Karloff, Christopher Lee, Barbara Steele, Mark Eden, Virginia Wetherell, Rupert Davies, Michael Gough.

The Devil Rides Out (aka The Devil's Bride)

Richard Matheson, whose most notable 1960s screenplays include those for various Roger Corman Poe Gothics and one underrated British chiller (*Night of the Eagle*), also toiled sporadically for Hammer Films. The British censor rejected his Hammer-bound screenplay "Night Creatures," an early adaptation of his classic novel *I Am Legend*, but the author did see his script for *Fanatic* make it to cinemas. Matheson next adapted Dennis Wheatley's popular 1934 novel *The Devil Rides Out*, for what was intended to be the first of a series of Hammer-Wheatley collaborations. The middling box office for the *The Devil Rides Out* movie effectively doomed the planned cycle (with Hammer belatedly unleashing the unloved *To the Devil a Daughter* during their dying days), though it did emerge in the same year that *Rosemary's Baby* heralded the start of Hollywood's Devil trend. *The Devil Rides Out* is one of the studio's most dynamically paced pictures as well as one of their most sinister with a pervading sense of all-powerful evil.

Christopher Lee has one of his best roles for the studio (reflected by his wholly positive attitude toward the project) as the Duc De Richleau, one of this actor's rare unambiguous Hammer good guys. He's a knowledgeable, authoritative figure whose presence in the story is to convince the rest of the cast of the evils at work. Lee and Leon Greene go searching for old chum Patrick Mower, and discover that he has joined a mysterious "astronomy" circle. When closer inspection reveals a basket full of nervous chickens and a black magic cult presided over by Charles Gray, the truth about Mower's pastimes becomes apparent. Rescuing Mower from becoming

The Devil Rides Out

part of a May Day ritual, and taking refuge at a friend's house, they are soon persecuted by Gray and his assorted diabolical instruments of terror.

This movie's genesis dates back to the first half of the 1960s, and it only emerged when censorship concerns about cinematic dabblings with Satanism had mellowed to a certain extent (the memorable "rape by the Devil" in Polanski's film was still considered excessive and reduced in British theatrical prints). Fisher avoids visceral horrors here: The Satanic orgy is among the most discreet scenes of its kind, and the only blood spilled appears during a mild animal sacrifice. The movie nonetheless evokes considerable mounting menace and urgency via James Bernard's suitably malevolent score and bursts of exciting action, including a country road car chase. Enhancing the intensity is the repeated use of Lee to stress the dire nature of the threat by sternly saying dramatic things like "The Devil himself" or ominously intoning, "It's not just your life you're risking, it's your very soul!"

Making the most of limited screen time, Charles Gray, with his icy cold blue eyes, wickedly charismatic charm and line delivery dripping with malice, is one of Hammer's finest villains. His fabulously intimidating warning "I shall not be back, but something will" paves the way for an unforgettable final half hour of sustained suspense. The typically under-funded nature of Hammer's special effects cannot dilute the impact of the scenes in which our heroes are assailed by a giant spider (a visual echo of one classic encounter in Matheson's peerless *The Incredible Shrinking Man*) and meet the "Angel of Death," a skeletal agent of Satan astride a winged horse.

With Vietnam-era horror films on both sides of the Atlantic (*Night of the Living Dead* and *Witchfinder General*) offering pessimistic or ambiguous resolutions to reflect the cynicism of the times, Hammer's later output—including Fisher's final Frankenstein movies—took a darker turn. Many of the studio's early 1970s movies (including *Blood from the Mummy's Tomb* and *Demons of the Mind*), overlooked at the time, no longer offered the comforting reassurance of good triumphing over evil as would be *de rigueur* in their early Gothics. *The Devil Rides Out*, in that sense, ends up sticking to the patented Hammer formula. The bravura child in peril finale is capped by a wholly traditional Hammer resolution, with evil purged by the winning team of fire and God ("*He* is the one we must thank!").

It may end conventionally, but there's nothing routine about *The Devil Rides Out*, which—markedly with Mocata's quiet invasion of the Eatons' home—generates frequent bona fide chills.
 -Steven West

Most people reading this will be aware of the film's origins, being adapted from one of Dennis Wheatley's many fine occult-based novels. Actually only a fraction of Wheatley's work is concerned with the occult, the larger percentage consisting mainly of suspense, adventure and romance stories, yet his knowledge, especially for a man who ("allegedly and supposedly") never took part in any magic rituals of either a black-or-white nature, was vast, and he invested all of his writings on the subject with an authenticity that many—including Terence Fisher and Christopher Lee—admired. What *The Devil Rides Out* has in common with more of his published work is not its subject matter but its characters: Simon Aron, Richard Eaton, Rex Van Ryn and, at the helm, the masterful Duc Nicolas De Richleau, and it is this role, portrayed authoritatively here by Lee, which is both the heart and the hub of the film and carries it forth with precision, gravitas and, most importantly, style—plus a superb moustache.

It is also to Lee's credit that, while the script makes several subtle "amendments" to Wheatley's original tale, his own portrayal of the Duc is never far removed from how his creator would have imagined him. Of course, knowing what a stickler for adherence to the text Lee could be, it's possible that his appearance in the film depended on it. Indeed, he has already informed us well enough of the chagrin he expressed when informed by an American distributor that they may have to change the title as the original "sounded too much like a Western."

Conversely, Patrick Mower, in the part of the vulnerable Simon, avoids playing him as a Jew (whether this was on purpose or not is unknown), yet simultaneously manages to convey the youthful fallibility and naïveté intrinsic to the character. In many of Wheatley's original novels—such as *The Forbidden Territory*, still sadly unfilmed—the plot revolves around the Duc, Rex and Richard having to "rescue" their young protégé from some unfortunate circumstance he had toppled into as a result of his own irresponsibility, and here is no exception, only this time the danger is greater, as he has fallen under the spell of the manipulative and thoroughly evil Satanist Mocata (Charles Gray) and joined what he refers to as "an astronomical society." Of course, the Duc knows better, and within five minutes of being in Simon's new house and finding that he and Rex are unwelcome because "There shouldn't be more than 13," he's onto the game and isn't going to stand easily by and see his friend follow the Left Hand Path.

The scene that ensues, most famously involving the discovery of a wardrobe full of hens and cockerels, is as iconic as any in the history of Brit horror, not least of all for the line "You fool! I'd rather see you *dead* than meddling with black magic!" followed by a swift Chris biff to Mower's upper jaw (but trust him, viewers, he's only doing it for Simon's own good). The Duc and Rex "kidnap" their errant friend, drive him back to London, hypnotize him (well, the Duc does; Rex just sits there nonplussed at the whole situation) and send him to bed, where, in the first of a series of set pieces that have yet to be bettered in *any* film since, he is almost asphyxiated by a crucifix placed around his neck for protection. Following his subsequent escape he is swiftly pursued back to his house by his friends, who stave off a grinning African demon that just might not pass "political correctness" muster in the present day, but has nonetheless terrified the living daylights out of everyone who has ever seen it.

It's a testament to the director's sheer skill, not to mention the superb cinematography of Arthur Grant (possibly Hammer's

greatest cameraman, and the man who would later apply a similarly purple hue to the underrated *Blood from the Mummy's Tomb*), that every overtly scare-based scene in this film still carries as much resonance as it did on original release. Even the obviously superimposed car chase between Rex and his love interest Tanith (also fleeing Mocata's clutches), and the quite badly magnified giant spider that terrorizes the young Peggy Eaton (future *Guardian of the Abyss* and *C.A.T.S. Eyes* starlet Rosalyn Landor in her earliest role) are imposingly effective, and whenever the special effects *do* show their obvious budgetary and technical limitations, it seems perfectly acceptable and almost adds to the surreal beauty of the picture.

Elsewhere the moonlit scenes of Devil worship (all right, hands up here, everyone aged between 30 and 50 who sat in their living rooms and replied back to Gray's cries of "Echo Babylon!" and "Echo Osiris!" with shouts of "Echo and the Bunnymen!"—oh, just me?) seem more credible than most, fighting shy of the clichés that would soon come to infest every film on the subject. Not to mention, of course, the epoch-defining appearance at this point of a certain well-known farmyard animal.

But, of course, no film, no matter how well photographed, could stand the test of time if the acting performances were below par, which is where *The Devil Rides Out* really shines, as Fisher seems to coax sterling efforts from all involved. Lee is at the top of his game here, dispensing suave, swift, no-nonsense, erudite pearls of wisdom in a way one would normally associate with his best friend and regular colleague Peter Cushing, and relishing his chance to play the hero for once, yet never losing the dark, imposing majesty that he naturally brought to his more evil cinematic doings.

But if anyone is in danger of stealing the show, it's Gray, subtly underplaying a part that seemed to have almost been designed for his steely Aryan gaze and impeccable sneering diction. He may have become more famous to subsequent generations of filmgoers as "that bloke who does the jump-to-the-left bits in *The Rocky Horror Picture Show*," but to a true genre addict he will always remain Mocata, the human personification of evil incarnate, who at several points in the film seems almost capable of outwitting the Duke, at least enough temporarily to worry the viewer out of his complacency. It's a tragedy that, with the exception of *Rocky Horror* and his appearances in more minor league Brit efforts such as *The Beast Must Die* (1974) and Richard Marquand's decidedly patchy *The Legacy* (1978), his undoubted genre potential went largely unused. He never really had a script as good as this again for the remainder of his career, except on occasions when called upon to revoice the dying Jack Hawkins

This neatly brings us to the one mystery surrounding the production: Leon Greene in the role of Rex Van Ryn. Ostensibly handsome and outwardly suitable for the part, this expatriate Aussie actor had already appeared in several high-profile TV roles since arriving in the U.K., including episodes of *The Saint* and *The Avengers*, and was obviously considered good enough by whoever cast the movie. Yet, for some bizarre reason, producer Anthony Nelson Keys chose to overdub him with the instantly recognizable voice of Patrick Allen, thus creating the only sight chink in the film's armor. Not that there is anything amiss in any way with Allen's voice—he's one of the true greats of British film and television, his warm yet somewhat foreboding tones (most famous of course to generations of terrified Brits as the voice of the *Protect and Survive* public information films) suit the character of Rex perfectly and add a familiarity for the viewer which many romantic leads of the day lacked, yet one can't help but wonder what was so wrong with Greene's own voice that it required substitution.

Maybe he was just *too* colonial to play such a quintessentially English gentleman? Particularly as leading lady Nike Arrighi is allowed to portray Tanith (not French in the book, although there are references to her having been in Paris with the sinister Countess, here portrayed by the ever effective Gwen Ffrancon Davies) with her real accent. It's a puzzler, although Allen being married to Sarah Lawson, who portrays Marie Eaton, may have had something to do with it.

As far as leading ladies go, Arrighi is not by any stretch of the imagination the best looking or the most charismatic, but somehow she just seems to *work*. Her romantic scenes with Greene (containing no nudity, leaving one to ponder what the producers would have insisted on two years hence), which are understated, tender without being mawkishly sentimental and, most of all, believable are also a tribute to the film's subtle

beauty. In fact, there's not a single member of the supporting cast who doesn't put in a stellar performance, but special mention must go to a pre-*Good Life* Paul Eddington, here cast in the role of the cynical, rational and therefore highly suggestible Richard, who spends large portions of his screen time stuck inside a chalk circle, and abides and endures some of the film's most genuinely dread-filled moments, including *that* appearance from the Angel of Death himself, who, as we all know, "once summoned cannot return empty handed." That the character seems both terrified and sanguine at the same time is surely testament to the late, great actor's skills, but also to the sheer plausibility of Matheson's script (and thus, Wheatley's original material).

There are very few genre pictures that can be described as practically perfect from start to finish, with which it is nigh on impossible to find fault. This film fits into that elite group. In terms of atmosphere, suspense, cinematography, dialogue, settings (okay, the roads around Elstree and Black Park again, but why change a winning formula, especially when it looks this good?), acting and horror, but also as a complete whole, it is near to unsurpassable. Hell (and yes, it was inevitable that I would have to mention that word at some point given the subject matter), even James Bernard's usually obtrusive score seems positively relaxed this time, to the point where I could almost bring myself to listen to it—possibly due to "supervision" from Phillip Martell, but I would prefer to believe that for once it was just a matter of the gods being in conjunction.
—D.R. Shimon

Credits: Director: Terence Fisher; Writer: Richard Matheson. **Leading Cast:** Christopher Lee, Charles Gray, Nike Arrighi, Leon Greene, Patrick Mower.

Dracula Has Risen from the Grave

This entry in the Hammer Dracula cycle gives Rupert Davies (as a Catholic Monsignor) the authoritative, stern Van Helsing-like authority figure role but, when he suffers a slight case of death before the final act, allows the youthful protagonists to step in and defeat the Count for the first time in the series. Perhaps reflecting Hammer's realization that their core audience was the young 'uns, the subsequent Dracula movies also featured teen heroes and heroines, though few got the blatant, shirtless introductory scene enjoyed here by Barry "Can shumone show me the way to the cashtle?" Andrews.

Francis' movie is significantly livelier than its immediate predecessor, reviving Dracula in half the time and giving him more to do, chiefly visiting the beautiful Veronica Carlson in her bed and grinning with pleasure as she unbuttons her nightgown in anticipation of penetration. The effective opening sequence—the discovery of a female corpse in a belfry—offers a neat summation of Hammer's principal ingredients (cleavage and blood) and leads nicely into the well-paced central scenario.

It has been one year since Dracula last died, but the local church remains permanently empty because the shadow of his castle looms large over it. A slightly twitchy priest (Ewan Hooper) literally stumbles over the Count's corpse entombed in ice, with the man of God's blood reviving you know who this time around. The Monsignor desecrates the castle to banish the evil forever, and this sets Dracula off on a mission of vengeance, using Hooper to get at Davies' nubile niece (Carlson).

This entry in the series provides a number of pleasing wrinkles on the well-established formula. Barbara Ewing, for instance, is excellent as a busty, flirty barmaid who, unusually for this series, is very much a sexual figure *before* the Count makes her a vampire slave. Her performance both before and after her transition represents a convincing balancing act between predatory lust and vulnerability. When Dracula makes it clear that he is pursuing Carlson, she insecurely asks, "What do you want her for? You've got me!", a moment that subtly reflects her earlier, pre-vamp jealousy of Andrews and Carlson being an item.

Andrews' character, although sometimes annoying, is also a departure from what has gone before. He's an atheist and, in a one film only addition to vampire mythology that displeased some, fails to achieve the desired effect of his climactic Drac staking, because of his inability to pray as a means of securing the dark dude's destruction. While adding to the vampire "rules," the film earlier breaks a long-established one for the sake of a cool shot (Dracula reflected in a pool of water).

Although Francis overdoes the amber filters, this is one of the best looking of all the Hammer Draculas, and its exciting bursts of action, notably a rooftop chase, rank as highlights of the series. Uniformly fine performances, including a characteristically jovial Michael Ripper as Andrews' boss, lend it further strength, and the frenetic climax is relishably gruesome: Dracula survives a bloody staking but winds up impaled on a crucifix in a moment that somehow was still allowed to remain in the G-rated American print!

The resolution, with Andrews apparently finding his absent faith, is never in doubt, of course, but Carlson is perhaps the loveliest of the series' heroines, and Lee asserts a remarkable presence as he booms out orders, slaps women around and seduces young girls in their rooms with minimum effort.
—Steven West

Credits: Director: Freddie Francis; Writer: John Elder [Anthony Hinds].
Leading Cast: Christopher Lee, Rupert Davies, Veronica Carlson, Barbara Ewing, Barry Andrews, Ewan Hooper, Michael Ripper.

The Lost Continent

At the time of its release, *The Lost Continent* must have been a pretty mind-boggling experience for contemporary audiences, once more demonstrating Hammer's fondness for juxtaposing the mundane with the extraordinary, as in *The Plague of the Zombies* and *The Reptile*, with their bizarre exotic cults

"DRACULA HAS RISEN FROM THE GRAVE"
(OBVIOUSLY)

operating in cozy rural Victorian England, *The Damned* and its seaside "Teds meet sci-fi" mix, the underrated *The Satanic Rites of Dracula*, blending espionage, germ warfare and vampirism, or *The Devil-Ship Pirates*, a film featuring seafaring Spanish rogues swashing their buckle along the unlikely locale of the Thames estuary.

The Lost Continent, based on the novel *Uncharted Seas* by Dennis Wheatley (which one of the characters is seen reading), starts out as a standard maritime adventure yarn as an ancient rustbucket sets out on its final voyage carrying a variety of characters with shady pasts. There's a memorably laughable scene near the beginning as the ship sails out of port, passing a flashing red light buoy, and it's painfully obvious that the ship's bridge is a standing set while the buoy is wheeled past the windows and the painted seascape beyond remains visibly static!

After surviving a hurricane which threatens to ignite the ship's illegal cargo of explosives (they detonate on contact with water), the vessel becomes ensnared in a drifting mass of carnivorous seaweed and it's at this point that the film changes tack from hokey shipboard adventure to wacko "Lost World" scenario as the hapless voyagers fall victim to an attack of the crabs (an occupational hazard for sailors, but in this case we're talking colossal crustaceans!), the onslaught of an outsized

Unnatural, appearing in the distinguished company of Erich Von Stroheim and Carl Boehm (of *Peeping Tom* fame) in the tale of "a totally evil and soulless seductress created by a mad scientist experimenting with artificial insemination!"

Carreras recalled in *Little Shoppe of Horrors*: "(Hildegarde) had an unhappy picture. She hated getting wet—and she did get wet a lot." However, I'm sure I'm not alone in thinking that her efforts, and those of the other cast and crew members, were well worthwhile in making *The Lost Continent*, with its atmospheric blend of miasmic mist, maniacal matelots and marine monstrosities, one of the most enjoyably bizarre pulp-fantasy adventures ever to grace late night television.
—Mike Hodges

Ladies and Germs, presenting *The Lost Continent*, or "The Maddest Story Hammer Ever Told." Featuring songs by the Peddlers that sound as if someone *on* speed accidentally selected the *wrong* speed on the turntable, this cheerfully loose adaptation of Dennis Wheatley's 1938 novel *Uncharted Seas* is one of Hammer's most bizarre pictures. A character reads the book on screen in homage to the project's originator, though it's a fair assumption that the notoriously curmudgeonly author would have chosen—by default—*The Devil Rides Out* if asked to pick a favorite Hammer interpretation of his work. Slow to start—it takes 50 minutes to get to the title location—this underappreciated oddity eventually turns into a genuinely loopy adventure flick that delights in defying description.

A ship carrying an illegal ten-ton cargo of explosives runs into Hurricane Wendy and gets dragged into the Sargasso Sea. Somewhat more of a concern than either the booty or the hurricane are the folks on board: Aside from inevitable old-faithful Michael Ripper and solemn-faced Eric Porter (his only other Hammer outing is the exceptional *Hands of the Ripper*), beware of man-eater Suzanna Leigh and piano-tinkling, womanizing drunk Tony Beckley ("You're a bore when you're sober").

This peculiar ensemble and others face mutiny, shipwreck, sharks and a lethal strain of seaweed that grabs and kills—for starters. Marooned on an undiscovered island, they also have to face El Supremo, an annoying adolescent boy who presides over a God-fearing cult. Said group feed those who "disappoint" to what looks suspiciously like a giant vulva dwelling beneath a trapdoor.

It's a fact that a movie wacky enough to feature religious cults, vaginal monsters and deadly seaweed is destined to be entertaining without further embellishments, though *The Lost Continent* adds a subplot involving Beckley's spirited efforts to get into the knickers of sexy island girl Dana Gillespie. This was Gillespie's second movie role in a modest career that nonetheless spanned from *The People That Time Forgot* to Nicolas Roeg's *Bad Timing* and the astonishing *Scrubbers* (a distaff *Scum* with the never to be repeated spectacle of Pam "Pat Butcher" St. Clement, Kathy Burke, Honey Bane and Robbie Coltrane in the same cast!). Fans of big, heaving, traditional Hammer boobs will find that *The Lost Continent* more than fulfills their needs.

octopus with a glowing green eyeball, an invasion of the aforementioned weed which penetrates Hildegard Knef's porthole (no, missus, don't titter!), and assaults from a bunch of nutters descended from the Conquistadors of Hernán Cortés, whose galleon was also stranded in the atrocious algae.

Our first sight of the horrific Hispanics, shambling across the fog-enshrouded carpet of weed decked out with huge round snowshoe affairs made from what appear to be rolled up dishcloths, and kept afloat by gas-filled bobbing balloons as they pursue the similarly attired Dana Gillespie (whose low-cut blouse reveals her own wonderful pair of bobbing balloons!), gives new meaning to the word "surreal" (and others like "ludicrous," "hilarious" or "What the hell...?" according to one's mood when watching).

The screenplay was written by Michael Carreras, not under his usual pseudonym of "Henry Younger" but that of "Michael Nash," a name he appropriated from his gardener. Carreras also directed the film, taking over early on from Barry Norman's dad, Leslie, and was also largely responsible for casting the picture, remarking that, alongside such True Brit stalwarts as Eric "*Forsyte Saga*" Porter and Nigel "Dr. Watson" Stock, he especially wanted Hildegarde Knef to bring what he termed "International Flavor" to the production. Ms. Knef already had the experience of working in odd films of a fantastic nature: In 1952 she starred in the German Gothic sci-fi/fantasy film

It is more than heartening to know that, in the late 1960s, Hammer managed to make a movie that not only bears all the hallmarks of having been created under the influence of illegal substances, but makes no secret of the fact. Faced with the onslaught of homicidal kelp, characters say things like, "We're surrounded by weed!" not to mention, "Now we go where the weed takes us!" and, of course, "Look, even the weed's burning!" Yeah, man, it was the 1960s!

You won't need anything illicit of your own to enjoy the film's cheerfully insane second half, which busies itself with giant rubber octopus attacks, characters inexplicably attached to oversize balloons and the endearingly absurd sight of a giant, barely moving crab battling it out with an equally lethargic oversize scorpion. The lack of enthusiasm displayed by both suggests they had earlier made passes at Dana Gillespie and had met with the worst kind of rejection. Nonetheless, the special effects are engagingly ropey in 1950's B-movie style, and the typically solid cast do their best to look genuinely surprised when a massive green-eyed mollusk somehow sneaks up on them. It's that kind of movie.
—Steven West

Credits: Director: Michael Carreras; Writer: Michael Nash [Michael Carreras].
Leading Cast: Eric Porter, Hildegard Knef, Suzanna Leigh, Tony Beckley, Nigel Stock.

Twisted Nerve

Down's Syndrome is a Red Herring. Down's Syndrome is a Red Herring. Down's Syndrome is a Red Herring.

In spite of, or perhaps because of, the carefully worded and yet rather hastily tacked on disclaimer at the beginning of *Twisted Nerve*, you might be forgiven for thinking that this sharply nasty, creepy little Boulting Brothers' gem is a politically incorrect "mongoloid"-as-killer thriller.

Martin (Hywel Bennett) is a bad lad. A cherub-faced girlie boy, as so many of the new breed of 1960's male icons were, he loves his mum (Phyllis Calvert) a little too closely, hates his step dad (Frank Finlay) a little too keenly, and dotes on his Down's Syndrome brother a little too morbidly. He slouches. He pouts. He listens to loud jazz. He's a typically spoiled, arrogant, little rich kid.

But Martin has a secret, an alter ego by the name of Georgie: a simple, mentally challenged, naïve man-child. And Georgie loves Susan (Hayley Mills), the pretty and innocent librarian who takes him in off the streets. Georgie might also love Susan's mum Joan (Billie Whitelaw), and that's when the horror really starts.

The oft-whistled Bernard Herrmann theme tune was used by Quentin Tarantino in *Kill Bill, Vol. 1*, and it's easy to see why. *Twisted Nerve* drips with foreboding, the crisp cinematography of Harry Waxman emphasizing every dark shadow of the mind and illuminating every bright light of the spirit. Compare Daryl Hannah's sexual predator of a nurse in *Kill Bill* with Billie Whitelaw's morally loose boarding house mum here, and you'll have a taste of the dank sexuality lurking beneath the surface.

Georgie's love for the almost saintly Susan is pure, while his love for his own mum, and the surrogate Joan, is twisted and Oedipal. Authority males are portrayed as coarse, rough and ego driven. Sex is a confusing mix of lust, duty and perverted morality. When Joan's motherly affection turns lustful in the shadowy confines of the garden shed, memories of bedtime with mummy and all that this implies come flooding back to haunt Georgie.

The film takes great pains to enunciate the nature of mental deformity, the twisted nerve of the title represented in a verbose verse about ganglions gone awry and the chaos they cause. The Oedipal tones are laid out in detail, too: the overly attentive mother, the absent father and the oppressively correct stepfather. It should be a simple case of "I love my mum/I hate my dad/my brain doesn't work/now the killing starts"—but it's not.

Why is Down's Syndrome mentioned in all this? Because Martin's brother has it. And because big brother has it, mummy has wrapped dear little Marty in cotton wool from the day he was born and treated him like a baby—to keep him perfect. The

condition is there to explain the relationship between mother and younger son—and that's it.

Martin's a good-looking young man. It's mentioned more than once what a "pretty boy" he is. Notice the bodybuilding magazines lying about hither and thither, but no bodybuilding *equipment*. Notice where he shoots his reflection: the mind, the heart and the genitals. I love my mum/I hate my dad/I should like girls—but I don't. And when they stick their delicate little paws on me, it drives me nuts—really nuts. We don't hear his full conversation with Susan when he botches a seduction attempt, but it ends with, "Most girls wouldn't understand."

Does the film tell you that the mentally challenged are psycho killers? Or does it tell you that homosexuals are? This was the time of debates on "Nature or Nurture?" widespread discussion of the Kinsey Report and so on. Homosexuality may have been legalized a year prior to *Twisted Nerve*'s release, but clearly attitudes didn't change overnight. Or as lecherous lodger Gerry (Barry Foster), the archetypal bloke in the street, might put it, "Well, it ain't natural, is it?"
—Sarah Edgson

> No puppetmaster pulls the strings on high,
> But a twisted nerve, a ganglion gone awry,
> Predestinates the sinner or the saint.

Twisted Nerve

Strange to think that relatively unknown screenwriter Leo Marks could be the man behind two controversies nearly a decade apart. Yet the outré stanza quoted above, taken from *Twisted Nerve*, echoes and recalls the furor and brouhaha caused by no less a milestone in British cinema than *Peeping Tom*, which the very same scribe was partially responsible for.

So what exactly were filmgoers and critics up in arms about in the summer of '68? Nudity? Well, okay, maybe some, but male, and more buttocks than anything else. Bad language? Not that much. Comic racism? That would have been par for the course then. Blood and gore? Surprisingly little. No, what made this particular British horror movie so much of a cause celebre was its central premise that a man related to a Down's Syndrome sufferer is capable of being a psychopath, sociopath and murderer, plus being able to split willingly into one of two personalities whenever it suits him. And all this was possible because, due to a defect gained at birth, it was predestined.

Twisted Nerve is a great film. Misguided it may be in the very basis behind its construction, but that doesn't detract one iota from its superb cinematography, excellent dialogue (the aforementioned segment notwithstanding), its beautifully executed sense of paranoia and foreboding, or the way in which it successfully captures the transition of suburban London (in this case the actual Mills family home in Twickenham) from the brown-hued, almost bookish color scheme of old to its newfound psychedelic trappings, something which Jack Clayton's *Our Mother's House* had hinted at the previous year and that Joseph Losey's *Secret Ceremony* concurrently tapped into—but, most of all, the flawless performances from all actors involved.

Hayley Mills, who would in 1971 marry director Roy Boulting (some 33 years her senior), is perfect as guileless heroine Susan Harper, who is ensnared right from the start in the killer's evil web when she is accused of helping him steal a toy duck from a department store, and seems unable, despite a background in academia and librarianship, to distinguish between the good and bad in people, even her own boyfriend, who seems uninterested in her other than as a sex object to place in his flashy car. Her trusting nature allows the film's events to happen, but at the same time Susan's concern for others proves ultimately her saving grace.

Barry Foster, as drunken, embittered, largely unemployed horror writer and lodger Gerry Henderson, a man with a neat line in political incorrectness and intolerance ("You can't really talk to 'em, can yer? No sense of 'umor, you see!"), is more sympathetic than unlikeable. This is largely due to the humanity he brings to even the most insulting dialogue, more often than not aimed at fellow boarder Shashie (Salmaan Peerzada), an educated Indian doctor who finds Foster's prejudice amusing rather than annoying. She takes delight in rebuking such jibes by explaining that Tarzan, an English lord by birth, liked nothing more than to "swing through trees with a bunch of apes."

Billie Whitelaw is a revelation as Mills' sex-deprived, near-menopausal mother (there is an inference that she and Foster have been sharing occasional "arrangements" with regard to his rent, but it's left pretty much to the viewer's imagination), oozing frustrated, womanly sensuality and setting a precedent for 40-something Brit sex-bombs that carries on today. Timothy West is a suitably grumpy police inspector, who gets one of the two best lines of dialogue in the whole film ("Watch it, this bloke's a nutter"), the other being "Sphericals!"—Foster's concise description of "bleeding heart" sympathies shown toward the criminal element. And in a brief cameo, Thorley Walters is his usual fusty, professorial self.

But the film undoubtedly belongs head and shoulders to its true star, Hywel Bennett. Mills may have been top-billed due to her celebrity post-*Parent Trap* and her romantic association with Boulting, but this is Bennett's movie through and through. He owns it from the very moment he first appears on screen, less than a minute in, as he stands gloomily in hospital grounds, throwing a ball to his mostly unseen brother.

His primary character, Martin Durnley, is a visibly troubled young man, the archetypal baby-faced killer who, although blessed with stunning good looks and a dress sense somewhere between Brian Jones and Scott Walker, seemingly has no friends, no social skills and is prone to spending hours in his room alone, rocking back and forth on a chair, cradling toys and listening to jazz. He also has a questionable penchant for collecting bodybuilding magazines and comparing his own physique to the photographs within, obviously a major bone of contention as in one scene we see him (implicitly) masturbating in front of a mirror that he has smashed in the middle, thus blurring his and our view of his genitalia.

There's always been something disquieting about angelic young boys in horror films, and Georgie is no exception: With his smiling, almost rodent-like features, he worms, smarms and giggles his way into your subconscious. The random moments—such as bursting into cackling laughter and declaring, "Batman is a fat man!" during a breakfast table discussion about comic books, or mounting and repeatedly whipping a rocking horse in the nursery while informing Susan that "Georgie always wins"—are disturbingly effective, largely due to Bennett's frighteningly convincing performance, and are capable of leaving the viewer agog in sheer disbelief at the implied evil within.

Some suggest that Martin's obsession with muscle magazines, his hatred of his own form in the mirror, and his retreat into "Georgie" (this is the bit where the theory falls down, as there's absolutely no logic to it whatsoever) are actually a veil for latent or denied homosexuality—and what he suggests to Susan is that she penetrate him in some way. Personally I see no alternative sexual orientation, unless one is to count that of a deranged psychopath or, more worryingly, an overgrown child. For this reason, the actor is probably the

most terrifying during this one scene than he has ever been at any other stage in his career, even outdoing his personification of sliminess in *Karaoke* (1996). Respite luckily comes soon in the form of the film's conclusion, of which I shall say nothing.

From whichever angle one comes at *Twisted Nerve*, its power cannot be denied or ignored. Whatever one may think of the flimsiness and medical questionability of its central tenet, it still packs one hell of a punch. A beautifully restrained and underplayed exercise in slow-burning Hitchcockian dynamics, although in no way is the film derivative of the great man, bearing as it does greater resemblance to the interpersonal dramas prevalent at the time in both Italian and Spanish cinema, and the kitchen sink drama that shaped Britain's aesthetic throughout most of the 1960s, indeed, the very same social realist style that had first brought Mills, Bennett and the Boultings together in *The Family Way* (1966). This attitude is apparent in most aspects of *Twisted Nerve*, from the camera work and décor, down to the themes of race and social background explored by Foster, Peerzada and housekeeper Clarkie (Gretchen Franklin), who even manages a pre-Ethel from *EastEnders* malapropism here by referring to the unnamed killer in the papers as "one of them psychoprats." Talk about setting the tone for your entire career.

Despite its "difficult" subject matter, the film evidently remains a popular and highly regarded one, hence not only its referencing by Quentin Tarantino, but also the Damned titling a song after it on their *Black Album* as far back as 1982, not to mention Mancunian psychedelic-progressive rock reissue supremos Andy Votel and Damon Gough, who named their label Twisted Nerve Records.

—D.R. Shimon

Credits: Director: Roy Boulting; Writers: Roy Boulting, Leo Marks, Roger Marshall.
Leading Cast: Hywel Bennett, Hayley Mills, Billie Whitelaw, Frank Finlay, Barry Foster, Thorley Walters.

The Vengeance of She

"Oh who is She, a misty memory?" asks the groovy theme tune to this 1968 Hammer sequel. The answer, after enduring this almighty borefest, is "Who cares?" Yeah, and the mistier, the better.

Hammer was talking about a follow-up to their hit *She* as early as July 1965. Ursula Andress wisely bailed out, and instead her role was assumed by the little-known Czech starlet Olinka Berova. They might as well have cast a block of wood. Despite looking pretty tidy (though not in Andress' league), Berova's acting "talent" is approximately nil. Costar Noel Willman said of her, "She was absolutely catatonic. I mean, she did not have a clue." And he wasn't wrong.

Things start unpromisingly when we realize the action has now been updated to modern-day Monte Carlo, at least to begin with. The monomially monickered Carol (Berova) hitches a ride with a lecherous trucker (always a wise thing to do) and narrowly escapes being raped when his own truck conveniently splatters him. Stripping down to her undies in a not altogether unpleasant scene, she wades into the sea and hitches a ride on a boat where things are swingin' big time, Daddy-O! The spectre of Andress looms large as Berova appears dressed skimpily in white. Unfortunately, Berova is less Honey Ryder, more Sue Ryder.

Carol doesn't exactly endear herself to the boat's passengers and crew; she doesn't know who she is, or why she feels compelled to follow a voice in her head that calls her "Ayesha." But what with her being "a young lady of considerable endowments," in the words of the boat's owner George (Colin Blakely), they allow her to stay. Big mistake, as when the boat alters course, she flips out and jumps overboard. For some inexplicable reason, George jumps in after her, promptly has a heart attack and dies. Edward Judd, as Philip, has a bit of a thing for our Carol, however, and continues to give the crazy bitch the time of day.

It transpires that, in the lost city of Kuma, the High Priest Killikrates has been convinced that dopey Carol is the reincarnation of his long-dead Queen (Andress, in the previous movie). Yes, it's at this point you realize you're watching basically the same plot as in the first film, but with the roles swapped. *Modesty Blase* co-creator and screenwriter Peter O'Donnell really knocked himself out the day it took him to cobble this shite together. From that point, it's interminable scenes of mystical mumbo-jumbo and Killikrates attempting to convince our Carol to step into "the blue flame," therefore securing her immortality. But you'll have lost the will to live by the halfway mark, trust me.

John Richardson reprises his role from the first film, though it seems he's forgotten any vestige of his previous existence as Leo Vincey. He's dubbed once again, as is Berova, and he has to suffer the indignity of wearing a skirt almost as short as hers! Noel Willman's and André Morell's final roles for Hammer are undignified send-offs at best (dig Willman's eyebrows). Derek Godfrey, as the duplicitous mystic Men-Hari, is at least given some cool facial hair.

There's no doubt about it, *The Vengeance of She* is one of Hammer's worst. The only conceivable reason for sitting through it is for a gawp at Berova's juddering chest puddings (one of which she gives a brief flash). Based on the flop of this film,

Hammer's latest star shone briefly, and she slunk off back to Czechoslovakia to be missed by precisely nobody—sad, really. —Jed Raven

Credits: Director: Cliff Owen; Writer: Peter O'Donnell. **Leading Cast:** John Richardson, Olinka Berova, Edward Judd, Colin Blakely.

Witchfinder General (aka *The Conqueror Worm*)

In the movie year of *Rosemary's Baby* and *Night of the Living Dead*, both triggering cycles and moving the genre in grim new directions, a young British director brought his own misanthropic worldview to the seemingly exhausted realm of the period horror film. It may feature the reassuring presence of screen veteran Rupert Davies, Hilary Dwyer's admirable heaving bosoms and even a tiny comic cameo from a face-pulling Wilfrid Brambell, but Reeves' famous swansong was a long way from the familiar world of homegrown Gothic horror that had been the speciality of Hammer and their rivals for more than a decade.

"SHE" USED SEX THE WAY MEN USE WEAPONS!

...to have her way with Empires and Kings!

Discover The Excitement of OLINKA BEROVA A New Screen Beauty In The Body Of A Woman!

THE VENGEANCE OF SHE

20th Century-Fox presents JOHN RICHARDSON · OLINKA BEROVA · EDWARD JUDD in "THE VENGEANCE OF SHE" co-starring NOEL WILLMAN starring COLIN BLAKELY Directed by CLIFF OWEN Screenplay by PETER O'DONNELL Produced by AIDA YOUNG Based on Characters Created by H. RIDER HAGGARD · COLOR by DELUXE · A SEVEN ARTS-HAMMER PRODUCTION

The unforgiving tone is set from the stark opening sequence. John Coquillon's camera catches a glimpse of glaring sunlight, a healthy looking English countryside, a serene herd of sheep and a pleading, screaming woman being dragged to her doom. Her shrill cries are swiftly replaced by the equally abrasive sound of her lifeless body swinging to and fro on the creaking gibbet. Subsequently the title sequence offers further gloomy hints of things to come: a series of monochrome images of tortured, pained, barely distinguishable faces. In 1968, as the American horror film began the boldest phase in its history, a filmmaker who wouldn't live beyond 1969 made a historical drama, Western and horror hybrid that consistently disturbs, even today.

Witchfinder General unfolds in 1645 in the midst of an ongoing civil war between the Parliamentary party and the Royalists. All over Britain, local magistrates dole out equal amounts of justice and injustice. The superstitions of many are exploited by self-styled crusader Matthew Hopkins who, with the law's blessing, makes a tidy profit as a "partner in extermination," solving alleged cases of witchcraft in the harshest possible terms. He claims to be doing the Lord's work and deludes only himself when describing his mission as a "noble thing." A grimmer truth becomes apparent when he proves unable to answer the question as to whether he enjoys the torture he liberally inflicts.

Deceptively, the early stages of the film offer pleasing, attractive sights and sounds that, were it not for that queasy pre-titles sequence, might lead us to expect a vastly different movie experience. Paul Ferris' score, infamously replaced for the film's pre-DVD American video releases, provides a gloriously lovely main theme, a piece rich with romance and heroism that wouldn't be out of place in an old-school Hollywood Western. This and the picturesque representation of East Anglia's green and pleasant land provide an ironically pretty counterpoint to an escalating sense of horror. Like the conventional Hammer horrors that preceded it, Reeves' film has, at its core, an appealing personification of Love's Young Dream: Cromwell supporter and farm boy turned soldier Ian Ogilvy, and the lovely niece (Dwyer) of chummy priest Davies.

In Reeves' cinematic world, however, aside from a trendy breast-baring love scene montage, the lovers appear doomed even before Hopkins arrives to dominate the picture. The gruesome resolution is foreshadowed early by a sequence showing Ogilvy killing a man (albeit justifiably) and by Dwyer's verbalized concern, after a moment of passion, that he's different toward her, a little on the rough side. The movie isn't even halfway through when Dwyer has been violated off-camera both by Hopkins and his assistant, while kindly Davies is repeatedly slashed and ultimately executed.

Formally and thematically, the film has echoes of the traditional Western. The emphasis on bloody mutilation, however (taken to the next extreme by the later, gaudier *Mark of the Devil*, among others), and the extended suffering of wounded characters position it somewhere between the post-Leone revisionist Westerns and the newfound explicitness in 1960s horror in the wake of *Psycho* and Herschell Gordon Lewis. A cause célèbre in its day, the film was memorably censored by (an admittedly reluctant) John Trevelyan, but Reeves never revels in brutality. A particularly distressing witch-burning sequence, for instance, plays out sans music and horrifies not because of any graphic gore shots, but because of the agonizing *length* of the victim's torment, punctuated by frequent cuts to the reaction of her anguished husband.

As in the outstanding mini-cycle of Pete Walker films to come in the 1970s, Reeves' pessimistic film depicts good people dying horribly and ugly violence permitted by a deeply corrupt system that lets everyone down. Just as Walker found disarming levels of malevolence within unlikely horror star Sheila Keith, Reeves, fresh from casting Karloff as a pussy-whipped pensioner in *The Sorcerors*, employs a horror icon beloved for his camp showman's presence in the genre and refuses to let him pander to the audience's expectations. Price, portraying the most callous and frightening bastard in his entire career, is stripped of all humanity and humor. An arrogant black clad bringer of death, he literally towers above all else in intimidating low-angle shots. Under the command of a filmmaker unhappy with the studio-imposed star (Reeves wanted Donald Pleasence), he is, simply, chilling. Typical of

the subdued evil conveyed by Price's portrayal is the mirthless half-smile he gives after witnessing a potential "witch" drowning, smarmily noting, with mock compassion, "She was innocent."

Like other key late 1960s films, in and out of the horror genre, *Witchfinder General* climaxes with a frenzied orgy of violence. By the end, Ogilvy is as single-minded and cold-blooded as Hopkins—a previously articulate, handsome young man reduced to an animalistic figure intent only on vengeance. The eruption of chaos in the closing scene includes a still startling bit of ocular violence and the jarring, once heavily cut, sight of a crazed Ogilvy whacking Price over and over with an axe. There are few moments in British horror as harrowing as the deranged stare in the blood-spattered Ogilvy's eyes as he reacts to a bystander's mercy killing of the barely alive Hopkins with the shrill fury of a madman: "You took him from me!"

And thus a remarkable movie ends, just as it began, with bloodcurdling screams: Reeves lingers longer than is comfortable on Dwyer's hysterical cries of anguish, which continue into the credits before fading into that lovely theme.
—Steven West

Credits: Director: Michael Reeves; Writers: Michael Reeves, Tom Baker.
Leading Cast: Vincent Price, Ian Ogilvy, Hilary Dwyer, Rupert Davies, Robert Russell, Patrick Wymark, Wilfrid Brambell.

1969

The Body Stealers

The Body Stealers was Tigon's attempt to make a science fiction movie that would appeal to the "family film" market. As with similar efforts from Hammer (*Moon Zero Two*) and Amicus (*The Terrornauts* and *They Came from Beyond Space*), the end result would try the patience of even the most indulgent 10 year old.

The initial premise is intriguing enough. British paratroopers are mysteriously disappearing into thin air (the film's working title) while in free fall. The MoD are seriously worried and call in troubleshooter, champion chain-smoker and God's gift to women, Bob "Born to Snog" Megan (Patrick Allen, giving it all he's got as a kind of upmarket Robin Askwith in suede jacket and purple tie), with lecherous leer and dodgy chat-up lines in overdrive. Most of his investigation is spent chasing Lorna (Lorna Wilde), a mysterious blonde "bird" he meets on a deserted beach somewhere on the coast of Elstree studios, while being relentlessly patronizing and lecherous toward a pretty lady scientist (Hilary Dwyer). Much time is spent embarking and disembarking from cars as Bob and assorted Army brass

endlessly rush to and fro between locations (the lab, the beach hotel and the airfield).

The main entertainment throughout the film's seemingly endless running time consists of some impressive footage of sky divers in action, including a few vertigo-inducing POV shots, documentary clips of the Red Arrows aerobatic team flying over a car park at an air show (count the Hillmans, Ford Cortinas, VW Beetles, Anglias, Wolseleys and Daimlers!) and an unintentionally comical ongoing scenario concerning a senior Civil Servant (Allan Cuthbertson) "working overtime" with his secretary.

Finally the alien (singular) behind the disappearances appears: an old duffer in a silver soccer shirt brandishing a Death Ray Pistol and moronic dialogue such as "My name is Marthas. I am from the planet Mygon." But Lorna, the beach bird, is also one of "them" (we already knew that because she's radioactive and also keeps vanishing into thin air) and saves our Bob's life (their nuclear couplings notwithstanding) before heading back to space in the model spaceship last seen in the Amicus film *Daleks' Invasion Earth 2150 A.D.* As this is a shoestring production, the borrowed craft doesn't even fly off, it just glows and fades away. The film's original cinema trailer disingenuously gives the cut price game away by posing the leading questions: "Do the space aliens take human form" or "Are the horrors from the sky invisible to man?"

In the final analysis, *The Body Stealers* is recommended viewing for aviation and skydiving enthusiasts, 1960s car buffs and students of social history wishing to observe the kind of blatant "male chauvinist" behavior which unctuous Jack the Lads were allowed to get away with 40 years ago. Other parties (especially horror and sci-fi fans), keep away!
—Mike Hodges

This report has been prepared in pursuance of my overall mission objective, to make a cultural assessment for the leaders of my planet on how the people of Earth interpreted possibilities of alien invasion in the seventh decade of their 20th century.

The film I have acquired as the focus of my study is one from the Earth year 1969 called *The Body Stealers*. I believe that my leaders will find an account of the events depicted in the story helpful to an understanding of the film's many flaws.

It would appear that a number of Earthmen are being mysteriously abducted by unknown forces. At first I thought that the abductees were performing a suicide ritual for the entertainment of spectators, but it transpires that they are parachutists (the aim of this bizarre sport seems to be to fall from a great height and to avoid death by unfurling a canopy of fabric just before impact—sadly by no means the strangest thing to be seen in this film).

These events are of some concern to various bipeds who make up the country's military and government forces. The militia are to be distinguished by their mode of dress—formal uniforms covered in stripes and medals—their strained clipped methods of speech and awkward gait, and their almost total inability to strategize against the problem in any effective way. The representative of the government is driven principally by a sexual urge towards the only female biped in the room, who provides secretarial services. This is a theme I will return to later.

These humans are obsessed with protocol and rank, and in preserving the divide between the government and the armed forces. This position seems ludicrous when we consider that Britain (where the film is set) had enjoyed peace for over 20 years when the film was made.

The filmmakers further appear to mock these symbols of authority by introducing a maverick human called Bob, whose strong jaw line and deep voice give him a feral quality, rendering him seemingly irresistible to women, and by showing the viewer that, despite many of his decisions being based solely on his desire for sexual congress with one or more females, he still manages more success than the authority figures in dealing with the problem of the missing parachutists. This is very troubling. To us, Bob appears crude, ungainly and primitive, but for the viewing audience of the time, and using the parlance of the period, he would be highly regarded as "a bit of all right" (I beg your pardon if the phrase fails to translate correctly).

It is quite logical that, with the primitive urge to the fore, one of the main alien protagonists responsible for the disappearances should appear in the form of an attractive female of their race, calling herself Lorna (attractive to humans that is; to us, she is — of course — repulsive). Bob immediately succumbs to this deception, but what is more troubling is that Lorna responds willingly to Bob's advances, and, in one scene, achieves intercourse in human form, which is simply not acceptable (nor biologically imaginable). In the next scene, Bob seeks to seduce a human scientist, Julie Slade, whom he leers over with similar intentions, but her professionalism provides her with at least temporary protection from a carnal intervention. That Bob is making advances to Slade while also seducing Lorna is already insulting to the depiction of a supposedly alien race — that an alien succumbs while a human resists is tantamount to a declaration of war.

The story behind the action in this film is perhaps, for our race, the most ridiculous aspect of *The Body Stealers*. The missing bodies are apparently being stored in the house of a Doctor Matthews, whose body has been taken over by the alien leader Marthas. (We never find out Lorna's real name.) The aim of the abductions is to build up a group of strong men, able to withstand the rigors of interplanetary travel, who can return with the aliens to repopulate their plague-ridden planet, Mygon. One look at the humans selected would render this premise completely implausible. Interestingly, in a couple of scenes humans are shown reacting to the Mygons in their "natural form" with horror — something we have encountered ourselves when confronted by other races — which clearly shows that the human form would be totally impractical for the purposes of planetary regeneration, what with them only having two legs and one head.

That the Mygons are able to occupy human form so naturally is also implausible. There would almost certainly be extreme discomfort in such occupation, and the body would be constantly awkward and restricted in movement. In fact, if our leaders consider the actor Neil Connery, who plays Jim Radford, his performance is far more accurate in portraying the woodenness associated with alien takeover.

That Bob and Julie contribute to the defeat of the Mygon invasion is, in the end, not down to the courageousness of either character but the treacherous act of Lorna in killing Marthas. Earlier Marthas states of the human race, "That's why these people are so backward, they're all heart and no brain," and we are supposed to understand that Lorna's relationship with Bob has left her with an essential humanity which gives her choice rather than obligation to her own race. Bob's offer to assemble a group of unsubjugated volunteers, to return to Mygon of their own volition, and Lorna's tacit agreement to this offer, is the final rivet in the burial tube of credibility.

In conclusion, my leaders, this is another example of how the people of Earth have failed to understand the nuances of alien invasion and of how easy they feel it would be for them to thwart the prospect of world domination. With the many similar examples of such stupidity gained from viewing countless other films of this time, I am confident that our current plans for the total domination of Earth in the next lunar year will encounter little practical resistance.

—Faaaaaaaaaaaaaaaaaaaaaaaaarg x
(Earth Mission code name: David Dent)

Credits: Director: Gerry Levy; Writer: Mike St. Clair.
Leading Cast: George Sanders, Maurice Evans, Patrick Allen, Neil Connery, Hilary Dwyer.

The Castle of Fu Manchu

Can a movie be too stupid or boring to be racially offensive? The question raises its head with drastic impertinence in *The Castle of Fu Manchu*.

There's a liner somewhere at sea with hordes of blissfully unaware passengers, and the nefarious Dr. Fu Manchu (Christopher Lee) and his diabolical cohort are — somewhere else. They turn on a machine after one of Lee's minions (Burt Kwouk; I hope he was paid well) tries to destroy it and is killed for his pains. As that happens, the contraption and an antenna on some hill blow up, and then an iceberg sinks the liner in stock footage-like scenes funny enough to later emerge on a 1972 *Monty Python* episode. It might have made a stirring, brilliantly edited action sequence, a là the assassinations toward the end of *The Godfather*, but obviously it doesn't. It eventually "boils" down to Fu Manchu's quest to blackmail the world with a machine that can turn the oceans to ice (and couldn't we use one of *those* nowadays?). Naturally, the only power in the entire world that can prevent such a dastardly cataclysm is Britain's own Scotland Yard (MI-5, MI-6, the army, etc., being too busy) and Fu Manchu's perennial and fervently bland nemesis, Nayland Smith (Richard Greene).

It might just be possible to watch the movie as a pleasant five-minute travel film of Istanbul with over an hour more of unaccountably attached explosions, poor fight scenes and mediocre villainy, but one fears the orthodox explanation would prove more insistent. The footage of Istanbul, where Fu

Manchu's trail leads, is pretty much the only good thing going, along with sexy Turkish bad girl Lisa (Rosalba Neri). As Dr. Petrie, Howard Marion-Crawford, so excellent in bad guy roles on *Danger Man*, echoes the buffoon he played in *Lawrence of Arabia* (repeating what people have just told him in a bulldog bark: "Opium"; "*Opium*?"), and nobody else (Greene included) is really of any consequence. Again, Lee's Fu Manchu comes across less as a mephitic mastermind and more as a vacationing banker tarting himself up as a "mandarin" several decades out of date. He doesn't even bother to try a Chinese accent, which on one level is a blessed mercy, but on another leads to frenzied head scratching.

Like *Fist of Fury*, the film seems to take place over several decades, which can't be right. There are a few terrible (as in "stupid and not very convincing") death scenes (one opium addict just shows up out of nowhere to be killed) and about 10 minutes of a boring heart transplant vitally important to the plot. Fu Manchu, of course, is defeated by the end, just as the film shoehorns in one spectacularly pointless, dumb (and badly filmed) demise right before time, but one is left to suspect the world hasn't heard the last from the evil mastermind (and shiver with terror at the thought of yet another sequel, though thankfully no more were made). Use this one as a beer coaster. —Wendell McKay

Credits: Director: Jesus Franco; Writers: Manfred Barthel, Peter Welbeck [Harry Alan Towers].
Leading Cast: Christopher Lee, Richard Greene, Howard Marion-Crawford, Tsai Chin, Maria Perschy, Rosalba Neri.

Frankenstein Must Be Destroyed

Having already *Created Woman*, Hammer's penultimate Frankenstein movie proved a worthy and thoughtful follow-up, which would have made a stunning swan song to the series. Comfortably in place are the elements we have come to expect: Veronica Carlson sporting *spectacular* cleavage during a nightgown sequence; throwaway comic relief featuring Thorley Walters as a fussy, snuff-snorting Inspector and Robert Gillespie as a deadpan mortuary attendant; and a stirring James Bernard score that in the memorable Hammer tradition spells out the syllables of the title in the main theme. Fisher's fourth Frankenstein flick, however, is otherwise far from being a formulaic entry in the franchise.

The exciting opening reel reaffirms the director's talent for rousing bursts of action, as Cushing's Baron, donning a grotesque horror mask, beheads a doctor with a sickle and narrowly evades capture. Subsequently, he moves in to lovely Carlson's guest house, where the regulars, unaware of his identity, routinely gossip about the Baron's earlier, now infamous exploits, referring to him as "one of the Devil's disciples." Discovering that a former colleague, and pioneer of a brain-freezing technique, is "incurable" at the local asylum, Frankenstein sets out to remove him from his cell and cure him, with the intention of working together. To this end, he blackmails Carlson and her doctor fiancé (Simon Ward), himself illegally supplying his ailing future mother-in-law with the drugs she needs, into assisting.

The most graphic surgery scenes of the series to date— paving the way for the bloody *Frankenstein and the Monster from Hell*—result in a "creature" (Freddie Jones) that, in the tradition of *Woman*'s Susan Denberg and *The Revenge of Frankenstein*'s Michael Gwynn, lacks overtly monstrous makeup or traits and is portrayed as a pitiful, hapless victim of the Baron's God complex. Unveiled 80 minutes in, Jones provides the film's most haunting moments. Fisher was clearly drawn to the tragedy of the Baron's subject reuniting with his grief-stricken wife (Audley): Jones' first action upon being cruelly reborn is a moving, tearful meeting with the woman who no longer knows who he really is. It's one of Hammer's least typical but most affecting sequences.

Destroyed is punctuated by some of the finest dramatic set pieces of the series, chiefly an asylum breakout featuring Colette O'Neil as a relentlessly screaming inmate, and a suspenseful bit of blackly comic Hitchcockian business involving a burst water main and an uncovered corpse in Carlson's garden. The moment in which the Baron callously stabs Carlson is among Hammer's most startling, and precedes a powerful fiery finale in which both he and his creation appear to perish. Prefiguring the subversion of the usual good defeats evil sense of resolution that would creep in to Hammer's often bleak early 1970s work, the ending shatters the studio's traditionally triumphant young romantic couple: At the end, Carlson is dead and Ward seriously wounded.

Cushing is, needless to say, superb as a Baron who veers from being charmingly humane to a cold-blooded rapist and murderer. The actor was seldom as sinister as he is in this film's infamous sexual assault on Carlson (though *Corruption* also offers the uniquely disturbing sight of Hammer's English gent as a predatory woman killer). Although it adds to the film's grim tone, this sequence is, of course, alarmingly out of context with what we've seen and known of the Baron over the course of the series. Shot at the last minute at the insistence of a studio-pressured James Carreras as a horrendously misguided means of injecting more sex into the picture, the scene remains uneasy to watch

Frankenstein Must Be Destroyed

for all sorts of reasons. As it was never conceived as part of the script, it exists by itself, with Carlson's character never displaying any subsequent reaction to what has happened to her. This unfortunate late compromise aside, the movie holds up superbly as one of the finest Brit genre flicks of its decade. —Steven West

Credits: Director: Terence Fisher; Writers: Bert Batt, Anthony Nelson Keys.
Leading Cast: Peter Cushing, Veronica Carlson, Freddie Jones, Simon Ward, Thorley Walters, Maxine Audley, Geoffrey Bayldon.

The Haunted House of Horror (aka *Horror House*)

Originally conceived as a vehicle for a pre-stardom David Bowie, with his songs punctuating the narrative, this swinging '60s shocker is not a supernatural chiller as the title suggests, but more like an early slasher flick. Prefiguring the American killer on the loose fare of the 1970s and 1980s, and such British equivalents as *Fright*, it showcases a whodunit plot, various red herrings, a knife-wielding ex-asylum patient, a screaming "final girl" of sorts and a couple of jarringly graphic murders probably modelled on *Psycho*'s classic set-pieces. Although rich with the kind of dialogue that characterizes yoof-centered genre pics of this period ("What

do you fancy, an orgy or a séance?" or "Come on, the moon is full, let's look for ghosts!"), this often atmospheric picture is considerably better than its reputation suggests.

To help sell tickets in the U.S., Frankie Avalon was cast as a (very obnoxious) character referred to as the "epitome of Swinging London." Richard O'Sullivan boogies on down to some groovy vinyl and sports funky sideburns that probably had their own appreciation society back in the day. Gina Warwick, as a brunette temptress, wears fetching miniskirts and decides she's bored with much older lover George Sewell ("I want someone young!"), who subsequently becomes a major red herring when he refuses to accept "It's Over."

Enduring a dull party, Avalon, Mark Wynter—a Carnaby Street player who is two timing Carol Dilworth with Warwick—and their friends (also including an unflatteringly cast Veronica Doran as a comedy fat bird who falls to pieces in the face of danger) decide to head to a "supposedly" haunted house just outside town for vicarious thrills. As usual in these movie scenarios, one of the group is fascinated with the macabre ("the way you dig blood anyone would think you're a vampire!") and everyone freaks each other out with stories of hack and slash murders that took place two decades earlier. When Wynter is violently killed, Inspector Dennis Price investigates while the nervous friends start to doubt each other's innocence.

Much of this plays like a dry run for the slasher cycle to come: a brief retelling of the location's grisly history; young

Credits: Director and Writer: Michael Armstrong.
Leading Cast: Frankie Avalon, Jill Haworth, Dennis Price, Julian Barnes, Mark Wynter, Richard O'Sullivan, Robin Stewart.

Justine (aka *Deadly Sanctuary*)

Following the death of their mother, sisters Justine (Romina Power, daughter of Tyrone) and Juliette (Rohm) suffer an additional blow when their father flees 18th century France in financial disgrace. Forced to leave the shelter of convent school, the girls end up in Madame de Buisson's brothel. Juliette decides to stay and embark on a career of lust, deception and murder, while Justine hits the road, encountering a succession of mostly reprehensible characters who use and abuse her for their own gratification and advancement.

Although *Justine* runs for over two hours in its complete director's cut, a 90-minute incarnation remained the most familiar for those lucky enough to cross its path. Franco's original version was made available on DVD from Anchor Bay in 2003 and the disc includes interviews with the director and his producer, Harry Alan Towers. Here, Franco is heavily critical of Romina Power's performance, revealing that Rosemary Dexter, his choice for the role of Justine, was passed over by the money men, who insisted it was "time for the children of the stars." For my money, Franco's outrage at being overruled by those "men in suits" heavily distorted his view of Power's abilities.

Yes, she was obviously inexperienced and a little wooden at times, but was she ever really given the chance to become the character that was originally intended?

During the course of the film, Justine is abused, blackmailed, deceived, literally branded a murderess and goes through a series of abductions that would tax the patience of even the most avid fan of *24*. Power is asked to run the full gamut of emotions and, if she's found wanting on more than one occasion, the blame should be mostly laid at Franco's door: At one point in the DVD interview, he confesses that many people believe she emerged with some credit and, con-

folks wandering around in the dark; false scares galore; and quickly edited knife killings. As in so many interchangeable later movies, the survivors make an uneasy pact that involves hiding Wynter's corpse to avoid becoming possible suspects in his murder. And, as in so many later flicks, the climactically revealed slayer (Julian Barnes) is a clean-cut loner traumatized into killing by a bad childhood (and adversely affected by the full moon, for some reason). Barnes' laughably wooden performance for much of the film actually segues into something fairly chilling during the final act.

This time capsule piece from a director en route to making the infamous *Mark of the Devil* makes effective use of its creepy backdrop—all foreboding candlelit rooms and creaking doors—and the murders (including a staircase stabbing) are startling for their time. The climactic assault on Avalon, for instance, is particularly bloody and incorporates a graphic groin knifing. The resonant final shot also adds to the lasting impact of this undervalued movie.
—Steven West

Japanese poster for *Justine*

ceding they may well be right, goes on to take responsibility for any moments of quality.

Maybe Power was unlucky to feature in a cast of seasoned performers who were far more familiar with the demands of this type of production: Klaus Kinski in demented form as the caged de Sade; Maria Rohm, excellent as usual, taking the role of wicked sister, Juliette; Sylva Koscina, who figures in a gripping game of "Poison Thy Spouse"; Mercedes McCambridge, toning up her tonsils for Billy Friedkin, who delivers a truly evil performance as the gravel-voiced Dusbois; and Euro-horror buffs will be delighted to see Rosalba Neri, one of a quartet of women who serve a sadistic group led by Howard Vernon. Franco also finds room for (by all accounts) a permanently blotto Jack Palance, and Horst Frank, who tries to implicate Justine in the murder of his wife. Rosemary Dexter? Well, she had to settle for a smaller role as Juliette's despicable tutor, and ensures her pupil passes with flying colors.

While *Justine* may not figure in the top drawer of Franco's filmography, an Altman-esque cast of Euro stars adds sufficient class to gloss over script deficiencies and make hay with the cruel, perverse aspects of this mostly absorbing tale. Applause also goes to another splendid score from Bruno Nicolai—not quite the Michael Nyman of exploitation cinema, but a wonderfully gifted composer in his own right.

—Steve Langton

Credits: Director: Jesus Franco; Writer: Peter Welbeck [Harry Alan Towers].
Leading Cast: Klaus Kinski, Romina Power, Maria Rohm, Akim Tamiroff.

Editor's Note: This review originally appeared in slightly different form at Darren Jones' "The Spinning Image" website and is reproduced here with the permission of the author.

Night, After Night, After Night.

Night, After Night, After Night served as director Lindsay Shonteff's initiation into sexploitation, having earned his horror film chops shooting *Devil Doll* and *Curse of Simba* for Richard Gordon earlier in the decade. After a disagreement with the producers in post-production, he had his name taken off the film, and the directing duties are credited to Lewis J. Force.

The end result of this troubled production gives the impression that a good deal has been lost to the cutting room floor (the Judge's wife gets her own signature tune, "Helena's Theme," but not the screen time to justify it, while a main character disappears around the hour mark, leaving a muddled film full of interesting contradictions). By rights, Police Inspector Rowan should be the film's hero but, blinded by vengeance, he emerges as a fascist bully, every bit the nightmare figure copper that longhairs would have dreaded being on their backs. The Judge is cowardly enough to let Pete stand trial for his own wrongdoings, even having the nerve to preside over the case. Despite the movie's distrust of authority figures, portraying them as hypocrites or with unjustified vendettas against youth,

persecuted Pete is no innocent flower child, but a *Clockwork Orange*-style violent little thug, whose switchblade and questionable attitude toward women gets him into trouble. Just to add to Pete's degeneracy, there is even a suggestion of underage sex, albeit off screen, in a fairly irrelevant scene in which Pete and a girlfriend disappear into the bushes followed by a curious and very young-looking girl. Youth, judges, the police, *Night, After Night, After Night* seems to piss on them all.

Some, not unjustifiably, find the film hypocritical for wallowing in X certificate territory while simultaneously telling the story of a man supposedly destroyed by pornography; but it is less porn that the film seems to be pointing to as the Judge's problem, and more the associated repression and dishonesty. Lomax's outward repulsion at any suggestion of sex (rejecting his hurt wife when she tries to please him by wearing a revealing dress) makes it harder for him to reconcile his secret habit. He keeps it all bottled up, hiring a grotty room which he has seen fit to decorate with girlie pictures. In the film's most unforgettable scene, Lomax paws and slobbers over the pictures and then destroys the room in a rage when self-disgust gets the better of him. One suspects that, as much as striptease scenes and shots of Pete Laver's hands disappearing up a girl's miniskirt gave value for money to a "dirty mac" audience, the film's subtext about outwardly respectable people leading pornography-obsessed double lives must have given them a feeling of unease.

Removed from the shadows, the Judge is merely a pathetic figure, offloading his marital problems at knifepoint on a terrified Soho prostitute. The later transvestite scenes, sometimes incorrectly written up as the character's fetish, seem a humiliating "slap in the face" punishment. By the film's end, the once respected, powerful and terrifying Judge is but a blubbering, dragged-up mess staggering around in a daze and reduced to the level of a sickly dog pleading to be put out of its misery. Working on the cheap, Shonteff shot the film without permits, and the spooked looks on the faces of passersby eyeballing Jack May bewigged, leather clad and staring into lingerie shops are all genuine. That he would agree to be filmed in such a public manner is a validation of May's "beyond the call of duty" commitment to the role.

As well as excellent character turns from May, Gilbert Wynne and Donald Sumpter, from a time capsule perspective, *Night, After Night, After Night* also offers everything you'd want to see in a film made in London circa 1969, with location shooting in Piccadilly Circus, Hyde Park, discothèques and the Old Bailey, as well as an archetypal "made entirely on location in London, England" opening of a couple embracing under the shadow of Big Ben.

Preceding Pete Walker's work in its anti-authoritarian bent, had *Night, After Night, After Night* been released a few years later, when Walker and Norman J. Warren were crafting innovative developments in British terror, chances are the film might be more well known today. At the time, it was sold pretty much as a sex item, and did the rounds at fleapits along with an import called *Days of Desire* before being dispatched to the provinces with a black and white West German horror oldie called *Cave of the Living Dead*. The film briefly surfaced on video in the early 1980s but, to all intents and purposes, has remained in limbo for the last 20 years. Those who have tried and searched in vain for the rights to the film come across a reoccurring story about the financer-owner later disappearing in "mysterious circumstances," while in the Far East, a grisly art-mirrors-life postscript that regrettably has consigned *Night, After Night, After Night* to rarely seen, minor horror gem status.

As was the case with many British skin flicks, B-level crime films and Hammer horrors of the day, a stronger "Continental" version of *Night, After Night, After Night* was made for the film's overseas release. This version drops around 10 minutes of narrative footage from the original film and replaces it with saucy scenes of the Killer Judge bedding various prostitutes, offering alarming glimpses of his leopard skin Y-fronts and hairy arse in the process. This footage was clearly filmed around the same time as the original film, either by Shonteff or someone the producers hired to shoot X-rated material, and showcases some hilariously stilted performances from 1960s glamour model-types who are given the briefest of dialogue in their hooker roles ("It's five pounds for a short time, ten pounds for all night and twenty for the special treatment") before taking off their clothes and ending up as the Judge's sexual conquests.

In addition, the raunchier edit of the film includes alternate takes in which the actors are wearing considerably fewer clothes than in the U.K. version, and near hardcore inserts to several of the film's sex scenes (whoever was responsible for the additional material appears to have been especially hung up on filming scenes of female masturbation).

Only one of the additional scenes is really in keeping with the original film, and sees the Judge (once again) visiting a prostitute, this time bringing his knife along, chasing the naked girl around her apartment and energetically butchering her. With Kensington Gore stage blood liberally splashed over the set and the actress, it's a scene reminiscent of the murder tacked onto the Euro edit of *Corruption* (1967), while predating the heavy bloodletting of the 1980s slasher boom by over a decade.

Of course it hardly needs to be said that the sexual material in the Continental version often seems at odds with the original film. Given the Judge's revulsion regarding female sexuality at several points in the film (especially the scene where his wife tries on the lingerie, and the scene in the whore's flat at the end), it is a little hard to believe the same character would be enjoying sexploits with harlots and generally behaving like some proto-Robin Askwith at the same time.

Slightly more intriguing, however, dialogue from one of the Continental version's prostitutes ("Hello Peter, you're early today; I was just having a cup of coffee, would you

like some?") suggests the Judge's Beatles Wig and Leather Jacket get-up is a deliberate attempt to impersonate Pete Laver and thus frame him for the crimes, something not explored in the original film, which sees the Judge adopt this guise before Laver is introduced or built up as one of the film's red herrings (the Continental version shuffles several scenes around to finger Laver as a suspect much earlier on).

Night, After Night, After Night has always seemed like it has one foot in the doorway of horror cinema and the other in the more shadowy world of sexploitation, so it's perhaps entirely appropriate to discover that, alongside a British version that plays like a horror film, there should have also been a lesser-known "dirty" version out there all along, offering a startling peek at some of the kinkiness that was being shot on the sly by certain Wardour Street veterans in the late 1960s.
—Gavin Whitaker

"I bang every bird I meet, and they enjoy it!"

In terms of its place in horror's chronology, *Night, After Night, After Night* is actually a seminal film. The Swinging '60s, most of which are still remembered in tinted monochrome, largely due to the epoch-defining work of David Bailey and Terence Donovan, were drawing to a close, and only two years after the Summer of Love that heralded a new beginning, the dream was already beginning to turn sour (something that would soon be cemented by Altamont and the Manson murders) and give way to a bitter cynicism about the supposedly brave new world.

How much of this was in part due to people who just hadn't been in the right place at the right moment, thus failing to benefit from what the counterculture had to offer is a moot point, but from the distinctly pessimistic tone explored by numerous U.K. filmmakers at the time, it would seem that, for every liberated swinging scenester merrily popping pills and cavorting his way through a dozen fluorescent Mod dens of iniquity, there were at least three or four more having a thoroughly miserable time and being exploited by the supposedly permissive and "laid-back" society. That's to say nothing of the sheer violence and nihilism depicted in contemporary American productions. And no film, with the possible exception of Peter Walker's sexploitation masterpiece *Cool It Carol* or Shonteff's own *Permissive* less than a year later, conveys this jaded mindset more effectively than *Night, After Night, After Night*.

From its opening credits depicting a Thames-side street scene highlighted by deliciously seedy, almost burlesque lounge music that one can imagine a million dodgy Cockney strippers called "Reenie" taking their kits off to (and, in this film, they do), it's clear that this is far from the cozy fireside horror of Hammer and their imitators. This is sleaze: One hundred and one percent, grade-A, flesh-crawling, "you'll need a good bath afterwards" sleaze.

Despite its obvious low-budget origins, several respectable names appear in the cast, not least of all top-billed Jack May, famous mainly for a lengthy stint in that most venerated of radio soaps, *The Archers*. The plot is fairly easy to follow: Some nutter is on the loose around Soho, Chelsea and various other "happening" London nightspots, stabbing and strangling young girls. Gilbert Wynne is the down-at-heel detective (he has a blonde wife with large knockers who smokes in bed) in charge of finding him. Said wife gets bumped off very early on, causing the thankless plod to take the whole case rather personally and persecute a young, long-haired "groovy" and, quite frankly, unpleasant individual (Donald Sumpter in his first major role, with *hair!*) who unfortunately happens to fit the description given by witnesses and doesn't do himself any favors by using phrases like, "I banged 'er in the bushes, copper!" and so forth. He's an obvious scapegoat, though, because—well, he's one of them 'ippies, innee? Or maybe he's one of them Mods. Either way, he's indecent, lives vicariously, wears leather and, worst of all (God forbid), he sleeps with women—regularly, and without being in a relationship. I mean, we can't have that, can we?

Meanwhile, a second plot unfolds, involving a prudish, cold, sexually repressed judge (May), the breakdown of his marriage to his "so vivacious, what's she doing with him, then?" wife, and his constant chastizing of his barrister (Terry Scully, also seen soon after in *Goodbye Gemini*). Scully is another possible suspect, because he goes to strip joints (cue more Reenies, Queenies, Yvonnes and Dorises flashing their bits to sub-Hawkshaw horn blarings) and reads *porn*—which, as we all know, turns you into a nutter.

There's a reason for these two stories linking together, of course. Have you guessed what it is yet? That's right. Sumpter, the obvious red herring, isn't the guilty man at all, as proved when the murders continue after he's safely locked behind bars. No, it's somebody else, it's—oh, come on, work it out for yourself. And that's when the screenplay's cynicism turns on its heels, criticizing the establishment with more venom than it had supposedly reserved for the permissive society.

This all leads to a slightly protracted (okay, let's not mince words—bloody overlong) final scene that runs for nearly a full half-hour, in which our man, his identity revealed, spends several minutes smearing on badly applied lipstick—like some kind of Brit Horror Robert Smith—snogs (and stabs) several photographs of nude ladies (we've seen his hands fondling them giallo-style earlier), and then proceeds to stagger through the streets of Mayfair and Pimlico in an ill-fitting black leather suit and Beatle wig, thus obviously hoping to throw the rozzers off the scent by convincing them that the murderer is one of them long-haired types that, you know, listens to beat combos in the hit parade and injects "marry-ju-warna."

Luckily for all concerned (including a frightened prostitute and, bizarrely, some queer-bashing queers, very confusing), someone has been following the loony all along and the incredulous cops, led by the beleaguered Wynne, are hot on his trail, but not before he gets the chance to utter one of the greatest lines of dialogue in exploitation history (*"So sweet, so beautiful, so EEVILL!"*) and indulge in some of the most ridiculous (not to mention utterly pointless, except in terms of plot expediency) transvestitism ever seen on screen, all the more incongruous considering the actor involved.

Thankfully for both the fictitious characters and the real-life viewers (it really has dragged on past its prime by this point), the whole shebang comes to a head where it began: on the banks of the Thames, in a sadly somewhat anticlimactic fashion, with the fiend expiring on a mudflat and a nondescript policeman delivering the ultimately unsatisfying final line, "I could have sworn he said, 'Help me'," seconds before the final credits roll. As for Sumpter (who would continue to play a variety of decadent roles in *The Black Panther*, *Our Friends in the North* and *The Buddha of Suburbia*, in which he found himself implicitly gobbled off by Naveen Andrews, a worse fate than prison, maybe?), his story remains unresolved and we never find out, in true "can't be bothered to tie up the loose ends" fashion, whether he was pardoned or not; but, then again, that's low-budget filmmaking for you.
—D.R. Shimon

Credits: Director: Lindsay Shonteff; Writer: Dail Ambler.
Leading Cast: Jack May, Justine Lord, Gilbert Wynne, Linda Marlowe, Peter Forbes-Robertson.

The Oblong Box

Like seemingly every AIP horror pic released in the 1960s, this disappointing farrago has Edgar Allan Poe's name above the title and Vincent Price in the lead role, though it's not worthy of either of them. Originally set to be directed by doomed potential genius Michael Reeves and shot by *Witchfinder General*'s John Coquillon, it also features that film's pretty heroine, Hilary Dwyer, dubiously cast as Price's fiancée. Much of the considerable talent behind and in front of the camera is sorely underused, including "Special Guest Star" Christopher Lee as a doctor who does dodgy deals with body snatchers.

Price is a Brit aristocrat who catches his brother in "the dark continent" of Africa ("a heathen place and no mistake!") indulging in the kind of goat-sacrificing voodoo shtick with which 1960s horror-movie Africans were always involved. When his brother Edward (represented initially by a subjective camera) dies, Price uses the services of the resurrection men to obtain a better-looking corpse for the funeral. Edward, however, is buried alive and, with a red hood covering his hideously disfigured face, sets off on a trail of throat-slashing vengeance.

The cast is fine: Price is worth watching in anything, though Rupert Davies is wasted and one would have liked to have seen more of sexy maid Sally Geeson, who blackmails

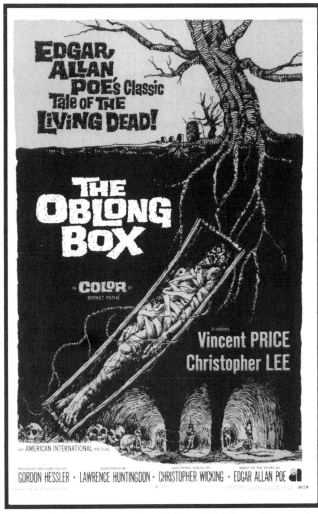

"I tried not to remember why I buried my horn..."

Two minutes or so into this, one of several partly British-funded films Jess Franco made in the late 1960s under the patronage of the notorious Harry Alan Towers, and we've already hit a double entendre. Start as you mean to go on, I say. "A guy like me without a horn is like a man without words..."

Maybe it's the translation to English that causes the intentional hilarity but, whatever the reason, the howlers keep on coming. Within the first 10 minutes, James Darren proceeds to hand us further pearls of wisdom such as, "When you don't know where you're at, I tell you, man, life is like an ocean" (do you think Ian Brown ever watched this?) and the all-time classic, "How can you run from a dead person unless you're dead yourself?" Do enlighten me. Not only that, but it takes almost 15 minutes before any actual dialogue between the characters is spoken!

I shouldn't be too unfair, though, because, on one level, *Venus in Furs* is a great film. It looks beautiful, sounds ace (with a soundtrack from Manfred Mann Chapter Three, how could it not?) and features all the requisite elements of a good cult movie. But it also makes about as much sense as the breakdown of my last phone bill, promising much, but in the final instance delivering little except confusion, disconnection and a general feeling of "erm, what happened?" And the old get-out clause of "it was the 1960s, they were all on drugs" doesn't hold water here, particularly as one can't imagine a hard-line exploitation taskmaster like Towers (still active in the business well into his 80s, up to the time of his death in the summer of 2009) tolerating such behavior. Mind you, it's the oldest rule in the business: Never allow the producer on the set; he might see what you're actually filming.

There *is* a basic narrative structure. I think. James Darren, in the role of jazz trumpeter Jimmy Logan, is suffering from amnesia, but something tells him that he's buried his instrument on the beach in Istanbul. Upon finding it, he also discovers a naked woman Wanda Reed (Maria Rohm, aka Mrs. Towers, also found in further Franco Britsploiters such as *Justine* and *The Blood of Fu Manchu*) washed ashore and remembers a series of immediately preceding events which link them together, involving a party thrown by "the Riviera Greek Island Yachting Crowd" (no, me neither), also attended by beautiful photographer Olga (Margaret Lee), billionaire playboy Ahmed (Klaus Kinski) and pervy art dealer Percival Kapp (Dennis Price).

At said shindig, the four (though not Darren himself) indulge in some BDSM [bondage and S&M] games that seem to get seriously out of hand, resulting in Rohm's death. Except that, as the film progresses, she may not be deceased at all, reappearing at other parties with a red bowl-cut, turquoise stockings, heels and a fur coat (a combination which set my pulse racing, anyway) and stalking the protagonists. It's therefore up to Darren, who doesn't even seem able to tell what year it is or what country he's in, to decipher the mystery. Unfortunately

Lee and finds the mysterious Edward alluring. Director for hire Gordon Hessler, whose *Cry of the Banshee*, released around the same time, is a significantly better movie, works in some fashionable bare breasts during a tavern interlude that ends in a silly brawl and splashes around some very fake blood during weak slashing scenes.

The plodding narrative, which has an inevitably patronizing view of African culture, struggles to overcome the dull nature of its verbose "monster," a pitiful Elephant Man-type figure. The much built-up melodramatically scored final unmasking reveals (dur, dur, durrrrrh!) a fairly ordinary bloke with a very half-hearted pancake-mixture makeup job on part of his face. Somewhat redeeming this generally lifeless movie is a grim closing scene that quite effectively heralds the downbeat spirit of genre movies to come during the next decade on both sides of the Atlantic.
—Steven West

Credits: Director: Gordon Hessler; Writers: Lawrence Huntington [Christopher Wicking: additional dialogue].
Leading Cast: Vincent Price, Christopher Lee, Rupert Davies, Sally Geeson, Alister Williamson, Peter Arne, Hilary Dwyer.

people keep dying or killing themselves, leading the police to think he and the supposedly departed Rohm are involved in something very suspicious.

In horror terms, *Venus in Furs* is neither that graphic nor particularly scary: In exploitation terms, the nudity and sex are more restrained and gently erotic than usual, though Franco would return to pure sleaze a year later with *Eugenie*. It *is* very atmospheric, but it's the heady atmosphere of Bohemian decadence that prevails. Performance-wise, Darren makes for a reasonably interesting male lead, and Rohm is smoldering sensuality incarnate (though Lee is more to my taste; I always did prefer British girls), but the show is stolen from under all their noses by the great American jazz singer Barbara McNair. In the role of the musician's long-suffering girlfriend Rita, she provides us with the one sympathetic focus in the whole movie and also gets to sing the fantastic title song. Backed by Mann, Mike Hugg and several leading lights of the British jazz-rock scene and cavorting in the most seductive of silver ball gowns, her voice ascends to heights others couldn't even dream of, practically validating the entire film single-handed.

"Guest stars" Price and Kinski appear onscreen so infrequently, one could almost forget they are in the film at all, though the former's demise makes for one of only two genuinely disquieting moments throughout, the other involving a rather messy suicide. I would never suggest that seeing "proper" actors appear in exploitation flicks is in any way depressing or demeaning, but, knowing what we do of Price's personal life, one can't help but feel a tinge of sadness at watching the man who once played the organ at Canterbury Cathedral, and who delivered the classic couplet "I shot an arrow in the air, she fell to earth in Berkeley Square," reduced to largely dialogue-free cameos in which his sole function appears to be to fondle the breasts and thighs of exotic women. On the other hand, given the opportunity, some might see this as the apex of their career. (Come to think of it, so might I.)

It's also interesting to realize that, at the time, even though it had already been released some three years before, absolutely no one outside of New York was aware of the fact that the Velvet Underground had recorded a tune of the same name, the lyrics of which, ironically, are a lot closer to Leopold von Sacher-Masoch's original text than anything contained within this picture's 86-minute running time. Let's be honest, Franco's script has nothing whatsoever to do with the original novel (a fact he and Towers presumably played

down during promotion). As has been pointed out, the dialogue leaves a little to be desired, but whatever else one says about Franco, he most definitely had a singular vision which, when given the necessary budget, has been allowed to create moments of stunning visual beauty. Some of those are on display here: the crumbling castles, the swirling red and purple hues, the long shots of Rohm walking barefoot across several plush carpets, all aided by Angelo Lotti's undoubted photographic skills; but unfortunately the effect is undermined by totally unexplained and random pink and blue filter shots or slow-motion sequences that do little or nothing to aid the story.

That's assuming, of course, that anyone is still following the story past the first 30 minutes. In the end, I enjoyed the whole experience more by giving up and immersing myself in the psychedelic spectacle. Perhaps that's what you're supposed to do? Ironically, during the last 20 minutes, this becomes harder to achieve as Franco introduces an almost conventional structure involving a police investigation and a chase scene worthy of *Dragnet*, complete with cheesy caper music, although upon entering a nearby churchyard, everything takes a turn for the nonsensical yet again. And while we're on the subject, why would a dead person have to run away from the police, anyway? Surely they'd just dematerialize. Unless they're *not* dead, in which case—oh, and hang on, we're back in Istanbul again. Or are we? I give up...

—D.R. Shimon

Credits: Director: Jesus Franco; Writers: Jesus Franco, Milo G. Cuccia, Carlo Fadda, Bruno Leder, Marvin Wald.
Leading Cast: Klaus Kinski, James Darren, Maria Rohm, Dennis Price, Paul Muller, Margaret Lee.

Whirlpool

Whirlpool is officially a Danish production, but was filmed in England: specifically, a quick stock shot of Trafalgar Square before the majority of the action takes place in typical Larraz country, i.e., a house in the bleak woods in close proximity to a picturesque river. It's here that this incredibly perverse tale of sex (possibly incestuous) and savage murder unfolds, with none other than 1960s supermodel Vivian Neves as the lovely central victim. Fans of Larraz won't be at all surprised that Karl Lanchbury is the menace, another in the long line of weird photographers in British horror movies.

For 1969, the sex scenes are hot stuff: We begin with a strangely

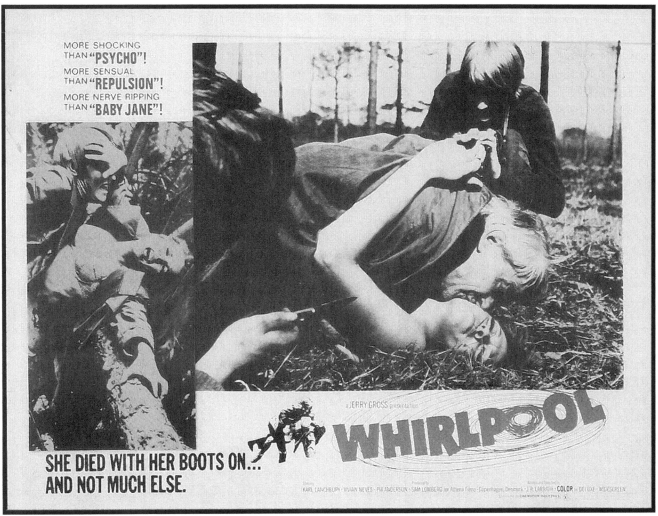

MORE SHOCKING THAN "PSYCHO"!
MORE SENSUAL THAN "REPULSION"!
MORE NERVE RIPPING THAN "BABY JANE"!

SHE DIED WITH HER BOOTS ON...
AND NOT MUCH ELSE.

a JERRY GROSS presentation

WHIRLPOOL

KARL LANCHBURY · VIVIAN NEVES · PIA ANDERSSON · SAM LOMBERG for Athena Films · Copenhagen, Denmark · J.R. LARRAZ · COLOR by DELUXE · WIDESCREEN

compelling game of strip poker and eventually progress into a really odd menage-a-trois, with Lanchbury ignoring the naked and alluring Neves in favor of giving the older Pia Andersson one (she's apparently his auntie) while Viv lies next to them in the same bed! Naturally it all ends up with a handful of murders, but the motivations for these are not your normal clichés at all, and there's a very odd revelatory flashback toward the finale that features a flute-playing tramp, among other bizarre aspects. As with Larraz's masterpiece *Symptoms*, it's all in the atmosphere and feel rather than the content; add *Whirlpool* to the list of semi-art, semi-exploitation movies (you know the ones: *Secret Ceremony*, *The Corpse*, *Mumsy*, *Nanny*, *Sonny and Girly*, *Performance*, *The Killing of Sister George*) made circa 1970, which somebody really ought to write a book about one of these days.

Neves looks fantastic throughout and gives a truly uninhibited performance. She's a little shaky during a very odd rape sequence which turns out, for once, to be utterly integral to the plot, but other than that she certainly surpasses expectations.

In the October 1971 edition of the *Monthly Film Bulletin*, Kenneth Thompson declared *Whirlpool* to be "a permissive updating of the best (or worst) Victorian melodrama, complete with over-emphatic gestures, pregnant pauses and sinister glances," adding "irrelevant appearances from one or two minor characters and the generally erratic continuity are the result of substantial cutting in the version showing here, which—after a sluggish exposition—gains in speed and impact for the later lurid developments." The MFB gave the film's running time as 70 minutes, chopped down from an original 90. *Whirlpool* remains officially unreleased on DVD, although bootleg copies pepper dealer's tables at film fairs everywhere. It's a lively, vivid movie, which will certainly appeal to admirers of Larraz's better-known fare.
—Darrell Buxton

Credits: Director: José Ramon Larraz; Writer: José Ramon Larraz.
Leading Cast: Karl Lanchbury, Vivian Neves, Pia Andersson, Andrew Grant.

Bonus Features

The following British horror films were made before the end of the 1960s but released during the early 1970s.

And Soon the Darkness

Cathy (Michele Dotrice) and Jane (Pamela Franklin) are two friends on a cycle holiday in rural France. They have a fractious relationship, Jane being super-organized and straight-laced, Cathy being more interested in catching some rays and eyeing up the local talent (assuming Sandor Elés qualifies as talent) than keeping to Jane's deadlines. Frustrated with her companion's procrastination, Jane cycles off, leaving Cathy on the side of the road, sunbathing. Regretting her decision, Jane returns to the spot where they argued, only to find her friend missing. Alone in an inhospitable environment and slowly grasping the fact that the area she is traveling through has been the site of an unsolved sex murder, Jane's panic and paranoia comes to the surface and she finds herself unable to trust anyone, whether it be the aforementioned Elés (claiming to be a detective investigating the earlier fatality) or the local gendarme (John Nettleton).

Directed by small screen veteran Robert Fuest and written by regular telly scribes Brian Clemens and Terry Nation, *And Soon the Darkness* does feel like a well-constructed, well-executed TV movie. Even for its time, the film is remarkably restrained and much of the suspense is generated by a script that concentrates on both the "fish out of water" paranoia that traveling through a foreign country and not speaking the language can generate, and by the beautiful but desolate French countryside. Ian Wilson's excellent cinematography and a spartan score from Laurie Johnson aid the oppressive atmosphere. The two lead performances are both excellent, as is the way their collapsing friendship is sketched out. From the start, Pamela Franklin's Jane is clearly a character who requires structure in her life, and when this is stripped away the suspicion and panic that are hinted at in the opening scenes rapidly bubble to the surface. She is also surrounded by unsympathetic characters that either do not understand her or treat her with outright hostility. Even those

who do try to help have murky motivations, and the viewer can't really establish whether Jane's suspicions have genuine merit or are a manifestation of her heightened state of alarm.

And Soon the Darkness is also a nicely deceptive title for a film that takes place largely in dappled daylight. It's one of a small group of horror films that generate a genuine sense of agoraphobia.

The open, deserted landscape of out-of-town France, with its empty roads and tiny, isolated settlements populated by terse, suspicious locals, becomes more unsettling and disorientating as the film progresses. The sunny wide open but empty vistas highlight Jane's deteriorating mental state in the same way that the sun-baked plains of the Texas panhandle underpin the downhome madness on display in Tobe Hooper's *The Texas Chainsaw Massacre* (1974), a film which utilizes a similar theme, subjects its heroine to great psychological stress and also uses its terrain to sinister, dislocatory ends.

And Soon the Darkness is by no means perfect. It's languid in terms of pacing, which in itself is no problem, but results in some sequences dragging a bit, particularly in the first half-hour. The finale is also a bit perfunctory and will be familiar to those who know Clemens' work (particularly his 1970s TV series *Thriller*); however, these are minor quibbles for a film that swims in an atmosphere of growing unease and stands apart from its British horror contemporaries by virtue of its restraint and reliance on fears of the unfamiliar and rustic, all aided by a very convincing central performance from the always watchable Franklin. *Champêtre terreur*, indeed.
—Neil Pike

Credits: Director: Robert Fuest; Writers: Brian Clemens, Terry Nation.
Leading Cast: Pamela Franklin, Michele Dotrice, Sandor Elès, John Nettleton.

The Body Beneath

One of the happiest accidents in the history of cinema is the fortuitous set of circumstances that brought one of the most notorious exploitation/ underground filmmakers to the U.K. to shoot some films, which are truly among the most vertiginous, schizophrenic productions ever committed to celluloid—in this case 16mm and probably scrounged short ends at that, which perversely makes them all the more irresistible to imbeciles like myself. The cinematic terrorist in question was the redoubtable Andy Milligan, brought to Blighty due to the successful exhibition of some of his (primarily sexploitation) films

SEXUALLY RAMPANT GHOULS, DEPRAVED SOULS... AND BLOOD-RED ROSES!

Filmed in the graveyards of England

THE BODY BENEATH

in BONE-CHILLING COLOR

Produced by CINEMEDIA FILMS
Released by NOVA INTERNATIONAL Productions Ltd

of deceit and lying. Reed is particularly, and entertainingly, verbose. "Really? I can't remember, I use so many sayings in my profession I lose track," he haughtily rejoins when asked if he has been quoting Oscar Wilde. Later, after kidnapping a young lady whom he proposes to use as breeding stock in order to further the vampire clan, he seems intent on breaking her resistance down by bombarding her with verbiage as much as anything else.

However, at one point, and indeed ironically, Reed tells another potential vampire-sirer that "words are nothing, my dear, actions speak louder" and *The Body Beneath* culminates in a tableau which has impressed even Milligan's detractors, the meeting of the vampire clan, in which the director combines day-for-night photography, a Vaseline-smeared camera lens and manipulation of the soundtrack which verges on the giddy (a gramophone recording of a church bell and classical music discordantly juxtaposed with horror library music). Milligan always loved playing two music tracks simultaneously to disorient and harangue the spectators.

—James McBean

Credits: Director and Writer: Andy Milligan.
Leading Cast: Gavin Reed, Jackie Skarvellis, Berwick Kaler, Susan Heard.

Editor's Note: Milligan's films *The Man with Two Heads*, *Bloodthirsty Butchers* and *The Rats are Coming! The Were-wolves are Here!* all contain material filmed in England, apparently during the summer of 1969, but none were released until the 1970s and, in some cases, may have had additional footage shot in Andy's home territory of Staten Island, so we've elected not to include full reviews here. (All complaints to me should come via the publisher, please.)

[Publisher's Note: We have a very large {but green} file 13 and aren't afraid to use it!]

The Corpse (aka *Crucible of Horror*)

When it comes to oily weirdos, there are few actors who can out-smirk Michael Gough. The British film biz quickly realized this in the early 1960s, and they shoehorned him into any film going. And much like Peter Cushing, he always delivered. *The Corpse* (often shown under its alternate title *Crucible of Horror*, which makes no sense at all) appears to have been written and made solely with him in mind, putting his character, Walter Eastwood, firmly at the forefront of the picture. Even when he's not on screen, his dominant presence can be felt, towering over his put upon family.

The Corpse is a peculiar example of that British horror film staple, the spooky suburban melodrama. It takes scenes of (almost) normal domestic life and suffuses them with a vague peculiarity that becomes more unsettling as the film moves on. Pete Walker would take up the baton thrown down by such films in the early 1970s and run with it with productions like *Fright-mare* and *Schizo*; but, where his "kitchen sink" horrors are more

in a cinema club. The first film Milligan concocted under the Cinemedia banner was a film with the, I feel, quintessentially Milliganesque title *The Body Beneath*. Milligan always seemed more drawn toward an opaque sort of title than the exploitative appellations splattered onto his films by the likes of William Mishkin.

Perhaps due to a slightly higher budget, *The Body Beneath* is, much of the time, the most "mainstream" of the four horrors that Milligan sprinted through during his stay in the U.K. (there's a fifth film, *Nightbirds*, also filmed while Milligan was still employed by Cinemedia, which is presumably still gathering dust in his biographer's garage, never having seen the light of day). *The Body Beneath* is a take on the vampire myth, with the magisterial Gavin Reed (Milligan really lucked out with most of the actors in these films) playing a Dracula-type character who has come to Britain on a similar mission. Crucially for Milligan, and like the protagonist in his subsequent American vampire film *Guru the Mad Monk*, Reed adopts the façade of a religious figure, the Rev. Alexander Algernon Ford. Milligan hated religion with a passion (not that there was much that he *liked*, right enough).

As Guru stated, "Talk comes cheap," yet talk is of crucial importance in Milligan's work and is one of the main conduits

178

open-ended and ambiguous. No explanation is given for the goings-on in *The Corpse*, but a healthy dose of black humor helps keep things bearable.
—Chris Wood

Credits: Director: Viktors Ritelis; Writer: Olaf Pooley.
Leading Cast: Michael Gough, Yvonne Mitchell, Sharon Gurney, Olaf Pooley.

Crescendo

An oddity, to say the least, *Crescendo* follows on directly from *Fanatic*, the first of Hammer's psycho-thrillers in color, bearing several of the hallmarks of every film in this particular subgenre, but is decidedly different in several ways, most noticeably in that, rather than this being a case of "they're trying to drive me maaaad," it's a case of "they're all stark raving bonkers." It also features florid and almost hallucinogenic cinematography (take a bow, the late Alan Gibson, the man who would within a year bring us the similarly psychotropic *Goodbye Gemini*, blow our minds two years later with the now-legendary kitsch piece that is *Dracula A.D. 1972* and even chalk up the trippiest entry in Brian Clemens' *Thriller* canon, *Sleepwalker*), plus far more explicit nudity, violence and even close-up heroin addiction (I kid thee not) than one would have expected from a Hammer production.

Several people have mistakenly credited it with being a TV movie and ironically it does seem like the missing link, both thematically and cinematographically, between the studio's "mini-Hitchcocks" and the similarly themed U.S. TV productions that followed a year or so later, such as John Moxey's *A Taste of Evil* (1971) written by Jimmy Sangster, the man also partially responsible for this, and most obviously Curtis Harrington's *How Awful About Allan* (1970) starring Anthony Perkins. Here, though, "The Sang" is aided by Alfred Shaughnessy, the man who would go on to write *The Flesh and Blood Show* and the rarely seen *Tiffany Jones* for Pete Walker, and his presence noticeably pushes the film in a more modern and less kitsch direction, although ultimately it never escapes its Grand Guignol origins.

Crescendo begins promisingly enough with a very eerie dream sequence in which a young man caresses his beloved on a lush mountainside beach before looking down to see that his fair maiden is in fact a grinning, rotting corpse, with eyes staring out of their crumbling sockets. If that wasn't enough, an exact body double of himself appears seemingly from nowhere and shoots him, causing him to wake

Crescendo

firmly rooted in realism, *The Corpse* has an air of late 1960s mysticism and experimentation about it that later films lack.

It begins with Gough, huge eyebrows aloft, gardening. His teenage daughter arrives home on a bicycle, and he immediately grabs its still warm seat. This in itself would be disturbing enough, but the audience is also being treated to some inappropriate musical climaxes and bizarre close-ups of people's faces.

Walter runs his family (wife, daughter and son) with a rod of iron. His wife is a wet blanket, son is a carbon copy of Walter (even working in the same place) and daughter is a bit of a rebel. It appears that, not only is she shagging Walter's friend from the golf club ("He just kissed me. He's got a moustache like a carpet sweeper"), but she's also a thief. And even a good horsewhipping by dad won't calm her down. It seems to shake mum out of her reverie, though. After the daughter has fronted him out following the thrashing ("I didn't want you to think me a coward") and father and son have gone off to work, mum whispers, "Let's kill him."

The Corpse is a very confusing film. It is never made clear whether much of what happens really *does* happen, post-punishment (there's a gunshot but no blood, and the action is interspersed with what looks like, but might not be, a flashback to a rape). A body appears, then disappears, and the surprise ending is made even more surprising because it's left

And... for Lovers of the Macabre

CRESCENDO

POWERS OLSON SCOTT LaPOTAIRE ACKLAND

Ackland, then berates him for "spending most of his life in asylums" before he practically shoves his fingers into her eyes and throws her bodily onto the sofa but *doesn't* have his wicked way with her, thus leaving her to get her small yet pert norks out in blurred focus (again) and jump into the heated pool, where she is subsequently stabbed in an orgy of frenzied bloody death that seems positively explicit compared to the quaintness of the studio's concurrent output.

There's also a ridiculous moment when Powers finds a photo album full of what are blatantly shots of her, only to be told by Scott that they are of Olson's former love, Catherine, who died mysteriously. "You do look somewhat like her," quoth the menacing matriarch. Of course she does, it's the same bloody woman! Do the alarm bells start ringing in our heroine's head here, maybe? Maybe being asked to come to dinner in a red dress for no apparent reason (except we've already seen the dead girl wearing it in the dream sequences) would arouse suspicions? No, it would seem not. Did they remove everyone's brain cells in the late 1960s?

The excitement then tapers off again (lots of walking about in the dark by people only seen from the waist down, giallo-style, abounds) before a half-nude Powers, now in bed with and planning to marry the hapless Georges, finally works out what the hell is going on and has to fight for her life. And yes, the build-up to the climax does actually resemble some kind of crescendo, just in case you wondered.

—D.R. Shimon

Credits: Director: Alan Gibson; Writers: Jimmy Sangster, Alfred Shaughnessy.
Leading Cast: Stefanie Powers, James Olson, Margaretta Scott, Jane Lapotaire, Joss Ackland, Kirsten Betts.

Cry of the Banshee

There was nothing the red-blooded male cinemagoer of the late 1960s and early 1970s liked more than watching a buxom wench get dragged along a muddy street before being stripped, whipped and set on fire. Or you may draw that conclusion, to judge from the number of films along the lines of *Cry of the Banshee* being released at the time. I certainly began to think it, as I gamely tried to stay awake through the first half hour of this effort. The whole shebang opens, extremely promisingly, with a title sequence devised and animated by Monty Python member and future director of renown, Terry Gilliam. It's mainly downhill thereafter.

Luckily, if you stick with it, it does improve. Price's witch-hunting gets him in bother with the real McCoy, and before he can say, "perhaps I shouldn't have raped and murdered all those girls," he's brought down a curse on his entire family—for curse, read Patrick Mower (which is pretty much the same thing). Patrick's a sort of low rent shape-shifter, his appearance signaled by the titular banshee wail, which sounds more like a werewolf, so why not call it *Cry*

from his fitful slumbers shortly before the title appears on the screen and we are shown the young heroine (Stefanie Powers, who had starred in *Fanatic* and should have known what she was in for by now) making her way along the coast road in a chauffeur-driven vehicle. As is oft the way with these films are we in the South of France again? Yes, indeed.

As for the plot, well, you won't be shocked to find that it involves an old country house near the sea; a mad bloke in a wheelchair (James Olson); his sinister and slightly mad mother (Margaretta Scott in a role that could have easily gone to Margaret Johnston or Brenda Bruce, and was in fact offered to Joan Crawford); a sinister, brooding, mad butler and chauffeur (Joss Ackland), who strolls around the house in the dark but doesn't appear to do any actual butling; Jane Lapotaire as a slutty maid par excellence; a room full of disfigured dolls (always a mark of quality); and a ridiculous twist in the tail which anyone who's ever seen any horror films or thrillers before can spot coming a mile off.

Our Stef is a music student who has met Danielle Ryman, a concert pianist's widow (Scott), at some grand gala concert, and has taken her up on her offer to spend a summer studying music with her and her disabled son Georges, also a musician but of less than scintillating quality (at least according to his overbearing mother) at their palatial villa. Even though the house is the kind of place that seems scary and uninviting even in blazing summer sunlight, and Lapotaire obviously resents her being there (largely because the hero inevitably finds himself drawn to our American starlet and therefore less inclined to let the sultry frog princess pump his arms full of heroin whilst nibbling his ear off). She stays, even though mysterious piano music plays by itself in the night, there's something so obviously up with the mother, and the sick "hero," whose haircut beggars belief, is prone to nightmares that constantly involve the same gun-toting body double and a dead woman—not to mention that his "disability" seems to come and go as it pleases. Or is that something to do with the twist in the plot?

This bloke's barnet: He has to be the most blatantly balding yet in denial principal male lead in any horror film, and his dress sense isn't up to much for 1969 (mind you, he is supposed to be a mentalist who lives indoors with his mum), yet the drop-dead gorgeous Powers falls for him, and not only that, the silly mare believes that his heroin fix is a prescription from the doctor! If women that beautiful can really go for blokes like that, then it gives hope to us all.

Still, it's not primarily a love story, it's a horror thriller. Things start to build up nicely when Lapotaire makes a pass at

of the Werewolf? (Editor's Note: Columbia had already used that title 1944.) Mower proceeds to munch his way through Vincent's family, until we reach a very nice little twist ending.

Unlike most films of the time, the special effects guys really understood the limitations of their craft, so we never actually get to see the avenging monster come out of the shadows, which is no bad thing by the look of his silhouette. Still, as *An American Werewolf in Paris* showed, in the main, furry lycanthropic beasts look crap anyway, even using today's computer technology.

The main problem with *Banshee* is the tone. Unlike most other witch-hunting films, the witches really are followers of Satan, which rather means that you're rooting for the bad guys. Burn the witch! And while you're at it, burn the script and then get someone to rewrite it—this time with a banshee in the storyline.
—Chris Wood

Credits: Director: Gordon Hessler; Writers: Tim Kelly, Christopher Wicking.
Leading Cast: Vincent Price, Hilary Dwyer, Carl Rigg, Elisabeth Bergner, Patrick Mower.

I Start Counting

When Jenny Agutter is mentioned to any man of a certain age, certain reactions (including drooling, dribbling and the emitting of noises) tend to occur. These are invariably followed by a discussion of her iconic (often naked) appearances in *Walkabout*, *Logan's Run*, *Equus* and *An American Werewolf in London*. Sadly, not as many have witnessed this groundbreaking, multi-layered and fascinating movie which belongs as much in the "once seen, never forgotten" category as it does in the ranks of "hard to see" British films.

Those lucky enough to have seen it often speak in almost hushed, reverential tones: For once, these are deserved. A film at least three years ahead of its time, it could even be said

(along with *Night, After Night, After Night*) to be the one that pointed the way for British horror and suspense in the ensuing decade. It was not the first film to openly embrace topics—drugs, rape, incest, teenage sexuality and blasphemy among them—which had been hitherto considered largely taboo in the nation's cinematic lexicon, but by transporting them from the liberated surroundings of central London's demimonde set to the concrete, disenfranchised suburban sprawls of Bracknell and Slough, it allowed audiences license to realize that these were issues affecting more than just one isolated group of individuals.

Sure, the gritty face of the northern kitchen-sink drama, as best envisaged through the eyes of Braine and Sillitoe, had already leered from screens for over a decade, but if *I Start Counting*—still essentially an exploitation film and thus not accorded the gravitas given to its monochrome predecessors—showed anything, it was that there was more to the seedy underbelly of this country than a class-based North-South divide. In an historical and cultural context it is equally significant: Not only does it point the way (like Lindsay Shonteff's aforementioned shocker) to the urban sleaze of 1970's Brit cinema, but its content seems to have laid the foundation for half the lyrics that the likes of Morrissey and Jarvis Cocker (himself an avid collector of cinema of this kind) have written over the past 25 years.

The story appears simple on the surface, but is revealed, especially after multiple viewings, as more multilayered and textured. Ostensibly it concerns a 14-year-old Catholic girl, Wynne (Agutter), growing up in this post-modern wasteland, who develops a crush on her much older adoptive brother (Bryan Marshall), one which perversely deepens and grows into infatuation after she starts to believe he is the local sex killer. This is an idea that makes you sit up with a jolt, but as the narrative develops, it continues not necessarily along a linear path but in several confusing and fascinating directions: The family's history (involving at least one spousal death discovered by the infant Agutter, detailed effectively in a chilling flashback during an improvised séance) is a chequered one, and has suffered at least one major relocation and upheaval in the past 10 years.

The brother's personal life seems to be one long catalog of tragedies, but aside from one angered outburst directed at Wynne's sluttily precocious friend, Corinne (Clare Sutcliffe), quite late on, he maintains a sense of calm throughout that creates confusion as to his true nature: Both Wynne's mother (Madge Ryan, drudgy as ever) and her grandfather (Billy Russell) seem like drained, useless couch potatoes whose social outlet is when Auntie Rene (there always was one back then, it seems) pops around to polish off the digestives, and her other brother (Michael Feast, a world away from the camp old roué of *Velvet Goldmine*) is a porn-collecting drug user who seems to spend his time hanging out with "the wrong sort."

Placed subtly in the midst of all this social commentary, not enough to be obvious at first glance, but by no means hidden from view, is the horror element: Murders of young girls have been occurring in the town (the very same locale in which

In the world of the nightmare, a little blood adds colour!

"I START COUNTING!"

JENNY AGUTTER · BRYAN MARSHALL

Agutter believes she sees the Christ figure in church weeping blood: By the time we acknowledge it, it's gone, but the seed has already been planted. Rarely in a genre production has the use of color and background been so important or effective in creating a uniformity of mood.

As to the powerful climax, it becomes pretty obvious with 20 minutes remaining (detractors may say even earlier, but that's missing the whole point) who the killer is, and that one character gets what some may consider to be his comeuppance. Some may consider the conclusion ambiguous, but the final shot of bulldozers trampling over fields and outhouses leaves us in no doubt as to its director's intent. The old world is dead, and the 1970s are around the corner. Admittedly never terrifying, but in equal measures fascinating, worrying, disquieting and enveloping, *I Start Counting* is as near-perfect an end to a decade as one could hope for—a genre essential.
—D.R. Shimon

Credits: Director: David Greene; Writer: Richard Harris.
Leading Cast: Jenny Agutter, Bryan Marshall, Clare Sutcliffe, Simon Ward.

Incense for the Damned (aka *Bloodsuckers*)

Chriseis? What Chriseis?

When Richard Fountain (Patrick Mower), Oxford scholar and son of the Foreign Secretary, goes missing in Greece, his pals from England band together to track him down. Enlisting the aid of the British military attaché Derek Longbow (Patrick-Macnee, having a ball), they are shocked to discover that the engaged but impotent intellectual has embarked on an affair with a jet-setting temptress, and that bloodied bodies are showing up at various locations Fountain is known to have visited.

Reportedly an extremely troubled production (Hartford-Davis removed his name from the film; some prints credit "Michael Burrowes" as director), *Incense for the Damned* may look rough-hewn and unfinished, and lurches along to a truncated 70 minutes or so plus credits, but has enough points of fascination to keep viewers attentive, especially those who may be seeking new twists on the hoary themes of vampirism. For here, as in Simon Raven's fine source novel *Doctors Wear Scarlet*, bloodsucking is seen to be the practice of the sexually liberated as opposed to the more traditional fanged creatures of the night. Indeed, this is one of those horror movies where the majority of the drama is played out amid sunny, outdoor settings, with beautiful scenery and architecture being used to the best advantage.

This backdrop of cloudless skies and azure seas gives *Incense* the air of one of Lew Grade's contemporary small-screen ITC adventure thrillers. Might Brett Sinclair from *The Persuaders*, or *The Champions'* Sharron Macready, be embroiled in espionage or derring-do behind an adjacent column or nearby ruin? Choreographed chase and fight sequences set to brash, blaring horns and lush string arrangements bolster such a comparison, and—perhaps befitting a film that treats its horrors in an unorthodox manner—action and exposition

Sidney Lumet's masterful *The Offence* was set three years later; just what is it with Bracknell, exactly?), and the older generation seemingly feel as powerless to intervene as they do in any of the other social changes with which they are confronted.

At the crux, however, it's the depiction of these social changes that make *I Start Counting* so fascinating and elevate its language far beyond the confines of the standard horror film. The major subtext—that teenage girls were maturing more quickly than before and developing full sexual and romantic appetites (even if in thought rather than deed), but were not possessed of enough discretion to make the "correct" choices—was a step forward for a genre in which its young females had previously been portrayed as bimbo victims (*Cover Girl Killer* and *The Night Caller*), but not one that all viewers would necessarily accept.

But most striking of all, and possibly the most enduring aspect, is the masterful symbolism that director David Greene invests in every shot. Every inch of the Kinch family's world—their house, walls and TV, Agutter's underwear, bedroom furniture and toys, Sutcliffe's clothes, Marshall's van, the local Catholic church, their town center, their record shop—is painted a bright, scintillating white which, by inference, is slowly becoming smudged and corrupted with the dirt of the outside world. White also symbolizes, of course, purity and innocence (two qualities Catholic schoolgirls are supposed to hold dear), and it is into this world of innocence that the ever-present red bus (a symbol of violation and penetration), conducted by the lecherous yet similarly juvenile Simon Ward, makes regular journeys. The allegory is further expanded in one scene where take precedence over chills and the arcane. The film strives to deny the extraordinary—as Macnee deadpans while strolling around a crumbling amphitheatre, "You can hardly believe that Minoan rites could take place at Oxford. Could you imagine the don being castrated by the Provost?"

As Chriseis, the alluring "threat" at the heart of the striking narrative, Imogen Hassall (all tan, eyelashes and kinky boots) is utterly captivating, her limitations as an actress being well disguised by Hartford-Davis' clever decision to pare back her dialogue and to concentrate on close-ups, or quick shots of her glancing, darting eyes, piercing and enigmatic. Not only does this make the most of Imogen's smouldering sexuality, it convinces us that Chriseis is capable of controlling everything surrounding her—a creature every bit in charge of her immediate environment as, say, Count Dracula. Mower, ubiquitous in genre fare at the time, is less successful in bearing the weight of the film on his shoulders, having to carry off some unconvincing mysticism, appear in hallucinatory sequences and attempt to convey the healing, restorative and combative powers of the Greek landscape (an unusual but very underdeveloped concept). It's Macnee who secures the pick of the good lines, and look at the fun he seems to be having in the couple of scenes where he has to ride a mule!

It's a courageous stab at filming a truly different take on accepted vampire themes, but one that clearly suffers from budgetary woes, uncommitted performers and production problems which leave the movie feeling sketchy and inadequate. In its favor, there's an exciting, expertly edited cross-cut sequence some two-thirds in which leaves us reeling at the surprise deaths of two major players in quick succession, Edward Woodward's sardonic cameo as an authority on the history of sexual deviancy ("You have your voyeurs, transvestites, narcissists, bestialists—aah, it's a funny old world") and a final freeze-frame which, while entirely negating the picture's previously ultra-modern approach to vampires, somehow seems shockingly satisfying. Fountain's climactic speech to the assembled cream of Oxford academia, in which he equates the dehumanizing educational process to leeching, comes as a damp squib, though. Impressively staged and with Peter Cushing in peerless form, the scene suffers from Mower's inexperience and inability to dominate the proceedings. It might have worked in the intended way had other hands been at the helm (imagine *If....*-era Lindsay Anderson and Malcolm McDowell let loose on such material) but, like most of *Incense*, falls a little flat.

Some versions contain an additional seven-minute sex and drugs orgy sequence (included as a separate extra on the British DVD), accompanied by an astounding guitar and sax wig-out typical of the times, and which is far more experimental and attention grabbing than anything in the remainder of the movie.
—Darrell Buxton

Credits: Director: Robert Hartford-Davis; Writer: Julian More.
Leading Cast: Patrick Mower, Alex Davion, Johnny Sekka, Patrick Macnee, Madeline Hinde, Peter Cushing, Imogen Hassall.

Legend of the Witches

From the perspective of a practicing witch, I have to say that my hackles were up right from the word Lucifer. "Here we go again," I thought. I remarked to no one in particular that I had a checklist in my head of "Inane Assumptions People Who Read the *News of the World* Have about Witches." Which this documentary then proceeded to tick, quite briskly and in Bristol-fashion, all puns intended.

Rather like an imaginary "Carry On Aleister Crowley," with the obligatory black-caped spooky types and boobs and bums a-plenty, Malcolm Leigh's grubby little offering gives us the following in vast, shaky camera, smudged black and white quantities (emphasis on the last two syllables, if you please):

Nakedness—all very well if you live in Baja, California, but not quite so condusive in the Home Counties of a wet mid-April afternoon. Trust me, even with global warming, nothing induces me to get my bazooms out in the fresh air of Blighty on an October eve.

Lucifer—Bloody Lucifer—and pigging bloody goats. What is this obsession with pigging bloody goats? Lucifer was a Judeo-Christian fallen angel. Witches are not Christians. They don't worship Christian deities—or shag bloody goats, kiss Satan's bumhole or a goat's bumhole, for that matter. But here we are again intoning and moaning and all-hailing dear old Luce in a circle full of "ahhs" and "ommms" and Ye Olde Latin. I rather fancy Pig Latin would be more apt, but there you are.

All the wittering about Black Masses: Hello, masses are Catholic. Maybe you were distracted by the nakedness and weren't paying attention.

"Diana represents the Moon." That's a fact, is it? Yes—ripped from your well-thumbed copy of "The Observer Book of Goat-Shagging Witches." All Goddesses represent the Moon, as it happens, and Diana specifically champions the hunt. Just so you know. I have never heard of any initiation ceremony where someone was led blindfolded through a forest, possibly in Buckinghamshire, Home of Hammer™. What absolute baboon's cobblers. Something for the gentlemen in the grubby macs at the back, I suspect.

The suggestion of orgies—dear, oh dear. Buy a copy of the *News of the Screws* and get it out of your system, there's a good boy. There is a Great Rite in Wicca, but 99.9 percent of the time it's conducted in private away from the rest of the coven. Sorry to disappoint anyone.

Ritual sacrifice: yawn. More nakedness: yawn. Curses and hexes: yawn. What goes around, comes around, mateys. And I've certainly never seen some spindly legged "Bad! Bad! Naked!" chartered accountant from Slough flopping himself down on Miss Sweden circa 1967 with a bit of shoelace sticking out of her mouth in order to piss off a traffic warden. Dear, oh dear.

The thing is, I'm as up for a laugh as anyone, and I seriously don't mind the "oo-ar titty witch wench torture"-style of Brit horror that we all know and love. It's the fact that this "documentary" is purported to be truth, and pretty po-faced at that, which gets my—pigging bloody goat, if you must know. —Sarah Edgson

Filmed in late summer 1969, *Legend of the Witches* is undoubtedly a product of its time—which is fine, of course, because those of us who like this sort of thing prefer our cinema as dated and authentic as possible. But the film (or, given its occult nature, should that be "thee film?") tends to walk a fine line between eerie and kitsch and occasionally ends up coming out on the wrong side.

The opening few minutes are as good a display of this as any: It's highly unlikely that so many female coven members would have looked as much like Mary Hopkin as half the cast here seem to, and knowing full well that the majority of practic-

ing Wiccans like to keep their activities secret and well hidden from the prying eyes of the media, it's doubtful that any members of the cast were genuine initiates. So, as we watch such an example of pulchritude (looking suspiciously like *The Flesh and Blood Show* actress Jane Cardew) blindfold her latest male conquest and then lead him over a cliff top via the skilful method of shouting "Michael" at him several times, we can be forgiven for not being entirely convinced! There is also a mildly humorous segment involving placing knives in cups ("As the knife is to man, so is the cup to woman, now let them be joined"), which makes Hitchcock's "trains and tunnels" symbolism in *North By Northwest* seem almost subtle by comparison. Yet none of this is to the film's detriment: Even after repeated viewings, it still makes for a highly enjoyable 75 minutes.

The narrator (whose name does not seem to appear on the credits, and who employs the quintessentially polite, Ealing-trained yet slightly foreboding tone of voice so beloved of most contemporaneous documentaries) delivers several pieces of information that, although maybe not entirely grounded in fact, seem well informed and at least blessed with a certain degree of enthusiasm for the subject. It's never clear which side of the fence Leigh stands on, other than that of an exploitation director looking for another marketable use of on-screen nudity and explicit sex for the delectation of the dirty mac brigade, who must have been disappointed by the relative lack of any steamy antics within, not to mention the fact that male buttocks are often on far more prominent display than female breasts. However, the dialogue pulls no punches in explaining how Christianity not only appropriated much of its iconography and ritual from witchcraft, but also committed vile acts of persecution against those involved, or indeed anyone interested in "something other than the dogmas of Christianity." This contradicts most of what appears in the recently published tome *The Kirk, Salem and Satan: A History of the Witches of Renfrewshire* (by Dr. Hugh V. McLachlan, a Christian), but then, again, it would, one supposes.

Mixed with the live footage are several sequences detailing ancient paintings and tapestries of occult scenes, which again must have either bored or confused its intended market in the Soho sex cinemas where it played but provided endless fascination for the more esoterically minded, during which it is revealed (once again controversially) that ritual magic in history did not include orgiastic sex acts. That said, there soon follows an extremely lengthy scene in which a man and woman tie themselves together naked in a circle and simulate the act of conception, apparently a very important symbol. It should be stressed here that my personal knowledge of "witchy things" is very limited: I have known (and on two occasions dated) several individuals who claimed to be fully paid-up adepts, but always found the imagery and paraphernalia more interesting than the actual subject, most of which bores me to tears.

One can't deny that the atmosphere engendered by the film is a powerfully persuasive one, in no small part due to the way Leigh's camera work uses mood and lighting (even if there is a tendency toward the occasional cheesy close-up). Sure, there are lots of churchyards, candlelight, windy trees and the type of chanting best described onomatopeically as "armineminuming" involved, but, come on, it's a British film about the occult from the late 1960s—what else would you expect? Apart, that is, from some amusing inserts of people engaging in modern-day superstition (which looks just as quaint now as the medieval sections), such as not walking under ladders, looking sorely afeared at the number 13 on their calendar, or wearing "End of the World" sandwich boards.

In the final sequence, which is arguably the essential one in terms of the film's continued relevance, Leigh almost single-handedly predicts the forthcoming 40 years of popular culture by demonstrating how rhythm, sound and the shamanistic nature of repetitive music can be used to induce a trance-like state. As a woman sits in a room listening to what sounds like Delia Derbyshire's pioneering electronic drone, with a disc depicting what appears to be the Vertigo record label swirling and whirling in front of her eyes, one can't help but question exactly how many people saw this film the first time around who just might have gone on to become major movers and shakers in both musical and cinematic fields! Even *Top of the Pops* seemed more interesting visually, post-1970—a coincidence?

Whether or not there's anything in this at all, it's undoubtedly a very forward-thinking concept. And it doesn't just end there. Strobes! Pyrotechnics! The underlying basis of live performance to come? Who knows? Ironically, several bands have used the film in recent years as a back-projection, so maybe we've come full circle. And maybe, just maybe, Leigh has answered his own question concerning the power of magic in the real world.

Legend of the Witches captures the essence of the subject that its obvious influence, Benjamin Christensen's *Haxan* (1922), also achieved—although it should be recognized that the name "Satan" (as opposed to Lucifer, "bringer of light") is not mentioned once throughout, displaying a tastefulness and understanding of the occult not often found in the genre. It also ends on a quite beautiful note, as a sun slowly rises into focus opposite a rural cliff top—a possible influence in itself, one might venture, on the camera work employed by Harry Waxman and Mike Drew in the closing scene of that veritable Brit horror behemoth, *The Wicker Man*? Who knows for sure?
—D.R. Shimon

Credits: Director and Writer: Malcolm Leigh.

While driving home one evening, business executive Harold Pelham (Roger Moore) takes on a Mr. Hyde-like aspect, as does his vehicle, which he imagines has transformed into a sleek metallic sports job, leading to an horrific accident. Pelham survives, although his operating surgeon notes that he had seemed, briefly and impossibly, to possess two heartbeats. Fit and working again, "Pel" (as he is known to colleagues and associates) comes to realize that he has been spotted in several places and indulging in a number of uncharacteristic antics of which he has no knowledge. What's more, he was on holiday in Spain when most of these alleged events occurred! Is there more than one Mr. P?

Combining the doppelganger themes of Poe's "William Wilson" with an industrial espionage plot, *The Man Who Haunted Himself* suffered a lukewarm reception on release, but hindsight reveals it to be one of the more challenging roles in the career of its star. The film's reputation has grown over the decades, and certainly the cleverness of the screenplay (credited to director Dearden and producer Relph but largely the work of Bryan Forbes) merits such increasing acclaim: The boardroom wheelings and dealings neatly mirror Pelham's predicament, with much talk of mergers and takeovers adding

layers of metaphor. It's surely no coincidence that the marine electronics firm for which Moore's character works is "*Freeman*, Pelham & Dawson" or that the competitor muscling in on their market is named "E.G.O."

Similarly, much of the dialogue comments with ambiguity on Pelham's dual dilemma, with the board chairman stating at a meeting that "I don't recognize the man sitting there," or his exotic lover remarking, "you're never the same man twice." Even one of his young sons seems to hit the mark, in a slightly different context, playfully quoting a two-line gag ("What lies on the bottom of the sea and quivers?" "A nervous wreck"), which again gets right to the heart of our tormented protagonist's situation.

Old faithful character players man the supporting roles admirably. There's Thorley Walters as an overbearing bore and practical joker, whose conspiratorial whispers about snooker sessions and illicit parties go over Pelham's head; Anton Rodgers as a fellow board member initially baffled by his friend's apparent craziness, before (in one of the movie's smartest and most subtle conceits) mistakenly hailing Pel's outrageous claims as being part of a masterful commercial gambit; John Carson as the slimy rival assistant boss; and stealing the show as ever, Freddie Jones, equipped with bow tie, shades and soft Scots brogue as a pill-popping shrink whose pop psychology includes advice like "Don't be a slave to convention" and who purposely attempts to draw out the shadier side of his patient's personality.

All leads inevitably to a big confrontation scene where the two Mr. Pelhams finally encounter one another, followed by a car chase through rain-soaked suburban avenues and country roads. There's both triumph and tragedy at the (literal) fade-out, but Moore's typically quizzical expression in the closing seconds leaves some doubt as to the ultimate fate of each of his manifested forms. In a spooky footnote, soon after the release of *The Man Who Haunted Himself*, writer-director Basil Dearden was killed in a road smash on the A40, close to the spot where Moore crashes in the opening scene.
—Darrell Buxton

Credits: Basil Dearden; Writers: Bryan Forbes, Basil Dearden, Michael Relph.
Leading Cast: Roger Moore, Hildegard Neil, Alastair MacKenzie, Hugh MacKenzie, Kevork Malikyan, Anton Rodgers, Thorley Walters, Olga Georges-Picot.

Mumsy, Nanny, Sonny and Girly (aka *Girly*)

A vast, secluded aristocratic pile somewhere that might well look familiar to viewers of other British horror films conceals dark secrets in this majestically offbeat little gem. Mumsy (Ursula Howells), Nanny (Pat Heywood), Sonny (Howard Trevor) and Girly (Vanessa Howard) are a "happy family" who don't like it when their "guests" don't follow "the rules," a grotesque array of tradition governing occasionally fatal childish games and dinner table manners. The cycle of guests—people Sonny and Girly ensnare on the street—par-

ticipating but failing to measure up to the family's exacting standards proceeds with sinister predictability until the pair entice "New Friend" (Michael Bryant) through blackmail to join in their dangerous activities. It quickly becomes apparent that they've gotten more than they've bargained for as New Friend masters the rules and then begins to introduce his own, leading to a reassignment of players.

Mumsy, Nanny, Sonny and Girly, based on the play *Happy Family* by Maisie Mosco, functions well both as a horror film and as a satire with the blackest of comic hearts. Even a foreigner like myself can't help but notice parallels to the British class system, as Sonny and Girly focus on tramps and transients for their fun-time torment, while the deceptively ever-faithful Nanny nurses a growing resentment for the silkily imperious Mumsy. Howells' performance as Mumsy is startlingly prophetic of Margaret Thatcher, shrugging off her own disobedience of the rules by saying, "They're for the children," and Bryant's groovy introduction with canned pop music represents the first real challenge to her family's Havisham-like existence.

In many ways, *Mumsy* is very reminiscent of cinema contemporaries like Lindsay Anderson's *If....* (Robert Swann, who had a major role in Anderson's film, gives a memorable but brief performance early in the proceedings here), savaging British (and Western) society of the time through tropes and costumes reminiscent of an earlier, more confident age. Even with its occasionally surrealistic nature, *Mumsy* presents a compelling horror scenario while suggesting that deeper themes lurk behind the shadows. The somewhat unsatisfying yet thought provoking ending offers a number of paths for the new players to take.

The dramatic heart of the film lies with Michael Bryant and Vanessa Howard. Bryant would go on to deliver one of British horror's all-time great performances in the Nigel Kneale-scripted telefilm *The Stone Tape* a couple of years later, and his steely, calculating cool is already on full display in *Mumsy* as he rallies against his appalling surroundings and turns the tables on his increasingly befuddled captors. Bryant would be much in demand, certainly in television, well after *Mumsy*, but the subsequent and inexplicable disappearance of Vanessa Howard, so good in *The Blood Beast Terror*, is a mystery, as she's absolutely mesmerizing in a way that only has a little to do with her beauty and tiny skirts. Girly starts out loving the game, but her feelings for New Friend—he *does* have quite a mustache—bring her to question the game's players, if not the rules. She has to master a number of different psychological states and nails them all, especially with a remarkably expressive two-minute take in which she learns a new game that New Friend has to teach her.

Mumsy, Nanny, Sonny and Girly is well worth seeking out for a number of reasons, but the sight of a lovely, talented actress giving a hypnotic, unique performance before completely vanishing from the cinematic scene within a matter of years is almost certainly at the top of the list.
—Wendell McKay

Pitched somewhere between an Aldwych Farce and the Theatre of the Absurd, the characters in *Mumsy, Nanny, Sonny*

everyone
is
dying
to
meet

Girly

"she's luscious, she's sensual,

she takes up where baby jane leaves off,

and she's SOME girl."

A RONALD J. KAHN Production **Girly**

MICHAEL BRYANT · URSULA HOWELLS · PAT HEYWOOD · HOWARD TREVOR and VANESSA HOWARD as 'GIRLY'
BRIAN COMPORT · BERNARD EBBINGHOUSE · RONALD J. KAHN · FREDDIE FRANCIS

R RESTRICTED
Under 17 requires accompanying
Parent or Adult Guardian

FROM CINERAMA RELEASING

the sprawling mansion inhabited by the family is the ubiquitous Oakley Court—and also of a certain type of understated English humor. Francis recalls that, when he showed the film to the crew of a subsequent movie, he urged, "You can laugh, it's supposed to be funny."

Mumsy can also be seen to have something to say about the era in which it was produced. As a satirical or sardonic reaction to, or reflection of, the Permissive Society that was under full steam in the Swinging '60s, the oft-repeated mantra "A Happy Family Must Have Rules" seems to sum up the dismayed perplexity felt by many people faced by the apparently rudderless drift of society, at a time when regulations, standards and "moral values" were being constantly challenged or overturned. When Mumsy (a classy and elegant Ursula Howells, mature but still decidedly bedworthy) transgresses one of the house rules ("You can have them, but you mustn't fancy them"), it signals the beginning of the end of the Happy Family, and initially it appears that the defenders of orthodoxy are to be vindicated. However, as it turns out, in this case the transgressor goes unpunished and a new type—in keeping with the times, a more "liberated" type—of family results.

Although a cult favorite among genre buffs, *Mumsy, Nanny, Sonny and Girly* certainly deserves greater exposure and represents one of Freddie Francis' best and most personal efforts in the horror field.
—Mike Hodges

Credits: Director: Freddie Francis; Writer: Brian Comport.
Leading Cast: Michael Bryant, Ursula Howells, Pat Heywood, Vanessa Howard, Michael Ripper, Imogen Hassall.

Scream and Scream Again

Scream and Scream Again doesn't make a whole lot of sense, but doesn't do so gloriously. A series of crazy killings in the decay of Swinging London alternate with sordid doings in what could be the post-1945 version of Anthony Hope's Ruritania, leading up to one of those usually annoying twist endings that have become de rigueur for Hollywood suspense in recent years with the advent of M. Night Shyamalan.

A number of young women are found murdered in London by the profane Superintendent Bellaver (Alfred Marks). An angry-looking young man (Michael Gothard) hangs out at the popular joint the Busted Pot, dancing to music by the Amen Corner. A series of high-ranking officials in "Nogoodnikgrad" (including Peter Cushing and Peter Sallis!) fall victim to one of their own with an ulterior motive. A British spymaster (Christopher Lee) is worried that one of his pilots is missing. A jogger is kidnapped and gradually dismembered. The police begin to suspect a respected—if hammy—surgeon (Vincent Price) for the killings. A "sensitive" doctor (Christopher Matthews) decides to take the investigation into his own hands. There are car chases, acid baths and autopsies. These plotlines repeat and alternate until the end, when they all come together for a "shocking" conclusion that's actually rather clever, and works all the better for the jerry-rigged plot.

and Girly behave in an outrageous fashion and utter the most ridiculous lines, but nobody bats an eyelid—even the friends' initial consternation at being forced to play (ostensibly) childish games evaporates remarkably quickly. The twee musical adaptations of nursery rhymes on the soundtrack, the absurd sight of young adults dressed in school uniform, Mumsy and Nanny sitting knitting and speaking in cloyingly adoring tones about the "dear little darlings," finishing each other's sentences in the baby talk that comprises almost the entire dialogue, may initially make the viewer squirm with embarrassment.

But as the story unfolds, the tone becomes edgy, tense, perverse and grotesque. It bears comparison to the uncomfortable sensations provoked by films like *The Baby*, *Freaks*, *The Mutations* and *American Gothic*. You feel you shouldn't enjoy watching this: Like Soldier, you are reluctant to join in as he says, "It's silly." But as the games become increasingly humiliating, the practical jokes sicker and the "children" increasingly homicidal, the film becomes absolutely compelling.

The very British hypocrisy of "double standards" and the juxtaposition of cozy domesticity, civilized behavior and respectability with violence, madness and murder in horror films is nothing new (indeed, it has been posited as one of the defining characteristics of British horror). *Mumsy* could be seen as a highly stylized caricature of the British horror film—even

This would be the only movie until *House of the Long Shadows* (1982) to feature all three horror "greats" (Peter Cushing, Christopher Lee and Vincent Price) but they have barely any time together, with Cushing delivering only a few lines. Lee glowers his way through the proceedings as usual. Price gives his regulation tormented mad scientist act, but it works here better than one would expect, thanks to the thought provoking (if clumsily presented) plot material.

Scream and Scream Again's greatness, though, lies with the supporting actors. Alfred Marks is fantastic, up there in the pantheon of lauded British cops like John Thaw's Morse and Donald Pleasence's Calhoun in *Death Line*. "Hey, man, I love you!" moans an American hippie about to be taken off to the nick. "Yeah, I'm mad about you an' all," Marks deadpans back. Christopher Matthews gives such a truly weird performance, combining brittle innocence with occasional mockery, that it's rather strange he didn't get more work during his career. One subplot—policewoman Helen Bradford (Judy Bloom) set up as a decoy for the killer, with the help of another copper (Clifford Earl) and to the consternation of her boyfriend, also on the force (Julian Holloway)—yields excellent results. Holloway's attempt to "get down" in the Busted Pot is so realistically dorky that it alone makes this worth watching; and Earl's sudden, wonderfully authentic laugh at Helen's faked explanation to

the killer as to why she dumped Holloway ("He wasn't very groovy") could equally apply to bemusement at the script.

Scream and Scream Again is breezily directed by Gordon Hessler (who'd also attempt to reign in Price for AIP's *The Oblong Box* and *Cry of the Banshee*); it doesn't really matter that much of it is nonsense, since it moves at a brisk pace and there are all those grand performances. The music is rather interesting, from the funky opening theme to the generic chase music, to the Amen Corner's extended jams in the Busted Pot, to the climax, where the variety of tunes come together with a bewildering swiftness (the trippy scene with Konratz walking through a series of TV screens is very well done). If stoned plot development and structure aren't an impediment, then *Scream and Scream Again* is worthy of the highest accolades. —Wendell McKay

Credits: Director: Gordon Hessler; Writer: Christopher Wicking.
Leading Cast: Vincent Price, Christopher Lee, Peter Cushing, Christopher Matthews, Alfred Marks, Anthony Newlands, Judy Bloom, Peter Sallis, Michael Gothard, Yutte Stensgaard.

Secrets of Sex (aka *Bizarre*)

There's a temptation for the genre fan to think that only one company was busy churning out compendium horror films during the 1960s and 1970s. After all, Amicus pretty much cornered the market with its brightly lit, comparatively bloodless little tales of murder and comeuppance. But the bigwigs at Amicus had only set out on that route after noting the success of *Dead of Night*, the grandfather of all portmanteau horror films. So it was only natural for people to see Amicus reaping its own success and wanting a piece of it.

All of Amicus' compendium films, although generally nasty, tend to steer clear of anything remotely approaching sex. There might be the occasional go-go dancer in a plastic bubble (*Torture Garden*), but in the main everyone keeps his/her paisley shirts and drainpipe hipsters firmly on. Usually, husband and wife relationships end with a bludgeoning long before they get anywhere near the bedroom (Joan Collins and poker in *Tales from the Crypt,* Richard Todd and axe in *Asylum,* Terry Thomas' forehead and hammer in *Vault of Horror*). What's more, watching a film in 15-minute sections means that you don't have to wait long for something to happen. Now, what *other* kind of genre would benefit from a short, episodic format? Why would anyone need to make a film where people might only want to sit in the cinema for a quarter of an hour?

With Amicus remaining resolutely prim on the sex front, the way was left wide open for the more shady entrepreneurs to have a go at livening up the anthology format. *Secrets of Sex* (aka *Bizarre*) isn't exactly what you would call "lively," but it is an anthology horror film that shows you everything. Whether that's a good thing or not is a matter of whether you like your ladies (and gents) "unaugmented" in the way

TRIPLE DISTILLED HORROR ...as powerful as a vat of boiling ACID!

SCREAM AND SCREAM AGAIN

VINCENT PRICE · CHRISTOPHER LEE · PETER CUSHING

JUDY HUXTABLE · ALFRED MARKS · MICHAEL GOTHARD · An AMERICAN INTERNATIONAL Picture COLOR BY MOVIELAB

MAX ROSENBERG and MILTON SUBOTSKY · CHRISTOPHER WICKING · GORDON HESSLER that only 1970's softcore films and those appalling phone chat satellite TV channels can present them—yes, there's a lot of droopy flesh on show here. And yes, for much of its length, *Secrets of Sex* is the kind of tawdry, adolescent fantasy fodder that makes you ashamed to be a heterosexual male (did anyone, *ever*, actually get off on watching this rubbish?). But when it veers into horror territory (it is from Antony Balch, the uncommon mind who brought us the sublime *Horror Hospital*), *Secrets* can be strangely effective.

The film's disjointed tales are linked by narration from the sonorous Valentine Dyall in the guise of a mummy who gradually deteriorates throughout the picture. Much of the film takes the form of strange, semi-coherent episodes that allegedly show the "age-old battle of the sexes," cut with strange visions of people (for want of a better phrase) having it off. After a weird introduction featuring three naked people and a quote from Milton's *Paradise Lost*, the first story unfolds: A judge in ancient times is told that his wife's lover might be in a trunk. He orders the luggage buried without opening it and throws away the key. Dyall's mummy (for 'tis him in the trunk) tells us, "For a thousand years these eyes have been hidden in the blackness of time. That is to say, a thousand of *your* years. But on certain occasions, I have been able to… observe the uncertain struggle of the battle of the sexes… The fruits of victory do not go to the strongest or the cleverest, as I myself have good cause to know!"

As a podgy stripper appears and begins to peel off her clothes, he continues: "Imagine this girl was making love to you" (no thanks), and the scene changes to a bunch of women (unconvincingly) disco dancing. Their clothes fall off, an unseen audience starts booing them and pelting them with cabbages (?), and a bunch of Robin Askwith-a-likes turn up and threaten them with guns. The girls respond by brandishing cut-throat razors. Aha! A battle of the sexes— as promised—and we're finally at the film proper, split into several untitled chapters.

Story 1: A kinky photographer gets her model to straddle a razor sharp "Spanish horse" torture device ("Come on, don't hang about," he complains. "This is torture!") and then attaches weights to his legs, leaving him alone to die.

Story 2: Mary Clare is a scientist and Sacha is her rich lover. He wants a kid—she gives him one. But she's not mentioned the congenital birth defect she's carrying, and he ends up with a monster for a child.

just when you thought you'd seen it all...

'DISTURBING' THE TIMES
'EROTIC' FINANCIAL TIMES
...*you've never seen anything like it* SCREW MAGAZINE

RICHARD GORDON presents
Antony Balch's

Secrets of SEX

IN *EASTMAN* COLOR

...about women and men

Starring
SUE BOND
MARIA FROST
CATHY HOWARD
DOROTHY GRUMBAR
YVONNE QUÉNET
LAURELLE STREETER

Story 3: A man catches a burglar at home and rips off his mask to reveal—"Christ! A bird!" She replies to his incredulity with, "Just a minute…you can deal with a girl, can't you?" before peeling off her PVC catsuit and going for a bath with her pants on. The story deteriorates into what appears to be an ad for lemon and cucumber soap, with him joining her in the shower. They wash each other, looking slightly embarrassed (but both keeping their pants on), before a quick chaste fumble in bed (still with both pairs of pants in place). This does lead to some very interesting ideas of what to do with a telephone receiver, before a vague "twist" at the end.

Story 4: Lindy Leigh (Maria Frost) is Special Agent 28, whose main talent appears to be the ability to "accidentally" shed her clothes at inopportune moments. The previous segment may have been slightly pathetic, but this looks like it was written and directed by a couple of 13-year-old boys with their hands down their trousers the entire time. The only possible saving grace for the whole embarrassing segment is that it contains the strangest "film within a film within a film" I've ever seen.

Story 5: A man phones for a call girl: "When do I want her? Right now!" His chubby escort arrives, and after squeezing her ample frame into his hotel room, he murmurs to her, "It's very fashionable, and it's very, very in today!" He shows her something, and she screams, "You're out of your mind…no one with any sense would go anywhere near that thing!" I'll leave it to you to find out what "that thing" is, but it's probably not what you're expecting.

Story 6: A woman who keeps flowers in a greenhouse is ruminating about her years in Monte Carlo to her new butler: "I ruined 17 men at those tables…and not one of them knew… At least, not until it was too late." She adds, "And now I've got them exactly where I want them!" indicating the flowers she's watering. Jeeves *isn't* impressed. "You filthy alien garbage heap!" he rather improbably interjects. "Misappropriation of men's souls is a very serious crime!"

The segments over, there's just time for a bit of gratuitous group sex. Or, as Dyall remarks, "And the battle goes on…" —Chris Wood

Credits: Director: Antony Balch; Writers: Antony Balch, John Eliot, Martin Locke, Maureen Owen, Elliott Stein.
Leading Cast: Valentine Dyall, Sue Bond, Maria Frost, Elliott Stein, Richard Schulman, Janet Spearman.

Tam Lin (aka The Devil's Widow)

A languid, hallucinatory gem and the only film to have been directed by the celebrated actor Roddy McDowall, *Tam Lin* (aka *The Devil's Widow*) had a troubled production history, received a belated and brief late-1970s release and has since disappeared without a trace. It's a great shame, for this updating of Robert Burns' famous "The Ballad of Tam Lin" to the age of Aquarius deserves to be seen, for a once in a lifetime gathering of young Brit starlets, endless bon mots and waspish dialogue, and a thrilling horror-chase climax every bit the equal of the flight of the children in Charles Laughton's *The Night of the Hunter*.

Anglicized to "Tom Lynn," the male lead here is a pre-*Lovejoy* Ian McShane in the days when he was something of a hot property and burgeoning star. Tom forms part of the entourage of sophisticated Michaela Cazaret (Ava Gardner), a middle-aged land owner who surrounds herself with a collection of bright young things, seemingly to ensure she remains similarly youthful and contemporary herself. The scene is slowly but carefully set, as life at Mrs. Cazaret's Scottish retreat appears to be a permanent round of relaxation, wine drinking and party games, interspersed with cutting comments from the acid tongue of Joanna Lumley or the world-weary viewpoint of Michaela's camp male secretary, Elroy (a magnificent Richard Wattis in the role he was born to play). The delicious Maddy Smith even squeals, "I'll swallow anything as long as it's illegal," summing up the decadent atmosphere in a single phrase while simultaneously managing to thrill every red-blooded male in the audience!

Tom makes the potentially fatal error of falling in love with the daughter of the local vicar (she's played by Stephanie Beacham, so why not?); Elroy delivers a coded warning that such romantic behavior will not be tolerated by their mutual benefactress, and that previous stray members of the household have wound up as victims of terrible road accidents ("You wouldn't believe…that a face could spread so wide," slimes Elroy, while displaying an horrific photo of one such calamity!), but Tom is smitten. Any doubt in his mind is settled when Tom discovers that his pregnant lover has traveled to Edinburgh for an abortion; but, meanwhile, Mrs. Cazaret has callously replaced her set of young swingers with an equally obnoxious bunch of new hangers-on, and the deadliest party game of all is about to commence, a chilling pursuit through daunting pitch-black woodland, with Tom, now drugged and experiencing a series of wild visions, as the prey.

Tam Lin may seem sluggish and uneventful on first acquaintance, but gets better as it progresses and improves immeasurably on repeated viewings, giving the opportunity to savor the ambience (mellow with a hint of bile) and the genteel savagery of this bitter and twisted group of frightful individuals. If *Gimme Shelter* cinematically signified the "end of the 1960s," this film perhaps offers the first hint that hippies turn into cabinet ministers when they grow up, and might even be said to predict the worst excesses of the "greed is good" 1980s. As for that alternate title, *The Devil's Widow*, such billing is fully justified by Gardner's grasping, evil performance, especially during a sly coda that repays careful attention.
—Darrell Buxton

Credits: Director: Roddy McDowall; Writer: William Spier. **Leading Cast:** Ava Gardner, Ian McShane, Stephanie Beacham, Richard Wattis, Cyril Cusack.

Taste the Blood of Dracula

The later Hammer Draculas have all come in for a great deal of bad-mouthing over the years, not least from their ever-cheerful title star, whose obvious contempt for the films is reinforced by contemporary publicity stills of him possessing the demeanor of a man who has just discovered a fresh cat turd in his morning cereal. The truth is, they are all worth revisiting and, yes, that does include *Scars of Dracula* with its posh Dennis Waterman and the once in a lifetime opportunity to witness Christopher Lee and Patrick Troughton indulge in a bizarre kind of sadomasochistic sex ritual.

Taste the Blood of Dracula's reputation has grown with the years to a much greater extent than the three subsequent Dracula outings, but is by no means as universally admired as the Terence Fisher classic that initiated the series in 1958. The most unpopular element of this fourth film tends to be the eccentric church-set finale, which involves rocks and debris being hurled at our heroes, before Dracula is overwhelmed by the sounds of God and topples off a ledge to another dissolve-decomposition. Even

She drained them of their manhood …and then- of their LIVES!

the story of the kind of woman few people even know exists

They call her… The Devil's Widow

AVA GARDNER · IAN McSHANE starring in a JERRY GERSHWIN - ELLIOTT KASTNER Production "THE DEVIL'S WIDOW" also starring CYRIL CUSACK · RICHARD WATTIS and STEPHANIE BEACHAM TECHNICOLOR® [PG] PARENTAL GUIDANCE directed by RODDY McDOWALL original screenplay by WILLIAM SPIER produced by ALAN LADD, JR. and STANLEY MANN executive producers HENRY T. WEINSTEIN and ANTHONY B. UNGER An AMERICAN INTERNATIONAL Release this oft-slated conclusion is a striking, unique element within a genuinely bold and impressive movie.

This film's notably tacky tagline "Drink A Pint of Blood A Day" may have hampered its chances of being taken seriously by critics of the time, though only a horror-hating cynic of the worst kind would deny the power of its atmospheric, well-remembered prologue. Traveling salesman Roy Kinnear gets stranded in the usual stretch of Hammer woodland and stumbles upon the Count's *Risen from the Grave* death scene, footage of which is thriftily recycled sans the cutaways to that film's protagonists. As appetite-whetting openers go, this sequence, deftly combining nervy humor and visceral horror, is up there with the best of them.

As in *Dracula—Prince of Darkness*, the film is half over before Dracula appears in a non-recycled fashion and, even then, he again is reduced to a sparsely scripted supporting role. The build-up and some unusually strong subplots easily compensate for Lee's token appearances.

In any case, the real monster of Peter Sasdy's beautifully shot sequel is played with sadistic relish by Geoffrey Keen, a bully-bastard of a husband and father in Victorian England. He condemns his pretty daughter (a radiant Linda Hayden) as a "harlot" for merely talking to her boyfriend (Anthony Corlan, less radiant, though not as punchable as some Hammer leading men) and yet displays an unhealthy level of drunken leering at his own kin when he invades her bedroom for a traditional thrashing.

On the last Sunday of each month, Keen and two other local pillars of the community (John Carson, Peter Sallis) slope off on the pretense of doing "charity work in the East End." This actually means enjoying a night at camp oddball Russell Hunter's brothel, where they can indulge in the decadent pleasures of booze and half-naked girls dancing with snakes. (These scenes, censored in American prints and early British video releases, feature the first nudity in a Hammer Dracula film.)

Keen and Company, however, grow bored of their monthly debauchery and are drawn to arrogant black mass-practicing Ralph Bates, who goads them into participating in a gruesome blood-drinking ritual. They get spooked to the extent that they casually kick and beat Bates to death. Dracula is revived regardless, reborn with a typically grim-faced attitude ("They destroyed my servant. They will be destroyed") and subsequently pops up intermittently to intone solemn things like "The First" and "The Second," as he sets out to off those responsible for Bates' death by manipulating their children. The plot doesn't hold up under close scrutiny but, crucially, it provides a stronger central narrative hook than subsequent sequels, without resorting to gimmickry.

Taste the Blood of Dracula possesses a thematic darkness and cynicism of the kind that were beginning to creep into the usual Hammer formula, reflective of the increasingly downbeat nature of the period's horror films worldwide. This undercurrent would dominate such impressive late-era Hammer entries as *Demons of the Mind* (which also has a very

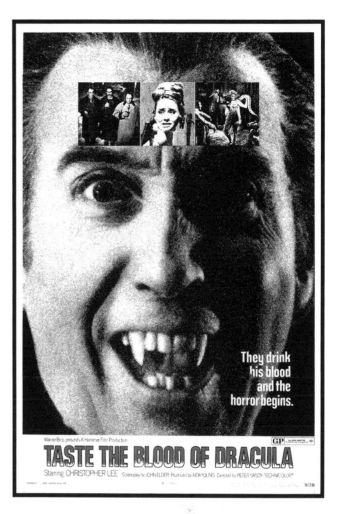

messed-up central family), *Blood from the Mummy's Tomb* and *Hands of the Ripper*.

Here, Gwen Watford's under-written but poignant portrayal of a downtrodden wife and mother, and Keen's hissably abusive Victorian patriarch provide the film with a surprisingly powerful emotional core. Their characters also contribute to a bleak overall tone that's only relieved by the lyrical whimsy of James Bernard's memorably beautiful, lilting love theme for Corlan and Hayden, and by Michael Ripper's trademark chirpy cameo as a joshing copper.

As in previous series entries, there is a great deal of pleasure to be had in watching the transformation of a fresh-faced Hammer beauty from simpering lovebird and victim to wanly smiling murderous slave of the Count. No previous film in the series, however, contains three (for the price of one!) potent, nasty scenes of patricide. In moments that err closer to the kind of personalized brutality on display in groundbreaking 1960s films like *Night of the Living Dead* than in previous Hammer movies, Hayden smashes a spade into Keen's skull with a relish shared by the audience; a vampiric Blair laughs malevolently as she stakes her sniveling coward of a father (Sallis); and the newly-turned Martin Jarvis is coaxed into stabbing Carson.

More subversive than it might first appear, there's a lot going on in *Taste the Blood of Dracula*, and it represented a strong feature directing debut for Hungarian filmmaker Sasdy. Though his later efforts, *Countess Dracula* and *Nothing But The Night*, are arguably noble failures, his place in Brit horror history is secured thanks to his sterling directorial work on the exceptional *Hands of the Ripper* and the BBC's unforgettable *The Stone Tape* (oh, and that Joan Collins vehicle *I Don't Want to Be Born*, with the horny dwarf and Ralph Bates sporting a comic Italian accent).
—Steven West

off his victims. Lee gamely does his best, and it's always a treat to see him in the Dracula guise, but the script lets him down badly. They also saddle him with the worst death scene in the series. Falling to his doom on a church altar after being "overcome" by the religious imagery is bland and confusing, to say the least.

So much for the bad news—this is indeed a good sequel. James Bernard created a softer, more melancholic score which sets the mood perfectly. As much as I like his usual bombastic style, he's equally as accomplished with the gentler stuff. Director Peter Sasdy seems more at home with the "family values" aspects than the horror elements: His direction is more relaxed during the dialogue passages, whereas the action and horror are played out without any great sense of urgency or style. Luckily for him, it's the Victorian family set up and its subsequent disintegration that makes the film shine.

By the time Hammer got around to making *Taste the Blood of Dracula*, Christopher Lee had already expressed his disappointment with the treatment of the Count in previous movies. That, coupled with his ever-increasing fee, made Hammer commission a script without him.

This new incarnation would see a younger, cheaper actor take over the role. Ralph Bates was assigned this dubious task but, before filming could begin, the American financiers declared that, if Christopher Lee was not available, the film would not get the go ahead. Several negotiations and rewrites later, Lee was on board, but the Dracula character was about to be placed further in the background than ever before.

This time the action centers on three Victorian "gentlemen," who are as puritanical as the period dictates at home, but venture out every night to indulge in the most basic pleasures. On one of their excursions they are introduced to Lord Courtley (Bates), who persuades them to purchase Dracula's ashes, cape and clasp from a dubious trader (Roy Kinnear) who had salvaged the remains in a great opening sequence depicting him witnessing Dracula's demise from the previous film.

As expected, things go badly: Courtley dies resurrecting Dracula, who then sets out to avenge his disciple by hunting down the three gents and their offspring. What motivates the Count to do this is very hazy, but it serves as a simple plot device, which offers as good an explanation as any.

Of all the Hammer Draculas, *Taste* features the worst turn by Lee's Count, which is odd because it's one of the best sequels. Maybe it's because the script was originally written to sideline Dracula, or maybe that the sub-plot is more interesting than the horror elements. Whatever the reason, this film works better when Dracula is off screen.

Hammer never really knew what to do with Dracula other than have him snarl on cue, and that's all he does in this movie. Considering how well the rest of the script is written, it's a shame and something of an embarrassment to hear him count

The three "gents" are a joy to watch: Keen, Carson and Sallis' portrayals of middle-aged men, perhaps closer to Jekyll and Hyde than the pillars of society they are perceived to be, are spot on. Sallis really stands out as the weaker of the three, who gradually crumbles under pressure as the consequences of his actions come back to haunt him.

Most of the younger cast, Dracula's intended victims, perform admirably but are difficult to accept as anything but aspiring juveniles. Maybe they were simply outclassed by the older generation. The exception, however, is Linda Hayden, excellent in a role that seems tailor-made for her unique brand of innocent sexuality. Her scenes with her father are very convincing as she struggles to grow up in a domineering and oppressive household. Similarly, when she is called upon to become Dracula's slave girl, she delivers the goods with a sultry abandon that would make the Count eager with anticipation.

The general feel is one of suppressed passion, whether from our trio of gentlemen or their screen children. It's an intriguing setting for such a highly sexual character as Dracula, and more could possibly have been made of his involvement, especially in the seduction scenes. Hammer settled for the Count as a bogeyman, which is what they thought the public wanted. If that's what you're intending, you have to make him scary and he simply isn't here, lit far too brightly and saddled with some truly awful lines.

It says a lot about the remainder of the film that it rises above the weakness of the titular figure, managing to engage the audience with a fully developed story and featuring some

of Britain's more eminent character actors. Even if Dracula is reduced to a guest star in his own movie, it's strong enough to entertain. Frustratingly enough, it gives us a tantalizing glimpse of what Hammer could have done with the Count if they'd taken as much care with him as they did with the rest of the cast.
—Matt Gemmell

Credits: Director: Peter Sasdy; Writer: John Elder [Anthony Hinds].
Leading Cast: Christopher Lee, Linda Hayden, Ralph Bates, Geoffrey Keen, John Carson, Peter Sallis, Isla Blair.

Trog

Oh, *Trog*. Oh Troggy, Troggy *Trog*—truly an ignominious end to the silver screen career of Joan Crawford, for sure. Bette Davis reputedly said that, if she'd been reduced to starring in *Trog*, she'd commit suicide. A bit harsh, perhaps, but Bette wasn't known for her diplomacy. And after sitting through this film, you can see her point.

Trog is a bad movie. And it's not "so bad it's good," it's just plain bad. But it will provide some deliriously goofy entertainment—if your expectations are pitched (very) low.

We begin with three potholers researching an underground cave. When they find a stream, two of them strip off to probe unexplored realms. And if that sounds a bit queer, it looks it, too. Maybe director Freddie Francis anticipated Joan's "gay icon" status, so provided a bit of lithe, young muscle, in the knowledge that *Trog* would need all the help it could get! Anyway, they pay for it, those silly, lunkheaded spelunkers, when one of them is killed by a shaggy, shammy-clad schlep with anger issues and bad teeth. The two survivors end up in the care of anthropologist Dr. Brockton (Crawford) who, somewhat conveniently, runs a facility nearby. She's intrigued by their reports of what she suspects might be "the missing link" and ventures into the cave, where she photographs the cut-price Captain Caveman. Inspector Greenham (Bernard Kay) isn't convinced and dismisses it as looking like "something out of a students' rag week," in a sly nod to the audience's incredulity. (The tatty costume, what there is of it, was a leftover from *2001: A Space Odyssey*!) But it's not long before TV crews converge on the cave, and their new star doesn't disappoint. He pokes his hairy head out, blinks once or twice and starts throwing cameramen around like rag dolls! And all they did was ask him where he bought his Ugg boots!

Dr. Brockton, ever ready with her "hypo-gun" and an array of blue and tan lab coats, stills the raging, reanimated rug and embarks on a mission to educate Trog, as he's christened, in a bid to "unlock the secrets of the past." This means sitting through increasingly ridiculous scenes of Trog playing with a doll, swaying to music (but not rock, the old fuddy-duddy; it makes him go-go berserko!) and taking a fancy to Joan's pink neck scarf. (Let's just pray Trog didn't delve any deeper into her drawers.) Amongst all this, Joan edifies the viewer with pseudo-scientific "poppycock" and "insane nonsense," all delivered with a commendably straight face.

But Brockton has her detractors: town busybody Sam Murdock (Michael Gough, who stops just short of foaming at the mouth) disapproves of the attention the doctor's experiments bring. There's some lip service paid to the evolution vs. creation debate, but not enough to outweigh the prevailing silliness. Things reach a nadir when Trog is hooked up to a machine that projects his memories, revealing he was around for the demise of the dinosaurs! (This is Ray Harryhausen stop-motion footage, spliced in from *The Animal World*.) Next thing you know, Trog is talking. "Unbelievable!" Joan declares. You're not kidding, love.

Of course, things go pear-shaped when the vindictive Murdock throws a (monkey) wrench in the works, freeing Trog to go for a butcher's around the village. A playground full of screaming brats later, and it's a front-page, stone age rampage! I won't spoil the end, but it involves a stalagmite that points out from the earth at a 45-degree angle.

Oh, Joan, did stardom mean *this* much to you?
—Jed Raven

Credits: Director: Freddie Francis; Writers: Aben Kandel, Peter Bryan, John Gilling.
Leading Cast: Joan Crawford, Michael Gough, Bernard Kay, David Griffin, Kim Braden, Joe Cornelius.

When Dinosaurs Ruled the Earth

When Hammer put Raquel Welch into a doeskin bikini and hired Ray Harryhausen to breathe life into the extinct dinosaur, it seemed like they had struck gold. *One Million Years B.C.* was a massive worldwide hit and, for that reason alone, merited a sequel.

While not a direct follow up to the previous film, *When Dinosaurs Ruled the Earth* inhabits the same territory, that of good-looking, scantily clad cave people living side by side with the odd T-Rex and Triceratops. Never one to let history or evolution stand in the way of a good story, Hammer more or less remade their previous film. No Raquel Welch this time, sadly and perhaps inevitably, but they did manage to find the lovely Victoria Vetri.

Chosen for her looks and figure, Vetri doesn't have to act, which is just as well, but simply has to run, jiggle and scream when the dinos turn up. She does this extremely well! Unlike Miss Welch's movie, this one goes for the pure exploitation angle. The women wear less and, in some cases, leave little to the imagination. The film was issued on Region 1 DVD with a G rating in 2008, and what a surprise it was to discover the nude scenes intact, as the uncut version was unleashed to the marketplace by mistake. Most were recalled and the disc is now a collector's item. The film isn't any better, but the cast is good to look at.

While Hammer had no problem in featuring anatomically beautiful people sharing the screen with dinosaurs they again drew the line at them spouting the Queen's English, which is a shame, that would have been great. What we do have is cave speak which runs to approximately 25 words, ranging from "ug" to, well, what does it matter?

One problem area is in seeing Patrick Allen squandered as caveman extraordinaire Kingsor. Mr. Allen was the possessor of one of the most recognizable voices on British screens, with an erudite manner of speech harking back to a golden age of British heroes with stiff upper lips. It's genuinely embarrassing every time he opens his mouth for nonsense like "zak" and "akita" to tumble out. Talk about a waste of talent.

Acting and script aside, there's only one reason to watch this, and that's the dinosaurs. Not forgetting Miss Vetri, oh, and Imogen Hassall and, before this turns into a *Life of Brian* sketch, I'll point out that, among the varied reasons to view, the monsters themselves are a saving grace. The special effects duties this time went to Jim Danforth, who turned in some fine-looking scenes. His stop motion may almost be on a par with the great Harryhausen, although his rendition of dinosaurs is a little childlike. They just don't seem real enough. I've heard that he tried to give each one a unique persona and facial expression. He might have achieved this but it made the monsters look, well, less monstrous. The plus side is that, whenever his creations are on screen, the movie comes alive. When we're not being treated to dino action or some naked cave girl, it's really hard to sit through. Mr. Allen's grunts and ugs are ridiculous, but the rest of the cast are just as bad. Then, again, how can you deliver lines (if you can call them that) like these effectively?

Val Guest was at the helm for this piece of prehistory. His documentary style of filmmaking had added a great sense of urgency to *The Quatermass Xperiment* and *Quaternass 2*, but there's little trace of his directing talent here. The connecting scenes between Danforth's stop motion endeavors are just plain dull. It was a good call to have so many scantily clad beauties on screen because, without them, the viewer wouldn't stick around until the next monster attack. I can only assume that it was an easy grab for the director, who had to pay the bills like any other person.

Ultimately, *When Dinosaurs Ruled the Earth* is a reasonably diverting exercise but one you wouldn't want to repeat too often. It's nowhere near as good as its predecessor and appears studio-bound all too often. There's an extended water-set scene that was obviously filmed in an indoor tank. The lighting doesn't even attempt to imitate real life. There's a lack of star names, Vetri didn't have the same effect or success as Welch, and the pace is ponderous. What we do have is a lot of eye candy, stop-motion dinosaurs and a terrific poster, which was distributed before the film was completed.

The unrated cut is definitely the more interesting version to seek out. While not a terrible movie, it isn't good enough to sit alongside the sparkle of *One Million Years B.C.* or the kiddie charm of *At the Earth's Core*. It's one of the few movies made by Hammer that has "cash in" stamped all over it.

—Matt Gemmell

Credits: Director and Writer: Val Guest. **Leading Cast:** Victoria Vetri, Robin Hawdon, Patrick Allen, Imogen Hassall.

Enter an age of unknown terrors, pagan worship and virgin sacrifice...

"WHEN DINOSAURS RULED THE EARTH"

VICTORIA VETRI

ROBIN HAWDON · PATRICK ALLEN · IMOGEN HASSALL

Afterword

by Jonathan Rigby

Not long ago, I was discussing the stage history of *Titus Andronicus* with a friend (as you do), and was trying my best to account for why it languished unproduced, after Shakespeare's death, for over 300 years. "Why, because it's a horror play!" I airily concluded.

A glib response, perhaps. But it certainly isn't difficult to see a familiar British thought process—simultaneously "knee jerk" and "nose in the air"—behind the play's comprehensive burial. Thanks to its brain-reeling body count, multiple dismemberments and concluding tableau of enforced cannibalism, high-minded critics have even gone so far as to exclude it from the canon, or else to dismiss it as sensationalist hackwork. Critical approbation and Grand Guignol extremism have seldom gone hand in hand in the U.K..

A spot of lateral thinking then took me to Robert Hartford-Davis, who was one of British exploitation's leading lights during the decade covered by this book. It was a period when filmmakers cheerfully raised two fingers to all forms of critical condescension, while at the same time pushing at the constraining boundaries established by the British Board of Film Censors. And towards the end of it—in 1969, to be precise—Hartford-Davis announced a cherished dream project that he presumably saw as the ideal follow-up to his recent "Peter Cushing with a severed head in the refrigerator" shocker, *Corruption*. What was that project? You guessed it—a film version of *Titus Andronicus*.

And here's a fact that I somehow failed to mention not only in *English Gothic* but even in my Christopher Lee biography: The film's proposed stars were Lee and 15-year-old Lesley-Anne Down, who had just appeared for Hartford-Davis in *The Smashing Bird I Used to Know*. Needless to say, the project never came to fruition, but what a loss. It could have been the definitive demonstration of a truth routinely denied by contemporary critics: that British horror's roots go extraordinarily deep, and that at least one of them has the name Shakespeare attached to it.

Never mind, though. Even without Lesley-Anne Down's hideously lopped Lavinia, British shockers of the 1960s were a bracingly varied bunch, ranging from delicately elliptical hauntings to scrapey sessions of late-Victorian brain surgery, from downtrodden zombies mining tin in darkest Cornwall to sexual dysfunction in swinging South Kensington. And the whole spread is mouth-wateringly arrayed in this bracingly varied book. Varied not merely because of the wide range of films covered, but also because of the intriguing Babel of competing voices brought to bear on them.

And with multiple contributors comes the bonus of multiple interpretations of what constitutes "horror." As a result, for every *Dracula Has Risen from the Grave*, you'll find something less predictable like *The Penthouse*; for every *Dr. Terror's House of Horrors*, a *Don't Talk to Strange Men*

or *Bunny Lake is Missing*. The tone ranges from nostalgic to thoughtful to irreverent, sometimes encompassing all three in the same critique. And, in the manner of many an Amicus anthology, if you don't particularly care for one you can rest assured there'll be another along in a minute. The whole thing has been put together, quite obviously as a labor of love, by the estimable Darrell "Pass the Marmalade" Buxton. And love is what these films—from classics to clunkers and all points in between—genuinely inspire.

How could it be otherwise? After all, a random flip through *The Shrieking Sixties* is guaranteed to bring back a host of deliciously macabre memories. A giant, ectoplasmic Martian devil holding sway over the Knightsbridge skyline? It's here. The basilisk stare of Vincent Price's implacable, parchment-faced Witchfinder? Ditto. The pitiful teleportation rejects stumbled upon in the outhouse by Carole Gray. The jaded witticisms of Alfred Marks as he sets off in pursuit of a lab-created bionic bloodsucker. A dustily resurrected Edgar Allan Poe surrounded by such brand-new compositions as "House of the Worm." The whirling cloud of vampire bats that smashes through the stained-glass windows of Château Ravna. The list goes on, and on it are some of the most indelible images in British cinema.

It was a vivid and vital period for Britain's film studios, and testament to the fact is provided by the vitality of the critical responses contained in this book.

—Jonathan Rigby
London
January 2010

Appendix 1

Short Films
compiled by Darrell Buxton, Paul Higson, and Gavin Whitaker

BREAKING POINT (1967)—black-and-white "haunted house" short by Guernsey-based amateur filmmakers Peter and Richard Rouillard. 'Ghost thriller'—www.theiac.org.uk.

CASTLE OF DRACULA (1968)—homemade short by the enthusiasts of the Delta Film Group, some of whom now organize Manchester's annual Festival of Fantastic Films.

CASTLE OF TERRORS (1964)—more from Delta Film Group; a wacky, almost Dick Lester-like horror comedy.

DEADLINE (1966)—(presumed short) directed by Geoffrey Arthurs, made by the High Wycombe Film Society. Once the guests have left, the host of a party is persecuted by the telephone, though no voice is heard (Paul Higson).

DEATH WEARS A MASK (1965)—14-minute short. "Scared to death by a ghost boy" (Paul Higson).

DREAM A40 (1965)—directed by Lloyd Reckord; homosexual couple speeding on the A40 are pulled over by a motorcycle cop and fantasize that he takes them to an oppressive, remote fortress "where nooses hang from the ceilings and the rooms are filled with nervous waiting men," with the younger of the pair revealed hanged at the end. "Crowds of zombie extras, a sub-Kafka regime of bureaucrats" (*Monthly Film Bulletin*, August 1971).

L'EREDITA DI DIAVOLO (196?)—short directed by Robert Wynne-Simmons. "Spoof horror shot at Castle Goring, Sussex, a Gothic folly built for Percy and Mary Shelley" (Wynne-Simmons' website).

FACE IN THE MIRROR (1969)—(presumed short) directed by Storm Thorgerson while at the Royal College of Art (Department of Film and Television). A woman, believing her husband is betraying her, dreams that she stabs him to death. On waking, she finds him in bed next to her with a stab wound (Paul Higson).

FLESH AND FANTASIE (1963)—almost wearing a negligee, lovely June Palmer is pursued around the corridors and stairways of Elm Manor Hotel by a balding, imposing vampire in this 5-minute sex-horror short from Harrison Marks. This has appeared on YouTube under the title "Elm Manor."

THE FOUR-POSTER (1964)—Harrison Marks-directed nudie short. "Another one of his horror-themed tits and bums shorts with Marks himself playing a maniac hunchback peeking in on, then trying to kill a nude Margaret Nolan in her pre-*Carry On* days" (Gavin Whitaker).

FRANKENSTEIN (1969)—directed by Alan Harrison, shot on 16mm, the work of students at Sheffield College of Art. "Reconstruction of scenes from James Whale's 1931 version" (Stephen Jones, *Essential Monster Movie Guide*).

FRANKENSTEIN'S XPERIMENT (1963)—more from the amateur Delta Film Group.

THE GAY GHOST (196?)—early 1960s short directed by a teenage Michael Armstrong, years before his career in British horror-exploitation. The spirit of murder victim takes vengeance on his killer by haunting a schoolboy.

HAUNTED ENGLAND (1961)—20-minute short directed by Michael Winner for Scimitar Films, produced by Winner and Pat Ryan. Re-enactment of true ghost tales from the U.K. Cast includes David Jacobs, Vera Gregory, Kenneth Lewis, David Lee, Tom Corbett, Mitzi Sanders, Irene Culyer, Emlyn Rees, Jenny Russell, Jimmy Jacobs.

HEX (1969)—Belgian writer and anthologist Michel Parry, a leading figure on the fringe horror scene in 1960s and 1970s Britain, produced and directed this short funded by a grant from the Belgian Film Institute and centred around black magic and human sacrifice.

THE IMAGE (1968)—directed by Michael Armstrong. David Bowie, pre-superstardom, stars in this rather good fragment from Armstrong, about an artist haunted by the apparition of a young man. New Musical Express made this available by mail order in 1984 as part of a VHS compilation called *Video Bongo*.

JACK THE RIPPER (1963)—in an early example of the pop video, Screaming Lord Sutch plays the maniacal killer in a short film accompanying his wonderfully over the top number, "Jack The Ripper."

LADY FRANKENSTEIN (196?)—"There was an outfit called Collectors Club based near Old Street in London that during the late 1960s into the 1970s...distributed 8mm copies of silent movies. They also had a series of glamour films that they produced themselves which included a title called *Lady Frankenstein* in which a hunchback brings a nude female to life—she runs around for a while before drinking a potion that turns her into a zombie, who turns on the hunchback" ("muswell," posted at "British Horror Films" website, February 2006).

LISTEN TO ME WHEN I'M TALKING TO YOU (1969-70)—"A surreal drama made by students from Sir John Deane's College. A girl walks down a path in Tatton Park and encounters various cultish activities. A man whips a woman (who transforms into a sheep) and people mime having sex with a tree and a cello, before the girl encounters a black mass which is to climax with the sacrifice of a child. The young woman rescues the child, and the cultists join her on the beach. Other scenes include schoolchildren killing a cat and a recreation of a World War II field hospital." (North West Film Archive). Twenty-six minutes of sex, violence, Satanism and the threat of child sacrifice. The film appears influenced by everything from Tigon Film productions and *Legend of the Witches* to *L'Age d'Or* and *Un Chien Andalou*. To add to the shock value, it is in color. I can't imagine what the college thought of it, but it matches the nihilism of Michael Reeves' *The Sorcerers* and *Witchfinder General* (Paul Higson).

MACABRE (1968)—Harrison Marks short with Monique Devereux and Howard "Vanderhorn" Nelson. "More horror than glamour—

Howard finds himself under the control of a black leather clad Monique and on the wrong end of her whip. Filmed on the dungeon set at Lily Place in September 1968." Genre historian Gavin Whitaker has suggested this may have been part of the rare Marks feature *Pattern of Evil*, although the quoted production date may indicate otherwise.

THE MUMMY (1966) — Harrison Marks 8mm short filmed on the set of *The Naked World of Harrison Marks*; a still on the official Marks website shows a topless girl being menaced by an ambulatory bandaged mummy. Part of a series of 8mm glamour films titled *Favourites of the Pharaohs* (advertised as "see six gorgeous girls depicting the glamour of ancient Egypt"), this final instalment sees a Mummy rise from his tomb to play peeping tom, or should that be peeping mummy, to several topless lovelies. The nude star of the film, 1960s glamour girl Teri Martine, recalled, "I was a slave girl and I get caught by the Mummy and laid on a slab. Tina McGowan was in that same scene with me, also playing the role of a slave girl. I recall being very scared as the guy playing the Mummy role was so realistic. The Mummy gets knifed by one of the pharaohs who saves me! *The Mummy* was a fun and scary movie" (Gavin Whitaker).

NIGHTMARE (1962) — "Non-professionally, I made a 20-minute horror called *Nightmare* in 1962, which was about a boy haunted by nightmares of a demon with glowing eyes trying to kill him—the twist being that in the real world he dies in front of the blazing headlights of a car as it runs him down in an accident" (Michael Armstrong).

PERCHANCE TO SCREAM (1967) — "Here is a weird, way out film for the viewer who wants something more than just glamour. Black magic, the occult, sadistic, it's all here, and there are six beautiful girls to put it across. Watch your pulse rate when you are viewing this one." A short girlie film made for the 8mm market by Harrison Marks. Partly shot in Marks' own house, and partly in the same dungeon set Marks used in his rarely seen feature film *Pattern of Evil* (1967) and 8mm short *Macabre* (1968), this sees model Jane Paul visiting a wax museum and then taking a bath, before being transported to a medieval torture chamber where an evil Inquisitor (Stuart Samuels) sentences topless women to be whipped and beheaded by a masked executioner. Jane eventually turns the tables and conjures up a crucifix that causes the Inquisitor to explode, leaving only a smoking skeleton. The same year Marks hooked up with *Corruption* director Robert Hartford-Davis to make a *Mondo Cane* variant titled *A Climate of Lunacy*, which Hartford-Davis would have directed, and Marks would have produced and starred in. Sadly, that film was never made (Gavin Whitaker).

THE PIT (1962) — BFI short based on Poe's "The Pit and the Pendulum" and directed by Edward Abraham.

PORPHYRIA (1959-60) — eight-minute, sound, black-and-white short. Artist kills model and then himself (Paul Higson).

SATAN'S CHILDREN (1960s) — stag short in which three young female satanists have sex with the Devil. The film features in *Classic Stags – Volume 267* and is covered by Dave Thompson in his 2008 book *Black and White and Blue: Adult Cinema from the Victorian Age to the VCR*: "Other Climax classics included…and, best of all, *Satan's Children*, a contrarily uncostumed drama built around the regular reports of sinister black-magic rituals being played out in the pages of Britain's Sunday tabloid press. Satan himself is clearly a skinny guy with what looks like a burlap bag draped over his head and a taste for waving his riding crop around; his children are three women, who in drawing such surprisingly copious amounts of communion 'wine' from

his erect penis, were essentially test piloting the first genuine 'special effect' in adult-cinema history—a thin tube, inserted into the mouth alongside the erect penis, through which a suitably coloured liquid (probably milk) was pumped at the moment of 'climax.' Unconvincing though they may be, the resultant cascades ensure that *Satan's Children* features some of the most electrifyingly messy fellatio scenes in stag history." The film features no fewer than four "money shots." The book includes eight images from the film (Paul Higson).

SON OF GODZILLA (1963) — the amateur Delta Film Group nabbed this title four years before Toho produced the official version of Godzilla's offspring.

TEENAGE JEKYLL AND HYDE (1963) — more work of the amateur Delta Film Group.

VAMPIRE (1964) — Harrison Marks' nudie short, black-and-white, with Wendy Luton. "One of Harrison Marks' newest and loveliest models features in this film, only a model of her beauty could put over a subject [such] as this..."

VIOLA (1967) — experimental short directed by Dunstan Pereira and Richard Davis. Man believes that his dead wife has returned in the form of a cat that pursues him. Music by Ravi Shankar.

THE WAGER (1969) — amateur short by Guernsey-based Peter and Richard Rouillard. "As a wager with the mysterious stranger George (Richard Rouillard), Lomax (Leonard Howard) agrees to stay overnight in a so-called haunted house"."

WORTHY OF THE DEVIL (1967) — (presumed short) 8mm amateur horror film made by members of the Skegness Cine Club. "Dark deeds in a churchyard, a palpitating human heart, a bestial claw that moves even though it has been severed from a body and a 'mad doctor' to boot! The color film, which was shown at the Lion Hotel, was devised by Jim Toyne who played the mad doctor, the only character in it"—*Skegness Magazine* website.

Short films directed by Roy Spence

Northern Ireland-based sci-fi and /horror buff extraordinaire Roy Spence kindly provided the following details of various amateur shorts he and his brother Noel filmed during the 1960s.

THE TOMB OF FRANKENSTEIN: A tale of revenge. A warlock uses witchcraft to restore life to the dead Frankenstein monster. He then uses the creature to take vengeance on two young thugs who had wronged him previously.

THE COMING OF THE BLACK DAWN: A young man travels to his uncle's castle to give him a rare tractate. His uncle enlists his help in trying to summon the demon, Cthulhu, using secret rites of black magic, which involve grave robbing and murder. As the demon is summoned the young man fears the outcome and inadvertently kills his uncle. He tries to escape the wrath of the demon but loses his own life in the attempt.

WOLVES OF DARKNESS: In an attempt to resurrect two former High Priests of the Brotherhood of the Wolf, a necromancer transforms a young artist into a werewolf, in order that the beast may assist him in the rites of Black Magic. The ceremony goes wrong at the last moment and the necromancer is carried off to another dimension.

197

Castle Dracula

A third snippet, from the same source, has a title card (all the titles look modern and have probably been added recently) that reads, "Purulent Putrescence Probed by Professor in Palmer Avenue SM3 8EF'." This one runs for 1:45 and features a mad scientist in a lab, unwrapping a severed head from a bag, digging into the brain with a knife, and placing a metal contraption and electrodes onto the object of his fiendish experiments. The YouTube info states this to be "the remains of a scene from an 8mm 'horror' film shot in Dave Longman's bedroom in 1966."

THE DEVIL'S WINDOW: The tormented ghost of a young woman, who had been burned at the stake by New England puritans, is laid to rest by a traveller who realizes the solution to her torment.

THE TESTAMENT OF CALEB MEEKE: A reclusive old man leaves behind his mansion to his nephew. The nephew arrives at the mansion only to find he has inherited a legacy of witchcraft and demonology, as his supposedly dead uncle uses him as a pawn in his dealings with the demon world.

THE CHANGELING: An East European peasant farmer exchanges his unwanted daughter for a son in a sinister bargain with the spirits of the moor. When the boy grows up to be a savage beast, the peasant tries to rescind the bargain, but ends up a broken and lonely man.

CASTLE DRACULA: A lawyer travels to Dracula's castle to do business with the Count but ends up victim to his grotesque host.

THE BEAST OF DRUIDS' HILL: An ancient beast, conjured to sleep by Druids in early times, is accidentally unleashed in a remote region of North Wales. A young student, the reincarnation of a previously sacrificed Druid, is offered up to once more lay the leviathan to rest.

YouTube Extracts

An excerpt from an 8mm amateur horror film shot by students on the Theatre Design Technician course at Croydon Theatre College in 1966 was posted on YouTube in August 2007. A title card reads, "Creepy Creatures Create Chaos in Croydon Crypt CR9 1DX," and the clip (approx. 1:20) depicts two white-clad vampire brides summoning a Dracula-like figure to rise from his grave.

A further excerpt, titled, "Evil Entity Exposed in Eerie Episode in Epsom KT14 4PF," was also posted at YouTube in August 2007. The accompanying notes read, "Epsom Art School students, Lew Coleman and Lin Valentine (plus some other friends) view the remains of an 8mm 'horror' film shot in Epsom Art School in 1965." The three-minute clip depicts a young woman in a negligee being menaced by a vampiric figure and a hunchback.

Appendix 2

Borderline/Problem Titles

ALL EYES ON SHARON TATE (1966)—ten-minute promotional film highlighting the tragic starlet, includes several clips from the then-in-production *Eye of the Devil*.

THE ANATOMIST (1956)—television play based on the Dr. Knox/Burke and Hare story; this was released to U.S. cinemas as a feature in 1961.

ANN WALKER (1964)—Harrison Marks nudie fare starring Ann Walker. "The Spanish Inquisition is the setting…a dungeon. Ann features in an unusual striptease and we can only urge you to view this provocative featurette, which, apart from showing this beautiful model at her best, provides an out of the run setting and some interesting close-up camera work."

THE ANNIVERSARY (1967)—eye-patch-wearing matriarch rules over her weak family. Hammer drama with Bette Davis.

ATLANTIS: CITY OF SIN (1967)—early work from prolific Britsploitation legend Michael J. Murphy. "By 15 I had made my first full-length Standard-8 epic: *Atlantis, City of Sin*. It was truly awful but showed at school and in my parents' dining room for over a month, one showing every night. It was very bloody with lots of model volcanoes and fireworks going off." (interview with the director by Paul Higson; see full review at the end of this appendix).

THE BED SITTING ROOM (1969)—end-of-the-world satire based on the John Antrobus-Spike Milligan play.

BEDAZZLED (1967)—Peter Cook and Dudley Moore in Faustian comedy. Cook makes a most entertaining Mephistopheles, especially while performing the title song (see full review at the end of this appendix).

THE BLOODY JUDGE (1969)—directed by Jess Franco, starring Christopher Lee. West Germany-Spain-Italy co-production, according to the 1993 publication *Obsession—the Films of Jess Franco*. The British Film Institute records some minor British production involvement and finance.

BLOWUP (1966)—enigmatic offering from Michelangelo Antonioni, with David Hemmings as a photographer who thinks he may have captured details of a murder, amid the indistinct details contained within a series of his pictures. Hugely influential on suspense and horror films ever since.

BOOM (1968)—from Tennessee Williams' play *The Milk Train Doesn't Stop Here Anymore*. Features Angel of Death character.

BY ONE, BY TWO, BY THREE (1965)—(presumed short) directed by Trevor A. Scott while at the Royal College of Art. Based on an Edwardian short story of the supernatural (Paul Higson).

CAN HIERONYMOUS MERKIN EVER FORGET MERCY HUMPPE AND FIND TRUE HAPPINESS? (1969)—indulgent fantasy directed by Anthony Newley; includes Milton Berle as the demonic "Goodtime Eddie Filth."

CAPTAIN NEMO AND THE UNDERWATER CITY (1969)—undersea adventure romp; sea monsters.

CASINO ROYALE (1967)—notorious Bond spoof; features brief appearance of the Frankenstein monster.

CASTLE OF THE LIVING DEAD (1964)—Italian horror film with Christopher Lee. Michael Reeves worked on this as assistant director. Sometimes listed in U.K. filmographies, seemingly by association.

CATCH US IF YOU CAN (1965)—the Dave Clark Five in pop musical directed by John Boorman; features fancy dress party with papier-mâché beast and Robin Bailey as the Frankenstein Monster ("How are my bolts?").

CEREMONY (196?)—8mm amateur porn short; ("muswell," posted at "British Horror Films" website, February 2006): "CEREMONY by Universal Pictures (not the Hollywood outfit I think) in which a naked couple are whipped and forced to copulate as part of a Black Magic Ceremony staged in a bedsit somewhere. This runs 200 feet and is staged in two shots, the continuous take adding immeasurably to the tension."

A CHRISTMAS CAROL (1960)—short version directed by Robert Hartford-Davis.

CIRCUS OF FEAR (1967)—circus murder mystery/crime thriller directed by John Llewellyn Moxey. Cast of Harry Alan Towers regulars includes Christopher Lee as an apparently scarred, hooded lion-tamer (see full review at the end of this appendix).

COFFEE BAR (196?)—early 1960s short from Rank's *Look at Life* series. Brief documentary about London's coffee bars; includes scenes shot in the horror-themed café Le Macabre, also includes a staged conversation between a producer and two young filmmakers discussing something called "I Was a Teenage Dracula from Outer Space!" (They describe a scene in which a girl is attacked by something oozing out of a plughole!)

COL CUORE IN GOIA (1967)—Tinto Brass-directed, giallo-style pop-art thriller filmed and set in London (aka *Deadly Sweet*).

THE COMMITTEE (1968)—"Unusual Hitchcockian thriller" (Internet Movie Database). "Murderous hitch-hiker" (Mark Coyle). Psychedelic rarity with Pink Floyd providing the soundtrack, and a brief appearance by The Crazy World of Arthur Brown. Directed by Peter Sykes.

EL CONDE DRACULA (1969)—Jess Franco's infamous take on Stoker, starring Christopher Lee. The book *Obsession—the Films of Jess Franco* credits this as a co-production from Spain, Italy, West Germany and Liechtenstein, but the British Film Institute's records indicate minor British production and finance.

COVER GIRL KILLER (1959)—Harry H. Corbett murders attractive young models in this early and recently reappraised psycho-quickie. Listed here, as it is occasionally given a "1960" production/release date. Directed by Terry Bishop.

CUL-DE-SAC (1966)—directed by Roman Polanski. "Nightmarish black comedy" (Ivan Butler, *Horror In The Cinema*).

DANGER TOMORROW (1960)—directed by Terry Bishop and starring Zena Walker, Robert Urquhart and Rupert Davies. Doctor's psychic wife "sees" murder in the attic.

THE DAY THE EARTH CAUGHT FIRE (1962)—Earth faces imminent destruction. Directed by Val Guest.

THE DAY THE FISH CAME OUT (1967)—strange apocalyptic comedy in which a plane carrying deadly nuclear device ditches into the sea near to a Greek island. Tourists flock there but ultimately realize they are infected and doomed to die.

THE DEVIL'S BITCHES (196?)—8mm amateur porn short, of the type sold privately for home viewing in pre-VCR days; ("muswell," posted at the "British Horror Films" website, February 2006): "*Devil's Bitches*, where three maidens service the high priest who has a ceremonial pillow case over his head."

THE DEVIL'S DAFFODIL (1961)—German/U.K. murder thriller based on an Edgar Wallace story.

DR CRIPPEN (1962)—with Donald Pleasence as the notorious true-life medic convicted of his wife's murder.

DR JEKELL AND MISS HYDE (19??)—(an advertisement for this title was originally placed in the June 1971 *Continental Film Review*, and later reprinted in *Absurd* fanzine #9): 8mm porno short, sold via mail order through London-based "Aphrodite Featurettes" and presumably dating from late 1960s-early 1970s. "Introducing the tantalizing Britt Marie—superbly directed by Svengali—for the discerning adult viewer." U.K production? Any significant horror content?.

DR STRANGELOVE: OR, HOW I LEARNED TO STOP WORRYING AND LOVE THE BOMB (1964)—apocalyptic nuclear comedy directed by Stanley Kubrick.

DR SYN—ALIAS THE SCARECROW (1963)—Disney family-orientated version of the smuggling yarn, starring Patrick McGoohan.

DRACULA (1968)—Denholm Elliott in feature-length adaptation of Stoker's vampire classic, made for ITV's *Mystery and Imagination* series.

THE EYES OF ANNIE JONES (1964)—directed by Reginald le Borg; girl speaks in dead woman's voice, exhibits other supernatural abilities.

FACES IN THE DARK (1960)—John Gregson as terrorized blind man. "Precursor of *Wait Until Dark* and *Blind Terror*" (Derek Winnert, *Radio Times Film and Video Guide*).

FAHRENHEIT 451 (1966)—François Truffaut's film version of the Ray Bradbury novel.

FIRST MEN IN THE MOON (1964)—Ray Harryhausen version of H.G. Wells' novel.

FRANKENSTEIN (1968)—Ian Holm as creature and creator in this feature-length adaptation made for ITV's *Mystery and Imagination* series.

FROZEN ALIVE (1964)—scientists freeze a human being.

THE FULL TREATMENT (1961)—Hammer psychological murder thriller, directed by Val Guest.

G.G. PASSION (1966)—directed by David Bailey; short film in which a rock star is hounded to death by mysterious assassins. Caroline Munro has a bit part in the film (Paul Higson).

THE GHOST GOES GEAR (1967)—pop musical starring the Spencer Davis Group. Haunted house (see full review at the end of this appendix).

GHOST OF A CHANCE (196?)—glamour short, possibly directed by Harrison Marks, possibly 1960s? (Gavin Whitaker).

GHOST OF A CHANCE (1968)—Children's Film Foundation featurette. Kids and ghosts team up to scare off a gang of property developers intent on destroying an historic old building.

GHOSTS AND GHOULIES (1967)—Children's Film Foundation short, from the *Magnificent 6½* series; haunted house.

THE HAND (1960)—low-budget programmer directed by Henry Cass. Wartime prisoner confesses to his captors, to prevent his hand from being severed—friends who have lost their own hands later track him down, intent on revenge.

THE HELL FIRE CLUB (1960s)—stag short including Satanic rituals made by Climax—Ivor Cooke's production company (Paul Higson).

THE HELLFIRE CLUB (1960)—directed by Robert S. Baker.

HEROSTRATUS (1967)—experimental feature directed by Don Levy, starring Michael Gothard. Young man intends to commit suicide and hires an advertising agency to publicize the event, in return for one month of luxury. Abattoir scenes and other violent imagery, along with the vaguely Faustian concept, have fans of this cult favorite comparing it to *Performance* and *A Clockwork Orange*.

THE HOUND OF THE BASKERVILLES (1968)—feature-length BBC TV version, from the celebrated television series which re-cast Peter Cushing as Sherlock Holmes.

THE HUNT (1968)—early 8mm feature, based on the Greek mythological tale of Theseus and the Minotaur, from director Michael J. Murphy, later to helm *Invitation to Hell* and various other British horror obscurities.

THE IMPERSONATOR (1960)—American airman, suspected of murdering woman in English village, helps to unmask the real killer, a deranged pantomime dame; directed by Alfred Shaughnessy.

THE INVADERS (c.1962)—early Delta Film Group short about alien invasion, made by Harry Nadler and Chuck Partington (Paul Higson).

A JOLLY BAD FELLOW (1963)—Leo McKern as university poisoner whose toxins cause victims to laugh uncontrollably before they die. Amusing black comedy.

JOURNEY INTO DARKNESS (1968)—the stories "Paper Dolls" and "The New People, "episodes of Hammer's *Journey to the Unknown* TV series, re-packaged as a "movie" for American television.

JOURNEY TO MIDNIGHT (1968)—more Hammer telly, re-packaged as a TV movie for the States. Stories "Poor Butterfly" and "The Indian Spirit Guide."

JOURNEY TO MURDER (1972)—stories "Do Me a Favour and Kill Me" and "The Killing Bottle," from Hammer's 1968 *Journey to the Unknown* TV show; screened as feature-length double-bill in the States.

JOURNEY TO THE UNKNOWN (1969)—Hammer TV stories "Matakitas is Coming" and "The Last Visitor," double-billed as a "movie" for U.S. small-screen consumption.

THE LAMP IN ASSASSIN MEWS (1962)—directed by Godfrey Grayson, a comedy of murder during the course of council attempts to improve a small town.

LET'S KILL UNCLE (1966)—directed by William Castle.

THE LONDON NOBODY KNOWS (1967)—James Mason takes us on a tour of the underbelly of swinging '60s London, including a visit to the site of one of the Ripper murders.

THE LONE RANGER (1968)—experimental short with music by Pete Townshend, includes a visual reference to Frankenstein's monster.

LORD OF THE FLIES (1963)—from the William Golding novel.

LOVING MEMORY (1969)—57-minute feature funded by the BFI, directed by Tony Scott. Elderly brother and sister knock down and kill a cyclist; taking him home, the sister dresses the corpse, makes him tea, and plots to kill her brother to prevent him from burying the body.

THE MAGIC CHRISTIAN (1969)—brief bit with Christopher Lee as a vampire.

THE MALPAS MYSTERY (1960)—thriller featuring man in "faceless" mask, based on Edgar Wallace's "Face in the Night."

MARAT/SADE (1967)—from the Peter Weiss play.

METAMORPHOSIS (1969)—(presumed short) directed by Carlos Pasini Hansen; the Kafka story adapted (Paul Higson).

THE MIND OF MR. SOAMES (1969)—Terence Stamp as revived coma victim, an infant in an adult body (see full review at the end of this appendix).

THE MONSTER OF HIGHGATE PONDS (1960)—directed by Alberto Cavalcanti; monster hatches from egg, has adventures with children.

MORGAN—A SUITABLE CASE FOR TREATMENT (1966)—crazy artist fixated on gorillas; clips from *King Kong*.

THE NAKED WORLD OF HARRISON MARKS (1967)—photographer fantasizes he is Dracula, James Bond, etc. (see full review at the end of this appendix).

NEGATIVES (1968)—couple's sex fantasies involve the husband impersonating Dr. Crippen. Directed by Peter Medak, with Glenda Jackson, Peter McEnery.

NIGHT OF THE BIG HEAT (1960)—90-minute Associated Rediffusion TV version of John Lymington's novel, later filmed by Terence Fisher.

NIGHTMARES (1964)—"Amateur short by Boys Club" (Paul Higson).

THE NINE AGES OF NAKEDNESS (1969)—directed by Harrison Marks; another sexploiter from Marks, includes caveman, Frankenstein sketches.

THE ONE-EYED SOLDIERS (1965)—scene with sadistic dwarf, torture chamber.

ONE OF THE MISSING (1968)—BFI short, one of the early works of director Tony Scott. Based on an Ambrose Bierce story, à la the author's celebrated "An Occurrence at Owl Creek Bridge."

ONE MORE TIME (1969)—sequel to SALT AND PEPPER, directed by Jerry Lewis. With Sammy Davis Jr, Peter Lawford; brief bit with Peter Cushing and Christopher Lee as Frankenstein and Dracula.

OUT OF THE FOG (1962)—former convict is chief suspect during a series of murders committed at the time of a full moon. Directed by Montgomery Tully.

THE PARTY'S OVER (1965)—controversial British drama starring Oliver Reed, features necrophilia and other depraved behavior.

PATTERN OF EVIL (1967)—directed by George Harrison Marks. "Aka *Fornicon*, a heavy S-and-M film written by the American novelist Lawrence Sanders, which features scenes of murder and Monique Devereux whipping Marks regular Howard "Vanderhorn" Nelson in a torture chamber. Shot for American backers and never shown in the U.K." (Gavin Whitaker).

PERFORMANCE (1968)—Nicolas Roeg and Donald Cammell's controversial classic, starring Mick Jagger and James Fox; much psychedelic and drug-induced "heightened reality" and a famous finale which appears to feature a body-meld/personality transfer.

THE PHANTOM (1968)—(presumed amateur short) directed by John Fahey Reilly. Boy tricks another boy into getting an electric shock and that night has a frightening nightmare (Paul Higson).

THE PIRATES OF BLOOD RIVER (1961)—Hammer pirate yarn; features death by piranha at beginning and end.

PRIMITIVE LONDON (1965)—*Mondo*-style movie, features a reconstruction of Jack the Ripper's crimes.

THE SCROLLS (1965)—short directed by Robert Wynne-Simmons. A totalitarian state takes voluntary sacrificial victims, but the tables are turned and the messenger is stoned to death (Paul Higson).

SECRET CEREMONY (1969)—Elizabeth Taylor, Mia Farrow and Robert Mitchum in *Vertigo*-like drama directed by Joseph Losey (see full review at the end of this appendix).

THE SECRET OF MY SUCCESS (1965)—three-part comedy with James Booth and Honor Blackman, including one episode with hero battling giant spiders.

THE SHE-BEAST (1965)—Michael Reeves' directorial debut, starring Ian Ogilvy and Barbara Steele. Filmed in Italy.

THE SILENT PLAYGROUND (1963)—listed as a horror film on the Internet Movie Database and in the Routledge book *British Horror Cinema*. The 1980 edition of *The Sunday Times Guide to Movies on Television* states, "Unpretentious little British thriller about some children in possession of dangerous drugs."

SLAVE GIRLS (1967)—hunter discovers lost tribe of primitive females. Daft Hammer exotica directed by Michael Carreras (see full review at the end of this appendix).

THE SPIDER'S WEB (1960)—directed by Godfrey Grayson; country house murder/hidden body. Based on Agatha Christie's play.

THE STRANGE CASE OF DR JEKYLL AND MR HYDE (1968)—Dan Curtis produced this two-hour version of Stevenson's horror classic, with Jack Palance in the title roles. U.S./Canadian production, shot in London and with many familiar British faces in the cast.

THE STRANGLERS OF BOMBAY (1959)—Hammer's thugee movie, given a "1960" date by many sources; Marcus Hearn and Alan Barnes' *The Hammer Story* states it was first screened in December 1959.

STRANGLER'S WEB (1965)—55-minute programmer filmed at Merton Park Studios, directed by John Llewellyn Moxey.

TALK OF THE DEVIL (1967)—directed by Francis Searle; Faustian comedy short with Tim Barrett and Hugh Latimer.

THE THIRTEEN CHAIRS (1969)—adaptation of the Russian novel *The 12 Chairs*; includes Orson Welles as manager of a Grand Guignol theater staging a Jekyll and Hyde-type show; Italian/French/U.K. co-production.

THE TIME MACHINE (1960)—George Pal's classic production of H.G. Wells' novel; listed (erroneously?) as a U.K./U.S. production by British weekly listings magazine *Radio Times* on more than one occasion.

TROUBLED WATERS (1964)—directed by Stanley Goulder; Tab Hunter as blond psycho released from prison who returns home and terrorizes his own family.

THE TRYGON FACTOR (1966)—directed by Cyril Frankel, German/U.K. production based on an Edgar Wallace novel.

2001: A SPACE ODYSSEY (1968)—directed by Stanley Kubrick; legendary science fiction classic which features killer computer HAL 9000 as a key "character."

UNCLE SILAS (1968)—feature-length adaptation of Le Fanu's novel, made for ITV's *Mystery and Imagination* series.

THE VALLEY OF GWANGI (1969)—cowboys versus an Allosaurus in this Ray Harryhausen monster Western. U.S. production shot in Spain, with Harryhausen's special effects and stop-motion work filmed in the U.K..

THE WATCHERS (1969)—short subject directed by Richard Foster, starring Helen Soroka; "a psychological drama with sf overtones—a schoolgirl has extraterrestrial visitations" (Paul Higson).

WE SHALL SEE (1964)—based on Edgar Wallace novel; scene featuring attempt to murder woman with bees.

WHAT A WHOPPER! (1961)—Loch Ness Monster comedy with Adam Faith and Sid James.

WHO IS MY NEIGHBOUR? (1967)—Mother's Union short film (19 minutes) and warning shot which includes a violent sexual assault sequence (Paul Higson).

WHISTLE AND I'LL COME TO YOU (1968)—Jonathan Miller's terrifying spin on M. R. James, starring an appropriately nervy Michael Hordern. Rarely have white bedsheets been so unsettling! 42-minute production filmed for BBC TV's *Omnibus*.

WITCHES BREW (1960)—Harrison Marks nudie short with "Rita Landre" (alter ego of the great Pamela Green). "The Queen of glamour photography makes her first appearance in cine film with this feature, and what an entrance…Night is mystic and who but the fabulous Rita would choose this time to weave her spell over the viewer? Watch her making her magic rites in preparation for the witches' sabbath and for anyone wanting sex appeal, which will leave them spellbound, this is the brew."

THE WRONG BOX (1966)—all-star black comedy based on the novel by Robert Louis Stevenson and Lloyd Osbourne; family members all try to maneuver and murder their way to a fortune; "Bournemouth Strangler" character.

YELLOW SUBMARINE (1968)—animated fantasy based on the songs of the Beatles; evil "Blue Meanies," brief bits with Frankenstein Monster and King Kong.

ZETA ONE (1969)—sci-fi sex comedy; race of alien females invade Earth, planning takeoverz

A handful of contributors to *The Shrieking Sixties* submitted full reviews of movies which only made it to our "Borderline" list, but which contain such valuable insights, quotes and other material that it seemed right to include them as an addition to this appendix:

ATLANTIS, CITY OF SIN is dated by its director Michael J. Murphy as 1967/68 and described as feature-length, though no approximation of the running time has ever been verified. It was never a theatrical release but an amateur production exhibited only in the local school and family lounge. The film is no longer in a condition that allows it to be seen, though it is hoped that it could be rescued with a little philanthropy. The only available independent reviews of the complete film are from the time, and the director has been able to supply the following local news article from his collection of clippings. The contemporary *Atlantis, City of Sin* review is by Charles H. Green, local drama critic, and appeared either in the *Portsmouth Evening News* or the *Hampshire Telegraph* in February 1968:

"Supping Full With Horrors"

To begin my film previews this week I am taking a long look into the future—films with the credit in big letters: produced and directed by M.J. Murphy. It could be. Sixteen-year-old Portsmouth Northern Grammar School fifth former M.J. (Michael) Murphy, judging by his full-length sound and colour film, *Atlantis, City of Sin*, certainly has the stuff of film-making in him; he has already grasped many of the tricks of the trade.

His film, in aid of Oxfam, admission by ticket only, had its "world premiere" on Thursday, but Michael invited me to a preview in his tiny "cinema"—the dining room of his home. "You will be the first person to see the film as a whole," he promised me. But so that I should not be lonely, he had also invited one or two friends—some members of the cast—to the preview.

Before *Atlantis, City of Sin* we were shown a trailer—of a film that will now not be made—called *The Torturers*. It was the longest trailer I have ever seen, but the shots and commentary were highly intriguing. Young Michael is catering for the taste of violence in films in a big way. Middle-aged "softies" like me might find this preoccupation with violence in such a young and pleasant film producer and director as Michael rather puzzling; but in *Atlantis, City of Sin*, he has set out to make a film which people will remember—and I shall certainly remember it. I came away feeling, like Macbeth, that I had "supped full with horrors," but Michael's script, written when he was 15, is exciting and filled with cinematic action.

The young director has created an undeniable atmosphere of claustrophobia, of a closed and decadent society whose destruction seems as inevitable as that of Pompeii. There is something rotten in the state of Atlantis—and it is the sin of murder, practised almost as a way of life. Michael admits that the dialogue is often corny—but it is spoken with conviction by the young actors and actresses; and also, by Michael's "gran," who appears in the film as an aged prophetess.

The boy is certainly persuasive—his "gran" took a great interest in the film, and he also gained the enthusiastic support of his sister, who plays the sister of the Boy King of Atlantis (Michael himself) and his sister-in-law, who is quite moving in her portrayal of the dumb Christian girl, Lydia. Locations like the steps of Portsmouth Guildhall (used for the Coronation scene at about 6 o'clock in the morning, when the city was sleeping), Portchester Castle, and the sand dunes at Hayling (scene of an exciting fight) are used effectively. Michael has used simple materials and textures

resourcefully and imaginatively and, with full credits and good use of music, the film, technically, ranges far above the average amateur effort. I hope that one day, at our Odeons and Essoldos and Gaumonts, we shall see those words in the credits: "Produced and Directed by M.J. Murphy."

Four minutes of footage from *Atlantis, City of Sin* are available on an excerpts compilation that has had limited circulation. It includes an erupting volcano (like a school science project), some crude split-screen and three or four scenes which may have been choice cuts determined by their gore content, or could very well be genuinely representative of the longer film. Each of the three gore scenes is moodily shot, swathed in shadows but the horrors enacted are never lost in the murk, Murphy's camera picking up every bloody detail. The first is a murder committed with a short trident (this is Atlantis, remember), the killer attacking his victim in the face then delighting in the blood-soaked body.

Murphy cast himself in the star role of the evil emperor of Atlantis in this, his first feature. Mike certainly clearly had to get some of the gorehound out of his system, and the fact that he did not have to run his amateur production by the BBFC meant that it could go much further. Speaking of his early excesses on local television (footage captured in the same excerpts compilation), Michael explained, "Well, at the time I really wanted to impress people by making the most controversial subject I could and didn't have any experience of filmmaking, so I thought blood and guts was the best answer."

The second scene is the murder of a young man sacrificially knifed in repose. The sequence continues in close-up as a pig's heart is wrenched from the bloody torso and then removed to a table for further preparation. One could swear that this scene was shot by Herschell Gordon Lewis, so reminiscent this gloating image is of *Blood Feast*, but as similarly captured as it is, it is unlikely that Murphy could have been familiar with the work of Mr. Lewis. The third notable example comes accompanying the destruction of Atlantis and is the most fascinating of the gore set pieces.

The insane emperor is not going to allow any natural catastrophe to dictate how and when he dies and commits suicide: by self-decapitation with a sword. He takes the weapon by both hands and places the blade to the back of his neck in order to bring it on through exiting at the throat. The first attempt fails and it wedges partway. There are three shots of note, a close-up on him, face front, as he begins to bring the blade the rest of the way through. Then there is an extreme close-up on the side of the neck as the sword works through the side of the neck to the throat. This is a real neck. The trick is very effective (particularly given that the sword is made of cardboard and aluminium foil), simply a cut-down of the "sword" at the hilt end scoring into the flesh, traveling the neck, impressing deeply but safely into the skin. It is a simple trick, but had a major film attempted it at the time, it would have been too effective and would never have been allowed by the British Board of Film Censors.

The next shot is back to a close-up, full face on, blood spilling out of his mouth, and Mike bringing the sword (the trick being in two halves) on through his neck, completing the decapitation. From there on it is the fake head falling to the ground and some sickly relishing of the bloody stump of the neck, the emperor's hands out before it, fingers frantic. The next shot is on to the fallen body and decapitated head. There is something to consider here. Not only did our 15-year-old director devise this entire sequence, but he was in front of the camera for it—and still got the required effective sequence of shots.

Murphy followed this with *The Hunt*, an 8mm feature-length telling of the legend of Theseus and the Minotaur. Murphy describes the

film as a fantasy adventure and not a horror, though it does reportedly contain some more examples of his early bloodlust.
—Paul Higson

BEDAZZLED? Just a comedy, isn't it? Pete 'n' Dud 'n' Ellie cavorting among Michael Bates' raincoat and Raquel Welch's boobs?

On one level, yes. But on another, there's a whole lot of darkness going on. And most of that darkness touches directly on all of us.

Look at Stanley Moon. Look at how he reacts to Devil Spiggott's ongoing "routine mischief." It all starts in small ways: scratching records, causing shopping bags to split but, at first, Moon, however meekly, if not wimpily, is dismayed, even disgusted by these acts—"'Ere, that's horrible"—especially in his outburst at Spiggott's disgraceful conning of a nice little old lady.

But Spiggott makes a valid point in riposte: "She didn't mind the idea of ripping off Fruney's" And he's right. Even this sweet little old granny will happily connive, manipulate and downright deceive to get something. We really are that venal.

And the last act of routine mischief that we see in the film is telling. Moore, in scuba gear, finds Spiggott, also in scuba gear, under water.

"What are you doing?"

"Drilling a small hole in this oil tanker..."

Suddenly, it's not about spilling groceries or nicking raspberries and cream. Now it's about real, albeit mundane, brutality. What if the hole somehow sinks the ship? How many lives will be lost? Even if the ship just quietly leaks oil, how many animals will die? How many livelihoods will be damaged, if not wrecked?

And Moon? Outraged? Appalled? Furious?

No. He's so wrapped up in his own desires and depressions that he doesn't even comment. He's our Everyman—ourselves—and any trace of anything even vaguely noble or decent has gone from him. We are, in a word, boned.

Grim as that is, it palls when placed next to the big picture. Spiggott and God have been having a wager—over collecting souls—in the same way that a couple of pub drunks would play a game of 501 to decide who buys the next round. And when Spiggott loses, the final moments of the film are nothing short of haunting—and disturbing.

"All right, you great git, you've asked for it. I'll cover the world in Tastee-Freez and Wimpy Burgers. I'll fill it with concrete runways, motorways, aircraft, television, automobiles, advertising, plastic flowers, frozen food and supersonic bangs. I'll make it so noisy and disgusting that even you'll be ashamed of yourself! No wonder you've so few friends. You're unbelievable..."

Spiggott is left hopelessly frustrated at the last in his attempt to secure Moon's soul. God is vastly amused by this, and booms his laughter at Spiggott, the only one who hears Him. And the thwarted, furious Devil responds to this in the way that any powerful supernatural being probably would: by shoving that anger right in His face, and damn the consequences to mere mortals.

The final shot of George gives him a certain air of tragic nobility that's hard to resist. Gazing at the sky, he sadly but defiantly wanders off through Piccadilly Circus, seen at best as a harmless loony by bemused passersby. And the end credits roll, and we realize that Spiggott wasn't making idle threats. Over the chaotically colored, whirling background, we hear ominous, industrialized sounds getting ever louder and more worrying: speeding traffic, violent demolitions, urgent emergency service sirens and finally the roaring swoop of an apparently diving aircraft, maybe carrying the very Bomb all ready to drop for all that we know.

And throughout it all, God Almighty guffaws like a good 'un. It's a sudden, unsettling twist to the comedy of the film that we've just seen. In His eyes, the Devil losing is a bloody good laugh, and even if we suffer because of His gloating triumph, He apparently doesn't give a celestial fig.

And that's Horror.
—Ken Shinn

CIRCUS OF FEAR is an old-fashioned potboiler that begins in surprisingly brutal fashion with an armed robbery on a pay van. One of the gang panics and a policeman is shot. The crooks then escape by boat down the Thames. Such action-packed thuggery is wildly out of synch with the rest of the film, which is exceedingly drab and genteel.

Investigating the crime is Inspector Elliott (Leo Genn), a refined old gent who drinks his tea in a cup and saucer. It's good luck for him there's no car chases, fisticuffs or fast women; his preferred beverage might slop out over the sides! Naturally he has a grouchy superior officer always badgering him to produce results while Elliott looks sardonic.

The trigger-happy gang member (Victor Maddern) has been silenced with a big blade in his back. The only clue leads Elliott to a circus full of intrigue where everyone is arguing, blackmailing or eavesdropping in an absurdly theatrical manner.

There's a seedy atmosphere to the real circus shot on location with its mangy animals. Among the performers are jealous knife thrower Mario (Maurice Kaufmann), blackmailing dwarf Mr. Big (Skip Martin) and Gregor (Christopher Lee), a lion tamer who, due to a terrible accident, always wears a hood. A handful of scenes with Klaus Kinski play as if the German guest star had wandered onto location by mistake. He thrashes around, "looking" for something, until he also gets dispatched with a knife.

The crime syndicate is forgotten as people start dropping like flies. The police aren't exactly a credit to the force. A woman is shown a murder weapon. She recognizes it but, instead of interrogating her further, the coppers take their leave, giving the killer time to silence her! There's a lot of ridiculous intrigue concerning a fatal crime from the past and the mystery about what's really concealed beneath Gregor's hood.

Finally the scriptwriter remembers the whole crime syndicate thing and the big cheese, of course, working with the circus, is dispatched in record time. The case solved, Inspector Elliott returns to the station for a fresh pot of tea.
—Gerald Lea

THE GHOST GOES GEAR, originally released as the support feature to Hammer's *One Million Years B.C.*, is a musical comedy vehicle for the Spencer Davis Group that depicts the band holidaying at the haunted ancestral home of their upper class twit manager (Nicholas Parsons). Typical haunted house hijinks involving the group, Parsons' butler (Jack Haig) and Polly the Maid (Sheila White) ensue, but the virtually plotless *The Ghost Goes Gear* is essentially a pop concert film with various "special guests" turning up in the form of Dave Berry, Mr. Acker Bilk, pop group also-rans the M6 and the St. Louis Union, plus the unbelievable girl group the Three Bells. Not wishing to be outdone, the Ghost (Lorne Gibson) also materializes to do a musical number.

Emmett Hennessy, an actor whose career includes everything from *Doctor Who* to appearances in Harrison Marks' 8mm films, had a brief role in the film and remembers shooting as "a whole day cruising on a barge on some river with a bunch of swinging '60s teens and the Spencer Davis group with a 16- or 17-year-old Stevie Winwood, who I overheard talking to another band member about his acne and the fact that the fans should only consider his musical talent, not his complexion! My little part was an exchange with Nicholas Parsons, as we were alighting from the boat and he was behind me and it was the corny old longhair joke where he thinks I'm a girl and says something to my back to that effect, and then I turn 'round all butch. Trouble was, after I got the part, I had to cut my hair for another role, so I had to wear a wig. Many years later, Parsons came to Trinidad for a golf tournament and was being interviewed on my wife's talk show, and when I saw him I flew down to the studio and reintroduced myself. Small world!"

—Gavin Whitaker

Whenever fans discuss the output of Amicus, **THE MIND OF MR SOAMES** is rarely mentioned. Described simply as "well intentioned" by Jonathan Rigby in his exhaustive tome *English Gothic* and steadfastly ignored by pretty much everyone else, *Soames* may be more sci-fi than outright shocker, but I'd contend that there is plenty for the horror buff here—it may even be seen as the studio's only stab at putting something akin to the *Frankenstein* story on screen. Set firmly in the groovy Amicus-land of the late 1960s, *Soames* is also the perfect antidote to the rest of the company's offerings of the time, with a thoughtfulness, languorous pace and quiet charm.

John Soames (Terence Stamp) is a man who has been in a coma since birth, meaning that although his body has fully matured, his mind has never been stimulated. Kept alive intravenously over the years, he lies in a glass coffin in a cold, sterile institute. As his 30th birthday approaches, moves are afoot to wake him up. A specialist, Dr. Bergen (Robert Vaughn) is brought over from L.A., and the owner of the facility, Dr. Maitland (Nigel Davenport), has arranged for the entire event to be broadcast live on television. In fact (in an accurate prediction of things to come in the real world), Maitland has decided that, once awake, Soames' life will be played out in front of the cameras. Neurologists, scientists and surgeons from all over the world attend the "birth," with the TV commentator giving a running commentary on the operation: "The drilling is about to begin… to form an entry to the brain…"

When, following the procedure, Bergen is congratulated on a "good show," he begins to realize that Maitland may not have his patient's best interests at heart; but by then it's too late, and all they can do is wait to see if their "baby" will wake up. There's a real sense of wonder as we wait with them, too. And when it happens, it's brilliant, with Bergen telling the new arrival, "Welcome to the human race, John Soames. Go on, let it out. It was never easy being born."

Soames is immediately put on an accelerated learning program, with his every move recorded for posterity. Maitland has set himself up as parent and teacher to the "child," but he refuses to allow Soames to deviate from his carefully orchestrated schedule. When Bergen discovers this, he brings in a variety of toys and games for Soames to play with ("Buckaroo," anyone?) and then (horror of horrors) allows him outside to muck about in the garden. Soames (resplendent in his big pink babygrow) is having a high old time until Maitland discovers what is going on, sending loads of burly security men out to drag him back inside.

This rough treatment has exactly the effect you'd expect: He's initially upset (heartbreakingly, when told he can go out again later, he replies "No. They will hurt me."), and then riled, killing a security guard to gain his freedom. Suddenly, Soames is off and into the big wide world, a grown man with a mentalist haircut, wearing a one-piece pink suit and unable to string a coherent sentence together. He finds a motorway ("red car!") and a pub, where he helps himself to a drink and a sandwich (a very 1960s choice, cheese or lettuce), but can't pay

and gets kicked out. He then joins in and ruins a game of football with some kids, and to top his big day, gets run over by a drunk driver.

The motorist takes him home (rather than admit to the authorities that he'd been imbibing), and Soames wakes up in a strange bed. Up until this point no one has recognized him, which seen in this day and age seems quite odd; after all, he'd be a celebrity in the 21st century. But the media have cottoned on (the *Daily Mirror*'s headline is "Can this baby kill?"), and the driver's wife knows who he is.

"Poor Mr. Soames, I don't know what they did to you," she tells him. "It was my useless, drunken husband that knocked you down. He's much more dangerous than you." He certainly is, because, although she's on Soames' side, the husband has phoned the authorities and the fugitive has to do a bunk and go on the run again. This time he gets onto a train, where he terrifies a mousy young girl by indicating he'd like her apple and blathering on about how "London is the capital of England" and that "there are many trees in the institute…I do not like the institute." (I have to say that I'd be scared at this point; in fact, you wonder on occasion exactly which course the filmmakers are going to pursue.) Soames ends up cornered by the police, the media and the scientists in a rain-lashed barn, where the glimmer of a happy ending can just about be ascertained through the murk.

As for those Frankenstein analogies? Well, consider Maitland as the Baron, a cold and ruthless man uninterested in his "creation," despite giving him life. Bergen is the more idealistic, thoughtful type of scientist, as so often drafted in to assist—in, say, Hammer's Frankenstein cycle—before the operation, he comments, "Are you sure we should try to wake him? He looks happier than most conscious people." Soames is the "monster," a child in a man's body, confused, angry, lacking self-control and, of course, eventually accidentally taking someone's life. And, if you substitute villagers for the TV crew and flaming torches for their spotlights, the parallels of this film's rain-soaked climax with the ending of many of Hammer's Gothic fantasies are striking.

And it's worth mentioning that Stamp's performance throughout is extraordinary. What could be an appallingly embarrassing turn (grown people playing children rarely works) just *isn't*, somehow. It's a testament to the man's talent that at no point do you consider him anything other than 100-percent genuine, whether he's making you laugh (the scene where he bounces a ball off Maitland's head is a comic high point!), cry (the moment before he makes his escape) or even unnerved (the scene on the train). *The Mind of Mr. Soames* is a dark little gem, and a worthy pretender to the British horror hall of fame.

—Chris Wood

THE NAKED WORLD OF HARRISON MARKS is a purported look at the life and business of the famed glamour photographer George Harrison Marks. "It would be wrong to think of Harrison Marks as a man who spends his days focusing on beautiful women," argues Valentine Dyall's narrator, somewhat unconvincingly given the amount of time the film dedicates to Marks snapping away at nude women either in his studio or on location.

Just to show there is more to the man than boobs, however, we get to see Marks judging a beauty contest and photographing cats; there are also fantasy scenes in which members of the public imagine what Marks' life must be like, which also provides a good excuse for Marks to dress up as a playboy, a gangster, Toulouse-Lautrec, while things take a detour into horror film territory when Marks is imagined as Count Dracula (incidentally, Marks had been the theatrical photographer during Bela Lugosi's ill-fated British tour as Dracula in 1951).

Considering the film mostly consists of topless nudity and slapstick comedy, *Naked World* ends on a surprisingly sinister note with

Marks experiencing a nightmare in which he meets a hooded ghoul in a graveyard, sees himself (quite literally) digging his own grave, and then finds himself in a dungeon surrounded by chained-up nude women. Their crime? Modeling for Harrison Marks! Marks is then put on trial for leading a "worthless life" before being dragged away by the vengeful nude ladies to be drowned.

The Naked World of Harrison Marks was initially rejected by the British censor but was swiftly passed with an A certificate by numerous nudity-loving local councils (the BBFC eventually relented and passed the film with cuts in 1968).

Teri Martine recalled, "I remember George taking me to see the preview of his feature film *The Naked World of Harrison Marks*. We were no sooner in our seats than George fell asleep, and was snoring so loud, I had to wake him up! Fond memories of the one and only George." —Gavin Whitaker

Where does one begin? Maybe not at the beginning. Viewing Joseph Losey's work in a linear context, and therefore judging him as you would judge any other director, is a tricky business, and never more so than when dealing with **SECRET CEREMONY**, a film which, 40-something years on, invites as much debate as when first released. Is it a work of genius? A byproduct of the era, perhaps, where precious little seemed to make sense? The ramblings of a lunatic? Or maybe all three? And, above all, what exactly is it *about*? I have to confess to moderate confusion myself, although I can't deny I find it captivating.

On the surface, it's about a prostitute (Elizabeth Taylor) having a nervous breakdown and attempting to come to terms with the death of her own (unseen) daughter. Or maybe, it's about Cenci (Mia Farrow), a troubled "teenager," who may in fact be considerably older, suffering delusions after the death (self-inflicted?) of her mother, and recovering from years of domestic sexual abuse at the hands of a sleazy stepfather (Robert Mitchum), thus transferring the need for love and affection onto someone who bears a passing resemblance to her departed parent, in this case, Taylor, whom she seemingly meets one day on a bus. At least I think so. But that only scratches the surface. There's so much going on underneath at any given time, so many hints, nuances, subtleties and allegories, that everything I've mentioned so far already seems oversimplified.

Is *Secret Ceremony* a horror film? Well, to some, it may be. At points it definitely feels like one, sharing both atmosphere and aesthetics with the likes of *Peeping Tom*, *Twisted Nerve*, *Season of the Witch*, *Fragment of Fear*, *That Cold Day in the Park*, *Repulsion*, *Symptoms* and *Images* (the last four also belonging in the subgenre of "female nervous breakdown" pictures, and the last three of which are the work of foreign directors in the British Isles), displaying some distinctly Bavaesque camera work and design, and dealing with topics of insanity, psychosis, delusion, delirium and murder, all common to the form. Don't forget that by 1968 the freedom afforded filmmakers by British producers, coupled with the experimental, pioneer spirit of the age, was such that genres were cross-pollinating and conjoining with alarming frequency, with an implicit understanding that any drama (and even some comedies) could plunge headlong into dark waters at a moment's notice.

Thus, "horror" could be the order of the day as easily as any other, although decidedly of the urban, psychological variety rather than the supernatural. On a basic level, what we have here is a psychological thriller; however, if that term could also be used to describe the likes of *Hysteria*, *The Nanny* and practically every giallo ever committed to celluloid, then by the same token this film belongs in this book. And whereas self-appointed arbiters of "serious" cinema have given the film a wide berth, British horror (and for want of a better term,

"cult movie") fans seem to have taken it to their hearts and given it the respect it deserves.

You *can* see how detractors (including seemingly every critic who reviewed it upon release, whose knives were obviously out after Losey and Taylor's previous collaboration on the misunderstood Tennessee Williams adaptation *Boom*) might make a point of its detached quaintness, pointing out that people in real life just don't talk or act the way the actors do here, and that even if they did, why should we be bothered about the mental anguish of some dotty heiress and her sluttish companion anyway? If anything, it has a timelessness some of its contemporaries *don't* possess, and even if it is a product, by its very nature, of the psychedelic age, it doesn't wear the 1960s on its sleeve. In fact, the one time a character is seen wearing a flower-power dress, it's shortly before they commit an unexpected act of violence, and "peace and love" don't appear to be part of the equation at all.

Then again, ambiguity and ambivalence seem to be the order of the day. The film's title could allude to a number of things: the knowingly pretend relationship acted out by Leonora and Cenci; Cenci's quasi-masturbatory fantasy of violation acted out on the kitchen table (whilst Leonora covertly watches from the shadows); the "role play" between Mitchum and Farrow which toys with the concepts of consent and rape to the point where they become worryingly intertwined; and the haziness of Ashcroft and Brown's "sisterhood." But, on a more subconscious level, could it not also describe the unacknowledged yet very real practice of pretence we adopt when entering any unhealthy liaison? We all wear a number of masks, wigs and hats at different times, but the blindfold we wear to shield ourselves from reality is the most potentially dangerous.

The women's relationship is conducted under this shield, and *is* ultimately unhealthy, leading inevitably to tragic consequences for one and uncertainty for the other—as well as the murder described earlier. The true "horror," though, is to be found in Losey's depiction of suicide, here portrayed as a squishy, swirly, quasi-hallucinogenic act that leaves an unpleasant jabbing sensation in the viewer's innards.

Yet despite all the unpleasantness, the after effect is actually one of quiet composure. Maybe it's because the two principal actresses give such serene performances. Although Taylor was well into her "mad bint" cycle by now (taking in *The Night of the Iguana*, the aforementioned *Boom*, *Identikit* and eventually full-on horror with *Night Watch*), here she is subtle, understated and, above all perfect for the part. Likewise, Farrow seems natural in her role, avoiding the occasional lapses into histrionic overacting that would mar an otherwise great performance in the later *Blind Terror*, and displaying the same mixture of vulnerability and near-evil she would put to great use the same year in *Rosemary's Baby* (and much later in *Full Circle*). —D.R. Shimon

Following some stock footage of African wildlife that opens **SLAVE GIRLS** (aka *Prehistoric Women*)**,** thoroughly decent chap and all-around good egg David is captured by a strange tribe of self-confessed "false idol" worshipers, who pray to a large statue of a white rhinoceros god. The poor fellow was only following a leopard to put it out of its misery after a bumbling oaf had failed to kill the beast on one of David's hunts, because, you see, our Bwana is a Great White Hunter.

Abruptly transported to the garden world of the *Prehistoric Women* (the U.S. title), he discovers the usual Hammer cave people's battle between the blonde-haired lassies and the black-haired ones. (See *One Million Years B.C.* and *When Dinosaurs Ruled the Earth* for similar, follicle prejudice-based shenanigans.) They also worship the same white rhino statue, and their world is currently ruled by the black-

haired women, with former Miss Jamaica Martine Beswick as their Queen, Kari. The men are "no longer men" and are locked in a cave, reduced to Monty Python-style "It's"-type creatures. (Thank goodness there are no brunettes or redheads around to confuse matters further.)

Needless to say, all the women in the film take one look at our brave British hero and want to shag him. Sadly, though, he seems to have fallen into a bucket of tits and come out sucking his own thumb. He finds Queen Martine's cruelty repulsive but is kept from his love at first sight, blonde slave gal Saria, by the tribe's rules and Kari's possessiveness. Surprisingly Kari reveals that once things were reversed, and "We dark ones were in bondage to the fair ones. You would have pitied me then." Much is made of what "the legends say" and what will happen if the old rhino god returns.

Despite a relatively short running time, not a lot seems to happen in the film. Large slabs are eaten up with lengthy dance sequences, or squads of girls parading round the rhino statue Nuremberg Rally style, and bowing obsequiously to it. *Slave Girls* never makes much sense, or generates enough tension or incident, to be a good adventure tale. Is it an early ecological awareness piece, an allegory of Britain's imperial past, a paean to manumission, an anti-feminist polemic or just a load of silly old tosh?

It's hard to see who the film was aimed at. Its theme, "Martine is chokin' for it, but her love slave fancies another," is a bit fruity for a Saturday matinee kids audience, who in any case would demand dinosaurs to accompany this sort of thing. Its execution is tediously tame for an adult audience, possibly expecting a bit more, well, thrills,

gore or nudity, of which there are none. At least our cave dwellers speak English this time, and are not "eeking" and grunting at each other. As they have mastered cloth manufacture and metalwork, it's hardly fair to call them "prehistoric," too. The picture's British title, *Slave Girls*, makes much more sense.

Its hero is played by Michael Latimer, a performer utterly lacking in any charisma, who would go on to enjoy a lengthy TV career in supporting roles. For some strange reason, Steven Berkoff suddenly shows up at the end as "John" and, while Ms. Beswick seems to have looked good enough, her dialogue has clearly been dubbed by somebody else. Of course, Martine is the only reason for sitting through this film. Her abs are truly objects worthy of adoration here, even ol' Latimer can't tear his eyes off them when he gets the chance. Efficiently shot by Michael Reed, mostly on just two sets with a bit of mucking about, the production was largely clamped in the tight fist of Michael Carreras, its writer, producer and director. It remains a hugely confused work in terms of tone and intention, possibly one reason for its remaining insignificance.

—John Rankin

Appendix 3

BBFC Film Cuts
compiled by Tim Rogerson

Approximately half of the films reviewed in this book were cut by the British Board of Film Censors (BBFC). This 50-percent ratio, the majority of which were X rated (under 16s not admitted), compares with a 48-percent ratio of X films cut overall by the BBFC in the period 1960-69.

Other British films that the BBFC considered needed cutting before they were deemed suitable to be seen by those aged 16 or over in the 1960s included *This Sporting Life*, *The Loneliness of the Long Distance Runner*, *Victim*, *Darling* and *Poor Cow*.

In addition to cuts made to finished works, the majority of British horror films had screenplay drafts or outlines submitted to the BBFC for preclearance and comment. This preclearance submission was commonly used in the period in order to identify potential censorship problems before filming started and thereby saved filmmakers the expense of shooting footage that the censors would not permit. Several of the films covered by this book were modified substantially in the preproduction stage following BBFC examiner comments on their scripts. Technically, however, these are not regarded as BBFC cuts per se and are not covered in this appendix.

Throughout the 1960s the prime objective of the BBFC, under its secretary John Trevelyan, was to avoid classifying anything that might result in the Board (and the film industry itself) being "criticized," a word often used in Trevelyan's autobiography. As applied to horror films, which normally did not contain any controversial political content, this meant scenes or themes that the Board considered to be "excessive."

The Board itself had no detailed "do" or "don't" rules—unlike its American counterpart the MPAA—but instead applied its own unwritten guidelines on a case by case basis. The advantage of this was that it gave Trevelyan and his team the freedom to treat more leniently the films which, in their opinion, had artistic merit but to come down more harshly on those which they felt had no such merit, or which they disliked. (Trevelyan described this as "intelligent censorship.") There are no prizes for guessing in which category most of the titles in this book fall. A notable exception was *Repulsion*, which escaped uncut because it was directed by Roman Polanski, whom Trevelyan considered to be an artist.

Areas of particular concern to the BBFC included "too much" blood, shots of severed organs and "excessive" soundtrack noises, such as screaming and sawing. Close-ups of stakes entering vampires were also generally prohibited until the X rating was raised to 18 years in 1970. A particular theme that runs through the Board's cutting of horror films is the presentation of sex. Trevelyan is on record as saying that he didn't like sex and horror to mix and consequently sex scenes in X rated horror films were treated much more strictly than similar scenes in non-horror films such as A-rated James Bond pictures. Essentially, Trevelyan didn't want anyone in the audience to get an erection while watching a horror film!

Listed below are details supplied to the authors by the BBFC, regarding the cuts the Board believe were made by them to the films covered in this book, where that information is still available. Most of the more severe cuts were made in the early part of the decade as part of the backlash following the extraordinary critical response to *Peeping Tom*.

Prior to the Video Recordings Act, 1984, there was no statutory requirement for the BBFC to keep records of cuts made to films they certified. Consequently, the information is sometimes missing, incomplete or vague due to lack of a full record of what was often a negotiation process with the filmmakers. Annotations have been made to this information where appropriate. In addition, the U.K. DVD status of these films (cut or uncut) has been noted. Where there is no U.K. DVD release, or the U.K. DVD is cut, overseas DVDs have been referenced as appropriate.

Our thanks in particular go to Jason Green of the BBFC for supplying most of this information to our various contributors.

1959

The Flesh and the Fiends
Classified X for its theatrical release in 1959 with the following cuts:
Reel 4: Shorten the scenes culminating in the death of Maggie. (*nb: shots substituted*)
Reel 6: Shorten the scenes culminating in the death of Mary.
Reel 7: Shorten the scenes culminating in the death of Jamie and reduce the shots of his dead body.
Reel 9: Remove the shot of Burke's dead face with the tongue protruding.
Comment:
The U.S. Image Entertainment DVD includes a "Continental" print which restores all of these cuts as well as the cut U.K. theatrical print.

1960

The Brides of Dracula
Classified X for its theatrical release in 1960 with the following cut:
Reel 7: Remove the shot of blood welling up from the wound after Lessing (*sic—actually Van Helsing*) has driven a stake into the Baroness' body.
Comment:
The U.S. Universal DVD, and the German Anolis DVD, are uncut.

Circus of Horrors
Classified X for its theatrical release in 1960 with the following cuts:
Reel 6 : Shots of woman with naked breasts in both the Adam and Eve and Sappho tableaux were removed. (*nb: substituted with alternate clothed takes*)
Comment:
All DVD releases are of the cut version. Screenwriter George Baxt has also claimed that a close-up shot of the knife embedded into Vanda Hudson was also cut but the BBFC do not acknowledge this.

Doctor Blood's Coffin
Classified X for its theatrical release in 1960 with the following cuts:
Reel 5: Remove shots of Peter making incisions in the body of the living man.
Reel 7: Remove all shots of heart, either in the body, being removed or being massaged.
Reels 9 and 10: Remove all CUs of the hand and face of the decomposed corpse. Distant shots may remain if the print is toned as to make the lighting dim. In the struggle between the corpse and the surgeon, remove all shots which clearly show the face and hands of the corpse.
Comment:
The U.S. Cheezy Flicks DVD is uncut.

The Hands of Orlac

Classified A for its theatrical release in 1960 with the following cuts:
Reel 3: The love-making on the bed between Stephen and Louise was shortened.
Reel 4: Shots of Nero holding a flick-knife towards Li-Lang were removed. (*nb: substituted with an alternate take of Nero slapping her cheek*)
Reel 5: The prostitute's question "Lonely, darling?" was removed.
Reel 10: Dialogue line "Or before he can get into bed with you—that's what's at the back of your mind, isn't it?" was removed. The first shot of the sword being thrust into the box was removed.
Comment:
The Spanish Devisa DVD is the alternate French version to which these cuts were never made. The old U.S. Rhino VHS appears to be the cut theatrical print.

Peeping Tom

Classified X for its theatrical release in 1960 with the following cuts:
Reel 1: Considerably shorten the episode of the murder of the prostitute.
Reel 2: Remove the shots of nude girls in an album. Remove, as far as possible, shots of girls bruises and references to them, reduce to a minimum shots of girls disfigured face.
Reel 6: Considerably shorten the murder of Vivian and remove emphasis on the spike.
Reel 8: Stop the conversation in the car between the two police officers at the point the inspector says "what!"
Reel 10: Reduce emphasis on spike in interview between Mark and Mrs. Stephens.
Reel 11: Remove the color transparency of a nude girl. Remove the shots of Millie on the bed.
Reel 12: Shorten Mark's suicide.
Comment:
Most, but not all, of these cuts are restored on the U.S. Criterion and U.K. Optimum DVDs, which are identical in terms of content.

The Snake Woman

Classified A for its theatrical release in 1960 with the following cut:
Reel 1: The scene in the bedroom between the doctor and his pregnant wife was shortened.

The Terror of the Tongs

Classified X for its theatrical release in 1960 with the following cuts:
Reel 3: Remove shot of first officer's mutilated hand. Remove shots of Helena's hand being held down by Tong men on a table and her reactions as her fingers are struck by axe.
Reel 7: There must be a considerable reduction in the torturing of Sale; in particular, remove all shots of the needles in contact with his flesh.
Reel 8: Remove shot of the torturer lying on the ground with axe in his body and blood all around it.
Reel 9: Remove CU of man's bloody body after it has been repeatedly stabbed and shot of his mutilated hand.
Comment:
The U.S. Sony DVD restores the shot of the first officer's mutilated hand, but is otherwise the cut theatrical print.

The Two Faces of Dr. Jekyll

Classified X for its theatrical release in 1960 with the following cuts:
Reel 4: Shorten the snake dance.
Reel 5: In the lovemaking between Hyde and Maria stop the first scene before he removes her cloak and shorten the second scene.
Reel 8: Shorten the scene in which Hyde rapes Kitty.

Yvonne Romain

Reel 9: Shorten the strangling of Maria.
Comment:
The Sony U.S. DVD, as well as more recent German and French releases, appears to be the uncut version except possibly for the first lovemaking scene in Reel 5, which ends on an odd dissolve.

Village of the Damned

Classified A for its theatrical release in 1960 with the following cut:
Reel 8: The shots of man's clothing on fire were removed.
Comment:
The Warner U.K. and U.S. DVDs are uncut.

1961

The Curse of the Werewolf

Classified X for its theatrical release in 1961 with the following cuts:
Reel 2: Remove MCUs of the Marquis's distressed face before sewing girl is sent to the dungeon. The scene in the dungeon must stop as soon as the girl is thrown into the cell and be resumed with the shot of her being released.
Reel 3: Remove whole scene in which Marquis waits for and attacks girl and is killed by her.
Reel 5: Remove all shots which show hair on Leon's hands.
Reel 7: The scene in the prostitute's bedroom must be considerably shortened.
Reel 8: Considerably reduce the throttling of Jose. Considerably reduce the loud groans and growls when Dominic is murdered.
Reel 10: Reduce the scene of murder of the beggar.
Comment:
There is some debate as to whether the rape scene in the dungeon and the stabbing of the Marquis were removed for theatrical release since these scenes, with some cuts, were relatively intact in the version of

209

Barbara Shelley

the film which used to screen regularly on U.K. television and which was released on U.K. VHS. In addition, the BBFC response doesn't refer to any cuts in the film's climax, in particular close-ups of the werewolf's dead face and of the impact of the bullet to his chest, which were missing from the TV/VHS version referred to above and cut for theatrical release according to Wayne Kinsey.
The Universal U.S. DVD, and the more recent Spanish and German DVDs, are uncut.

Konga
Classified A for its theatrical release in 1961 with the following cuts:
Reel 7 : The scene in which Bob tries to throttle Decker was shortened.
Reel 9: The shots of Sandra being seized by an insectivorous plant were reduced to one, and the sound of her screams was considerably reduced. The CUs of a woman in the crowd and the sounds of her screams were reduced to a minimum.
Reels 9/10: CUs of Konga in these reels were reduced.
Reel 10: Shots of the dead Decker lying on the ground were reduced to a minimum. The amount of shooting at Konga was reduced.
Comment:
The U.S. MGM DVD appears to be uncut.

Mysterious Island
Classified U for its theatrical release in 1961 with the following cuts:
Reel 3: Remove CU of the girl when she is attacked by the ostrich bird and when she is making sounds of fear.
Reel 4: Remove the large CUs of the bee (where it fills up the whole screen) before the bee seals the man and girl up in the honey cell.
Comment:
The U.K. Sony DVD is uncut.

The Shadow of the Cat
Classified X for its theatrical release in 1961 with the following cuts:
Reel 1: The murder of Aunt Ella was shortened.

The Tell-Tale Heart
Classified X for its theatrical release in 1961 with the following cuts:
Reel 1: The scene in which Edgar looks at a woman's legs through the window of a bar was shortened, and the shots of his face as he looks at the woman's knees when he is inside the bar and shots of her knees were removed. Shots of nude pictures were reduced.
Reel 2: Shots of Betty undressing (while Edgar watches her) were reduced.
Reel 4: The episode of Betty sitting on a bed in a seductive pose and reading a book was removed.
Reel 6: The murder of Carl was considerably shortened.
Reel 8: The shots of Carl's dead face were shortened. Shots of Edgar working his knife round in Carl's corpse were removed and shots of his lifting out the heart were shortened. Shots of the heart in Edgar's hands were removed.
Reel 9: The shots of Carl's dead face were reduced.
Comment:
The U.S. Alpha DVD is uncut.

What a Carve Up!
Classified U for its theatrical release in 1961 with the following cuts:
Reel 5: Remove "I don't mind you sleeping in my bed." Remove "No peeking, Sid."
Reel 6: Remove "I thought you wanted to have a little game."
Reel 8: Remove all shots of coffin lid moving up and down and opening; and all shots of Ernest with his head shrouded in a sheet. Remove all shots of mask being removed from the corpse's face in the coffin, and all shots of the corpse's face.
Comment:
The U.K. Anchor Bay DVD is the cut theatrical print.

1962

Maniac
Classified X for its theatrical release in 1962 with the following cuts:
Reel 4: The love scene on the beach between Eve and Geoff was considerably shortened. In the scene in which they make love in bed, all shots of them embracing were removed except when only their hands and shoulders are seen.

The Phantom of the Opera
Classified A for its theatrical release in 1962 with the following cuts:
Reel 1: Pre-credit "shock" shot of masked face with its gleaming eye was removed. The incident of the man hanging above the stage was shortened, removing sight of the man swinging backwards and forwards, and should only establish that there is a corpse.
Reel 2: The shot of the dwarf stabbing the rat-catcher in the face and the shot of his bleeding face immediately afterwards were removed. The big CU of the masked man where details of the mask are not clearly seen was removed. The similar shot in brighter lighting remained.
Reel 3: When the dwarf appears at the woman's window, the shot where the window is opened and the dwarf thrusts his head forward was removed.
Reel 5: The shots and sounds of the Professor's agony after the acid has spurted into his face were shortened. Shots of the Professor hitting his head against the wall after the accident were reduced to an absolute minimum. All shots of the Professor's face without the mask were

removed. As many of the shots immediately following the removal of the mask were removed.

Comment:

The R1 Universal DVD is uncut.

Vengeance

Classified A for its theatrical release in 1962 after cuts, but there is no information available on the material cut from this film.

1963

Devil Doll

Classified X for its theatrical release in 1963 with the following cuts:
Double Reel 2: Considerably shorten the embrace between Mark and Marianne in the car. Also remove shots of him kissing her breast and putting his hands up her leg.
Double Reel 4: Remove the shots in which Marta's bare breasts are seen.

Comment:

The U.K. 2 Entertain DVD is uncut. The U.S. Image DVD is also uncut and includes an alternate "Continental" version.

Jason and the Argonauts

Classified U for its theatrical release in 1963 with the following cut:
Reel 6: Shorten considerably the fight between three Argonauts and the skeletons; particularly remove CUs and front views of the skeletons.

Comment:

The U.K. Sony DVD is uncut.

The Kiss of the Vampire

Classified X for its theatrical release in 1963 with the following cuts:
Double Reel 3: The scene in which Ravna puts a surplice on the apparently naked Marianne was removed.
Double Reel 4: Dialogue line "She was riddled with disease" was removed. Dialogue line "I want only you" was removed.
Double Reel 5: The episode in which bats attack the vampire people was considerably shortened, in particular shots where women's bare legs and thighs are seen and as many as possible of the bats attacking women and of their sucking blood were removed.

Comment:

The U.S. Universal DVD and the previous U.S. Image DVD are identical. They appear to have some minor cuts to the bat finale but all other cuts are restored.

Nightmare

Classified "X" for its theatrical release in 1963 with the following cuts:
Double Reel 1(a): Janet's hysteria and screams were shortened, as was the mad laughter of her mother.
Double Reel 1 (b): The visuals and sounds of the episode in which Janet sees her mother standing over her murdered father were both reduced.
Double Reel 3 (a): The scene of Janet cutting her wrists with a piece of glass was reduced. The scene in which Janet stabs Helen was shortened.
Double Reel 5 (b): The sequence in which Grace kills Harry was shortened.

Comment:

The U.S. Universal DVD appears to be uncut.

The Old Dark House

Classified A for its theatrical release in 1963 with the following cuts:
Reel 2: All CUs of Casper in his coffin were removed.
Reel 3: All CUs of the body in the coffin were removed.

Kiss of the Vampire

Reel 4: All CUs of the body in the coffin were removed.
Reel 5: All CUs of Aunt Agatha's dead face were removed.
Reel 6: Two shots of hyena slavering on the body were removed.
Reel 7: All CUs of Jasper in the coffin were removed. Shot of Roderick trying to close the eyes of the corpse were removed. Shots of corpses in chairs were removed.
Reel 9: CUs of the Aunt in the coffin were removed. CUs of Roderick in the coffin were removed.

Comment:

No DVD release but the U.K. Columbia VHS release was uncut.

Paranoiac

Classified X for its theatrical release in 1963 with the following cuts:
D. Reel 3: The shot of Harriet caressing Simon's chest was removed.
D. Reel 4: The episode in which Simon embraces the nurse before he drowns her was shortened.
D. Reel 5: The number of shots of the mummy were reduced, especially when Simon drags it about.

Comment:

The U.S. Universal DVD appears to be uncut.

Unearthly Stranger

Classified A for its theatrical release in 1963 with the following cut:
Reel 4: The scene in which Lancaster and Davison struggle with secretary as they chloroform her was reduced.

The Very Edge

Classified A for its theatrical release in 1963 with the following cuts:
D. Reel 1: In the episode of husband and wife in bed, remove all shots of them except one shot of them lying motionless, the shot of her stopping the alarm clock and the shots of her turning back to her side of the bed and then getting up out of bed. Very considerably shorten the intruder's chase of Tracey and his attempted assault on her. Remove "I can't touch you with all those clothes."
D. Reel 2: Remove "The only real cure for frigidity is the right kind of love." Remove the Inspector's words "This is a nasty business."
D. Reel 3: Remove the man's words, on the telephone "I want you without clothes."
D. Reel 5: In the scene between the husband and his secretary, remove the references to impotence and the idea that the two go to bed together (except that the shots of her drawing the curtains and of the telephone being taken off its rest may remain). Shorten the episode in which the intruder chases Tracey across the roofs.

1964

The Black Torment

Classified X for its theatrical release in 1964 with the following cut:
Reel 1: Remove all shots in the precredit sequence from the moment the man first stretches out his hand towards his victim.
Comment:
The U.K. Odeon, U.S. Redemption and German EMS DVDs are the cut version.

Devils of Darkness

Classified X for its theatrical release in 1964 with the following cut:
Reel 8: Episode in which the snake-dancer dances was reduced to a bare minimum.
Comment:
The U.K. Odeon DVD restores the BBFC cut but is missing about 40 seconds of other footage due to print damage. The U.S. MGM DVD has this other footage but the snake dancer scene has been cut.

The Evil of Frankenstein

Classified X for its theatrical release in 1964 with the following cuts:
Reel 1: Remove all shots in CU and MCU of heart in and out of tank, being placed in tank and when seen with Baron Frankenstein's bloody hand or hands.
Reel 4: Reduce monster's beating up of Burgomaster.
Comment:
The U.S. Universal DVD and the U.K. Slam Dunk DVD are uncut.

The Gorgon

Classified X for its theatrical release in 1964 with the following cut:
Reel 5A: Darken the shots in which the Gorgon's severed head is seen in fairly CU.
Comment:
The U.S. Sony DVD shows the shots undarkened.

The Horror of It All

Classified A for its theatrical release in 1964 after cuts, but there is no information available on the material cut from this film.

The Masque of the Red Death

Classified X for its theatrical release in 1964 with the following cuts:
Reel 1: Reduce shots of person on fire. Reduce shots and dialogue showing Alfredo's interest in the female dwarf.

Reel 2: Remove all shots and dialogue in which Scarletti offers his wife to Prospero in return for admittance to the castle, and Prospero's reply "I have already had that doubtful pleasure." The whole scene in which Giuliana offers herself to the Devil should be removed.
Reel 3: Remove Giuliana's references to her conversion to Satanism, her forthcoming wedding to Satan and her loss of innocence.
Reel 4: Remove the whole scene in which Giuliana intones prayers to Satan and drinks from a chalice. Remove the entire dream sequence. Reduce to a flash the birds' attack on Guiliana, removing in particular all shots of her bloodstained throat, shoulders and chest. Remove all shots of the "ape" struggling with a girl on the ground.
Reel 9: Reduce to a minimum shots of Alfredo (in the ape costume) catching fire and burning.
Comment:
The U.K. MGM DVD is uncut regarding these BBFC trims (although it appears to be missing some other footage).

Witchcraft

Classified X for its theatrical release in 1964 after cuts, but there is no information available on the material cut from this film.

1965

Curse of Simba

Classified A for its theatrical release in 1965 with the following cut:
Reel IIA: Remove the shots of a woman taking off her dress and about to take off her bra.
Comment:
The U.S. Image DVD, titled *Curse of the Voodoo*, is uncut.

Curse of the Fly

Classified X for its theatrical release in 1965 with the following cut:
Reel 7: The shot of what remains of the "teleported" bodies of Samuels and Dile, as seen in a glass cabinet in Albert's laboratory, was reduced to a flash.
Comment:
The U.S. and German Fox DVDs are uncut.

Dracula—Prince of Darkness

Classified X for its theatrical release in 1965 with the following cuts:
Reel 5: Remove shot of Alan being slashed (when he is hanging up) (*nb: cut does not appear to have been made*); also remove shot of blood pouring from him and shot of blood flowing into or congealing in the sarcophagus. (*nb: one shot out of three of blood pouring actually removed*)
Reel 9: Shorten the struggle between Helen and her guards (*nb: cut does not appear to have been made*). Remove the shot of the stake being driven into her and the shot of blood spouting from the wound. Remove the shots of Dracula trying to make Diana suck the blood on his chest. (*nb: shot reduction made only*)
Comment:
The U.K. DVDs are all uncut. The U.K. VHS releases were the cut version.

The Face of Fu Manchu

Classified U for its theatrical release in 1965 with the following cuts:
Reel 1: Remove shots of corpse's head being taken away in a basket and shots of the decapitated body.
Reels 2 and 3: Shorten the fight between Carl and Smith in laboratory.
Reel 4: Remove all the preparations (tying up, baring of back, handling of lash) for the flogging of the Chinese girl.

Reel 5: Remove all shots of her from the moment she is put into the water chamber. Remove Maria's screams. Remove kick in warehouse fight.

Reel 8: Remove "bloody cold" and "bloody frozen." Reduce the shots of corpses in Fleetwick. Remove the incident in which Gaskell stabs himself.

Comment:

The U.K. Momentum DVD is uncut.

Fanatic

Classified X for its theatrical release in 1965 with the following cuts:

Reel 5: The whole incident in which Pat is stabbed by scissors was reduced to a minimum. CUs of the blade embedded in Pat's bare flesh were removed.

Reel 6: The scene in which Harry chases Pat around the garden (after she has fallen through a greenhouse roof) was considerably reduced, especially removing CUs of Harry's face with its sadistic and lecherous expression. (There was a suggestion that the sound effects in this scene may have to be adjusted.)

Reel 7: Fight between Anna and Pat was reduced to a minimum. Shot of Anna kicking Pat was removed. The following scene in which Anna is twisting Pat's arm and Mrs. Trefoile is threatening to disfigure her with a broken saucer was reduced. Harry's attempted rape of Pat was reduced; the scene can start with him forcing her onto the bed and should cut immediately to Mrs. Trefoile entering the room.

Reel 8: At the start of the reel, scene in which Mrs. Trefoile picks up bloody knife and puts it to her lips was removed with the fade going to her going upstairs with bloody hands. Shock shots of Harry's face as his dead body lies under running tap were removed.

Reel 10: There was a suggestion that the scenes involving shots of Mrs. Trefoile with her hands cut or with blood on them may have to be reduced in color.

Note: These cuts were transcribed from handwritten notes in the file. These cuts were suggested when the film was submitted incomplete—there was no soundtrack—and in black and white at the end of 1964. A color print was submitted in February 1965. From the handwritten notes, it would appear that these cuts were made—or at least the film was now in an acceptable version—as only one cut was now proposed in Double Reel 4 to the shots of Harry bleeding from the mouth after he has been shot. The distributor appealed the cut on the grounds that it was an impracticable one as it would cause a jump in the scene. The BBFC accepted the difficulty of the cut, and waived it.

Comment:

The U.K. Sony DVD, under the *Die! Die! My Darling!* title, is uncut.

Invasion

Classified U for its theatrical release in 1965 with the following cut:

Reel 6: Shots of doctor's dead body on bonnet of car were shortened.

Comment:

No DVD release. The U.K. Warner VHS is uncut.

Rasputin—The Mad Monk

Classified X for its theatrical release in 1965 with the following cuts:

Reel 2: Remove the shot of a severed hand falling on the straw. (*nb: cut appears to have not been made*)

Reel 4: The scene where Rasputin embraces Sonia must stop before he undoes her shirt and reveals her naked to the waist. (*nb: dissolve put in at this point in the cut print*)

Reel 7: Considerably shorten Sonia's hysterical attack on Rasputin and remove shots of his holding the flask of acid near her face when she is bent backwards over a bench. (*nb: cut appears not to have been made*)

Reel 8: Reduce to a minimum Rasputin's attack with acid on Peter,

including shots of the injured face. (*nb: one shot of the injured face was removed and one reduced*)

Comment:

The U.K. Studio Canal DVD is uncut. The U.K. VHS releases were the cut version.

She

Classified U for its theatrical release in 1965 with the following cuts:

Reel 1: Reduce to a minimum shots of the dancing girl with only stars on her breasts.

Reels 8 and 11: Remove the shots of a group of men falling down into the pit of fire.

Reel 11: Shorten the disintegration scene and darken the shot in which the head appears as a skull.

Comment:

The U.K. Studio Canal DVD contains the Reel 11 shots of men falling into the pit of fire but is otherwise cut as above.

A Study in Terror

Classified X for its theatrical release in 1965 with the following cuts:

Reel 1: The episode in which a woman is murdered in a horse trough was considerably shortened. The first flurry of blood staining the water was removed and the shots that suggest repeated stabbings were reduced. Sight and sound of the struggle which ends in the death of the third prostitute (who wears a red dress and bonnet) was considerably shortened.

Comment:

The U.K. Fremantle DVD is uncut.

Ten Little Indians

Classified A for its theatrical release in 1965 with the following cut:

Reel 8: Remove shot of a man taking a woman's towel off her.

Comment:

The U.K. Orbit Media DVD is the cut version.

1966

The Brides of Fu Manchu

Classified U for its theatrical release in 1966 with the following cuts:

Reel 1: Remove the whole incident in which a girl is tied up by her hair over the snake pit and then, when her hair is cut, falls screaming into the pit. Remove also the shots of snakes and sounds of her screams.

Reel 6: Remove the whole incident in which a girl is dragged to the snake pit, and held screaming over it; and all shots of the snakes.

Reel 9: Shorten the fight between the girls and the Chinese.

Comment:

The U.K. Momentum DVD is uncut.

Island of Terror

Classified X for its theatrical release in 1966 with the following cut:

Reel 6: The shot of the stump of Dr. Stanley's arm spurting blood was removed.

Comment:

The U.K. DD Video DVD is the cut version. The German Cult Cinema DVD is uncut.

The Reptile

Classified X for its theatrical release in 1965 with the following cut:

Reel 7: Remove the close shot of the incision in Harry's neck when he returns home and is lying on the bed.

Comment:

The U.K. Studio Canal DVD is uncut.

Theatre of Death

Classified X for its theatrical release in 1966 with the following cut:
Reel 10: Reduce to a minimum the back view shots of the female dancer when she is nearly naked.
Comment:
The U.K. Momentum DVD appears to be uncut.

1967

The Deadly Bees

Classified X for its theatrical release in 1967 with the following cuts:
Double Reel 2: Shots where the bees are seen all over the woman's face and hands were removed. Shots of her face after death were removed.
Comment:
The U.S. Legend DVD appears to be uncut.

Dance of the Vampires (The Fearless Vampire Killers)

Classified A for its theatrical release in 1967 with the following cut:
Reel 2: The second shot of Dracula *(sic)* attacking Zara in her bath was reduced, and shots of him afterwards when he has blood on his mouth were also shortened.
Comment:
The U.K. Warner DVD appears to be uncut.

The Mummy's Shroud

Classified X for its theatrical release in 1967 after cuts, but there is no information available on the material cut from this film.

The Shuttered Room

Classified X for its theatrical release in 1967 with the following cut:
Reel 5: All shots of the gang driving up and down taunting and threatening Mike when he is trussed up in the net were removed, except the last shot when he frees himself.
Comment:
The U.S. Warner DVD is uncut.

They Came from Beyond Space

Classified A for its theatrical release in 1967 with the following cut:
Reel 2: Shots of faces with plague spots on them, in particular CUs, were reduced.
Comment:
The various U.S. "public domain" DVDs appear to be uncut.

The Vengeance of Fu Manchu

Classified A for its theatrical release in 1967 with the following cuts:
D Reel 2: Remove shot of branding iron in contact with girl's flesh (and accompanying scream), and shot of her back afterwards.
D Reel 3: Remove CUs of man's clutching hand before the murder and of girl's face as she is murdered.
D Reel 5: Shorten the torture of Maria, in particular removing shot of threat with branding iron by Roddy.

The Sorcerers

Comment:
The U.K. Momentum DVD is uncut.

1968

The Blood of Fu Manchu

Classified A for its theatrical release in 1968 with the following cuts:
D Reel 2: Remove all shots and sounds of tortured girls including the naked girl—before Lin Tang enters.
D Reel 3: Considerably shorten the whole episode in which Sancho's men attack a village and assault the women or make love to them. Remove also the shot of Uma when her breasts are partly visible.
D Reel 4: Remove "Doubtless he is proud of being a man" (when Sancho is tortured).
Comment:
Oddly, the BBFC cuts list does not mention the scene in which a naked woman is tortured by having a snake pressed against her breasts, which occurs just under an hour into the film on the U.K. Optimum DVD. This was cut when the film was first certified on video. Possibly this scene was precut by the distributor for theatrical release. The U.K. Optimum DVD is uncut (all previous U.K. releases were cut).

Corruption

Classified X for its theatrical release in 1968 with the following cuts:
Reel 4: The attack on and murder of a girl on a train and the subsequent shots in the railway carriage were reduced. The attack on and murder of Terry was reduced.
Reel 5: The incident of the man holding a glass over Lyn's face was shortened. Shots of girl's severed head after the girl has unwrapped it were removed.
Comment:
The Spanish Sony DVD includes all of the BBFC cuts but is missing the entire Soho murder.

Curse of the Crimson Altar (The Crimson Cult)

Classified X for its theatrical release in 1968 with the following cuts:
Reel 1: Remove whole scene of the flagellation, including all shots of woman wielding a whip.
Comment:
The U.K. DD Video DVD is the cut version. The German EMS DVD is also the cut version but has an uncut version of the relevant scene as an extra.

Dracula Has Risen from the Grave

Classified X for its theatrical release in 1968 with the following cut:
Close-ups of Dracula trying to pull out the stake that transfixes him.
Comment:
The U.K. Warner DVD is uncut.

The Vengeance of She

Classified A for its theatrical release in 1968 after cuts, but there is no information available on the material cut from this film.
Comment:
According to Wayne Kinsey's *Hammer: The Elstree Studios Years* (page 68), the proposed cut, to remove the dialogue "a floating bloody

knocking shop," was never made.

Witchfinder General

Classified X for its theatrical release in 1968 with the following cuts:

Double Reel 2: Substantially reduce the spiking of Lowes in the back, and reduce his screams. Remove the whole episode of a woman being hit and half-strangled in a cell; there should be no shot of her at all.

Double Reel 3: Reduce the ducking of the parson and two women. Reduce to a minimum the burning of Elizabeth Clark, including shots of her being dragged to the gibbet: there should be only a distant shot of her in the flames.

Double Reel 5: Reduce the episode of Sara being tortured with a spike and screaming. Substantially reduce the shots of Richard chopping up Matthew with an axe.

Comment:

The U.S. MGM DVD is uncut. The U.K. Redemption DVD restored the cuts by insertion of inferior video footage and also contained an alternate Continental version of the film with the same restored inserts.

1969

The Body Stealers

Classified A for its theatrical release in 1969 with the following cuts:

Reel 3: Remove shot of Lorna's naked breast as she removes her dress and the ensuing MCU of her approaching the sea (the longer shot as she enters the sea can be allowed).

Reel 4: Remove the whole of the love scene between Bob and Lorna from the point where he removes his shirt.

Comment:

This film was originally passed uncut with an X. The U.K. Anchor Bay DVD is the cut A version.

Frankenstein Must Be Destroyed

Classified X for its theatrical release in 1969 with the following cuts:

Entire scene in which Frankenstein attempts to rape Anna.

In the scene where Frankenstein operates on the heads of two men—sounds of sawing, the shot of the first man's bleeding head after the operation, and the shot of Frankenstein trying to lever off the top of the second man's head and carrying that part away (the portion of the head is out of shot).

Comment:

The U.K. Warner DVD is uncut.

Night, After Night, After Night

Classified X for its theatrical release in 1969 with the following cuts:

Double Reel 2: The love-making between Pete and his girlfriend on the grass was shortened; the shots of his rolling over and over with

Veronica Carlson

a second woman were removed entirely. The whole of the stripper's strip in a nightclub after she has begun to take off her bra was removed.

Double Reel 3: The murder of the car prostitute was considerably shortened.

Double Reel 5: The scene in Lomax's room was considerably shortened, removing as far as possible the shots of his kissing the photographs of naked women and the shots of his slashing them.

The Oblong Box

Classified X for its theatrical release in 1969 with the following cuts:

Double Reel 3: The incident in which Edward kills Mark was reduced, including the shots of the dying or dead man.

Double Reel 4: Shots of Edward squeezing Heidi's breast and of the breast being bared were removed. One of the shots of Edward cutting her neck was removed.

Double Reel 5: Shots of Edward's bloodstained mouth and face after he has bitten Julian were removed. *(nb: this cut does not appear to have been made)*

Comment:

The U.K. Optimum DVD is uncut.

1970

Legend of the Witches

Classified X for its theatrical release in 1970 with the following cuts:

Reel 5: remove "as will be the person whom it represents" (after "The image is drowned").

Reel 6: Remove "The corresponding organs of the victim will suffer" (after "These are pierced and mutilated").

Secrets of Sex

Classified X for its theatrical release in February 1970 with the following cuts:

Reel 1: Remove shots of two naked men and one naked woman together. Remove the shot of the naked boy rolling over in the hay *(a replacement shot was substituted)*. Reduce the CUs of female strippers being pelted with tomatoes.

Reels 2 and 3: Substantially modify the episode in which a woman photographer is taking torture pictures, lessening the implication of sadism and entirely removing the final part of this episode.

Reel 3: Drastically reduce the sketch about the kinky female burglar; in particular, remove the sequence in which the woman does a striptease in the bathroom and is then joined by the "Host" who is her victim. The ensuing sex scene must be considerably reduced.

Reel 5: Reduce the sequence of the old lady in the greenhouse, particularly removing the middle section in which she and the butler watch the naked couple making love in the straw. Substantially reduce the orgy sequence, removing as many as possible of the shots of couples embracing on the floor. Remove final sequence of the nude man and woman, and the shots of the two nude men and women similar to those which open the film.

Also classified X for theatrical release in August 1970 with the following cuts:

Reel 1: Drastically reduce the sequence in which the mummified commentator keeps repeating, "Imagine you were making love to this girl... this boy... this girl" ending with "Imagine this boy making love to you"; this involves a drastic reduction of the visuals backing this commentary. Reels 2 and 3: Substantially modify the episode in which a woman photographer is taking torture pictures, lessening the implication of sadism, and entirely remove the final part of this episode.

Comment:

The BBFC informed us "as to why the film was submitted twice, and received different cuts, I'm afraid we do not know, as—despite extensive searching—there appears to be no extant file for the work." This was likely to be due to the X certificate age limit being raised from 16 to 18 in the intervening period (increasing to 18 on July 1, 1970). The distributors may have resubmitted the film in the (successful!) aim of restoring some of their more controversial moments.

Taste the Blood of Dracula

Classified X for its theatrical release in 1970 with the following cuts:
Shots of Oriental man in brothel cubicle with a bare-breasted woman.
Shots of Dracula's bloodstained teeth in the scene when he kisses Lucy. (*nb: shot was reduced but not removed entirely*)
Shot of blood spurting from Paxton's chest as Lucy hammers a stake into it (*nb: substituted by softer take*), and shots of his face spattered with blood immediately afterwards. (*nb: appears not to have been cut*)

Comment:

All DVD releases are of the cut version. Note that the U.K. VHS release was the U.S. "PG" print which was cut further.

When Dinosaurs Ruled the Earth

Classified A for its theatrical release in 1970 with the following cuts:
Reel 1: Considerably reduce shots of monster's head in flames, and sound of its howls.
Reel 2: Reduce fight between two girls. Remove incident of man being killed by snake.
Reel 3: Remove incident of girl being engulfed in man-eating plant and cutting off her hair to free herself from its clutches.
Reel 4: Shorten the fight between man and pterodactyl, removing all CUs. Remove shots of man's agonized face as he floats out to sea on a burning raft.

Hazel Court

Raquel Welch

Reel 5: Remove first shot of man being caught by giant crab.
Correspondence on file indicates that the sex scenes and "nudity" in the film, particularly the naked swimming in Reel 8, were retained.

Comment:

According to Wayne Kinsey's *Hammer: The Elstree Studios Years*, quoting BBFC correspondence, the cuts above are actually proposed cuts for a U in 1973 and that the actual cuts made in 1970 were to some of the film's nude scenes, although some nudity was retained. However, when queried on this point, the BBFC specifically confirmed to our contributor that these violence cuts above and not the sex cuts were made for the film's A classification.
The U.S. Warner DVD is uncut and restores all the violence and all the sex material which Kinsey states was originally cut.

Whirlpool (*She Died with Her Boots On*)

Classified X for its theatrical release in 1970 with the following cuts:
Reel 3: Dialogue "I promise you an extra special night tonight," "She'll soon learn" and "A threesome is more exciting" was removed.
Reel 4: The scene in the wood in which Theo photographs the girl apparently being raped by another man was reduced, in particular removing shots of his pulling off her underwear. The scene in which Theo makes love to Tullia and Sarah in succession on the same bed was re-edited so as to eliminate entirely his lovemaking with Sarah, and also the suggestion that she is watching him make love to Tullia. Shots of Tullia writhing and panting were also removed, retaining only the subsequent shots of the man making love to her.
Reel 5: The stabbing of the woman was reduced to an absolute minimum; the sexual element was to be eliminated as far as possible and the stabbing should be as brief as possible.

1971

The Corpse (*Velvet House*)

Classified X for its theatrical release in 1971 with the following cuts:
Reel 1: The word "fucking" in Janet's remark to Rupert was removed (*nb: substituted by "bloody"*).
Reel 2: Shots of the father whipping his daughter were shortened as far as possible, or the sound was reduced.
Reel 3: The scene of the mother and daughter using a funnel to force whisky and drugs down the throat of Walter when he is unconscious was shortened.

Comment:

The U.S. Trinity DVD titled *Crucible of Horror* has the "bloody" substitution but it is unclear whether the other cuts were ever made, since the old U.K. Intervision VHS titled *The Velvet House*, which uses "fucking," has identical content in the other two "offending" scenes.

Incense for the Damned

Classified X for its theatrical release in 1971 with the following cuts:
Reel 2: Drug orgy was drastically reduced, in particular shots of drug being administered on dropper; all CUs of lesbian love making, all shots showing more than one couple in frame love making and shot of girl pouring wine down her naked body were removed.
Reel 5: Shot of man kissing woman's breasts while she is being held by another man was removed.
Comment:
The U.S. Redemption DVD, titled *Bloodsuckers*, the longest available version of the film (83 minutes), is the cut BBFC version. It runs longer than the recently screened BBC version under the *Incense of the Damned* title, which was missing the end credits. Most of the shots cut by the BBFC can be found in a U.S. release from Something Weird, titled *Freedom Seeker* (although

Quatermass and the Pit

called *Bloodsuckers* on the DVD cover), which runs 80 minutes and contains a much shortened version of the orgy scene, albeit with some alternate takes to those found in the Redemption release. The U.K. DVDs, from Metrodome and Prism, are missing the entire 7-minute orgy sequence, which is included as a "deleted scene" (this is the *Bloodsuckers* edit of the sequence).

Justine (*Justine and Juliette*)

Classified X for its theatrical release in 1971 with the following cuts:
D Reel 4: Remove "It's never been so exciting. I find it stimulating to make love to one who will so soon be dead." Considerably shorten the incident in which Juliette drowns Claudine, leaving only enough to establish what has happened.
Comment:
The U.K. Anchor Bay DVD is uncut. The version released in U.K. cinemas, according to the *Monthly Film Bulletin* (May 1972), was about 20 minutes shorter than the Anchor Bay DVD, and the BBFC certified an edited version, although the nature of those edits is unknown.

Portrait illustrations by Jed Raven; other illustrations by Sam Trafford

About the Editor

Hailing from the city of Derby, England, Darrell Buxton has been hooked on motion pictures since childhood, having been transfixed by the eyes of Kaa the snake in Disney's *The Jungle Book*. A contributor to various publications including *Samhain*, *Shivers*, *Creeping Flesh*, *We Belong Dead*, *The Dark Side* and *Giallo Pages*, Darrell also maintains the British horror website *Pass The Marmalade*. He unearthed the rarely screened sociopolitical shocker *Sleepwalker* (1984) from obscurity and assisted director Saxon Logan in bringing this undeservedly dormant production to a new audience.

Buxton appeared in the 1997 film *I Zombie: The Chronicles of Pain* and co-wrote the 2007 short *The Opening*. He regularly lectures on cult/fringe cinema, penned two essays for the DVD release of acclaimed drama *This is England*, and saw his popular presentation on the life and work of Johnny Cash play to sellout crowds. He achieved a long-held ambition when he interviewed his hero, actor Robin Askwith, live on stage at Manchester's Festival of Fantastic Films.

Buxton's chief obsession is with the music of Mark E. Smith/The Fall, and his favorite British horror movie remains *The Devil Rides Out*. He continues to contribute to several terror/cult movie-related websites and lives in hope that his retro-Gothic, feature-length screenplay *Horror of the Witches* might one day reach the big screen.

Photo by Andreas Beck

Plague of the Zombies

Glossary of Brit Slang

absobloodylootely: absolutely

after: bars open after normal closing time

all over the gaff: unorganized

arse: butt

arse-over-tit: tumbling over

babygrow: babies onesie

ballistic: wild

balls-up: (vulgar) error, mistake

bangers: sausages

barmy: crazy

barnet: hair

bedsit (or bedsitter): one-room apartment that serves as a bedroom and a living room

berk: a mildly derogatory term for a silly person

biff: hit

biro: pen

blimey!: Oh geez!

bloke: a male

bob: shilling

bobby: policeman

bollocks: bullshit

bolthole: safe place to run to

bonce: the head

bone-idle: lazy

brilliant!: great! awesome!

Bugger: damn or fuck

Bugger off: go away

Buggers: irritating creature; can also mean to ruin or damage

Bum: butt

cabbage: a slow person

cack: crap (What a load of cack, mate!)

cakehole: mouth (Shut your cakehole!)

charlie: crack, cocaine

cheeky: impertinent, fresh

chin-wag: talk

chips: french fries

chokey: prison

chunder: to throw up

ciggy: cigarette

claret: blood (They were copping it up, claret all over the place!)

cod: joke

cop a feel: to feel someone up

to cop it: to get in trouble

copper: policeman

crikey!: My God!

damage: cost

dicky: feeling unwell

dischuffed: disappointed, unhappy

doddle: something easy (It was a doddle to get the Charlie.)

dodgy: shady

done over: beat up (He was done over by that bloke.)

Doris: a plain woman

dosh: money

duck and dive: to run from the police

earner: a dishonest laborer

eppy: a fit

faced: drunk

fannying: fooling around

five finger discount: shoplifting

flim-flam: crap (Cut out this flim-flam, you wanker!)

flip-sidding: turn over

flippin: freakin'

folding: paper pound-notes

Frenchy: a french kiss

full monty: the entire take, all that is desired

gab: to talk a lot

gander: to look at

geezer: charming scoundrel

get the nod: to get permission

git: an unlikeable person

gnashers: teeth

gob: mouth

goppin': gross

greaser: a '50's style person, usually a man

grub: food

gutted: choked up (He was gutted at the funeral, mate.)

hacked off: annoyed (He was really hacked off at that copper.)

having it off: a term for intercourse

headcase: a nutcase

hold it down: keep the noise down, control yourself

hooter: nose

ickle: small, tiny (I like that an ickle bit, mate.)

in stook: in financial trouble (Your uncle's in stook, mate.)

inside: imprisoned (Barry's inside again.)

jammy: lucky

jar: a pint of beer

jock: a Scottish man

jugs: breasts

juiced up: very drunk

kick it off: start something, a fight with another Brit perhaps

kip: sleep (I need some kip, mate.)

knackered: tired

knock-up: to wake someone up

knobbing: having sex

lairy: loud, brash

larging it: to live large

lech: sexually lust

lip: smart talk

loaded: very rich

lock-in: a term for late-hours in a pub

lolly: money

lost the plot: gone mad

mate: address for a friend

matelot: sailor

mental: crazy

miffed: fed up

minger: an unattractive girl

mitts: hands

mog/moggie: cat

monkey: 500 pounds

moose: an ugly girl

mudflat: tidal plain

mullered: drunk

munch: food (Time for munch, mate!)

naff: nasty, in poor taste (That's naff!)

nipper: a small child

norks: breasts

nosh: food

nutter: a crazy person

offed: killed

offie: a place where off-license alcohol is sold

off your face: very drunk

out of the tree: nuts

parky: chilly (Parky weather today.)

pea-souper: foggy

pebble dash: to vomit on

perspex: Plexiglas

plank, a fool

ponce: a slacker

poof: homosexual

radio rentalist: crazy person

ramped: drunk

rat-arsed: drunk

readies: cash (Have any readies? I'm all out.)

rozzers: police

ruck: a fight

rug: wig

saucepot: sexy woman

scrounge: to beg food, materials

shafted: screwed, betrayed

shag: sexual intercourse

sheety: ghostly

shell-like: ear (Can I have a word in your shell-like?)

shite: shit

skirt: a young woman

snog: a french kiss

sprog: child

squire: minor nobleman can also be a term for a working man

sussed out: figured out

tanked: drunk

tarting: dressing up

toerag: a tramp

tom: a prostitute

tonto: crazy

top!: wonderful

trainspotter: a nerd, geek

trots: an upset stomach

undercooked: under done, undeveloped

up for it: enthusiastically available

up the duff: pregnant

wank: to masturbate

wedge: money

wind up: to tease

wittering: talking endlessly

Y-fronts: men's underwear briefs

If you enjoyed this book

visit our website or call, write or e-mail for a free catalog:

Midnight Marquee Press, Inc.
9721 Britinay Lane
Baltimore, MD 21234

www.midmar.com

410-665-1198

Made in the USA
Charleston, SC
17 December 2012